ANTI-
MEMOIRS

Other books by André Malraux

ANDRÉ
MALRAUX

ANTI-
MEMOIRS

TRANSLATED BY
TERENCE KILMARTIN

HOLT, RINEHART AND WINSTON
NEW YORK   CHICAGO   SAN FRANCISCO

Published simultaneously in Canada by Holt,
Rinehart and Winston of Canada, Limited.

Library of Congress Catalog Card Number:
68-24751

First American Edition, October, 1968
Second Printing, November, 1968

Designer: Robert Reed

SBN: 03-072565-8

Printed in the United States of America

FOR MRS. JOHN FITZGERALD KENNEDY

Contents

The elephant is the wisest of all the animals,

the only one who remembers his former lives;

and he remains motionless for long periods of

time, meditating thereon.

—BUDDHIST TEXT

1965, Off Crete.

In 1940 I escaped with the future chaplain of the Vercors.* We met again shortly afterward in the little town in the Drôme where he was parish priest and where he used to hand out baptismal certificates wholesale to Jews—on condition, however, that they let him baptize them: "Some of it may stick, after all . . ." He had never been to Paris, having completed his studies at the seminary in Lyons. We talked far into the night, as friends do when they meet again, amid the homely village smells.

"How long have you been hearing confessions?"

"About fifteen years."

"What has confession taught you about men?"

"Oh, confession teaches nothing, you know, because when a priest goes into the confessional he becomes another person—grace and all that. And yet . . . First of all, people are much more unhappy than one thinks . . . and then . . ."

He raised his brawny lumberman's arms in the starlit night: "And then, the fundamental fact is that *there's no such thing as a grown-up person* . . ."

He died on the slopes of Glières.†

To reflect upon life—life in relation to death—is perhaps no more than to intensify one's questioning. I do not mean death in the sense of being killed, which poses few problems to anyone who has the commonplace luck to be brave; but death as it manifests itself in everything that is beyond man's control, in the aging and even the metamorphosis of the earth (the earth suggests death by its age-old torpor as well as its metamorphosis, even if this metamorphosis is the work of man) and above all the irremediable, the sense that "you'll never know what it all meant." Faced with that question, what do I care about what matters only to me? Almost all the writers I know love their childhood; I hate mine. I have never really learned to re-create myself, if to do so is to come to terms with that lonely halfway house which we call life. I have sometimes managed to act, but the interest of action, except when it rises to the level of history, lies in what we do and not

*Mountain area of southeastern France, one of the principal maquis strongholds. (Tr.)

†Plateau to the north of the Vercors, scene of a savage battle between German forces and maquis in March 1944. (Tr.)

in what we say. I do not find myself very interesting. Friendship, which has played a big part in my life, has never been leavened with curiosity. And I agree with the Glières chaplain—though if he insisted that there were no grown-ups, it was because children are assured of salvation . . . Why should I remember?

Because, having lived in the shifting realm of intellect and imagination all artists share, then in the realms of combat and of history—having known, at twenty, an Asia whose death-struggle threw new light on the meaning of the West—I have experienced time and again, in humble or dazzling circumstances, those moments when the mystery of life appears to each one of us as it appears to almost every woman when she looks into a child's face and to almost every man when he looks into the face of someone dead. In the multifarious forms of that which drives us on, in all that I have seen of man's struggle against humiliation, and even in that sweetness which one can scarcely believe exists on this earth, life, like the gods of vanished religions, appears to me at times as if it were the libretto for some unknown music.

Although the East I knew in my youth could be likened to an old Arab on his donkey sleeping the inviolable sleep of Islam, the two hundred thousand inhabitants of Cairo have since become four million, Baghdad has substituted motorboats for the baskets of reeds and pitch in which its Babylonian peasants used to fish, and the mosaic gates of Tehran are now buried in the middle of the town like the Porte Saint-Denis in Paris. America had had its mushroom towns for a long time, but they did not obliterate an older civilization, they did not symbolize the metamorphosis of man.

That the world has never changed so much in a single century (except by destruction) is a fact with which we are all familiar. I myself have seen the sparrows swooping down on the horse-drawn buses at the Palais-Royal—and the shy and charming Colonel Glenn on his return from the cosmos; the old Tartar town of Moscow—and the pointed skyscraper of the university; all that the little railway engines in Pennsylvania Station, with their bell-shaped funnels so beautifully polished, evoked of the old America—and all that the Pan-American Building symbolizes of the new. How many centuries is it since a great religion shook the world? This is the first civilization capable of conquering the entire planet, but not of inventing its own temples or its own tombs.

Not so very long ago, a journey to Asia was a slow penetration into space and time combined. India after Islam, China after India, the Far East after the Middle East, Sinbad's vessels lying abandoned off an East Indian harbor in the gathering dusk, and after Singapore, at the entrance to the China Sea, the first junks like sentinels.

Now, on doctors' orders, I resume this slow penetration, and contemplate the upheavals which have punctuated my vain and turbulent life as they have convulsed Asia—on my way to rediscover, at the other end of the earth, Tokyo, where I sent the Venus de Milo; Kyoto, changed beyond recognition; and Nara, almost intact despite its gutted temple (all three revisited not long since by air); and China, which I have not yet seen again. "As far as eye can reach, the ocean, smooth, lacquered, without a ripple . . ." The sea brings back to me the first sentence of my first novel, and the telegram board on the boat reminds me of the message which forty years ago heralded the reemergence of Asia: "General strike declared in Canton."

How then does my life respond to these dying gods and rising cities, to this tumult of action which seems to beat against the liner as though it were the eternal uproar of the sea, to so many vain hopes, so many friends killed? This is where my contemporaries begin to tell their little stories.

In 1934, at his flat in the Rue du Vieux-Colombier, Paul Valéry and I once happened to be discussing Gide: "Why," I asked him, "if you're indifferent to his work, do you rate his Conversation with a German so highly?" "What's that?" he asked. I reminded him. "Ah, yes! It must be because it has a beautiful example of the imperfect subjunctive." Then, with the relative seriousness he was wont to mix with his patrician slang: "I'm fond of Gide, but how can a man allow young people to be the judges of what he thinks? And anyway, I'm interested in lucidity, not sincerity. Besides, nobody gives a damn." Thus did he often dismiss ideas which, in Wilde's phrase, he regarded as the stuff of drawing-room conversation.

But what Gide called youth was not always restricted to young people, just as Christendom in the broad sense was not always restricted to the faithful. The demon loves collectivities, assemblies even more; grandeur too. I lived up to the age of thirty among men who were obsessed by sincerity—because they saw it as the opposite of lying, and also (they were writers) because ever since Rousseau it has been a privileged concern of literature. Added to which there is the aggressive self-justification, Baudelaire's "hypocrite lecteur, mon semblable, mon frère . . ." For it is not a question of conveying a particular knowledge of man, but rather a question of unveiling a secret, of *confessing*. Christian confession was the price of absolution, the path to repentance. Talent is not a form of absolution, but it acts in an equally profound way. Supposing Stavrogin's confession—from *The Possessed*—was really Dostoevsky's own, what he did was to transpose the appalling event into tragedy, and Dostoevsky into Stavrogin, into a fictional hero—a transposition that is perfectly expressed by the word "hero." No need to modify the facts: the guilty man is saved, not because he has imposed a lie, but because art and life are on different planes. The proud shame of Rousseau does not destroy the pitiful shame of Jean-Jacques, but it brings him a promise of immortality. This metamorphosis of a fate undergone into a fate transcended is one of the most profound that man can create.

I admire the confessions which we call memoirs, but they only half hold my attention. Nevertheless, the analysis of an individual, apart from the effect it has on us in the case of a great artist, raises an intellectual problem which interested me a great deal at the time of that conversation with Valéry: how to reduce to the minimum the theatrical side of one's nature. This involves the subjugation by each of us of a fictional world which is not strictly ours but which we wallow in and hate to see challenged. It is the basis of the theater of comedy from Molière to Labiche, typified by Victor Hugo's indignant orator who bravely gives the king a piece of his mind—a character who has played such a perennial and futile role in the politics of Mediterranean countries. But to fight against playacting is to fight against weaknesses, whereas the obsession with sincerity is the pursuit of secrets.

The individual took on the status he now occupies in memoirs when they became "confessions." (Those of St. Augustine are not confessions at all, and they end with a treatise on metaphysics.) No one would dream of calling Saint-Simon's *Memoirs* confessions: when he speaks of himself, it is simply to court admiration. Once, Man was sought in the great deeds of great men; then he was sought in the secret actions of individuals (a change encouraged by the fact that great deeds were often violent, and the newspapers have made violence commonplace). The memoirs of the twentieth century are of two kinds. On the one hand, the reporting of events—in some cases, such as General de Gaulle's *War Memoirs* or *The Seven Pillars of Wisdom*, the account of a great enterprise—and on the other, introspection conceived as the study of man, of which Gide is the last great exponent. But *Ulysses* and *A la recherche du temps perdu* took the form of novels. Introspective autobiography has changed its character, because the confessions of the most provocative memorialist seem puerile by comparison with the monsters conjured up by psychoanalytical exploration, even to those who contest its conclusions. The analyst's couch reveals far more about the secrets of the human heart, and more startlingly too. We are less astonished by Stavrogin's confession than by Freud's *Man with the Rats*; genius is its only justification.

Although nobody now believes that the object of the self-portrait, or even the portrait, from the effigies of the Egyptian sculptors to the Cubists, was simply to imitate nature, people still believe it of literary portraiture. Thus the more "like" it is the better, and the less conventional it is the more like. This is the definition suggested by the realisms which have nearly always developed in opposition to the idealizations. But if the idealization of Greece and the Renaissance represents one of the major achievements of European art, its supposed counterpart, literary idealization, bears little relationship to Leonardo or Michelangelo except in the characters of the tragic theater. Yet Joinville's St. Louis or Bossuet's portraits are undoubtedly as valid as the characters in the *Goncourt Journal*, even though their authors intend them as exemplars. Truth above all? I doubt whether Michelet's *Napoleon*, a fairly poor lampoon, is truer than his *Joan of Arc*, an admirable panegyric. We know how Stendhal loved minor details about the great; why not major ones? To re-create the Napoleon of Austerlitz is at least as worthwhile as to reveal his habit of smearing his son's face with jam. And the victory of Marengo may well have had other causes besides Josephine's adultery. To reject the major facts about a man out of contempt for convention can lead to an exclusive preoccupation with the minor. Admittedly the truth about a man lies first and foremost in what he hides. A remark of one of my characters has been attributed to me: "A man is what he does." Of course he is not only that; the character was in any case replying to another who had just said: "What is a man? A miserable little pile of secrets." Gossip provides on the cheap the titillation we expect from the irrational; and with the help of the psychology of the unconscious, what men hide—which is often merely to be pitied—is too easily confused with what they do not know about themselves. But Joinville did not claim to know everything about St. Louis, or indeed about himself. Bossuet knew a good deal about the Great Condé, whom he had perhaps confessed; but, speaking in the presence of death, he attached little importance to what were then called weaknesses. Like Gorki speaking of Tolstoy.

Gorki in his youth was in the habit of secretly following people to use them as characters in his novels (Balzac did it too). He told me he had once followed Tolstoy in the forest of Yasnaya Polyana. "The old man stopped in a clearing by a smooth rock on which a lizard sat watching him. 'Your heart's beating,' Tolstoy said to the lizard. 'The sun is shining. You're happy.' And after a pause, gloomily, 'I'm not.'"

We had just chopped down a small tree—a curious afterlunch custom at the Gorkis'. He stood there in his little Tartar cap, silhouetted against the vast backdrop of the Black Sea. And he went on reminiscing about the old "genius of the Russian earth" conversing with the beasts in his forest like an octogenarian Orpheus.

"Sincerity" has not always been sought after for its own sake. By each of the great religions Man was, so to speak, "given"; memoirs begin to proliferate when religion loses its power. Chateaubriand converses with death, with God perhaps; certainly not with Christ. If Man becomes the object of a search and not of a revelation—for every prophet who reveals God reveals Man by the same token—there is a great temptation to drain him dry, to assume that the more copious all the memoirs and journals the better we will know him. But man can never plumb the depths of his own being; his image is not to be discovered in the extent of the knowledge he acquires but in the questions he asks. The man who will be found here is one who is attuned to the questions which death raises about the meaning of the world.

Nowhere does this meaning haunt me more insistently than in the contrast between the transformed Egypt or India of today and the razed cities of Europe. I have seen German cities covered with white flags (sheets draped from windows) or completely pulverized; Cairo risen from two hundred thousand inhabitants to four million, with its mosques, its citadel, its City of the Dead, and its pyramids in the distance, and Nuremberg so shattered that its central square had vanished. War puts its questions stupidly, peace mysteriously. And it is possible that, in the realm of human destiny, the depth of man's questioning is more important than his answers.

In the creation of fiction, in war, in museums real or imaginary, in culture, in history perhaps, I have found again and again a fundamental riddle, subject to the whims of memory which—whether or not by chance—does not re-create a life in its original sequence. Lit by an invisible sun, nebulae appear which seem to presage an unknown constellation. Some of them belong to the realm of imagination, others to the memory of a past which appears in sudden flashes or must be patiently probed: for the most significant moments in my life do not live in me, they haunt me and flee from me alternately. No matter. Face to face with the unknown, some of our dreams are no less significant than our memories. And so I return here to certain scenes which I once transposed into fiction. Often linked to memory by inextricable bonds, they sometimes turn out, more disturbingly, to be linked to the future too. The scene which follows is reproduced from *Les Noyers de l'Altenburg*,* the first part of a novel of which the Gestapo destroyed too many pages for me to rewrite it. It was called *La Lutte avec l'Ange*, and what else am I undertaking? This suicide is my father's; this grandfather is mine, though doubtless transfigured by family folklore. He was a shipowner of whom I drew a closer likeness in the grandfather of the hero of *La Voie royale*†—specifically his old Viking's death. Although he was prouder of his master-cooper's certificate than of his fleet, most of which had already been lost at sea, he liked to keep up with the rites of his youth, and had split his skull open with a blow from a double-edged ax while symbolically putting the finishing touch to the figurehead of his last boat in accordance with tradition. This Fleming from Dunkirk became an Alsatian because the first German gas attack took place on the Vistula, and I needed a character who had served in the German army in 1914. These timber sheds where the clowns flit among the stacked trunks of great fir trees are the sheds where the sails used to dry; the forest has taken the place of the sea. I knew nothing of Alsace. I had spent five or six weeks as a hussar in Strasbourg, in the yellowing barracks of Napoleon III, and my forests are based on a vague memory of the forest of Sainte-Odile or Haut-Koenigsburg. The family is called Berger because this name can be either French or German according to pronunciation. But it later became mine for two years—some friends in the Resistance gave it to me as a pseudonym, and it stuck. Then I was asked by the Alsatians to command the Alsace-Lorraine brigade, and I took part in the fighting round Dannemarie some days after the death of my second wife in a clinic on the Avenue Alsace-Lorraine in Brive. My third wife lived on the Rue Alsace-Lorraine in Toulouse. Enough. There are a great many streets by that name in France.

It has been noted that Victor Hugo wrote *Marion Delorme* before meeting Juliette Drouet. No doubt whatever prompted him to write it made him more susceptible to the life of Juliette Drouet than a man who kept actresses would have been. But are such premonitory

---

**Les Noyers de l'Altenburg* (a part of *La Lutte avec l'Ange*). Lausanne, Yverdon, Éditions du Haut Pays, 1943. (*The Walnut Trees of Altenburg*. Translated by A. W. Fielding. London, J. Lehmann, 1952.)

†*La Voie royale*. Paris. B. Grasset, 1930. (*The Royal Way*. Translated by Stuart Gilbert, 1935. New York, Random House; Modern Library, 1955.)

creations to be explained by the fact that the virus of daydreaming gives rise to action too, as T. E. Lawrence asserts? And what if there is no action, but only those prophetic lines which Claudel compiled in anguish or in which Baudelaire and Verlaine presage their disasters? "Mon âme vers d'affreux naufrages appareille."*

It was the Alsace-Lorraine brigade that recaptured Sainte-Odile, and Colonel Berger who salvaged the Grünewald altarpiece from the cellars of Haut-Koenigsburg. The boat on which I am writing this is called Le Cambodge; the toothache which the central character of Le Temps du Mépris† suffers during his escape prefigures the pain I suffered from wearing shoes too small for me when I escaped seven years later. I wrote a great deal about torture at a time when no one was particularly concerned about it, and I was to come very close to it myself. Hemingway, throughout the curve which begins with the young man in love with an older woman, then with a younger one, and ends—after God knows how many instances of impotence and suicide—with the sixty-year-old colonel in love with a young girl, never ceased to foreshadow his own fate. And what of Chamfort? And Maupassant? And Balzac? Nietzsche wrote the last line of The Gay Science—"Here tragedy begins"—a few months before meeting Lou Salomé—and Zarathustra.

What interests me in any man is the human condition; in a great man, the form and the essence of his greatness; in a saint, the character of his saintliness. And in all of them, certain characteristics which express not so much an individual personality as a particular relationship with the world.

The gnostics believed that the angels put to every dead person the same question: "Where do you come from?" What will be found here is what has survived. Sometimes, as I have said, only by going out and finding it. The gods do not seek relaxation from tragedy only by resorting to comedy; the link between the Iliad and the Odyssey, between Macbeth and A Midsummer Night's Dream, is the link between tragedy and a realm of magic and legend. The human mind invents its Puss-in-Boots and its coaches that change into pumpkins at midnight because neither the believer nor the atheist is completely satisfied with appearances. I have called this book Anti-Memoirs because it answers a question which memoirs do not pose, and does not answer those which they do; and also because it is haunted, often in the midst of tragedy, by a presence as elusive and unmistakable as a cat

*"My soul sets sail toward terrible shipwrecks."
†Le Temps du Mépris. Paris, Gallimard, 1935. (Days of Wrath. Translated by Haakon M. Chevalier. New York, Random House, 1936.)

slipping by in the dark: that of the *farfelu** whose name I unwittingly resurrected.

Jung, the psychoanalyst, was once on a visit to the Indians of New Mexico. They asked him what was the animal of his clan. He answered that Switzerland had neither clans nor totems. When the discussion was over, the Indians left the room by a ladder which they descended as we descend a staircase: with their backs to it. Jung went down, as we do, facing it. At the bottom, the Indian chief silently pointed to the bear of Berne embroidered on his visitor's jacket: the bear is the only animal which climbs down with its face to a tree trunk or ladder.

*A favorite word of the author's, spurned by the major French dictionaries, Littré and Robert, but now in fairly widespread usage, meaning whimsical, eccentric, dotty, bizarre, fey. Its etymology is obscure, but it seems to have been resuscitated by André Malraux in an early book, a quasi-surrealist fantasy entitled *Royaume-Farfelu*. He uses it constantly in the present book not only as an adjective but as a noun designating a particular kind of crazy quixotic adventurer. (Tr.)

The Walnut Trees of Altenburg

1

1913, Alsace. My father had been back from Constantinople for less than a week. There was a ring at the door very early. In the half-light of his bedroom, the curtains not yet drawn, he heard the maid's footsteps approach the front door and stop, and her grief-stricken voice repeat, without a word having been spoken by the person who had rung, "My poor Jeanne. My poor Jeanne."

Jeanne was my grandfather's servant.

A moment's silence: the two women were embracing each other. My father listened to the sound of a four-wheeler receding in the dawn, having already guessed what had happened. Jeanne pushed his door open gently, as though she was now afraid of all bedrooms.

"Is he dead?" my father asked.

"They've taken him to the hospital, sir."

My father has described to me the gravedigger of Reichbach, up to his waist in the pit amid the smell of sun-warmed clay, looking up and listening to one of my uncles saying, "Come along, Franz, hurry! It's one of the family." We had some twenty cousins in the neighborhood, and the gravedigger bore a striking resemblance to my dead grandfather.

"I've heard a great deal of nonsense about suicide," my father used to say, "but for a man who kills himself resolutely I've never come across any other feeling but respect. Whether suicide is an act of bravery or not is a question that can only concern those who haven't killed themselves."

Most of my uncles and great-uncles had not met for years. They had been kept apart not so much by circumstances as by the hostility between those of them who accepted German domination and those who rejected it—although this hostility had never gone so far as open rupture. Several of them now lived in France. They had all forgathered at the home of my uncle Mathias, who helped to run my grandfather's factory. Only my great-uncle Walter had failed to turn up. Was he really abroad for some months? For fifteen years he had been estranged from his brother Dietrich, my grandfather, but however harsh and obstinate he was made out to be, his traditions forbade him to bear malice toward the dead. Nevertheless he was absent, and his absence intensified the hostile feeling which had always surrounded his name, and surrounded it still: my grandfather had always spoken of him with greater animosity—and also with greater alacrity—than any of his other brothers, but he had appointed him (as he had appointed my father) his legal executor.

My father did not know him. Unable to acknowledge any member of his family who did not treat him with the deference due to the chief of the tribe, Walter was not hated, but was surrounded with the respect which attaches to the passion for authority when it has been exercised unremittingly for forty years. Having no children of his own, he had adopted one of my cousins and developed an austere and exacting affection for him. When the child was barely twelve years old, he used to send him a brief letter every morning, full of peremptory advice, insisting on an answer from him before he went off to school. At the age of twenty, after an argument about some girl, my cousin left home. Uncle Walter, in spite of his wife's distress, had never answered his letters. The cousin, whom he had dreamed of making his heir, became a foreman. Walter never spoke of him, and his brothers, who were aware of his grief, saw it as evidence of enough warmth of heart to make them wonder that in other respects Walter had none.

It is true that if ever their brother proved too intolerable, they were all prepared to say, "With a disease like his, it's a miracle he isn't worse." All his photographs showed him standing, his crutches concealed by a long overcoat: both his legs were paralyzed.

As the *foie gras* succeeded the crayfish and trout and the raspberry brandy the Traminer wine at the funeral dinner, the reunion showed signs of developing into a festivity. Thousands of years have not sufficed to teach men how to observe death. The smell of pine and resin drifting in through the open windows, and the innumerable objects made of polished wood, united them all in the memories and secrets of a common past, of childhoods spent in the shared surroundings of the family forestry business; and as they recalled my grandfather, they vied with one another in the affectionate deference which death permitted them to show unreservedly toward the rebellious old burgher whose inexplicable suicide seemed to crown his life with a secret.

Already old when, for a consideration, the Church granted certain concessions in the Lenten rules, my grandfather had protested furiously to the parish priest, who was a protégé of his since he was mayor of Reichbach (ineradicably: in this region covered with vestiges of the "Holy Forest" of the Middle Ages, the townships still own huge tracts of common land, and Reichbach had ten thousand acres which provided the best part of the municipal funds; my grandfather's professional qualifications were unchallenged). "But, *monsieur le maire*, surely a simple priest must bow to the decisions of the Vatican?" "Then I'll go to Rome myself."

He had made the pilgrimage on foot. As chairman of various charitable organizations, he had had no difficulty in obtaining an audience with the Pope. He had found himself with a score of the faithful in a room in the Vatican. He was by no means shy, but the Pope was the Pope, and he was a Catholic: they had all knelt down, the Holy Father had come in, they had kissed his slipper, and they had been dismissed.

After recrossing the Tiber, filled with holy indignation fanned by the sacrilegious multitude round the fountains, the indifferent shadow on the streets without sidewalks, the antique pillars, the red plush tea shops, my grandfather rushed off to pack his bags, and left by the first express.

On his return, his Protestant friends believed he was ripe for conversion.

"A man doesn't change his religion at my age."

Thereafter, cut off from the Church but not from Christ, he attended Mass every Sunday outside the building, standing in the nettles in one of the angles made by the junction of the nave and the transept, following the service from memory and straining his ears at the stained-glass windows to catch the frail sound of the handbell announcing the Elevation. Gradually he grew deaf and, afraid of missing the bell, ended up by spending twenty minutes on his knees in the summer nettles or the winter mud. His enemies said he was no longer in his right mind, but such unyielding perseverance is not readily dismissed, and for most people this figure with the short white beard and frock coat, kneeling in the mud beneath his umbrella, in the same place, at the same time and for the same purpose for so many years, seemed not so much a crackpot as a just man. Alsace is impressed by faith, and in those days she had good reason to appreciate fidelity too.

Nevertheless it needed all my grandfather's authority, all the success with which he managed his factory (people believe most readily in the madness of the unsuccessful), to survive the consequences of his Roman adventure. The lease between the Jewish community and the owner of the house in which they had set up their synagogue having expired, the owner refused to renew it, and no one was willing to take his place as their landlord. My grandfather proposed to the municipal council that they should lease one of the council buildings; he was met with a flat refusal.

"Gentlemen, can you not see that this is unjust!"

Steadfast silence: an Alsatian pigheadedness equal to his own. He was almost an anti-Semite, but that very evening he summoned the rabbi and offered him free of charge a wing of that very house, echoing with beams and exposed rafters behind its massive door of Louis XVI ironwork, in which my uncles were now finishing their banquet.

It was the same story with a circus to which the council had refused permission to camp on Reichbach territory: my grandfather gave them a home in the timber sheds behind the house.

And my uncles, sipping their raspberry brandy from their fluted glasses, shook with brotherly merriment at the memory of the famous night when they had all gone out together to untie the animals and, Mathias having opened the great door which had been secretly oiled, had ridden off, one on the performing donkey, another on the dressage pony, a third on the camel, and my father on the elephant. Oblivious of the screams of their new masters, the animals had fled into the forest, and the whole village had to be mobilized to bring the mayor's criminal children back to him.

Whereupon, at the arrival of the next circus, he had locked up his children and provided the same hospitality.

In the vast house where a whole exotic menagerie slept in the rooms closed for the summer amid the cicada drone of the sawmill, one of the circuses had left behind a green macaw. My grandfather had taught it, ironically perhaps, the words, "Do your duty." Whenever one of the boys was punished, Casimir (the parrot) seemed to know all about it; as soon as the child came within earshot of the perch, the bird would flap its wings and screech, "Do your duty! Do your duty!" And the child, looking daggers, would run off for some parsley, which is poison for parrots. This one ate it, grew fat on it, and ended up by loving it.

How many summer evenings had this courtyard fallen asleep to the muted hum of the saws and the smell of the warm wood, with Jews flitting stealthily past, bejeweled like Rembrandts, clowns harnessing bears, a kangaroo hopping across the mountainous stacks of timber? Since my grandfather's body had been brought back there, the macaw, now old and freed from its cage, fluttered clumsily through the dark rooms, screeching into the void like the spirit of the dead man: "Do your duty . . ."

My grandfather had made no mistake: the inheritor of his lordly despotism was indeed the absentee, his brother Walter. Themselves manufacturers and businessmen, my uncles revered him as a distinguished scholar. (Perhaps only my father commanded the same degree of respect from them at the time.) After a fine career as a historian, which would have been a dazzling one had he not been Alsatian, he had founded the "Altenburg Conferences" to which none of those now celebrating the funeral banquet at Reichbach had been invited, and which enjoyed considerable social prestige in their eyes. A persistent and no doubt cunning organizer, he had collected the necessary funds to buy the historic priory of Altenburg, a few kilometers from Sainte-Odile, and every year he gathered there some of his more eminent colleagues, intellectuals from various countries, and the most gifted of his former pupils. Papers by Max Weber, Stefan George, Sorel, Durkheim, and Freud were born of these discussions. Finally—and this, for my father, was not without interest or glamour—Walter had been a friend of Nietzsche.

A strange character, what with the memory of Nietzsche and the anecdotes related at this supper table. After Agadir he had had the audacity to organize a discussion on "Nations in the Service of the Intellect," but every one of his brothers (and still more all his nephews) remembered that when still a little boy—it was between 1850 and 1860, and Alsace still belonged to France—he had replied to someone who asked him what he wanted to do "when he grew up":

"I shall work at the Académie Française."

"What the devil will you do there?"

"There'd be M. Victor Hugo, M. de Lamartine, M. Cuvier, M. de Balzac . . ."

"And you?"

"I should be behind the desk."

"What the devil would you do behind the desk?"

"I'd say to them, 'Take it back and do it again!' "

My father claimed that Altenburg was the product of that early dream never, alas, realized.

The following week he received a letter from Walter, who had just returned to Altenburg to supervise a conference, and was expecting him there.

The library at Altenburg was superb. A central pillar thrust the medieval vaults high into the shadows where the bookshelves were lost to view, for the room was lit only by electric lamps set below eye level. Darkness glowed through a huge stained-glass window. Here and there were a few Gothic sculptures, photographs of Tolstoy and Nietzsche, a showcase containing the latter's letters to Uncle Walter, a portrait of Montaigne, the deathmasks of Pascal and Beethoven (almost members of the family, my father thought). In a deep recess his uncle awaited him behind a desk that looked like a kitchen table, deliberately set apart, resting on a wooden dais one step high, which enabled him to tower above his interlocutor. Thus, from a proudly humble cell, did Philip II look down on the splendor of the Escorial.

My father had seen Walter on the platform when the train stopped: although he did not know him, he recognized him by his crutches. Very erect, flanked by two acolytes, his uncle watched him approach in the strange rigid stance he adopted to disguise his infirmity. A very high collar and a small black tie were visible under the light Byronic cape which reached below his knees; gold-rimmed spectacles perched on his broken Michelangelo nose—Michelangelo at the end of a long university career. A greeting in the grand style had been followed at once by: "We get up at eight."

To my father's astonishment, they had set off on foot, the acolytes walking behind. The solemn rows of fir trees under a somber sky of broken clouds driven by the breeze of that poor summer, the clip-clop of the horses' hooves and the muffled creaking of the carriage following behind matched the silent tread of the rubber-tipped crutches. At last, four hundred yards in front of them where the dark lines of the valley converged, the priory came into view, a building of austere and massive beauty. Walter Berger, propped up on his left crutch, had stretched out his right arm: "There." And then, modestly, "A barn, just a barn."

"It's just a barn . . ." he had repeated, brushing all comment aside. And finally they had climbed into the carriage.

Walter looked at the badly lit portraits and the rows of books in the shadows, as though he expected this cloister of learning to put my father in a state of grace. The light shone on his face from below, accentuating its rough-cast quality. He had put down his spectacles, and this low light, throwing his face into relief, brought out the features of his dead brother. This was the man my grandfather, after fifteen years' estrangement, had wanted as his executor—and it was in order to send them on to him that he had bought the reviews that spoke of my father's work in the Orient.

"I was fond of Dietrich," Walter said in the tone he might have used for bestowing an honor, but not without emotion.

There was something abstracted both in his voice and in his expression—as though he were afraid of committing himself, or as though what he was about to say was hardly more than a continuation of his own musings. Nevertheless he went on:

"He had prepared some poison, I'm told, in case the veronal had . . . no effect?"

"His revolver was under the bolster, with the safety catch off."

Standing every week, for so many years, at the same time, in the same place outside the church . . .

Walter started to speak, stopped, finally made up his mind. "Are you in a position to enlighten me—I merely say enlighten—as to the reasons which could have driven Dietrich to this . . . misadventure?"

"No. In fact I should say, on the contrary. Two days before his death we dined together. We happened by chance to discuss Napoleon. He asked me somewhat ironically: 'If you could choose another life, whose would you choose?' 'What about you?' I asked him. He thought it over for some time and suddenly said, solemnly, 'Well, you know, whatever happens, if I were given another life to live, I would want none other than Dietrich Berger's.' "

" 'I would want none other than Dietrich Berger's . . .' " Walter repeated softly. "It's possible for a man to go on caring deeply about himself, even when he has already detached himself from life."

From outside, borne on the rainy evening air, came the inane shrieks of hens. Walter stretched out his hand toward my father in a gesture of interrogation: "And you've no reason to think that during the following day something . . ."

"Suicide was implied by his 'whatever happens.' "

"Nevertheless, you guessed nothing?—I merely say guessed."

"I was convinced that those who talk about suicide never kill themselves."

The one man in the world, my father reflected bitterly, to whom my few moments of success really brought some joy or pride.

In a tone of reminiscence, the immobility of his lips accentuated by the low light, Walter murmured, "Yet one comes to recognize death when it has already struck many times."

"I had never seen a man I cared about die."

"But in the East—all that violence and agitation . . ."

"I've been in Central Asia. Life for the Muslims is a random chapter in the universal destiny—they never commit suicide. I've seen many of them die, but none of those who died were my friends."

Outside, the raindrops pattered on to the flat leaves of the spindle trees as though they were paper; at regular intervals a heavier drop, falling from some gutter, rang out.

"When I was a child," said Walter in an undertone, "I had a terrible

fear of death. Every year that has brought me closer to it has made
me more indifferent toward it. I think it was Joubert who said, 'The
evening of life brings its lamp with it.' "

My father was sure Walter was lying: he could sense the anguish
below the surface.

"Why," the old man asked, "did Dietrich want a religious burial?
It's strange—I merely say strange—and not easily reconcilable with
suicide. He was quite aware that the Church allows suicides a religious
burial only in so far as it judges them . . . irresponsible."

He seemed jealous of the resolution with which his brother had died
—and at the same time proud of it.

"Irresponsibility," said my father, "was not his forte. But after all,
he repudiated the Church, not the sacraments."

He paused, and then went on: "I find what happened extremely
painful. You know the will was sealed. The sentence 'It is my express
wish to have a religious burial' was written on a loose sheet of paper
which was lying on the bedside table beside the strychnine. But what he
had written first was, 'It is my express wish *not* to have a religious burial.'
It was only afterward that he crossed out the negative, with several
strokes. He probably didn't have the strength to tear it up and write
it out again."

"Fear?"

"Or the end of rebellion: humility."

"In any case, how can we ever know? Essentially a man is what he
hides . . ."

Walter shrugged his shoulders and brought his hands together like
a child making a mud pie.

"A miserable little pile of secrets . . ."

"A man is what he does!" my father answered sharply.

By temperament he was irritated by what he called "the psychology
of secrets," which he spoke of as he might have spoken of pickpocketing.
Supposing there had been a "cause" for my grandfather's suicide, that
cause, whether it was the most tragic or the most commonplace secret,
was less significant than the poison and the revolver—than the determination with which he had *chosen* death, a death that resembled his life.

"In the shadow of secrecy," he added in a more temperate tone,
"men achieve equality a little too easily."

"Yes, you're what I believe is called a man of action . . ."

"It wasn't action that made me understand that 'essentially,' as you
say, man is more than his secrets."

He remembered his father's room, the deathbed disarranged by the men from the hospital who had just removed the body, and timorously rearranged by Jeanne, with the hollow in it like the hollows that sleepers always make, the electric light still on as if no one—not even himself—dared to drive death away by drawing the curtains. In the half-open wardrobe there was a little Christmas tree, with many tiny candles. An ashtray lay on the bedside table, with three cigarette ends in it: my grandfather had been smoking either before taking the veronal or before falling asleep. An ant scuttled across the rim of the ashtray and, continuing its course in a straight line, climbed on to the revolver which lay beside it. Apart from a distant car horn and the clip-clop of a carriage in the street, my father could hear nothing but the remorseless sound of the traveling clock, which had not yet stopped. Mechanical and alive like this ticking, the community of insects stretched across the earth, indifferent to the mystery of human freedom. Death was there, in the disturbing light of electric bulbs when daylight is visible through the curtains, and in the imperceptible traces left by men who remove corpses; from the living world outside came the regular hooting of the car horn, the sound of a horse's hooves receding, morning birdcalls, human voices—muffled, strange. At this hour, the donkey caravans would be wending their way toward Kabul or Samarkand, the clatter of hooves drowned in the lassitude of Islam.

The human adventure, the earth. And all of it, like his father's fulfilled destiny, might have been other than it was. Gradually he was overcome by an unknown sensation, as he had once been at night in the Asian highlands by the sense of some ineffable presence, while the velvet wings of the little sand-owls fluttered noiselessly round him. It was a renewal, in a much more profound form, of the intoxicating sense of freedom he had felt that evening in Marseilles as he watched the shadowy figures flitting past in the faint fumes of cigarettes and absinthe—when Europe had seemed so unfamiliar to him and he had watched it as, released from time, he might have watched an hour from a distant past glide slowly by, with all its weird pageant. Now, in the same way, he felt as though the whole of life had become unreal; and suddenly he felt released from it all—mysteriously remote from the world and astonished by it, as he had been by that street in which the men of his rediscovered country glided across the green grass.

He had finally drawn back the curtains. Beyond the huge iron doors with their classical spirals the leaves shone with the vivid green of early summer; a little further down the darker foliage began, culminating in the rows of near-black fir trees. He gazed at the infinite multiplicity of this familiar landscape, listening to the long, drawn-out murmur of

Reichbach awakening, just as, in his childhood, he had gazed at smaller and smaller stars beyond the constellations until his eyes gave out. And from the mere presence of the people hurrying by in the morning sunshine, as alike and as different as leaves, there seemed to emanate a secret that did not spring only from the presence of death still lurking behind him, a secret that was far less the secret of death than of life—a secret that would have been no less poignant if man had been immortal.

"I have known that . . . feeling," said Walter, "and I sometimes think I shall experience it again, when I'm old . . ."

My father looked at this seventy-five-year-old who said, "When I'm old." Walter gazed back at him intently, then raised his hand:

"They tell me you once gave a course of lectures on my friend Friedrich Nietzsche to those . . . Turks, was it? I was in Turin—in Turin, by chance—when I heard he had just gone mad there. I hadn't seen him: I had just arrived. Overbeck, who had been notified, dropped in on me, so to speak, from Basel: he was to take the poor fellow away immediately, and didn't even have enough money for the tickets. As usual! You . . . know Nietzsche's face"—Walter pointed to the portrait behind him—"but no photograph can convey his expression: it had an almost feminine sweetness, in spite of his . . . bogeyman mustache. That expression had vanished . . ."

His head was still motionless, his voice still withdrawn—as though he were speaking not to my father but to the books and the famous photographs in the shadows, as though no listener was quite worthy of understanding him; or rather as though those who might have understood what he was about to say were all of another age, as though no one, today, would be willing to understand him, and he was speaking only out of a weary politeness and sense of duty. In his whole attitude there was the same arrogant modesty as was expressed by his little raised desk.

"When Overbeck, overcome with emotion, cried 'Friedrich!' the poor fellow embraced him, and immediately afterward, absentmindedly asked, 'Have you ever heard of Friedrich Nietzsche?' Overbeck pointed at him awkwardly. 'Me? No, I'm a fool.' "

Walter's hand, still raised, imitated Overbeck's gesture. My father loved Nietzsche more than any other writer—not for what he preached, but for the incomparable generosity of spirit which he found in him. He listened, ill at ease.

"Then Friedrich talked about the ceremonies that were being arranged for him. Alas! We took him away. Luckily we had met a friend of Overbeck's, a . . . dentist, who was used to madmen. I hadn't much money on me, so we had to go third class . . . It was a long journey, from Turin to Basel. The train was practically full of poor people, Italian workers. His landlord had warned us that Friedrich was subject to fits of violence. We managed to find three seats. I remained standing in the corridor, Overbeck sat on Friedrich's left, Miescher, the dentist, on his right, and there was a peasant woman next to him. She looked like Overbeck, the same grandmotherly face. A hen kept poking its head out of her basket, and she kept pushing it back again. It was enough to make one go berserk—literally berserk. What it must have been like for a . . . sick man! I expected some appalling incident.

"The train entered the St. Gotthard tunnel, which had just been completed. In those days it took thirty-five minutes—thirty-five—to get through, and the third-class carriages had no lighting. In spite of the rattle of the train, I could hear the hen pecking at the wickerwork, and I was on tenterhooks. How to cope with a fit of violence in that darkness?"

Except for the lips, which scarcely moved, his whole face was still motionless in the theatrical light. But his voice, punctuated by the raindrops falling from the gutters, betrayed the vindictiveness that underlies certain forms of pity.

"And suddenly—you know, of course, that a number of Friedrich's writings were still unpublished—a voice rose in the dark, above the clattering of the wheels. Friedrich was chanting—with perfect articulation, although in conversation he used to stammer—he was chanting a poem which was unknown to us; and it was his last poem, 'Venice.' I don't much care for Friedrich's poetry. It's mediocre. But this poem was . . . well, by God, it was sublime.

"He had finished long before we reached the end of the tunnel. When we emerged from the darkness, everything was as before. Just as before. It was all so . . . fortuitous. And Friedrich, much more disturbing than a corpse. It was life—quite simply life. Something very strange was happening: the poem was as powerful as life itself. I had just discovered something. Something important. In the prison of which Pascal speaks, men succeed in drawing from themselves a response which, so to speak, imbues those who are worthy of it with immortality. And in that railway carriage . . ."

For the first time he made a fairly broad gesture, not with his hand but his fist, as though he were wiping a blackboard.

"And in that carriage, do you know, and sometimes since—I merely say sometimes—the infinitudes of the starry sky have seemed to me to be as far outshone by man as our own petty destinies are outshone by the stars."

He had stopped looking at my father, to whom his sudden eloquence, seemingly absentminded, was all the more disturbing for being so alien to our family. But already Walter had resumed the strangely disdainful tone which seemed to be aimed beyond my father at some invisible interlocutor:

"Gratified lovers—'gratified,' I believe, is the word?—set up love against death. I've never experienced it. But I know that certain works of art can withstand the vertigo that comes from the contemplation of our dead, of the starry sky, of history. There are some of them here. No, not those Gothic pieces. You know the head of the young man in the Acropolis museum? The first sculpture to represent a human face, simply a human face; freed from the demons, from death, from the gods. On that day, man also fashioned man from clay. That photograph there, behind you. I have sometimes scrutinized it after having spent some time looking through a microscope. The mystery of matter doesn't touch it."

The vast and infinitesimal hiss of the rain on the leaves as it grew gradually finer, like the sound of burned paper uncurling, could still be heard outside; the large drops continued to form and to ring out at regular intervals as they splashed into a puddle. Walter's voice grew still more remote.

"The greatest mystery is not that we have been flung at random between the profusion of matter and of the stars, but that within this prison we can draw from ourselves images powerful enough to deny our nothingness. And not only images, but . . . well, just look . . ."

Through a skylight somewhere, the mushroom scent of the trees dripping in the still warm night drifted in with the rustle of the forest silence, mingling with the dusty smell of bookbindings in the ill-lit library. And in my father's mind Nietzsche's chant above the din of the wheels mingled with thoughts of the old man of Reichbach waiting for death in the room with the curtains drawn, the funeral banquet, and the clanking of the handles of the coffin borne on the men's shoulders.

This human gift which Walter spoke of, how much more potent it was against the heavens than against sorrow! And perhaps it might even have prevailed over the face of a dead man had it not been the face of one he loved. For Walter, man was no more than the "wretched pile of secrets" destined to cherish these works of art which peopled the deep shadows surrounding his motionless face; for my father, the whole starlit sky was imprisoned in the feeling that caused a man already possessed by the desire for death at the end of an often painful life to say, "If I could choose another life, I would choose my own."

Walter drummed his fingers on the book on which his hands had fallen. Once more my father saw that face on which suicide was attested only by a poignant serenity, a smoothing of the wrinkles, the heart-breaking youthfulness of death. And he looked at the almost identical face in front of him, the boldly chiseled features, the fixed, glassy eyes, and on the table, in the full light, Walter's trembling hands, the same hands as his—only stronger—the forester's hands of the Bergers of Reichbach, with their gray veins and gray hairs.

My father was to attend an afternoon session of the congress, half out of courtesy, half out of curiosity, and leave in the evening. That morning one of his cousins, Walter's factotum, a jolly fat man with a natty bow tie who bounced through the corridors of the priory like a ball, told him when he asked about his uncle's connection with Nietz-sche: "I think Walter's role, not so much in relation to Nietzsche himself but in that circle, was that of the useful bore: fairly rich, capable of pulling strings to get people jobs, pensions, and the like. He's both mean and generous (and he's not alone in that). He prides himself on having brought him back to Basel, but in cases like that you could just as well be taken home by the hallporter. As for the letters he received from Nietzsche, which are the pride of his library but which he'll never show you the contents of, my dear chap, they're nothing but complaints."

When the congress opened, my father realized that he had for-gotten the extent to which intellectuals are a race apart. Because in their thinking they seek consensus rather than conflict, because they refer to books rather than experience; but books, after all, are nobler and less garrulous than life. The theme of the conference, which was to last six days, was the permanence of man through the rise and fall of civilizations. Of the discussion, as futile as all ideological discussions —its interest lay in the individual speeches—my father remembered only a few flashes. A shaggy little bearded fellow, buried in his white locks like a cat's paw in a ball of wool, had said: "It is worth remarking that the three great novels celebrating the reconquest of the world were written by a former slave, Cervantes, a former convict, Dostoevsky, and a former victim of the pillory, Daniel Defoe." But it was Professor Möllberg's contribution that had really interested him.

In spite of his title, Möllberg had long since given up teaching ethnology. He had just completed a three-year mission in Africa, from German East Africa to the territory of the Garamantes administered by the Turks. My father had had occasion to facilitate his mission, but had never met him. With his protuberant skull, his slanting eyes and pointed ears, he looked like a vampire from some German romance. He had aroused passionate interest when he outlined some of his researches into protohistoric societies:

"Above the ruler-priests was the king. His power waxed with the moon: invisible at first, he began to show himself when the new moon appeared, and performed minor acts of state. Finally the full moon made him the true king, the master of life and death. Then, painted or gilded (looking, perhaps, like a pre-Columbian king), decked out in the royal jewels, reclining on a raised couch, he received the sacred ablutions, the blessings of the priests. He administered justice, distributed food to the people, and offered the solemn prayer of the kingdom to the stars.

"The moon began to wane, and he was confined to the palace. When the moonless nights came round again, no one had the right to speak to him. All mention of his name was banned throughout the kingdom. Abolished! Daylight was denied him. Hidden away in the dark, even from the queen, he was deprived of his royal prerogatives. He no longer issued orders; no longer gave or received gifts. The only remnant of his former status was this sacred seclusion. Throughout the land, crops, marriages, births were all bound up with these events. Children born during the moonless period were killed at birth."

Here he had raised a lean finger, as sharp and pointed as his ears.

"The wedding of the king and the queen—always his sister, always—was celebrated on top of a tower; sexual intercourse between the king and his other wives was linked to the movements of the stars. As the life of the king was linked to the moon, that of the first queen was linked to Venus—the planet, of course!

"Now then. When Venus, the evening star, became the morning star, all the astrologers were on the watch. If it coincided with an eclipse of the moon, the king and queen were taken to a cave in the mountains.

"And there they were strangled.

"They knew their fate as surely as a cancerous doctor knows the outcome of cancer: chained to the heavens as we are to our germs. Nearly all the court dignitaries followed them to their deaths. They died from the death of the king as we die of a clot on the brain.

"The king's corpse was tended with the greatest devotion until he rose again with the new moon in the shape of a new king.

"And everything began all over again."

In this vast room filled to the ceiling with books, it was as though Africa itself were thinking aloud.

"And all this survives even into historical times: as you know, a representative of the king used to be ritually strangled in the center of Babylon at the birth of the new year, and meanwhile the real king, the all-powerful one, was stripped, humiliated, scourged in a dark corner of the palace.

"There's no question of this king being likened to a god or a hero. He was the king in the same way as the queen termite is queen. This is a civilization of total fatalism. The king is not sacrificed to a moon-god: he is at one and the same time himself and the moon, as the panther-men of the Sudan are at one and the same time themselves and panthers—and almost, quite simply, as children are at one and the same time themselves and d'Artagnan.

"We are in a cosmic realm, a realm older than religion. The idea of the creation of the world has probably not yet been conceived. They kill in the eternal. The gods have not yet been born."

And after an analysis of the "great mental structures," the sequence of which he regarded as forming the human adventure, he had concluded:

"Whether we consider the link with the cosmos in these early societies, or God in later civilizations, each mental structure regards as absolute and unassailable a particular manifestation which orders life and without which man could neither think nor act. (A manifestation which does not necessarily guarantee a better life for man, which may well, indeed, contribute to his destruction.) It is to man what the aquarium is to the fish swimming inside it. It does not come from the mind. It has nothing to do with the search for truth. It seizes and takes possession of man, whereas he never entirely possesses it. But perhaps these mental structures disappear without a trace like the dinosaur; perhaps civilizations must go on succeeding one another only to cast man into the bottomless pit of nothingness; perhaps the human adventure can only be sustained at the price of a relentless process of metamorphosis. In which case, it matters little that men hand down to one another their concepts and their techniques for a few centuries: for man is an accident, and the world, essentially, is made of oblivion."

He shrugged his shoulders and repeated, like an echo, "Oblivion . . ."

"Fundamental man is an intellectual's dream relating to peasants: just try and dream up a fundamental industrial worker! Do you maintain that for the peasant the world is made of anything but oblivion? Those who have learned nothing have nothing to forget. I know what a wise peasant is; he's certainly not fundamental man! There is no such thing as fundamental man, enhanced, according to the age he lives in, by what he thinks and believes: there is thinking and believing man, or nothing. Look!"

He had pointed out, on the main wall, where once, perhaps, a crucifix had hung, a carefully polished ship's figurehead of Atlas, in the crude, bold style of nautical carvings, and below it, two Gothic saints in the same dark wood.

"Those two Gothic statues and that figurehead are, as you know, of the same wood—walnut. But what is beneath those forms is not the basic tree, but logs.

"Outside thought, we have sometimes a dog, sometimes a tiger, or a lion if you like: always an animal. Men have hardly anything in common but sleep—when they sleep without dreams—and being dead. What does it matter if the world is everlasting nothingness, when the tenacity of the best only achieves what is most perishable . . ."

"That tenacity at least is lasting, my dear professor," Walter had interjected. "Something eternal lives in man—in thinking man. Something that I would call his divine self: his capacity to call the world in question . . ."

"Sisyphus too is eternal!"

The discussion over, someone had asked Möllberg in the vast corridor when his manuscript would be published.

"Never. All said and done, it was a struggle with Africa. Its pages are hanging from the lower branches of various types of trees between Zanzibar and the Sahara. In accordance with tradition, the victor wears the spoils of the vanquished."

My father had set off across the fields, which stretched behind the priory between two clumps of forest, speckled with the stars of wild chicory which were the same blue as the evening sky—a sky now as transparent as the sky at high altitudes—across which fleeting clouds were drifting. Everything that grew out of the earth was wrapped in a radiant calm, basking in the early evening haze; the leaves still glistened in an atmosphere quivering with the last cool breezes born of the grass and the brambles. At Kabul, at Konya, my father was thinking, the only talk would have been about God. How often, in Afghanistan, had he dreamed of what he most looked forward to again! The smell of train smoke, sun-baked asphalt, cafés in the evening, chimneys under a gray sky, bathrooms! Coming down from the Pamirs, where the lost camels bellow through the clouds, returning from the southern deserts where, in the thornbushes, crickets as big as crayfish raise the antennae on their knight's helms as the caravans go by, he would reach some town the color of bleached bones. Under a gateway made of clay and bristling with beams, tattered horsemen sat dreaming, their legs stretched out in their stirrups, and in front of dwellings veiled like the women a horse's skull or the skeleton of a fish glinted in the sand of the windowless streets. Outside, not a leaf; inside, not a stick of furniture: walls, sky, and God. After a few months of Central Asia and the endless trot of Afghan ponies, he used to dream of billboards plastered with multicolored posters, or of inexhaustible galleries covered with pictures right up to the ceiling, like the art-dealers' shops in Dutch paintings. But on arriving back in Marseilles in a blue haze similar to the one that was now rising from the Rhine, he had discovered that first of all Europe meant shop windows.

Some of them were still familiar: chemists', antique dealers', butchers', grocers' (but how red the meat was, how small and pale the peaches!). Others surprised him at first: chiropodists, orthopedists, florists, corset shops, a hairdresser's with the notice—new to him— "false chignons," and a window full of funeral wreaths. In a large mirror, women gazed at themselves as they went by. My father now had time to examine them: he was astonished at their swinging hips, the immodesty of these clinging dresses which he had not yet seen in Europe and which were unknown in the world of Islam. He remembered frilly cloche hats, and now saw odalisques in toques or wide-brimmed hats, their hobbled steps suggesting the crippled feet of Chinese women as they made their way among the men in their elastic-sided boots—all those boots!—and fine-checked trousers and panamas and boaters. No Muslim woman wears a hat. The familiarity of these women in their carnival costumes gave every face he glimpsed the sort of blank conviction one sees on the faces of lunatics. And yet, in the absence of the Muslim veil, in the apparition of these exposed faces, Europe took on a poignant innocence. What stamped these faces was not their nakedness, but work, worry, laughter—life. Unveiled.

Was it because, after six years, fashion had transformed people's clothes, or because of a suggestion of obscure haste in the nonchalance of evening, that he felt, watching this once familiar race swarming round him in the Vieux-Port, with its walking sticks, its mustached mannequins, its tangos, its warships in the distance, that not only was he returning to Europe, but that he was also reentering Time? Like a castaway on some shore of eternity or the void, he observed its chaotic flow—as divorced from it as from those who had passed by, with their forgotten sufferings and their lost legends, in the streets of the early dynasties of Bactria and Babylon, in the oases overlooked by the Towers of Silence. Through the strains of music and the smell of warm bread, housewives hurried past with shopping bags on their arms; a chandler was putting up his multicolored shutters caught by a last lingering ray of the setting sun; a steamer's siren seemed to be the signal for a shop assistant in a skullcap to lift a tailor's dummy on to his back and take it into the shadowy interior of a narrow shop—on earth, toward the end of the second millennium of the Christian era . . .

The sun was setting over Alsace, burnishing the red apples on the apple trees. How many successive inquiries had been pursued with the same passion beneath the vaults of this priory? Vain thought, orchards eternally reborn, kindled time and again by the same anguished questioning as though by the same sun! Thoughts of long ago, of Africa, of Asia, thoughts of this rainy, sunny summer day, so fortuitous, so strange —like the white race rediscovered that evening in Marseilles, like the race of men outside the window of the dead man's room, the overwhelming, commonplace mystery of life in the uneasy light of dawn . . .

He had reached the big trees: firs already plunged in darkness, a raindrop still glistening at the end of each needle; lime trees chattering with sparrows. Finest of all were two walnut trees: he was reminded of the statues in the library.

The splendor of these venerable trees arose from their great bulk, but the effort by means of which the twisted branches emerged from the enormous trunks, and the way the dark leaves burst forth from this wood, so old and so heavy that it seemed to be sinking into the earth rather than dragging itself out of it, created an impression at once of endless will and endless metamorphosis. Between them the hills sloped down to the Rhine. They framed Strasbourg Cathedral far off in the serene twilight, as so many other trees framed other cathedrals in the fields of the West. And that tower stretching upward like a one-armed man at prayer, and all the evidence of human patience and labor in the waves of vines reaching right down to the river, were no more than a backdrop to the ageless thrust of the living wood, the two thick, gnarled trunks dragging the strength out of the earth to display it in their foliage. The sun, now very low, threw their shadows across to the other side of the valley, like two broad furrows. My father thought of the two saints and the Atlas; the tortured wood of these walnut trees, instead of supporting the weight of the world, blossomed into ever-lasting life in their glossy leaves silhouetted against the sky and in their ripening fruit, in all their solemn mass above the wide ring of young shoots and the dead nuts of the past winter. "Civilizations or the animal, like statues or logs . . ." Between the statues and the logs were the trees, and their design, as mysterious as that of life itself. And the Atlas, and the faces of the saints consumed with Gothic fervor, were lost therein like the human intellect and all that my father had just heard —buried in the shadow of this benevolent statue which the forces of the earth carved out for themselves, and which the sun, now at hilltop level, spread out over the sufferings of men as far as the horizon.

It was forty years since Europe had been at war.

2

1934 / 1950 / 1965. Art and death are all I hope to rediscover here.

Memoirs rarely bring us the author's encounters with the ideas which are to permeate or guide his life. Gide explains to us how he discovered that he was a pederast, but it is his biographer who attempts to explain to us how he discovered that he was an artist. Yet in my mind—and in the minds of most intellectuals—there are ideas the first encounter with which remains as immediate as if they were persons. I use the word encounter advisedly, because excogitation, the process of elaboration and development, comes later. Nevertheless we sense at once the fecundity of these ideas—which were once called inspirations. And it was in Egypt that I encountered those which for years have governed my thinking about art.

The first of them was born of the Sphinx. It was not yet completely uncovered; no longer buried, as in 1934, but still speaking the noble language of ruins which are in process of being transformed into archaeological sites. It was in 1955 that I wrote the following beside it:

"The weathering of the stone, by reducing its features to the verge of formlessness, gives them an aura of devil-stones or sacred mountains; like the wings of a barbarian helmet, the side pieces of the headdress frame the huge worn face which is further obliterated by the approach of night. This is the hour when the oldest regulated forms reanimate the spot where the gods once spoke, drive out the formless immensity, and command the constellations which seem to emerge from the night to gravitate around them.

"What then is there in common between the sense of communion that arises from the penumbra of medieval naves and the seal with which the monuments of Egypt have stamped the immensity of time and space—between all the forms that have captured a portion of the ineffable? For all of them in differing degrees reality is appearance; and something else exists, which is not appearance and which is not always called God. The harmony between man's eternal drifting and what directs or disregards it gives them their power and their impact: the rugged headdress of the Sphinx harmonizes with the pyramids, but these giant forms rise together from the little burial chamber beneath them, from the embalmed corpse which it was their mission to unite with eternity."

It was then that I distinguished two languages which for thirty years I had been hearing as one. The language of appearance, the language of a crowd which no doubt resembled what I saw in Cairo: the language of the ephemeral. And the language of Truth, of the eternal and the sacred. No doubt Egypt perceived the unknown in man as the Hindu peasants perceive it, but the symbol of his eternity is not some rival of Shiva resuming his cosmic dance in the constellations over the trampled corpse of his last enemy; it is the Sphinx, a chimera whose unreality is still further enhanced by the mutilations which make it a colossal death's head. Then I began to realize that this is also true of the cathedrals of Europe, of the grottoes of India and China; and that art is not an end product of the ephemeral in peoples' lives—their houses, their furniture—but of the Truth which they have each in their turn created. Art does not depend on the tomb, but on eternity. All sacred art is opposed to death, because it is not an adornment of the civilization it represents, but the expression of its highest values. At that time I did not think of the word sacred as having any funereal overtones. The Greek Winged Victory seemed to me a sphinx of the morning. The only enduring realism is otherworldly, and I began to see that, taken as a whole, even modern art is a fabulous beast. I was to go on discovering it for years.

At the time the Sphinx towered over the village and the little temple. Its paws were still buried in the sand, giving it the aura of a sculptured mountain. But the ruins, the true ruins which made the crumbling temples one with the abandoned prisons of Piranesi with their gibbets supporting colossal lanterns, are gradually being transformed into archaeological sites. We shall never see the Sphinx buried again, with a few soldiers perched on its ears like the soldiers of Bonaparte or Nelson; nor shall we ever see again that Athens "which was, alas, no more than an Albanian village." We shall not see much longer those sphinxes sunk up to the neck in the Nubian Desert, nor those that the wind-blown sand has gnawed at until their heads resemble the stumps of the oldest olive trees.

In the Great Pyramid, the funeral chamber of the pharaoh is now accessible.

It was said to be from here that Hitler took his inspiration for the chamber where he used to commune with himself before his speeches at the Nuremberg Stadium. The pillars of the Nazi monument do indeed resemble those of the Temple of Granite, excavated in front of the Sphinx. But the path which leads to the pharaoh's tomb has nothing in common with the path marked out by the geometrical pillars of Nuremberg. First there is the complex labyrinth uncovered by the tomb-robbers—modern robbers, Islamic robbers in the service of the mad caliphs, and above all those who in ancient times groped their way toward the gold of death by the light of their sputtering torches. Their path lay through crevices between the close-knit stones, like prehistoric tunnels, and you expect to make out on these rocks the faded bison of Font-de-Gaume, the traces of formless millennia, when the pharaonic gallery, which cannot be entered standing upright, suddenly appears climbing straight up into the darkness. In Upper Egypt, at the end of even narrower galleries than this, the skeletons of treasure-seeking robbers who were unable to turn round have been found jammed between the walls bristling with mummified baby crocodiles · piled up like bottles.

Fate, with its blind man's gestures, has never ceased to shuffle the dominoes of the sarcophagi of the kings—at Thebes as well as here. Under the Twenty-second Dynasty, the mummies of the great Theban kings were bound up again by the priests and gathered together in a small number of tombs. At the end of the nineteenth century there were found "thirty-three kings, queens, princes and high priests of Amon—together with ten personages of secondary importance . . ." A ship loaded with pharaohs made its way back up the Nile, and disheveled women wailed as it went by, as if at a funeral. While these transfers were being made, many bodies were put into coffins that were not their own. And among the coffin lids that were found was that of Ramses.

Last year I went to inspect the domain of the abandoned shades of Versailles. Little Venice, which used to be inhabited by gondoliers from the Grand Canal; the remains of the menageries with their stone animals and of the maze with its mythical creatures made of lead; the tiny theater of the Trianon where Marie Antoinette played *The Barber of Seville* for her friends (and for Beaumarchais, who was then taken back to the Bastille). The storehouse for the little theater's scenery seemed unduly large. I gathered that its doors had not been opened since the Revolution. A little girl with plaits like tiny horns brought us an enormous key, and the workmen managed to drag the doors open. In an explosion of coughing, clouds of dust enveloped the courtyard where wives of the staff grow geraniums in windowboxes; and the shafts of a carriage draped with spiders' webs like the sails on the galleys of death crashed down on the cobblestones, sending a bevy of black cupids with silvery wings flying among the turkeys.

"They've been looking for that at the Invalides for fifty years," cried the curator. "It's Napoleon's funeral carriage!"

Cleaned up, it resembled nothing so much as the hearse drawn by thirty-six black-caparisoned horses in front of which went Berlioz, his wild hair tossed by the winter wind. And in this gallery of the pharaohs which mounts straight up into the darkness, so close to Bonaparte's pyramids, I think of the day when he tore open the first packet of mail on St. Helena—to find, instead of the news-sheets he was expecting, bundles of love letters from women offering to share his life.

Here is the burial chamber, majestic in its proportions, in the inspired severity of its architecture—these stones seem to have been carved with a razor, like those of the monuments of Mexico—and in the baleful, closed-in character of the place. We have climbed a long way up, and the air is as rarefied as in an atomic bunker. But the rooms in such bunkers lie in the depths of caverns lined with interminable pillars whose preadamite arches are lost in the gloom, with the headlamps of some weird vehicle shining on the white gauntlets of a motionless soldier. Here, the stifling geometry of the pyramid which encloses us emphasizes the purity of the burial chamber and of death. The sarcophagus was destroyed or stolen long ago: its absence proclaimed by the ruined casing is more in accord with these incorruptible walls than its presence would be. One is reminded of the Indian tale about the prince who, after the death of a beloved wife, labors for years to build the most beautiful tomb in the world. The monument completed, the coffin is brought in, but it destroys the harmony of the burial chamber. "Take it away," says the prince. Here the tomb is enough; it is the tomb of Death. Our caves, with their flint implements and their generators, remind us that man invented the tool—but it is in Egypt that we are reminded that he invented the tomb.

One approached Hitler's sanctum down a spiral staircase, of gray marble, I think. Near the still intact ramparts that encircled shattered Nuremberg, where our tanks could not even find the central squares, skeletons greeted us from a balcony: it was the Museum of Natural History, whose windows had been blown in by a shell. The stadium was not destroyed. The lateral salients on which the fires used to burn while Hitler spoke, the rostrum, and even the monumental corridor reminiscent of the Temple of Granite, were still standing. Twisted fragments of the bronze eagle from the pediment were strewn over this ground so recently ravaged by the gods and demons of Germany, as if the Third Reich had gone out with the high beams of the searchlights that had crisscrossed the night sky at the hour when the fires were lit. Afternoon silence, the silence of razed towns after the corpses have been buried. We started down the spiral staircase, dimly afraid that it might be mined. Soon our flashlights were unnecessary; a red glow was rising from the depths, and a faint chorus rose toward us like the voice of this minute conflagration. It was as though the earth of this haunted city, the city of the Horsemen of the Apocalypse and of Hitlerian memories, were determined to preserve an echo of the great scourge, the fiery trail that had ravaged Europe as far as Stalingrad and even now was setting Berlin ablaze: oil tanks like the pyres of Hindu gods with their five-mile-long black plumes, burning farms reflected in the snow at night, cities flaming from phosphorus bombs. As we descended toward that motionless glow, sacred as the flames I have seen in the mountains of Persia where once the altars of the magi were raised, it was as though we were descending not toward the vaguely legendary study of the dictator but toward a fiery sanctuary that had accompanied him through the years as the patient pyre had awaited Hercules. And as it waited it sang, not with the crackling voice of flames but with the gentle roar of a baker's oven at white heat. And the song pierced us like a distant benediction. The horror that we knew only too well (we had opened up extermination camps) still hung over the stadium, over the cities transformed into heaps of rubble and the jagged fragments of the great bronze eagle. Here, in the depths of the earth, an unpeopled twilight throbbed with this inexplicable lullaby for the death of Germany.

We went on down. Beyond the last steps, which hid what seemed to be the debris of a huge red mirror—piles of opened sardine tins lit up by electric lamps with little crimson shades (Hitler's?)—a bunch of Negro soldiers from the first American unit to reach Nuremberg were dancing an impromptu ritual dance and humming a marvelous spiritual. It was the song of the plantations at nightfall, a sorrowful chant improvised long ago by some Southern slave as he listened to the paddle wheels, and it still reached us faintly when we were back among the geometrical pylons modeled on the Temple of Granite.

It was springtime, for as I emerge from the tomb-robbers' passageway and return to the Nile under its sandy haze, I remember, beneath the skeletons leaning across the balconies, a solitary, smiling fat lady jolting over the rubble of deserted Nuremberg on a bicycle, her handlebars weighed down with lilac.

* * * *

In Cairo the poincianas are in flower. I had almost forgotten that color which evokes the tropics as the smell of opium used to evoke China, just as I had forgotten that I had never seen these countries in this season. Pink acacias, cascades of bougainvillaeas, and the three crimson blooms of a pomegranate tree in an ochre courtyard which might have been in Isfahan.

Here is the museum. Thirty years ago there stretched in front of it one of those desert-like areas that the English, though so knowledge-able about lawns, bequeathed to Islam. Its sleeping dust was in keeping with the shadowy figures who sidled up to me one night, one after another, listlessly offering obscene photographs—as it was in harmony with the old Shepheard's Hotel where I stayed before setting out at daybreak with Corniglion in search of the ruins of Sheba. In a world of plush and dust, the colossi of Akhnaton loomed out of the Pompeiian red of its walls with a weird power, on the fringes of a sleepwalking nation, its pleasure-loving pashas and its City of the Dead.

I went back ten years ago and found the dusty museum and the desert-like square again. Today it is Liberation Square; the new, vigorous Cairo rears its squat skyscrapers all around me, and the enormous Hilton Hotel which flaunts its own view of Egypt against the slow soaring of two sparrow hawks, descendants of Horus. At the other end of the square, where the fountains play, the same spiritual presence fills the rooms of the museum, which would be provincial if they did not contain some of the masterworks of humanity—a spiritual presence, and something more disturbing. At the time of its inauguration at the turn of the century, the attendant journalists suddenly saw the officials, in their fezes and frock coats, in full flight, their speeches cut short; the mummy of Ramses, the tragic sorcerer with the parrot's head, white plumes waving in the breeze, was slowly lowering its arm toward them.

A ray of sunlight, striking the mummy and causing one of the joints to swell, had loosened the forearm that once bore the scepter.

How many museums abandoned to their worn plush hangings have I visited, from those in British colonies, where the stuffed birds watch the motionless Dances of Death, to the Breton collections with their accumulations of model ships which sea captains used to present to shipowners, like the ones my grandfather left me. The little Gallic museum whose name I forget, among its flowering hawthorns so simple they have a Celtic air and seem to spring from a soil enriched by the forty thousand hands that Caesar cut off; and the Etruscan museum at Volterra, all its denizens drawn up in rows on little flower-covered terraces as if for a Last Judgment that the Judge has forgotten (with the cries of the market offstage); and the Sicilian villas where the hunchbacks in three-cornered hats look as though they might come down from the walls at sundown to join the night birds. The samurai in court dress in the palace of Kyoto, visible only from the rear, whose dummies tremble imperceptibly at the noise of feet on the parquet, deliberately constructed so that its sound should alert the Emperor's guards. And the Museum of Costumes in Tehran, its wax figures emerging from the gloom in corpse-like attitudes as the neighboring tea merchant opens one by one the windows that are forever closed, as if the Persia of Gobineau were carrying on a secret conclave in the shadows where waxen children in tall bonnets weave carpets that will never be completed. And the patio of the old museum of Mexico City —the Mint built by the Viceroys—where the Aztec gods, which the new museum spurned, punished by having to stand facing the wall under the arcades, surround the garden now gone to seed. And in Cairo itself, the house of the Cretan lady with its divans in screened alcoves and, in the middle of a crazy Mehemet Ali drawing room, in a cage shaped like a mosque, a tropical bird, featherless as a tiny vulture, which the curator used to wind up—and which sang.

I like eccentric museums, because they seem to be playing a game with eternity. None of them could touch our old Trocadero, where you had to crouch down and use your lighter to see the icons from Abyssinia —our Trocadero, or rather its storerooms. I think the aquarium below already existed; and the sculptures seemed to glide in the half-light of the attic like melancholy fishes. The most important pieces (Khmer and pre-Columbian above all: this was before the Dakar-Djibouti expedition) had been rescued by a zouave with a passion for fetishes who was said to have inscribed "Breton Art" under the Mexican masterpieces in such beautiful lettering that no one would have dared (for fear of an outcry from Breton members of parliament?) to dislodge them from these heights. The dummies that had once displayed the imagined costumes of savages and mandarins were stuffed into corners, a gorgeous plumed helmet from Hawaii on a wooden head, or a jade scepter in a wooden hand. And on wires stretched across this attic absurdly modeled on that of a palace in Cadiz, among the clothespins like swallows on telegraph wires, a dusty heap of turquoise and coral feathers hung like the pelt of the Bluebird of the fables, above the only label with a gilded border: "Montezuma's Diadem."

The Cairo Museum is akin to these haunted places. The sarcophagi have had to be moved closer together to make room for the treasures of Tutankhamen. The labels have yellowed. Masterpieces are lined up like figures in a junk shop. But here are the companions of the tricorn-hatted hunchbacks, of the sugar skeletons of Mexico, of Montezuma's diadem: pink cardboard sarcophagi and all the confectionery of Hellenistic Egypt in decay are thrown together higgledy-piggledy in deserted rooms with Fayum portraits and heads from Antinoe still stuck to their shrouds. O soldiers of Islam digging trenches for Saladin's dog roses, O soldiers of Napoleon digging in the dunes to find pharaohs—and unearthing these Horuses dressed as harlequins, these great cardboard figures with hypnotic eyes! A wild-looking princess loses the pink sequins from her Bengal Lancer costume in the sand, to make the trench reach to the Tartar rosebushes.

The tourists move on to Tutankhamen, after a glance at the crocodiles sprawled on top of the cupboards. Around the funerary furniture, gilded, orderly, alarming, the museum is no more than a royal store-house.

In the real tomb, at Thebes, all these furnishings, these golden sarcophagi encased one within another, were watched over by the exemplary black Anubis who symbolizes the king at the moment when he emerges from death to enter eternal night. The frescoes on a yellow background, almost popular in style, painted in haste (no one had foreseen the young pharaoh's death) side by side with those depicting the apes of the sun, are very different in tone from the luxurious funerary objects. Tradition has it that the archaeologists who discovered the tomb died mysterious or violent deaths, but the animals that went in with the humans have proliferated: on the yellow frescoes, the pharaoh's eternal companions no longer have feet, for the passage of rats has rubbed them off. The alabaster cup, which looks almost commonplace in the museum, was found on the threshold of the ante-chamber facing toward the Valley of the Kings: "Mayst thou drink for eternity, turned toward thy beloved Thebes . . ." But here are the dried cornflowers which made it possible to deduce that Tutankhamen died in March or April, and here is the box containing the toys he played with as a child.

Food for the dead—labels written with as much care as went toward the composition of these offerings. Here, the different kinds of fowl, onions and grapes made of stone; there, the menus of banquets without guests (Egypt has no representations of meals until the Amarna epoch) with pigeons and quail. There is a gastronomic meticulousness reminiscent of the Japanese in all this, but more, there is the invisible hand offering for the last time the gifts of the earth. Over all this dust of nothingness hovers the gesture, at once attentive and hesitant, of mothers putting toys into the tombs of children. Here are the triangular loaves of the dead, and all these seeds which are said to germinate when they are planted, and the "mummified flowers," no longer distinguishable from their brown leaves. Why are these dull bouquets so moving? Is it because flowers generally bring to the dead the perfection of the ephemeral, whereas here they were decked out for eternity?

Here is a pink leather dog collar, here are the "heart scarabs" which were placed on the breast of the deceased to adjure his heart not to impugn him before the divine Judges; here is the scarab which assiduously commemorates the killing of two hundred lions by Amenhotep III, here the cosmetic spoon decorated with the figure of a golden jackal holding a fish in its mouth; the down cushion of a child-princess; the blue figurine that women wore around their necks, with the inscription, "Rise up and bind him whom I behold, that he may by my lover." (It bears the date 1965, *Twelfth Empire*. Time's symmetry has often haunted me. What were the events of the year 1965 B.C.?) Here are the castanets and checkerboards, the wooden tortoise stuck with cat-headed pins, here are the mummies of ibis, of monkeys, of fifteen-foot crocodiles and *aha* fish which might have been invented by Jarry, of a gazelle "which belonged to a princess of the Twenty-first Dynasty." And the labels, inscribed by a poet who rivals the zouave in the Trocadero: "Wooden bottles from an embalmer's secret store—magnificent forked implement—various objects, purpose unknown—skeleton of the earliest mare, Eighteenth Dynasty —sarcophagus of a brother of Ramses II, but the bones found in it are those of a hunchback—small box, the property of Her Majesty [which?] while still a child—lock of Queen Tiye's hair: all that remains of that great queen." Further on, the sarcophagi whose dead occupants had to pull or push the bolts, painted for their journeys or their sleep; the mirrors in which the dead might see themselves; and, in a commonplace showcase, the golden nail which closed the coffins of the kings.

Egypt has the oriental taste for gold, but the race that inhabits the museum is made of ochre, of stone and turquoise against the background of desert sand, like the cities of Persia.

Here, now, are the birds with human heads, images of souls. Möllberg, he with the pointed ears, used to say that Egypt had invented the soul. What is more certain is that she invented serenity. For the feeling which strikes me here is not to be confused with the feeling of death. Not even with the contagiousness of that funereal serenity which I once experienced at Thebes. The word death irks me, with its gong-like boom. The soul of a religion can be transmitted only through its survivors—and the religions of the ancient East have been effaced by Islam. I am as profoundly ignorant of ancient Egypt as a man would be of love if he had not experienced it, however much he might have read; as profoundly as each of us is ignorant of death. All that I know of it are these figures which I contemplate as I pass by. Europe has made them a race of corpses, for the companions of Bonaparte instinctively compared the sculptors of Memphis with Michelangelo, Canova, or Praxiteles, whereas I should compare them to their counterparts in the sacred caves, and above all with our Romanesque sculptors. Beside our statue columns, what becomes of the corpse-like rigidity which the Book of the Dead seemed to corroborate? If the "Crouching Scribes" I pass in front of now were imitating life, they would indeed be corpses. We had been studying this sculpture for a hundred years, but we did not see it until the time of Cézanne. Baudelaire still spoke of the naïveté of Egyptian art. Even when carved out of the side of a mountain and sheathed in robes that wrap them round like bandages, the queens of Egypt, by comparison with the queens and Virgins of Chartres, have the curves of an amphora.

There is no Egyptian Baroque, only a decay of the Egyptian style. For three thousand years, almost totally estranged from history, it sheds the selfsame phosphorescent glow over the forms which it unites in the selfsame eternity. Its rigidity is a language. To be sure, this sculpture is magical and not aesthetic, and its figures are intended to insure the survival of perishable bodies. But not because they resemble those bodies: on the contrary, through that which, in these doubles made in their likeness, does not resemble them. If the function of these statues is to insure survival, that of their *styles* is to cut them off from mortal appearance, in order to give the dead access to the beyond.

I cannot find the Hellenistic statues which represented gods and monsters "realistically." What have they done with the "exquisitely feminine" harpy? And the Anubis—a debonair jackal's head on top of a toga-clad figure. Egypt invented Anubis because he *cannot* exist in the world of the living—into which the art of Alexandria strove in vain to introduce him and produced instead an absurd figure in a carnival mask. Ah, here he is, under the stairs.

He would converse with the queens of the old empires in the way puppets converse; but the scene in which the hawk-headed god leads

Nefertari, wife of Ramses, toward the other gods is one of the high
points of art, for this hawk's head surmounted with the pharaonic
crown is no more conceivable outside the Egyptian style than Mozart's
Don Juan outside the terms of music, or the Greek Victories outside
the terms of sculpture. He leads the queen by the hand, yet without
actually touching her, toward a beyond of which the style that unites
them is today the sole expression. The queen is far less the wife of
Ramses than of the god, who invests her with the majesty of the
shades. The creative process spiritualizes the queen as the Tuscan
genius idealizes Venus. And this stylization does not work alone; it
is only here that the queen expresses the quality that makes her one
with the Winged Victory of Samothrace, the Mona Lisa, the giant
faces of the grottoes of India, the exaltation of Western music—with
everything in art that is not completely explicable by art. I only dimly
remember the tomb, which opened at ground level opposite the Valley
of the Queens. That day the sparrows were twittering in the Ramesseum
as they do in the lime trees of France on summer evenings, and I
thought of that murmuring as of bees that rises from the dead, according to the funerary texts. Birds had made their nests in the wings
of the sacred falcons on the bas-reliefs. At Thebes, the sun lit up the
Goddess of Silence and made the Goddess of the Eternal Return
stand out from the dimness of her hypogeum like a hesitant gray
flame. Above the marvelous formlessness of the colossi of Memnon
wheeled a flight of migrant hawks. I have forgotten the tomb, but not
the queen who appeared again on wall after wall in the course of her
funeral journey, with the same divine majesty—until the scene in
which, seated alone before a chessboard, she staked her destiny as a
dead woman against her dissolution into nothingness, face to face with
a void that represents an invisible god.

Here, though, in glass cases, are the remains of men. So much less
meaningful than their images, in spite of their enamel eyes. Ramses's
mummy will menace inaugurations no more. He was ninety-six years
old, I believe. Next to him lies a young princess, more disturbing than
the others because injections of wax have preserved the shape of her
cheeks; she was called Sweetness.

I am overcome with a feeling as powerful as that which I felt before
the Sphinx, when I heard for the first time the separate voices of the
ephemeral and the sacred. It is the mummies that reveal to me my
profound relationship with the statues. Nearly all small figures from
life—wooden Egyptian boatmen, Tanagra statuettes, terra-cotta Chinese
dancers—are funerary figures; but they are not presented to us with

skeletons. Here (and where else?), almost side by side, the gods created by men and the emperors created by gods have crossed the centuries. What has become of the real Ramses, of all the pharaohs whose sarcophagi have never been found? A more or less bloodless corpse, a more or less fallen glory; we have known it for a long time. But we also think we have known for some centuries that a work of art "survives the city" and that its immortality is something more than the paltry survival of the embalmer gods; and what now strikes me, in this doomed museum, is the precariousness of artistic survival, its complexity. For at least a thousand years, throughout the entire world, the art of Ramses was no less forgotten than his name. Then he reappeared as a curiosity, in the same way as the arts we call Chaldean, and all that the Bible encompassed. Then the curiosity became an object of scientific or historical research. Finally what had been an effigy, then an object, became a statue and found a *life* again—for our civilization, perhaps for those that follow it, but for no other. It is not through the Koran that Egyptian Islam brings Egypt back to life, but through the Louvre, the British Museum, and the Cairo Museum. And already this museum is no longer an assurance of survival. Tomorrow, the colossi of Akhnaton will be in a modern museum, and doubtless in the museum of the imagination, where they will no longer be quite what we now see— just as they are now not what artists saw during the primacy of Greek art. The world of art is not a world of immortality, it is a world of metamorphosis. Today metamorphosis is the very lifeblood of a work of art.

In the bookshop at the back of the hall, where the two wings of the museum meet, there are all kinds of books about Mexico, with photographs of the pre-Columbian monuments. The pyramids of Mexico seem at home here; and even more the geometrical perspectives of Monte Alban, the little angular temples of the Plaza de la Luna, all the "modern" architecture, without lotuses or fluting, which links the temples of the warriors of Yucatan with the private temple of Giza and the rostrum at Nuremberg; and the austere architecture which reigned over the dead of Mexico with that which reigned over the Egyptian dead. But let these dead appear, and the accord is broken. Here are photographs of the Mexican Day of the Dead, the inexhaustible appeal of the skeleton. How many peoples have lived on familiar terms with the dead, mingling the black gloom of the grave with a macabre and compassionate humor! The photographs of funerary

loaves in the shape of skulls provide food for thought in this Cairo
where the funerary loaves are in the shape of triangles—as do the dogs
of Mexico skulking in the cemeteries, in this place where the jackals
are mummified; and death, in this Egypt where immortality seems to
lose Man somewhere on the way.

In Mexico City I had seen the image that Eisenstein pinned down
once and for all: one by one, in a slow jig, across the faces of smiling
children, pass the menacing shadows of skeletons revolving on a little
merry-go-round. Mexico . . . the inns of the dead, the frenzy of the
bone-players, and that straw mermaid with the long, sinuous body
beneath a tiny skull that someone once wanted to present to me like
a skeleton in a dream. Nothing could be more foreign to ancient
Egypt, whose art is funerary but in no way funereal—it has neither
corpses nor skeletons. What the voice of the great Egyptian doubles
and the chattering of the little race of death's familiars that then surrounded me called to my mind was not Mexico, where stillborn children
turn into hummingbirds, the Mexico of the longest Feast of the Dead
the world has yet known; it was the Indian world of Guatemala, perhaps because there death has no other form than that of flame, perhaps
because there it plays among flowers.

Flowers of Sicily, Arabian flowers in rocks and adobe houses; flowers
without leaves, orange bougainvillaeas as thick as ivy, huge mauve
trees, sword dahlias as red as Bohemian crystal, which the Conquistadores mistook for agave flowers. I remembered yellow churches
at the end of multicolored streets, pre-Romanesque chapels, a black
funeral that sobbed as far as the fourth row, smiled in the back ones,
and lorries transformed into religious floats with pretty little Indian
girls motionless under placards reading Virgen or Fortituda. This
procession followed a village idiot sitting back to front on a donkey
and wearing the mask of death—as if the corpse of Don Quixote were
leading the saints of Paradise through the volcanoes. Swarms of little
Indians in gaudy costumes were coming down from the forests. My
companions were talking about them: "I said to the woman, 'Why
isn't the last little animal as carefully embroidered as the others?' and
she told me, 'You must always leave one like that, so as not to annoy
the gods. Perfection belongs to them.' " On the base of a Maya idol
towering over a lake, a dog pricked up its ears at the noise of our
passing. "When the people of the north came here, Quetzalcoatl
pointed to his warriors and said, 'I shall conquer with this army.' To

which our Maya chief replied, showing him a newborn child, 'And I shall conquer with this child . . .' " The curator of the museum smiled, and said, "Our leader sent quetzals, which are as beautiful as dream birds; the men of the north killed them; and our people left, saying that they couldn't live in a country where people killed birds." "The Indians are our little brothers," the assistant curator said, without a smile. My three companions were mestizos. We were coming into Antigua, a background for viceroys with its captaincy general, its old university, its fountain with black basalt nymphs on the Plaza Real whose giant trees watched over the sleepers. It might have been a town in Mexico or Peru, were it not for the staked-up flowers in the inhabited patios and the crumpled flowers in the abandoned ones; and above all, were it not for the atmosphere of cataclysm left by the earthquake. Here I remembered that my plane had come in through a sea of cloud broken by the peaks of volcanoes. I thought of Noto in Sicily, with nothing standing above the second story, and so yellow above its immense stairways and its almond blossoms. But Noto has been cleared, whereas the debris of colossal archways fills the open spaces of Antigua, beneath the benign volcano, possibly extinct. The Indians pattered through these streets in which the wind swept up the bougainvillaea blossoms along with the dust. Avalanches of carnations and armfuls of irises covered the dried armadillos in the market. In a section of catacomb, the sanctuary of the marketplace, a solitary infant toddled between the rows of short candles set on the flagstones, and the ice-cream vendor's rattle came like the handbell of the dead.

Behind a still intact façade stretched the nave of the cathedral, eviscerated like the churches of Spain during the Civil War but filled with the cosmic ruins of earthquakes. In the middle a stairway leading down to the crypt, and then the crypt, scarcely higher than my head, with candles that seemed as though planted in the ground, an invisible crucifix, and a single Indian at prayer, holding the hand of a child as small as the one I had seen wandering between the lights in the market sanctuary. I could hardly make out the crucifix, but the walls bore the marks of white hands like those of the Magdalenian hunters on the bison of the palaeolithic caves. The prayer of the motionless, prostrate Indian filled the crypt as palpably as the candlelight.

I was to come across this magical prayer again in the heart of the Indian country, at Chichicastenango. Two sugar-candy churches sparkled against the luminous blue sky, at the top of steep flights of steps. Between them, a colorful marketplace traversed by a procession of black-clad figures escorting the Blessed Sacrament; their conical hats emerging above the tangle of Indian heads made their way toward the pyramid steps where men-bulls and dancers of various confraternities were milling around a sacred figure invisible inside a glass case crowned with enormous feathers. The sound of a marimba could be heard from the cloister nearby, and firecrackers exploded amid the copal tree smoke that rose from the censers like the smoke of a house on fire. All this otherworldly carnival was being played out on the steep steps, as in former times on the steps of the temples of the Mayas.

The high vault of the big church, the Christs with real hair, enamel eyes, and velvet robes, were lost in shadow. Only in Antigua had I seen these short candles bedded in the ground, but now it was more than a faint catacomb glow that confronted me; it was a blaze of light, stretching beneath me like the trembling lights of a town at night as one comes in to land. The air which came from the open door, laden with copal fumes, made all these flames flicker. I thought of the firmaments of fireflies over the marshes of Annam, of Cuban shanties lit by gauze bags full of bees with phosphorescent abdomens. Three beds of candles covered the flagstones of the nave, from the main portal up to the altar, among the kneeling Indians. What I had never seen, even in Peru, was the harmony of these lights with the people who surrounded them, the wave of movement that made the faithful immerse themselves in darkness when the flames bent over. In the first bed of candles, interspersed with ears of maize, the flames seemed to burn to the rhythm of a litany; those of the third, among the rose petals being thrown toward the altar, accompanied an incantation. But the Indians were not reciting: they were talking. The sense of a magical presence —of a sacred madness, profound and tender—stemmed from the solitude of each of these conversations with the unknown, and the fact that here these Indians without villages formed a crowd.

"It's very interesting," said a voice at my side.

The Father Superior, lit up from below, stiff in his soutane buttoned to the neck, as Spanish as a painting.

"It's very moving," I replied.

He looked at me attentively. Behind him crouched thirty or so Indian women, with the heads of babies reaching up above their shoulders like the heads of little devils. They were saying nothing.

"It's for the baptism," he went on.

"You baptize collectively?"

"Most of them are not Christians. Superstition is still very deep-rooted here."

"That sort of superstition doesn't disturb me, Father. The Middle Ages may have been filled with it . . ."

The murmuring lapped round us up to the waist, and I had to raise my voice for the priest to hear me:

"Isn't this a petitionary prayer?"

"The ones who are praying in front of the ears of maize are asking the Lord to bless their crop. But after that, they light a second candle. Those are the ones all around you. They ask for nothing. The flame is the dead person whom they loved best. It is to him that they are talking."

Whence this fervent buzz of voices, so different from the drone of responses to a litany: it was a dialogue with the dead.

"I had to take a lot of trouble to see they weren't stopped. After all, what is prayer? It's a conversation, isn't it? And that's all they're up to. I tell them that when they have finished talking to their dead, they must not forget to talk to Our Lord, to ask his mercy. I think they do so."

"I'm told that vocations are becoming more numerous."

"No. I have eight thousand Indians under my care. It isn't only a question of vocation. All this has an effect on our priests, even the purest. They have to be recalled to Spain, replacements have to be found. For centuries . . . The Indians say something very interesting when we don't understand their conversation with the dead: they say the priest is not a Catholic."

I thought of the days of the catacombs of Asia, when the lights of Chaldea and Phoenicia still burned—"He descended into Hell, and rose again the third day"—and the words of the priest echoed in my ears: "I tell them that when they have finished talking to their dead, they must not forget to talk to Our Lord." This whispering suggested that for them (and only for them?) the Lord was infinitely closer to the dead than to the living.

"When I arrived here," the priest said, "it was on a day like this, a big baptism, many Indians. The nuncio had come with me. Perhaps he knew it wouldn't be easy. I said to him, 'But what am I here for, what am I here for, Monsignor?' He answered gently, 'Close your eyes, stop up your ears—and little by little you will understand.' "

Near the main door, the women had regrouped without putting down their infant burdens. None of the babies was crying. Between the holy tumult of the Maya steps—shouts, flutes, and Indian songs such as were doubtless heard by Alvarado's Spaniards before the final battle—and the faint murmur of the dead receiving their benison in the depths of the invisible nave, not a cry.

"Did the nuncio," I asked, "think that God would do the work himself—but not alone?"

"As always."

He too would soon have to be recalled to Spain. He left me at the top of the steps, in front of the veil of copal floating wispily over the frenzy of the square. He advised me "to go and have a look at the idol." Three hundred yards higher I found a basalt figure, vaguely Mayan, on which pine needles were falling, surrounded by stones and guarded by a drunk Indian. The copal smoke rose over the village, the sugar-candy churches, and a patch of sword dahlias glowing like a shard of red glass.

I hear the impatient drivers blowing their horns outside the Cairo Museum. And somewhere in a country of plumes and ponchos, near Oaxaca where the forest has covered the skeletons of Conquistadores in their black armor, or near the High Andes where the skeletons of the sun virgins lie stretched out on the snow with their white parrots on their shoulders, little kneeling men murmur to the candle flames and a transistor radio plays jaunty Spanish dances in a deserted Indian marketplace.

I hear the murmur of the Indians at prayer, buried in the funereal darkness around the candle flames. They will gutter and die, but their ever-renewed flickering will last longer than the eyes that gaze at them. Corpses folded into jars, musical skeletons and death's headed mermaids flutter around the invulnerable dead of Egypt.

The museum bookshop also has on display my speech about the preservation of the monuments of Nubia, and big photographs of the work in progress. I remember the rounded black rocks of Aswan reflected in the Styx-colored Nile. They had probably not changed a great deal since the time when the young Flaubert caught syphilis there from a girl whose name, Kutchek Hanem, dazzled him as though it were the Queen of Sheba. I believe it stands for "Little Lady." She was caressing a sheep spotted with yellow henna and wearing a black velvet muzzle. Here are photographs of the work on the high dam— seventeen times taller than the pyramid of Cheops—which will give birth to a three-hundred-mile lake and the destruction of which by an atom bomb would annihilate Egypt. The yellow crane at Abu-Simbel lifts up to the sky a bas-relief of prisoners, as if to dedicate it to the sun-god. Here the enormous red saws, and the pieces of the temple transferred to the biblical mountain over the Nile bank on which the Nubians used to light their fires in front of the colossi and the wild mimosas. How strange it is to reread here that speech delivered in 1960 against the background of the Algerian war. "The first world civilization claims the world's art as its indivisible heritage. The West, at the time when it believed that its artistic history began with Athens, looked on indifferently as the Acropolis collapsed . . ."

But when Nubia comes back to me, with its assegais and its black monkeys, it is not Abu-Simbel that I think of: it is a domain of which I was unaware when I came here before, and whose subterranean sorcery pervades the museums of Egypt: animism.

For a long time I had dreamed of the Casamance River. Because of the word romance, and the *Chansons des Iles?* But in the background of its engravings, instead of slim schooners, was the mass of Africa; and the picturesque pavanes of Gorée, the Marquis de Boufflers and his *signares*, mulatto women with veils of tulle over their hooped skirts and magicians' hats on their heads—and such a moon above Cape Verde! (I have seen them since, with Senghor, after he became President of Senegal, thanks to a *Son et Lumière.* The picture-book moon threw the silhouettes of the high-pointed bonnets onto the arabesques of the balconies; and the mad rush of a stray dog into the middle of a pavane was enough to turn the ballet dancers into a ballet of shadows. The night wind was rising over Gorée.)

I had expected to see a few distant processions of muslins and mauve cottons under the bougainvillaeas—a Senegal of another age, asleep on the banks of its delta creeks. But the Casamance is a river-lake, a Niagara, with little sea waves lapping its banks. In the forest, ageless villages of a disturbing cleanliness, for cleanliness seems to us a modern trait. They have kept their priest-kings, whose power is now only spiritual, but whose prestige survives because of the way they are elected. When the king dies, the tribe designates his successor. "But I am not worthy . . ." He is then beaten to the point of death. If he survives, he is king—which carries with it the duty of making sacrifices and which gives him the right to have his way with any girl touched by his straw scepter.

The first king I met was quite young, draped in a spahi's red coat under which he hid his scepter, and surrounded by a tatterdemalion court in European dress of ancestral nobility. After exchanging salaams, I asked him if his spiritual power was waning.

"The missionaries are powerless against the magic trees. And important personages still come to visit me: the British ambassador last week; you today."

A truly regal answer. And above this court of holy tramps, the sun of Africa beating down through the trees.

At the next village, no one to be seen: the women were fishing, the men working on the palm-wine harvest. An old king was playing with a child on top of some high steps. He took our tobacco and watched us depart through long dust-free courtyards.

Then we came to the realm of the queen. In the corridor of her thatched earthen palace, with its wooden pillars, she hastily donned a pistachio-green pleated toga (I had never before seen a pleated toga) which fell into place to reveal the face of a cheerful visionary. A host of familiars surrounded her—her family, the village children, and those who had come with me. She stood with the bearing of a priestess, her forearms raised as if making an offering. Then she spoke.

"Tell General de Gaulle that he is in my thoughts," the interpreter repeated.

"He will be most honored, Queen Sebeth."

Why not? The British ambassador (or perhaps some governor of Gambia?) had presented her with a bottle of whisky: "Her Gracious Majesty presents to Your Majesty the finest liquor in the world."

"Thank you."

I said to the Senegalese prefect, surprised but not displeased, that in these music-hall ceremonies she had more dignity than the ambassador or myself. She had taken me by the hand. "She is leading you to the fetish," the interpreter murmured.

I had been expecting carved figures. The queen's fetish was a tree, something like a giant plane tree. An open space had been cleared around it, so that it was possible to see how it towered over the forest. Out of a tangle of gnarled roots, separate trunks rose up as straight as walls, coming together in a colossal bole which blossomed out majestically a hundred feet above. The angle of two of these trunk walls, over fifteen feet high, formed a triangular chapel, separated from the surrounding area by a little barrier that the queen alone might cross, and with a floor kept scrupulously clean like the floors of the village huts; for the rest of the clearing was covered with the silken snow of kapok, which drifted down continually. In this setting of dreamlike purity, the congealed blood from sacrifices streamed from the tree.

For me, the spirit of the sacrifice was much more powerfully embodied in this majestic column than in any temple I had known. It was not only a splendid tree, a prince among trees, that I was looking at, but a tree that evoked a world into which men were supernaturally drawn, as the gods of Egypt evoked the dead. All at once, the queen threw her arms round my neck and kissed me.

"Does the power of the tree protect the dead?" I asked her.

We were on our way back to the palace, and her cat was following her, an Egyptian cat the size of a lynx, wild and black as our witches' familiars. The children had stopped talking, and their silence seemed to emanate from the unreal cleanliness of the village. The queen did not reply.

"The dead must not be spoken of," she said at last in a tone that brooked no argument. Was it the secret voice of the queens who had succeeded one another here for so many centuries, conferred upon them by that murderous ceremony which Sebeth had lived through?

A quotation stirred in my memory. "And Brunehaut's torture was to be tied to the tail of a horse by her white tresses . . ."

When we left, the old Merovingian queen, standing on the steps of her earthen palace, stretched out her arms in a gesture of benediction. The silky snow of kapok was still falling solemnly from the great tree, and it gathered on the green toga under which her necklaces tinkled in the silence.

In the Cairo Museum it was the dead who spoke. And I realized why it was that I remembered Queen Sebeth. Her tree reminded me of the walnut trees that I had not forgotten, but these were attuned to the rhythm of human life, while the sacred tree was suggestive of a geological rhythm, in which man flitted past like a butterfly. The feeling that had overwhelmed me was one of profound reverence for that seal with which the unknown gods affirm their incarnations. (I had forgotten that Helen of Sparta had been the incarnation of the plane tree.) I had experienced nothing of this kind before the gods who accompanied Queen Nefertari into the beyond; or even before the Goddess of the Eternal Return, scarcely visible in the darkness of her hypogeum at Karnak. Only before the Sphinx. But through the Sphinx, it was indeed the gods of Egypt that the queen's tree in its mountainous majesty evoked. Not only did I have the feeling that Horus and Anubis had lost their souls, as the sacred tree would lose its soul when it was no more than a dead trunk hemmed in by the forest. The gods do not die because they lose their kingly power, but because they lose their property of belonging to the domain of the all-unknowable that was theirs. Whether they were born of the Egyptian nether world, or whether it was born of them, abstracted from it they were no more than fish out of water, fairy-tale characters, figureheads. What did our successive interpretations of Horus and Osiris matter? The gods have no meaning if Olympus no longer has one; Anubis the embalmer has no meaning if the world of the dead no longer has one. Each of the gods had belonged to the impenetrable world of Truth that men adored. Egypt had called Osiris back to life through its prayers, and we called him back through his form and his legend—through everything except prayer. He was born again not in Truth or in the unknown, but in the splendid halls of the world of art which was to inherit this cargo of centuries from a ship of pharaohs wrecked among the pashas. The metamorphosis of the doubles of the Egyptian dynasts descended the melancholy staircase of the Cairo Museum, between the priestly wigs and the panther skins studded with golden stars, through a cemetery of gods.

In a few years' time each of these masterworks, isolated, specially lit, will grace the white rooms of a new Cairo Museum. From the nether world into the world of form, the metamorphosis will be complete. Up there, near the citadel, an edifice of glass or an emir's palace will welcome the masterpieces now slumbering in their Victorian plush. It will rival the flowered museums of Rabat and Damascus. Through vast windows the illustrious figures, from Cheops to Queen Nefertiti, will watch the City of the Dead—as if over the centuries Islam had constructed its greatest necropolis in homage to the tombs of the pharaohs. On the charred panther skins the great gold stars will glow gently in an artificial gloom, reminding me, perhaps, of Hitler and his soothsayer. On the bas-reliefs, the bark of eternity will glide through the thickets of papyrus. And the pyramids will stand out in the distance through the sand haze still quivering in the heat over the Nile as in the days of the sun worshipers.

Queen Sebeth will be dead, and under her tree another survivor of the rites of torment will officiate. Near Mexico City, on the Plaza de la Luna where little temples will still play their forgotten game at the foot of the other pyramid, the sails of dust dismasted by the wind will be torn to shreds as they swirl like the incense on the vertical steps of the Indian churches; the canal on whose banks Montezuma built the garden where the Conquistadores discovered such "beautiful flowers, singular animals and melancholy dwarfs" will rock the tourists' fake empty gondolas in front of an Aztec flower-seller's boat, loaded with violets; and an archaeological expedition will advance among the corpses of the monkeys wiped out by yellow fever. The "little brothers" will speak softly to the flames who are their dead, and the abandoned dead of Egypt will watch the doubles of the ancient civilizations descend the staircase of the new museum, where stuffed birds will doubtless be mixed up with the mummies of ibises. Behind them will descend the god who presides over the most profound metamorphosis of all, that which will have changed the empire of death into a modern museum. If I am still alive, I will come back to see the museum of dust and plush. In the great patch of sky where the two birds of prey are still wheeling, other descendants of Horus will hover; and at Thebes the old funereal murmur will merge with the sound of wings unfolding in the bird-haunted Ramesseum.

3

1934, Sheba / 1965, Aden. How did I take
it into my head, thirty years ago, to search for the Queen of Sheba's
capital?

At that time geographical adventure exerted a fascination that it has
now lost. Its glamour dates from the days of the *Belle Epoque*, as so
many novels testify: Europe had had no great wars for a hundred years.
The eighteenth century, and the early nineteenth, had been responsive
to the historic adventures of a Clive or a Dupleix, but had regarded
solitary travelers in the unknown with a mixture of curiosity and amuse-
ment. Gobineau, as French envoy in Tehran, invited to dinner a
European lady who had walked from Constantinople to Bukhara and
was then on her way back from Samarkand, and was not in the least
surprised that she should talk to him mainly about the care with which
she had clung to her virginity. Such people were just picturesque
lunatics—until they became transfigured by romanticism and by the
familiarity of Europeans with the confines of civilization, the lands
beyond the mountains; the supreme adventure became the penetration
of a forbidden world. At that time the appeal of Arabia lay in its holy
cities and in the independent emirates whose isolation the British were
helping to insure. (Our steamship is now heading for Aden, whence
Rimbaud set out for Abyssinia; and it has just come from Jidda,
whence T. E. Lawrence took off into the Arabian Desert.)

What gave Sheba its poetry—and still does? Queen Balkis? She is
one of the few women who appear in the Bible, arriving out of the
unknown with her elephant crowned with ostrich feathers, her green-
clad horsemen on piebald steeds, her bodyguard of dwarfs, her fleets
of blue wooden ships, her coffers covered with dragon skin, her ebony
bracelets (the sky seemed to rain with her golden jewels!), her riddles,
her slight limp, and her laugh that has echoed through the centuries.
And her kingdom is among the lost civilizations.

The ruins of Mareb, the ancient Saba or Sheba, lie in the Hadhra-
maut, south of the desert, northeast of Aden. No European had been
able to reach them since the middle of the last century; no archaeological expedition had been able to study them; the site was known
only from written accounts. This was enough, however, to allow the
ruins to be located from the air, if the expedition were carefully prepared, and then to be photographed, even if the aircraft could not
land. Since the British objected to flights over their territory, the departure point would have to be Djibouti. I had at my disposal a single-

engined plane, lent to me with trusting generosity by Paul-Louis Weiller. It carried fuel for a ten-hour flight, together with reserve tanks (Mareb was nearly five hours from Djibouti, and it had to be found first; but the return flight would be easy, with the coast of Africa as a landmark). I was no pilot. Mermoz and Saint-Exupéry were tempted; the airmail company refused. Seetzen and Burchardt had met their deaths trying to reach Mareb overland. We would probably be shot at, and the reserve tanks were slung under the wings, but it was practically impossible to hit a plane with the rifles the Arabs possessed. Corniglion was attracted by the idea, and he was not dependent on an airmail company. (Mermoz and Saint-Exupéry crashed at sea; I represented General de Gaulle at Corniglion's funeral at the Invalides.)

What was it that attracted him? Friendship, perhaps, or what the airmail company regarded as the "frivolousness" of the expedition; in other words, the romance.

For more than two thousand years this land has been a land of legend. Such it was for the Romans, and for the writers of the Bible and the Koran, and such it still is for the storytellers of Ethiopia and Persia. I have listened to the latter in the days when the caravans still crossed the main square of Isfahan (preceded by their little guide donkeys with collars of blue beads, amid the sound of cattle bells, each traveler protected by the most efficacious talisman—a fox brush, or the shoe of a Christian child), telling how the Roman army of Aelius Gallus lost its way when it was looking for the coast after being repulsed outside Sheba. "A very bad desert," they would say. According to them, it was the curse of the stargazers of Sheba that made the legions lose their way; and it is true that they wandered for months in this wilderness, led astray by their Nabatean guides, at one time less than sixty miles from the coast that would have saved them. They found only the inland sea, with its motionless waves and beaches covered with bluish shells.

Just as Xerxes had had the Aegean flogged, their general decided that, having failed to take the city, he would take the sea. Crazed by the sun-god, he dreamed of returning to the Capitol with his army laden with the shells in which he saw the spirit of this sea that no Roman had ever beheld. He drew up his troops in order of battle facing the waves. The beetles of Rome entered the tepid water at the command of the war trumpets; each soldier stooped, cuirass flashing in the sun, filled his helmet with shells and went back without breaking ranks, holding a helmetful of echoing murexes or conches, to meet death by sunstroke.

For two centuries Arab travelers reported seeing an army of skeletons buried up to their breastplates in the sand, each with its skinny fingers holding up toward the sun a helmetful of shells. Since they could not have the sea, the setting sun gave these dead legionnaries the entire desert, casting their shadows far across the flat sands, some of them with hands open over helmets they had let fall—open, with fingers infinitely elongated over the sand, like the fingers of misers.

This region plays a prominent role in the popular imagination of Persia, perhaps because the mountain Yemenis are Shiites. And the storytellers of Isfahan (alas, no more to be seen in the square) used to describe the death of Solomon, which the Bible ignores.

For years, Solomon had shunned Jerusalem. Servants of the seal whose last character only the dead can read, his daemons had followed him across the desert. And in a valley of Sheba, leaning on his tall wanderer's crook with his chin resting on his crossed hands, the king who had written the world's greatest poem of despair watched year after year as the daemons built the queen's palace. He no longer moved, but his forefinger still pointed at the all-powerful seal. Every evening his shadow, like those of the half-buried legionnaires, stretched far across the desert, and the daemons of the sand worked on, envying their free brothers shrieking over the desert with the voice of the whirlwinds.

An insect came in search of wood. It saw the royal staff, waited, grew more confident, and began to bore. Staff and king dissolved into dust: the Lord of Silence had wished to die standing, so that all the daemons he ruled might be forever enslaved to the queen. Released, they ran to the town. It was already in ruins, and the queen had been dead three hundred years. They looked for her tomb, until they found the famous inscription:

> I have laid her enchanted heart among the roses, and
> I have hung in the balsam tree a lock of her hair.
> And he who loved her clutches to his breast the lock of
> hair, and breathing its scent, becomes drunk with sadness . . .

And they fled across the desert, after finding the queen with the legs of unequal length buried in a coffin of crystal watched over by a jeweled serpent, motionless and immortal.

These lands of legend attract eccentrics. While I was looking for documents about Mareb, Charcot, my sponsor at the Geographical

Society (which used to house, and doubtless still does, the authentic deathmask of Napoleon), drew my attention to the reports of Arnaud, the first European to reach Mareb.

Onetime chemist with the Egyptian regiment stationed at Jidda, where in 1841 he set up as a grocer, Arnaud had heard the natives speak of Mareb as the city of the legends. He went to Sana with the Turkish mission, and reached Mareb in disguise. There he found fifty-six inscriptions—of which he made rubbings with a shoebrush— and a hermaphrodite donkey.

Leading the donkey by its halter, he took the road back to the russet coast, hiding the rubbings which the Arabs might have taken as a clue to buried treasure, and pursued by the tragic vagaries which seem to have afflicted all who tried to approach these ruins. He passed himself off as a candle merchant (wax is plentiful in these mountains). He had to protect his candles against the greed of the Bedouin, who thought they were eatable; instead of helping him to earn a living, they were tucked away in well-wrapped bundles in his caravan with the secret rubbings. In order to eat, he became a showman, and made his dogged way from village to village toward the coast from which he would be able to make good his escape, exhibiting to the natives his hermaphrodite donkey, which had become his saviour. In this way he was to reach Hodeida, where he once more became a grocer before he was able to get back to Jidda. A hostile dervish smelled out the infidel in him and roused a mob, and he had to flee once more, taking his inscriptions and his donkey with him in a boat, while his enemies celebrated by the modest light of the candles they had looted from him.

He suffered from ophthalmia, and by the time he reached Jidda, where Fresnel was consul, he was blind. He gave his inscriptions to Fresnel, who translated them and sent them to the *Journal Asiatique* and then asked Arnaud to draw up a plan of the dam and the sand-covered temples of Mareb. The blind hand could only trace meaningless butterfly patterns on the paper. Arnaud then took Fresnel by the shoulder and told him to lead him to the beach. There, lying on the wet sand, prostrate in front of his guide who wondered what he was up to, with groping hands he reconstructed the dam, traced out the oval temple of the sun, dug holes with his forefinger to represent the broken bases of columns. The Arabs watched this man making sand castles, filled with a new respect for him because they thought him mad, while Fresnel hurriedly transferred to his notebook these structures that would soon be washed away by the sea, as if everything to do with Sheba were doomed to be restored to eternity.

Arnaud was to remain blind for ten months. He came back to
France, gave the donkey to the Jardin des Plantes, and was sent on
missions to Africa and Yemen. After innumerable adventures, he returned to Paris in 1849 with his collections. The last throes of the
Revolution of 1848 had so impoverished the state that it could not
afford to buy anything, and Arnaud, pursued by a fate almost biblical
in its capriciousness, finished up in Algeria a poor and disappointed
man. The donkey starved to death in the Jardin des Plantes and the
last traces of Sheba disappeared among the political pamphlets in the
cemetery of the riverside bookstalls. The *Journal Asiatique* published
the corpse of so many dreams—the inscriptions and Arnaud's report,
highly regarded by the specialists, in which I read: "Leaving Mareb, I
visited the ruins of ancient Sheba, which in general have nothing to
show but heaps of earth . . ."

I should like to have known Arnaud, with his zouave beard, his
solemnity, his candles, his casual heroism, his simple and charming
genius for adventure. Perhaps, unwittingly, I went to Sheba to look for
his ghost? Or for that of his donkey, which I would have liked too,
and which probably died among the polar bears and the penguins,
delighted with this donkey paradise promised by Allah, but unable to
understand, utterly unable to understand, why it was being held prisoner
there and why they had stopped feeding it.

Anxious but excited, Corniglion and I repeated to each other, "which
in general have nothing to show but heaps of earth . . . ," as we revved
up the engine on the airfield at Djibouti. The military pilots wished
us luck, and we watched the clouds and the sky with the solemnity
of Chaldean astrologers and the weariness of shepherds. Then we left,
casting no shadow in the morning twilight. Behind us, the invisible
waves of the Gulf of Tadjoura broke over the corals, playful dolphins
doubtless skimming through them. That long jellyfish, flaccid and rust-
colored, stretching into the infinity of mist and sky was Arabia—a white
mosque and the walls of scattered palaces. As a boy, I used to look up
romantic cities in the encyclopedia, and I can still smell the sawdust
in the café where I used to read: "Mocha, magnificent palaces falling
into ruin . . ." Here the vessels of Sheba took shelter, and the
Phoenician ships that brought the queen "the little Syrian rose trees,
all spangled with roses . . ."

The anxieties of the shepherd were succeeded by those of the navi-
gators of antiquity. Thirty years ago an aircraft was a big blind beetle

as soon as it lost touch with the ground. The European airlines offered some security because of radio transmitters, but in these parts there were no such things, and in any case our plane was not equipped with a wireless. So we had to rely on the compass and our registered speed to get our bearings.

An endless mist had replaced the straggling clouds like tattered Islamic standards, merging with the sand haze into which we were now plunging, and the crosswind might take us seventy miles off course without any indication from the compass. Whether a plane is flying crab-wise or straight ahead, the needle still points north in the same way. The instrument for calculating the angle of drift took its bearings from the ground, which only appeared now and then through gaps in the mist. As for speed, the speedometers of touring aircraft only showed it *in relation to the wind*. At the moment, ours showed 120 m.p.h. What was our true speed, with this crosswind? About 100, as at the start? Or 130? At last, at the top of a peak identical with so many others, a geometrical shape appeared. Another illusion? No, it was a fort. In Yemen, only Sana is overlooked by a fort. And suddenly a cleft in the mountains revealed, less than a mile away, the valley of Sana, cultivated to the last patch of earth, and in the middle the town inside its sloping walls, with the remains of Rauda nearby, like the shed skin of a snake—Sana, round, built entirely of stone, arid and magnificent, a bowl of white and crimson crystals at the foot of its steep mountains.

Now it was a question of following the valley of the Kharid as far as the Valley of the Tombs, from which we hoped to see the ruins. The mist was thinning. According to the map, the Kharid was quite near, beyond several other rivers. But we could not see a wadi, and we finally realized that the dotted lines meant that these rivers were subterranean: there was no Kharid. We had brought fuel for ten hours, we had been traveling for five, we no longer had any ground bearings. But as we flew on we drew further and further away from the mist, and soon it was behind us. We were over the Kharid! The river ran underground, but in this almost barren region a dark green line of vegetation followed that of the water.

Beyond the Kharid stretched the great southern desert where the kingdom of Sheba lay. It was not yet a desert of long soft dunes, like the north Sahara, but rocky or flat, completely bare and fleshless, a white and yellow skeleton of the earth, full of shadows and doubtless abounding in mirages. No valley, no tombs. It rejected all precise forms, as though embattled against the human eye intruding on its planetary solitude. It seemed as if innumerable rivers, dried up geological aeons ago, were engraved on the sand, ramifying like leafless trees or a network of veins as far as the horizon where whirlwinds raged. The wind carried the sand in flattened swirls; each engraved branch ended in a quivering veil of flame. The whole forest of the desert blazed, a forbidden kingdom in whose depths there surely reigned some sacred scorpion, its scales reflecting in turn the baleful sun and the constellations of the Babylonian sky. Yet the mind soon began to grow accustomed to it all. So did the eye: in front of us, to the right, what was that collection of huge boulders?

We could see the ground more and more clearly as we flew lower, struggling with the viewfinder, as the plane tilted over, like agitated waiters in a café juggling with their trays. We were no longer over the desert, but over an abandoned oasis showing traces of cultivation; only to the right did the ruins encroach on the desert. Those massive oval ramparts, whose debris was clearly visible against the soil, could they be temples? How to make a landing? To one side lay the dunes, in which the plane would overturn; to the other, a volcanic soil with rocks projecting from the sand. Closer to the ruins, the ground was caved in everywhere. We flew still lower, and went on photographing. The horseshoe walls opened on empty space: the town, built of sun-dried bricks like Nineveh, must have similarly reverted to the desert. We turned back to the main mass: an oval tower, more ramparts, cuboid buildings. Tiny flames flickered against the dark patches of Bedouin tents scattered outside the ruins. They must be firing at us. On the other side of the walls we began to make out the mysterious traces of things whose purpose we could not fathom. That flat *H* on the tower overlooking the ruins, what did it represent? Part of an observatory? The terrace of a hanging garden? They were still common in the high Yemen, these gardens of Semiramis now reduced to humble kitchen gardens, but covered with dream-grass, the hemp of the Old Man of the Mountain. A pity it was impossible to land! We flew on, gaining height to fly over another ruin, small and of little interest; then turned back over the town. Like the amorphous hands of the gods of Sheba, aroused too late, mist and clouds began to cover over this shipwreck stranded there like a Babylonian vessel laden with broken statues.

It only remained for us to make our way back in time (but now the wind was behind us); there is no reprieve for running out of fuel over the sea. On the crust of the desert there gradually unfolded the curve of an immense obsidian dagger made of volcanic rocks, glittering with black facets. It was the Valley of the Tombs, which we had missed before, the valley of the Adites where legend has it that the kings of

Sheba are buried, their slate tombs sparkling in square facets like the windows of towns at sunset.

They say there is treasure buried under these slates. I have come across again since then the astonishing glitter of black minerals under the tropical sun. The Bedouin have not yet found their way into the tombs. (They should go and learn in Egypt!) But for them, as for us, this valley of Tantalus remains impregnably guarded; it has delivered up neither its inscriptions nor the names of its illustrious dead surrounded by the corpses of the pre-Islamic warrior-poets:

"How often have I left the husband of a beautiful woman stretched out on the sand by opening the veins of his neck in a wound no bigger than a cracked lip!

"I have left him as food for the wild beasts, who tear him to pieces, gnawing his fine hands and his magnificent arms.

"And under the arrows, falling like clouds of locusts on the damp meadows, the coats of mail flashed like frogs' eyes in a windswept pool!"

Since many more years will go by before the excavators come and fling their spadefuls of mysteries at this sun that once conquered the Roman legions, let that slightly larger tomb, the one on the right, remain the tomb of the queen.

Can it be that the gods of Sheba are not to be aroused in vain? The very day on which the press published our pictures of the ruins saw the army of Ibn-Saud marching against Yemen.

We had reached Djibouti in time: the compass, rudimentary for the purpose of locating a particular site, was adequate for finding the Gulf of Tadjoura again.

The return journey to France was to bring me, in a more commonplace but profounder sphere than that of Sheba, the experience of a lifetime: for the first time I was to encounter the cosmos of the *Iliad* and the *Ramayana*.

We had set off from Tripolitania for Algiers, though the weather forecast was not promising; as we flew over Tunisia, the weather grew steadily more disturbing. We struck cloud, and after a long smooth stretch where the map showed scarcely a hillock, vertical crests, still snow-covered, suddenly loomed up against a continually darkening sky. It was the Aurès.

We were at least seventy miles off course, plunging into an immense cloud, not calmer or stiller at this height, but poised like an animal ready to pounce, compact, alive and murderous. Its flanks advanced toward the aircraft as if it were hollowing itself out at its center, and in the immense, slow deliberation of its movement it seemed to be girding itself not for an animal combat but for some inexorable cataclysm. The brownish-yellow outlines of its frayed flanks, like a glimpse of headlands in a foggy sea, merged into an unending gray, seemingly boundless because cut off from the earth: for the dark cotton-wool of cloud had now slid beneath the plane, hurling me into the realm of the sky, itself occluded by the same leaden mass. I felt as if I had escaped from gravity, as if I were suspended somewhere between the worlds, grappling with the cloud in a primitive combat, while below me the earth continued on its course, which I would never cross again. In the darkness that now filled the cockpit, this tiny machine hanging on like grim death to these clouds now all at once given over to their own uncontested laws seemed unreal, submerged beneath the primitive voices of the hurricane. In spite of the pitching of the aircraft, which dropped at each squall as if on to a solid floor, my whole attention would have been frozen on to this blind engine drawing me forward, if the aircraft had not suddenly begun to sizzle.

"Hailstorm?" I yelled.

Corniglion's answer was inaudible. The metal plane was ringing like a tambourine above the crackle of the hailstones on the cockpit windows: they were beginning to find their way through chinks in the cowling, riddling our faces and eyes. Blinking rapidly, I saw them hurtling across the windowpanes and ricocheting off the steel grooves. If a window burst, it would be impossible to fly the plane. I pressed with all my strength against the mounting of the window and held it rigid with my right hand. Our line of flight was still due south, but the compass was beginning to show east. "Left!" I shouted. It was useless. "Left!" I could scarcely hear myself, shaken, uprooted, submerged under a volley of hailstones which drowned my voice and made the plane jump like a whiplash. With my free arm I pointed to the left. I saw Corniglion push the joy stick as if for a 90 degree turn. We looked at the compass. The plane was turning right: the controls were no longer responding. It was trembling along its entire length, imperiously motionless all at once in a heavy shuddering. The hail, and the never-ending black fog—and at the center of it all the compass, which was our sole link with what had been the earth. The needle revolved slowly to the right, then under a stronger blast it began to turn and turn until it made a complete revolution. Two. Three. At the center of the cyclone, the plane was turning full circle, making level turns around itself.

And yet it seemed as stable as ever; the engine was determined to drag us out of the cyclone. But this revolving dial was more powerful than the sensations of my entire body: it proclaimed the life of the machine just as the still living eye proclaims the life of a paralytic. It whispered to me the secrets of that vast and fabulous organism that was buffeting us just as it bends trees, and the cosmic fury was refracted with precision inside its tiny circle. The plane went on turning. Corniglion was clenched to the controls, at the highest pitch of concentration; but his face was a new face, the eyes smaller, the lips puffed out—the face of childhood. It was not the first time I had seen the mask of childhood overlay a man's face in the presence of danger. Suddenly he pulled the joy stick toward him; the plane reared, and the compass dial jammed against the glass. We were seized from below like a whale in the grip of a tidal wave. Still the same regular breathing from the engine, but my stomach was falling through my seat. Looping or climbing? Between two fresh whiplashes of hail, my breath returned. I realized that I was trembling, not in my hands (I was still holding the window) but in my left shoulder. I scarcely had time to wonder whether the plane was back on even keel when Corniglion pushed the stick forward and cut off the engine.

I knew this maneuver: lose height, take advantage of the force of gravity to burst through the storm, and try to pull out again close to the ground. The altimeter showed 6,000 feet, but I knew how much reliance could be placed in the accuracy of altimeters. 5,200 already; the needle was dancing as the compass dial had done earlier. If the mist extended all the way to the ground, or if the mountains were still below us, we would crash. Now that the plane had ceased to be passive in the struggle, my shoulder had already stopped trembling; all my senses were now gathered in a tension that could only be described as sexual. We were plunging with all our weight, breath held back, bursting through squalls as if through layers of canvas, in the endless stygian gloom which was savagely alive in the tearing sound of the hailstones.

 3000
 2800
 2700
 2550
 2400
 2250 (I felt my eyes bursting out of my head, in their frantic fear
    of suddenly seeing the mountain—and yet at the height of
    exaltation)
 1800

1650
1500
12—

The plain! Not horizontal and straight ahead as I expected, but far off and at an angle. I hesitated before the unreality of this 45 degree horizon (the plane had been falling at a tilt) but already everything in me had recognized it, and Corniglion was struggling to right the aircraft. The earth was still far off beyond this sea of obscene cloud—floccules of dust and hair—that had already closed round us again, and then opened up once more; and suddenly, 300 feet below us, a leaden landscape loomed up through the last shreds of mist, black splinters of sharp hills around a pallid lake which spread its tentacles out into the valley and reflected the sullen sky with a geological calm.

The battered aircraft crawled under the storm, 150 feet above the peaks, then over bleak vineyards and across the lake, which rippled in the wind that skimmed over its surface. At last I took my hand away from the window, and remembered that my lifeline was long. On this land where the ever more numerous lights seemed to spring out of the winter mist now merging with the twilight, roads, rivers, the scars of canals were no longer visible except as the gradually fading network of wrinkles on an immense hand. I had heard it said that the lines on the hands of the dead fade, and as if to see this last manifestation of life again before it disappeared, I had scrutinized my dead mother's palm for a long time; although she was hardly more than fifty, and her face and even the back of her hand had stayed young, her palm was almost that of an old woman, with its fine deep lines intersecting indefinitely. And now it began to merge with all the lines on the earth below me, devoured by the mist and the gathering darkness. The calm of life rose up from the still livid soil toward the exhausted plane, pursued by the trickling of the rain like an echo of the hail and the hurricane that lay behind us; an immense peacefulness seemed to bathe the newfound earth, the fields and the vineyards, the houses, the trees and their sleeping birds.

It was then that I first experienced the sense of "coming back to earth," which has played a big part in my life and which I have often tried to express. I translated it direct from life in Le Temps du Mépris. It is the feeling that any man experiences when he comes back to his own civilization after being bound up with another, that of the hero of Altenburg on his return from Afghanistan, that of Lawrence of Arabia (though he said that he had never become English again); but if the wonderment seems the same, death is more foreign to us than foreign parts—especially when it is bound up with the elements. Later on I took part in air battles; I know what it means not to be able to fire on an enemy (three seconds . . .) because he is the first you have seen wearing a beard under his mask, and his beard turns the battle into murder. But the forces of nature stir up inside us the entire past of humanity. It was at Bône that I came back to earth on that occasion. Warm southern voices at once acclaimed "our performance": they mistook us for some other airmen. By the side of the road there was a gate without a fence, as in a Chaplin film, with an inscription in huge Second Empire characters: *Ruins of Hippo*. In the town, I passed an enormous red hand which was the glovemakers' sign in those days. The earth was peopled with hands, and perhaps they might have been able to live by themselves, to act by themselves, without men. I could not recognize the shops, this furrier's window with a little white dog trotting between the dead skins, sitting down, then setting off again: a living being, with long hair and clumsy movements, which was not a man. An animal. I had forgotten animals. This dog was strolling around quite calmly in the shadow of death, whose fading rumble still reverberated inside me: I found it hard to sober up from the intoxication of the void.

People still existed. They had gone on living while I had descended into the blind kingdom. There were those who were happy to be together, in semifriendship and semiwarmth, and no doubt those who sought, whether patiently or forcefully, to extract a little more consideration from their companions; and at ground level all those tired feet, and under tables a few hands with their fingers intertwined. Life. On the human stage the sweet drama of evening was about to begin, the women round the shopwindows fragrant with the perfume of leisure.

Shall I not come back at such a time—to see the life of men well up little by little, as steam and drops of moisture cloud over an iced glass —when I am really killed?

Aden. From a distance, it is still the rock that Rimbaud saw—of which it is hard to say whether it belongs to Dante or to Gustave Doré—but with the anachronistic air that characterizes these imperial rocks of the former queen of the seas in the age of atomic submarines. The ship's loudspeakers announce: "Because of the situation in Aden, passengers who wish to go ashore do so at their own risk." The British want to make Aden the capital of a federation of the sultanates of South Arabia, to which they will grant independence in 1968. The Arabs who are hostile to the sultans, supported by the Egyptians who are training them in Yemen, want to throw the British out at once.

A motorlaunch from the French consulate awaits us.

As everywhere in the East, a new town has sprung up: the asphalt roads of what was once the British Empire, bordered by South American houses colored by the Indies: Nile green, salmon pink, ash-blue. In the center of the town, a garden unusual in this aridity, with poincianas and oleanders in flower (a placard forbids the removal of leaves). In the center of the garden, the little museum.

It is the traditional museum of the British colony, a neatly kept jumble, with stuffed birds casting a beady eye on a collection of crystals, some costumes, a few seeds and archaeological remains. Better to be on all fours to look at these, as in the old Trocadero Museum. The bas-reliefs, carved on the sides of stones, are ranged like books, so that you can only see the edges. But at knee height there are many alabaster figures. Not excluding Constantinople and Philadelphia, this is the most important collection of sculptures from Sheba.

The Bedouin bring them here one at a time; a rich Arab trader collected a large number of them and bequeathed them to the museum. For Sheba, or Mareb, whatever one wishes to call it, is still in the hands of the dissidents. They have resisted the emirs, the Yemenis, the Egyptians, and what was even more difficult, the oilmen, whose fairly recent expedition failed. The British? They probably learned from their native agents just how far they could go. But in any case, in this part of the world archaeology was not the main preoccupation of their special services. One day, perhaps, a scientific expedition from independent Aden will clear up the "mystery of Sheba"—ironically invulnerable in this museum haunted by the ghosts of the chemist Arnaud and his donkey.

"And the men of Dabar placed the objects they had erected under the protection of the gods, guardians, kings, and peoples of Sheba; whoever defaces them, whoever dislodges or removes a single sculptured image or a single idol, may his race perish!"

If I were a lizard, I would appreciate this inscription. But I like the ones that have to do with those disquieting gods: the moon-god Sin, who is masculine here—though feminine in other mythologies—Dat-Badan, the sun-goddess, and Ouzza, the masculine Venus-god, mentioned in so many inscriptions but still unknown. In this poor museum

where the gallant little flowers are overwhelmed by the water from
cyclopean cisterns attributed to Queen Balkis, set in gorges worthy of
Dante's Inferno, one wonders at the sexuality of a people that conceived of Venus as a man, saw in the sun the feminine sign of fertility,
and in the moon a clement and pacific Father. Was it from the desert
that this benediction of the night was born? But the other peoples
of the desert, during the same epoch, saw the moon as a cruel god.
What cloudy or pure sexuality made this vanished race—whose legend,
confirmed by no historical evidence, affirms that it was always ruled by
queens—see things in the opposite way to everyone else?

At Constantinople, in addition to the collection in the museum,
there was a series of those estimable fakes which, far from imitating
authentic works, invent an art. Here, the statuettes found by the
Bedouin are genuine architectural statuettes, like certain Sumerian
and Mexican pieces, in which the figure is at once worshiper, god, and
temple: and vaguely lifelike kings—much later, perhaps of Parthian
influence? In the second room, a mustachioed king is displayed before
an improvised black velvet drape. How many centuries between these
savage architectures and these vaguely Roman, Parthian, or Palmyrian
faces, whose labels innocently vaunt their "finesse"? And what does it
matter? These are the last envoys of the queen whose perfumes pervaded the Bible, and of whom there remains only a burst of laughter
across the wilderness: "Laugh then, fair hermit!"

Was her crypt ransacked by graverobbers and her mummy sold? Is
all that remains of it a fallen eye, of bone and lapis lazuli, like that of
the pharaoh's queen in the Cairo Museum which was found on the
staircase of a tomb among the mummies of alligators and long-eared
cats? Shall we ever find the thin pressing that covered her face, the
clumsy hollows of metal pressed down with the thumbs to retain the
imprint of her still warm eyelids? Or some ill-cut gold trapezium like
the one in the old Athens Museum that bore the dusty and spurious
label: "Mask of Agamemnon"?

Among the curios, with no particular explanation, there is a gold
hundred-franc piece, bearing the effigy of Napoleon. I remember his
mask at the Geographical Society, in the half-light behind Charcot
when he was telling me about Arnaud. Arnaud writes that when he
arrived in Mareb, another white man had been there before him: the
Arabs remembered his light complexion and the strangeness of his
visit. Mistaken for the Mahdi, the long-awaited prophet, he spent the
evening with the sheik, and distributed to those around him eleven
large gold pieces. After the sunset prayer, though he knew no one

there, a letter was brought to him. He read it and said, "My brother is dead"—then he got up and left. The next day, on the enormous shattered feet of the only statue in the ruins were found eleven "phantom gold coins"; and soon afterward it was discovered that the unknown traveler had been murdered by a neighboring tribe.

Arnaud had one of the coins brought to him: it was a hundred-franc gold piece bearing the effigy of Napoleon. The other ten were still in the Mareb bazaar, though they often changed hands; the sheik had forbidden the gold of this traveler who seemed to possess the wisdom of Solomon to be taken to Sana. Arnaud then asked to see what the Arabs called a phantom coin, and they brought him a wafer-seal. These seals, unknown in Arabia, must of necessity have been brought by the mysterious traveler. Why had the latter invented the phantoms after handing out the coins?

Today, let Sheba, still inviolate, be dedicated to that adventurer who appeared for a moment and vanished at once to his death; so that there where his bones lie—for he is surely one of those adventurers without a grave, passionately caught up in the fascination of chance, and returned to the realm of chance—he may play, as those dead men play who were brave and frivolous throughout their lives, among its flowerless terraces, its crumbling observatories, its perfume stores, and its ruins that seem to quiver with solitude under the silent blur of birds; so that together we may hold in our ghostly hands one of the last mysteries, which will be a boon to us in the endless boredom of death.

A polite curator points out to me through a window the cisterns attributed to Balkis. He talks about King Akram, who fled with his people one night after seeing a rat loosening with its tiny paws a block of the Mareb dam that twenty warriors could not have budged—that dam whose destruction was to deliver up to the sand the wealth and the life of the kingdom of Sheba.

Forbidden city or open city, city of ruins or of bricks returned to clay like those of Nineveh, I shall never see Mareb again. Here are its statues, its inscriptions, perhaps its flowers. The myrrh tree in front of the museum merges into the zinc palm tree, which, when our plane took off from there, was the only tree in Djibouti (now it's a town) with its flocks of goats and its black shepherds in the whiteness of the salt pans, a last glint of sunlight on the heads of their spears. Here is the Negus in the royal guébi. He is seated on a Galeries Lafayette sofa in front of his toga-clad dignitaries. While the interpreter calls Corni-

glion-Molinier "Monsieur de la Molinière" because the Negus with
the sad smile had received some Junkers two days earlier, the roar of
the lions of Judah can be heard through the windows. For centuries,
their cages have lined the great avenue of the palace of the emperors
of Ethiopia, who number the queens of Sheba among their legendary
ancestors. Here is the desert, and the sand haze that is the same color
as the ruins, the dead Solomon surrounded by his daemons, jealous
of the capricious whirlwinds, and a loud cry from the queen who plays
the harp under the constellations with insects' names. Poetry of dead
dreams. For there are dreams that have crumbled to dust—the noble
savage, for instance; and paradises that remain invincible, like justice,
or timeless, like liberty or the Golden Age, and a world of ardent
dreams whose ashes turn into poetry as those of the gods turn into
mythology: chivalry, the Thousand and One Nights. All those other
minor worlds meet and mingle, the ruins of Mareb with those of the
Nuremberg Stadium, the two stone piers which held the torches between which Hitler invoked Germany in the night; with the great
flames of the ancient altars of the Magi in the mountains of Persia;
with the burial chamber of Cheops in the pyramid; and with death,
lying in wait up there among its stellar plains, which caused the network of the veins of the living earth to appear to me like the lines on
my dead mother's hand. With an affectionate irony I contemplate this
outworn dream, for which after all I risked my life, in this little
museum which absorbs it in much the same spirit as the dog roses in
a priest's garden in Damascus once hid the onyx slab under which the
glory of Saladin lies. Across the doorway flits the shadow of a hawk, its
wings outstretched, like a remote and silent guardian.

The curator shows us some butterflies. Did they come from Sheba
to be impaled on these corks? I like to imagine Balkis greeting Solomon
with an oriental obeisance, a butterfly on her nose. I think of the old
queen of the Casamance beside her sacred tree under the silky flakes
of kapok in the same tropical sun. It is midday. We must leave. The
museum will go back to sleep at the foot of the giant cisterns, under
its handsome trees that have no scent and no monkeys.

In the town, a string of grenades has just exploded. Sirens. Shrieks
and yells reminiscent of an Arab rodeo fade away into the ancient
silence. The car takes us off, flying the French colors. Traffic jams and
ambulances in the place where the grenades were thrown. The street
we turn into to avoid the crowds is blocked, but there is another. From
every house Cairo Radio can be heard from sets turned up to maximum

volume, screaming that the British torture the independence fighters.
We are back on the British residential avenue. It is called the Maallah,
but is better known as "Murder Mile." A British radio station is talking
about Yemen.

Four years ago, the Imam of Yemen, recently allied with the United
Arab Republic, broke with Syria by a great dithyramb against Nasser.

"Laugh then, fair hermit!"

ANTI-
MEMOIRS

1

1923 / 1945. In 1923 I expected Ceylon to be a more dazzling version of North Africa. The junk merchants had boarded the steamer yelling like pirates and carrying dainty baskets from which they drew their sparkling trinkets with the solemnity of guardians of the crown jewels. Once on land, I found houses all covered with green on the side facing the monsoon, vast, almost flowerless gardens, palms dripping after the rain; then, toward evening, the Brahman quarter, a glimpse of India in a narrow square with its bearded patriarchs like characters out of Homer in front of a tower pullulating with blue carved figures; and at night the sculptured prows of Arab dhows beneath the ancient light of torches swinging back and forth like hanging lamps—the forgotten vessels of Sinbad.

It was not until much later that I was to become familiar with southern India. In 1929, apart from Benares, I saw only Muslim India. I had arrived in Afghanistan (the Afghanistan of *Altenburg*) by way of Tashkent, already Sovietized, and Termez where caravaneers from Samarkand or Bokhara with their pumpkin turbans and flowered robes, squatting in the meager shade of spiny trees, seemed to have been left behind by the Orient of fantasy beside the Russian airfield. The long landing strip disappeared in the early morning twilight, and already the heat felt murderous. To shield himself from it the pilot had plunged into the well, from which he emerged clad only in his mustache, and ran to play on a swing with a no less naked friend who was also a friend of mine (Boris Pilniak! ha-ha etc.*). The swing was a cooling substitute for wind, and you had to be in good shape to cross the Pamirs; a dozen or so pilots had been killed there—for lack of a swing, no doubt.

Kabal, still almost a forbidden city, was open to the Indians, who had made of it a corrugated iron suburb of Lahore or Peshawar. I wondered whether Lhasa was equally dingy. But after Ghazni, huddled inside its earthen walls, the lavender steppes began, a delicate blue that merged in the early morning with the blue sky over the Pamir foothills. For me, the Afghanistan of 1929 suggests civil war, the usurper boiled in oil (poor Habibullah, with his Minister of Agriculture looks†),

*Boris Pilniak was a well-known Soviet writer of the twenties who wrote books glorifying the Revolution and in particular the industrial achievements of the USSR. He disappeared during the purges in 1935 and is thought to have been shot somewhere in the Urals. (Tr.)

†The reference is to M. Edgard Pisani, Gaullist Minister of Agriculture

those vast blue fields; and on the whitewashed walls of the bazaars, all
those slippers curved and black like commas, and those musical instruments of Aladdin whose sound was never heard. An ossified Islam
was the sole backbone that kept this sleepwalking people erect among its
ruins, between the bareness of the mountains and the solemn palpitation
of the white sky.

I had come from Moscow by airplane, but I reached India by road.
What was the name of that earthen township where I occupied a royal
caravansery with a marvelous ornamental pond full of evil-smelling
water? I can only recall the night of central Asia, the mingled sound of
horses and lorries of the Afridis clattering down the mountain slopes
as in Kipling's time into some Afghan or Indian town, and the caravan
of an archaeologist who had just discovered several hundred Greco-
Buddhist stucco statues. He had shown me how ingenious a bachelor
can be when it comes to keeping his clothes pressed: dew gets the
creases out of jackets. But somewhere near the Khyber Pass he had
unpacked his finds, brought on camelback from Hadda, in order to
replace the cocoons of lavender in which they were wrapped with
European packing materials—and also perhaps for the pleasure of seeing
his statues again. By daybreak that same dew, vanquishing the stucco
which the sand had protected for sixteen hundred years, had transformed these Greco-meditative Bodhisattvas into little heaps of plaster,
which the puzzled camels gazed at as they ambled by as if they were
incinerated souls. Then came the Pass, the asphalt tracks of the British
Empire, peaceful as the roads of the Romans. T. E. Lawrence had
spent some months in one of these forts.

The route through the Khyber was at that time one of the symbols
of British resolve. "And I have done this to show what an Englishman
can do," the dying Scott had written at the South Pole. Those who had
"done" this epic route did not die, but they had truly written the name
of England over the Pamirs. This was the battleground for their
skirmishes with the Afridis or the Kafirs, who used to topple whole
chunks of Himalaya onto the British columns; it was here that a non-
commissioned officer, the only survivor of an ambush, when asked
"Where is the column?" had replied with the voice of Sparta—and the
voice of English humor, too—"I am the column." I think of you now,
my English friends killed in the Battle of London, of the voice of

1961–66 (and then Minister of Housing until his resignation in 1967), a
well-known figure on the French political scene with his black beard and
thick spectacles. (Tr.)

Churchill in the night. In 1929, England seemed invulnerable, and it was not of that England that I was thinking.

Peshawar was truly the capital of the Frontier Provinces: there in the rugged Islam of the mountains sprang up the luxuriant architecture of the Moguls, at once epic and sugary where it is not now in ruins. Then Lahore, the tomb of Jahangir, with its first courtyard in marble for maharajahs, and its second in clay, lined with motionless ranks of waiting vultures summoned from some tower of silence.

Was it near Lahore, or in Kashmir, near Shalamar, that I first came across vegetable ruins? Beyond the historic gardens, the black marble pavilions, the heronries, a vast commonplace orchard stretched over the reddish bronze of fields of amaranth. And all at once, between the apple trees, there appeared a mile-long corridor: an imperial avenue had existed here in the days of the Moguls, and trees no longer grew in the soil which had once been tamped down. Although there were no ruins to be seen, these vanished avenues suggested an unbreakable accord between the earth and death, a Versailles which kept only the existence of emptiness alive. This phantom parkland is vaguely associated in my memory with the observatory at Jaipur, the most dreamlike place of all. I did not think of astrology, for this gigantic construction toy abandoned by the jinns suggested a modern "set," the model of a palace for a Méliès film, rather than the elemental but inviolable domain of the pyramids; I did not think of astronomy, since for us the astronomer's instruments are not built of stone. These sections of staircase aimed at the stars suggested an inaccessible firmament, as the empty spaces of Shalamar suggested the vanished park. And these long triangular ramps were oriented toward the most unreal city of Muslim India. Not only because the Palace of the Wind, an organ in pink stone, is as strange to us as a cathedral is to an oriental; not only because an entire street consisted of painted canvas façades resembling the Arabian Nights scenery of our traveling fairs and hiding perfectly ordinary houses; but because suddenly the populace of melancholy monkeys who seemed to be the true inhabitants of this unpeopled city slowly crossed the street. It was noon, and the sun's shadow, too, was about to change pavements. One avenue led to Amber, which has been waterless for two hundred years. Temples, red marble palaces, roofless houses with wild flowering shrubs growing in the corridors— everything was returning to nothingness in a profusion of plant life, of stone masks grinning through palms, with more monkeys perched on window ledges and peacocks fluttering heavily down through the silence. More dead cities, more red forts, and along the roads those scrawny, docile animals—then the Taj Mahal, where the tall cypresses were not yet dead, and all the little squirrels with short tails and two stripes down their backs.

And finally Benares, its hotels closed at that season; a resthouse where old ladies operated the punkah all night long as in the days before the Mutiny; narrow lanes between high walls of gray stone, erotic sculptures on temples where eroticism seems to be a ritual; the temple of Hanuman where monkeys pursued mysterious errands around a sacrificial stone from which the blood still trickled, drawing back in fear from offerings of tuberoses—all this in a mist drifting down from the Tibetan marches, whose sticky clouds lingered around the flames kept burning in front of the idols. The world toward which those unreal stairways led remains in my memory as a world of lichen-covered walls like those of abandoned ruins in deep forest, beneath which little lights continually glowed while sacred animals made their way through the fog—and all the time, framed in low doorways, brahmans with dripping torsos under their garlands of frangipani, and blood, the lingam, mist, and shadow. Below, the Ganges under the monsoon clouds, with its funeral pyres still dimly flickering in the fog; and an ascetic dancing and laughing his head off, shouting "Bravo!" at the illusion that is the world.

That was the extent of it until, at the end of 1958, General de Gaulle, once more Prime Minister, decided to improve relations with various Asian countries, India among them, which had been more and more neglected for the past twenty years.

My ties with General de Gaulle were already of long standing, although the traditional account of our first meeting is pure invention: the General certainly did not say of me in Alsace what Napoleon said of Goethe, since Colonel Berger was never introduced to General de Gaulle in Alsace. He received me for the first time at the War Ministry, after my speech at the Congress of the National Liberation Movement.*

In 1944 the communists were determined to gain control over all the Resistance organizations. This movement was a coalition of all those which they did not yet control. Their strategy was simple. At least a third of the executive committee were secret members of the party. They urged the unity of the Resistance through amalgamation with the Na-

*Mouvement de Libération Nationale (MLN). (Tr.)

tional Front, already to a large extent communist-controlled. Thus the leadership of the unified Resistance would fall into their hands. General de Gaulle had been humoring them because he was determined to use every means at his disposal to put France on her feet (not one strike occurred from the time of the Liberation until his departure). They for their part were humoring him, relying on time and on the black market to erode past glory. They had wanted to arm the *milices patriotiques,** which their opponents christened the "Mil-pat" (*Mille-pattes*: centipedes), "against the internal enemy." The General wanted to amalgamate all fighting units with the regular army against the Wehrmacht; army or police, the defense of the nation was a matter for the state alone. He alone had opposed the arming of the militiamen and they had not been armed. The communists intended to set up in opposition to him the entire strength of the unified Resistance of the Interior as soon as they could. And we all felt that what was at stake went deeper than politics.

The MLN had asked me to join its executive committee, and in January 1945 I attended its Congress. The leaders of the organizations, the principal combatants, were anticapitalist out of indifference to money, hatred of Vichy, and contempt for the men of the Third Republic. The dialogue between Camus and Herriot was significant. *Combat*, then run by Pascal Pia, had written: "We want leaders who no longer make us laugh." The editorials in *Combat* were unsigned; Camus, when the first attack came, had replied: "This newspaper is edited by a team which is jointly responsible for all its editorials; with that premise understood, I wrote the article," whereupon Herriot had written an article entitled "Reply to a team-man," and we all thought France aspired to be governed by men who did not make her shrug her shoulders. A lot of people would have been delighted to see De Gaulle replaced by a Herriot, but not the Resistance. In spite of Vichy, there had been no shortage of reactionaries either in the concentration camps or in coffins; but in general the organized Resistance was left-wing. Hostility to communism, among those who opposed capitalism, was primarily a hostility toward Stalinism; they far preferred a more or less socialized capitalism to a regime in which the secret police would be the Fourth Estate, and perhaps the first if occasion permitted. It was also hostility toward a mendacious propaganda that might work in closed societies but was ineffectual in western Europe: the line about

*Paramilitary force recruited by the communist-controlled Resistance network at the time of the Liberation. (Tr.)

communist resistance in 1939, the communist call to arms in 1940, the arranging of the Paris truce by the Gaullists in order to save the Germans, the seventy-five thousand communists shot when there were only twenty-five thousand all told, and so forth. The Communist party's acceptance of the Nazi-Soviet pact had not been forgotten, and many people thought that it would submit even more readily to the Red Army when it came to the point. Members of political parties were few in the France of 1939; most of the men of the Resistance belonged to none. They were, in the main, liberal patriots, and it is for this reason that the Resistance never found its own identity, politically speaking. In the eyes of these men, Stalinism was the negation of everything they had fought for. The speakers I was about to oppose at the Congress nearly all denied their party affiliations, only to appear in their true colors the following year. Six months earlier I had had a secret lunch in a country bistro with four non-communist delegates whose groups would soon be amalgamated to form the French Forces of the Interior. Having settled the matter—without controversy—we discussed the future autonomy of the Resistance, then went our ways. I walked through the rain with the Paris delegate along a provincial Station Road. We had done some fighting together. He said without looking at me: "I've read your books. I must tell you that at the national level the Resistance movements have been infiltrated through and through by the Communist party (he put his hand on my shoulder, looked at me, and stopped), of which I have been a member for seventeen years."

He walked on again. I remember the tranquil rain on the slate roofs, and that hand on my shoulder. And also the huge Mutualité assembly hall where we had made so many speeches in the days of the World Committee against fascism, and where this time I was to address the Resistance fighters; but already the political game had started up again. This woman had rescued her husband, submachine gun in hand; this youth had been a member of a group which had attacked a Gestapo van in front of the Palais de Justice; that man had escaped twice—not like myself, but from a prison cell. And it seemed as though these delegations of the night, now that the dawn had come, represented nothing but a dream.

Although most of the Congress members were ex-fighters, their deeds of valor did not exempt them from the feeling of inferiority that the Girondin feels toward the Montagnard, the liberal toward the extremist, the Menshevik toward anyone who declares himself a Bolshevik. While the fellow travelers took heart from joining forces with a party which was beginning to speak of General de Gaulle as if he were a Kerensky, the non-communists were groping because they failed to understand that during these months any movement born of the Resistance must be Gaullist if it did not want to be communist: only the General was really prepared to set up an independent state and nation as an alternative to a communist state. They hardly knew him; he had done nothing to win them over or even to get to know them, had more prestige than popularity, and perhaps believed that they were already in the hands of the communists. My speech was addressed to the Resistance as a whole, and they knew that the following day I was returning to the front.

The Resistance had mobilized the energy of France; it must do so again, or risk becoming no more than an old soldiers' association. We had represented France in rags; our significance did not spring from the action of our networks, but from the fact that we had been *witnesses*. The coal mines of the Nord and the Pas-de-Calais had been nationalized on December 13; Renault, on January 16. These were not right-wing measures. The decisive step, everyone knew, would be the nationalization of credit; if the government took it, it had to be allowed a fair chance to govern, and we would have to define ourselves in terms of a national, not a political, task. There had been talk of the troubles that the repatriation of the prisoners would bring in its wake. Let the movement reestablish all its sections, from the Rhine to Paris, and put them at their service. Let the National Front join with us, if it genuinely wanted to, *for the common good*. Then we would see. "A new Resistance is beginning . . ."

After ten or a dozen speeches, and "fraternal" visits from communist or para-communist delegations, amalgamation was defeated by a vote of 250 to 119. The Communist party would not be able to make use of the Resistance against General de Gaulle. But on my way back to the front through the snow-covered countryside of Champagne, I thought of my communist comrades in Spain, of the epic of the Soviet achievement, in spite of the OGPU; of the Red Army, and of the communist farmers of Corrèze, always ready to help us in spite of the Milice* on behalf of this party which no longer seemed to believe in any other victories but those won by subterfuge. I thought of the hand on my shoulder in that Station Road where the slates gleamed in the rain.

*Paramilitary corps set up by the Vichy Government in 1943 to help the German occupation forces against the Resistance. (Tr.)

2

1945 / 1965. I used to go to Paris occasionally, for a number of matters were still in the hands of the War Ministry. There I met Corniglion again; he had become a general and a Compagnon de la Libération, and was soon to take command of air operations against Royan, one of the last German strongholds in France. Meanwhile he was writing a humorous book in collaboration with Dr. Lichvitz, whom I had known in the 1st DFL,* and who had become General de Gaulle's physician. With unquenchable good spirits, he would read chapters aloud to Gaston Palewski (after some dispute or other in London, this born ambassador had left for Abyssinia to conquer Gondar, before becoming head of the General's Secretariat), Captain Guy, and a few others. This was how I came to know the famous Gaullist "entourage."

A few days after the MLN Congress, we talked about elections; people are always talking about elections. I felt no desire to become a member of parliament. But I had a pet idea about the transformation of education by the widespread use of audiovisual aids. Only films and radio were involved at that time; television was a long way off. The idea would be to broadcast especially chosen master courses, whether to teach reading or the history of France. The schoolmaster's task would no longer be to teach, but to help children to learn.

"In other words," Palewski said, "you want to record Alain's lectures and broadcast them in all the schools?"

"And replace the lesson on the Garonne by a film on the Garonne."

"Sounds splendid, but I'm afraid you don't yet know the Ministry of Education . . ."

We also spoke of Indochina. I had said, written, proclaimed, ever since 1933, that the colonial empires would not survive a European war. I had little faith in Bao-Dai, and still less in the French settlers. I was familiar with the servility which, in Cochin China as anywhere else, brings the middlemen crawling around the colonizers. But well before the arrival of the Japanese army, I had seen the birth of the paramilitary formations in the mountains of Annam.

"Well then," I was asked, "what do you suggest?"

"If you're looking for a way to keep Indochina, I have nothing to suggest, because we won't keep it. The only thing we can save is a kind of cultural empire, a domain of values. But we would have to

*Première Division Française Libre, formed after the Liberation of France to carry on the war against Germany. (Tr.)

repudiate the sort of 'economic presence' represented by the slogan that the principal Saigon newspaper has the nerve to print on its masthead: 'Defense of French *interests* in Indochina.' And ourselves bring about the revolution, which is inevitable as well as just—first cancel the extortionate loans, nearly all Chinese, which are crippling the peasantry of a peasant country. Then distribute the land, then help the Annamite revolutionaries, who are certainly badly in need of help. Soldiers, missionaries, teachers, none of them are bound to the settlers. Perhaps not many Frenchmen would remain, but France might.

"I detest moneygrubbing colonialism. I detest our petty bourgeois in Indochina who say: 'Out here, we can really hold our heads up high,' as if they were veterans of Austerlitz, or even of Langson.* It's true that Asia needs European specialists; it doesn't follow that they should be imposed on her as masters. I doubt if empires can long survive the victory of two powers who proclaim themselves anti-imperialist."

"I didn't become His Majesty's first minister to preside over the liquidation of the British Empire," Corniglion said, quoting Churchill.

"But he's no longer Prime Minister. And you know Labour's position on India."

"All the same," Palewski said, "you surely can't expect our administration to do an about-face like that?"

"France still has the men to form a liberal administration. And another thing. To make Indochina a friendly nation, we should have to help Ho Chi Minh. It would be difficult, but no more difficult than it's been for the British to help Nehru."

"We're a good deal less pessimistic than you."

Which brought us to the subject of propaganda. The Ministry of Information was in the hands of Jacques Soustelle, who wanted to change ministries.

"In effect," I said, "the sources of information at your disposal haven't changed since Napoleon. I think there's one that's more efficient and more accurate: opinion polls."

"Doesn't the Ministry of the Interior use them?"

"It 'has its sources.' But it doesn't make use of sampling techniques, without which precision isn't possible."

In France at that time the Gallup system was known only to experts. I outlined it briefly.

"Do you believe in it?"

*Scene of an engagement between French and Chinese forces in Northern Tonkin in 1885. (Tr.)

"I believe it would be possible to forecast the effect of the women's vote, or the response to the referendum you're preparing—provided you only employ politically neutral investigators. Opinion polls are like medicine: less scientific than they claim, more scientific than any alternative.

"And then, there's the problem of keeping the country informed— in other words, publicity. Now, American publicity methods can only go so far; as for totalitarian propaganda, I think it's inseparable from a one-party system. I doubt whether General de Gaulle is prepared to create such a party. He will accept neither the state at the service of a party, nor a party as the state's main instrument of action. He wants an army, not a militia; a national police force, not a party police force.

"The first objective of your propaganda should be to put him across to the people, because, surprising though it may seem, no one knows a thing about him. But I think the country's energies can be mobilized not by opposing one set of myths by another set of myths, but by offering a program of action. The General's strength lies in what he has done and what he is doing. What are the real forces at the moment? You, and the parties to the extent that the Resistance has disinfected them. The Radicals are going to collapse."

"And the MRP*?"

"It's a safe bet: the country regards it as the General's party. If the communists are your only serious opponents, it's not because of Marx, but because of Lenin. Let each of your Ministers say to the country, 'Here's my most urgent task. I am accountable to you for it, and I won't speak of it again until it's completed.' Wouldn't that work?"

"Perhaps that's one of the keys to fascism . . ."

"After all," Corniglion replied, this time quoting, ironically, Napoleon, "War is a simple art; it's all in the execution . . ."

I was living in the big Dutch-style house at Boulogne where some years later the young Delphine Renard was almost blinded by OAS explosives. It must have been after nine o'clock, for the summer evening was turning to night over the pillbox shelter built by the Germans at the corner of the garden. The telephone rang.

"I have an important message for you," came the voice of one of my regular contacts. "Can I see you in an hour or two?"

"By all means."

* * * *

Mouvement Républicain Populaire: the democratic Catholic party which grew out of the Resistance. Its first leader was Georges Bidault. (Tr.)

"I'll be round about eleven."

At eleven o'clock a military car pulled up outside the house. I opened the door. We were alone. The man who had telephoned did not cross the threshold of the huge studio, which was still only dimly lit.

"General de Gaulle asks you in the name of France if you will help him."

It was an odd way of putting it. But in London one of the General's first speeches to his officers was something like, "Gentlemen, you know where your duty lies." The tone of today's message was identical.

"It goes without saying," I answered.

"I'll tell you what time tomorrow."

We shook hands. The car, which had turned round, skirted the little pillbox and disappeared in the direction of the Seine.

I was surprised; though not excessively so—I have a tendency to think myself useful. But after my first escape, in November 1940, I had written to General de Gaulle, assuming that the Free French Forces could use any airmen they could find. No reply. Since he was said to have rejected Pierre Cot, I supposed that he found my support unwelcome because of my participation in the Spanish Civil War; no rancor was involved, however, for later on, before the creation of the Alsace-Lorraine Brigade, our maquis group had always found General Koenig—and behind him De Gaulle—ready to help. I was summoned to the War Ministry. In the waiting room I found a genial visitor who spoke with a shrewd and polite good sense that intrigued me, for in spite of his dress I guessed that he was a soldier. Soon he was sent for: it was Marshal Juin.

The office, decorated in a resplendent Empire style, which had once belonged to Count Daru, had been allocated to Palewski. On the other side of the monumental staircase was an anteroom where the aides sat, and then General de Gaulle's room. "It's far from settled," one of the officers, a friend of mine, said to me. I was shown in as the clock struck; some large ordnance survey maps on the walls gave the room a working atmosphere. He motioned to me to sit down to the right of his desk.

I had retained an exact memory of his face: in 1943 Ravanel, then chief of the *groupes francs*,* had shown me a photograph of him that had arrived by parachute. It was a head-and-shoulders picture; we did

*Resistance commandos. (Tr.)

not even know that General de Gaulle was very tall. I was reminded of the delegates of the Third Estate who were stupefied the first time they saw Louis XVI; up to 1943 we had not known the face of the man in whose name we were fighting.

What struck me now were the ways in which he did not resemble his photographs. The real mouth was a little smaller, the mustache a little darker. And films, although they convey all sorts of expressions, only once caught his dense, heavy gaze—much later, during an interview with Michel Droit, when he looked straight into the camera and seemed to be looking at each individual viewer.

"First of all, the past," he said.

A surprising introduction.

"It's simple enough," I replied. "I engaged in a struggle for—let's call it social justice. Perhaps, more precisely, the aim was to give men a chance. I was president of the World Committee against fascism with Romain Rolland, and I went with Gide to deliver to Hitler—who refused to see us—a protest against the Reichstag Fire trials. Then there was the Spanish Civil War, and I went to fight in Spain. Not with the International Brigade—it didn't yet exist, and it was we who gave it the time to exist: the Communist party was still thinking it over. Then came the war, the real one. Then defeat, and like so many others I became wedded to France. When I got back to Paris, Albert Camus asked me whether we would one day have to choose between Russia and America. To me, the choice is not between Russia and America, but between Russia and France. When a weak France finds herself face to face with a powerful Russia, I no longer believe a word of what I used to believe when a powerful France faced a weak Soviet Union. A weak Russia wants popular fronts, a strong Russia wants people's democracies.

"I once heard Stalin say: 'At the beginning of the Revolution we looked to European revolution to save us, and now the European revolution waits upon the Red Army.' I don't believe in a revolution in France brought about by the Red Army and kept in being by the OGPU—any more than I believe in a return to 1938.

"From a historical standpoint, it seems to me that the essential lesson of the last twenty years has been the primacy of the nation—which is not the same as nationalism: it's a matter of individuality, not superiority. Marx, Victor Hugo, Michelet (who went so far as to write, 'France is a person') all believed in a United States of Europe. In this context it wasn't Marx who was the prophet, but Nietzsche, when he wrote that the twentieth century would be the century of national wars. Did you hear the *Internationale* when you were in Moscow, General?"

"It wasn't mentioned: it had gone sour."

"I was there when the Russian national anthem became the official ceremonial music. For some weeks *Pravda* had been using, for the first time, the phrase 'our Soviet fatherland.' Everybody knew what it meant. And I realized that what was happening was that at last Russia had found in communism a way to assert her position and prestige in the world—a successful Orthodoxy or Pan-Slavism."

He was looking at me attentively, with no sign either of agreement or disagreement.

"Because, even if one disregarded Lenin, Trotsky, and Stalin—which would be difficult—communism would still come nearer than anything else today to expressing the revolutionary impulse, which the French Revolution expressed in its time."

"What do you mean by the revolutionary impulse?"

"The provisional form which the demand for justice assumes—from peasant risings to revolutions. In our century, it's a matter of social justice, which is no doubt partly due to the decline of the great religions; the Americans are believers, but American civilization is not a religious one.

"The National Front is para-communist, on the way to being openly communist; my friends are para-labourites, on the way toward a social democracy which doesn't yet exist and which they don't know whether to look for from themselves, from the Socialist party, or from you."

"What do they want to *do?*"

"The same as in 1848 and 1871—play out a heroic drama called revolution. Honorably, in the case of the genuine ones, not those who came out of the woodwork when the army arrived. To paraphrase—Clausewitz, wasn't it?—I should say that for them politics is a continuation of war by other means. Unfortunately it isn't true. For me (as for you, too, I think, and even for the communists) politics means creating a state, and then making it work. Without a state, politics is in the future, and more or less boils down to a system of ethics. Which is something that the Resistance organizations seem quite unaware of. If it isn't a question of revolution, what is it? For the politicians, whether of yesterday or tomorrow, it's a question of joining the party, or forming a new one. The communist sympathizers in the Resistance will end up as party members or belonging to some front organization. The others will end up God knows where, because, as I've told M. Palewski, the parties need disinfecting. But if there were Radicals in the maquis, the maquis isn't Radical. A party must have objectives. The Resistance had one: to help liberate France. As a whole, the men of the Resistance were liberal patriots. Liberalism is a sentiment, not a political program—a sentiment that can exist in several parties, but cannot create one. That is the current dilemma of the Resistance, as I discovered at the MLN Congress.

"Its members aren't against communism. As an economic doctrine, fifty per cent of them are for it. It's the communists they are against, or rather the Russian element in French communism. They don't see the energy they admire in the Russian party as being inseparable from all the accusations, the equivocations, the expulsions—not to mention the trials—that they hold against it. The secret dream of a good many Frenchmen, and most French intellectuals, is a guillotine without the victims. What fascinates them in communism is all that energy in the service of social justice; what alienates them is the means by which that energy is applied. Liberalism is by no means dead. None of the parties had many members before the war, and what I have seen of the atmosphere of the Liberation, in the provinces and on the newsreels, suggests a victorious Popular Front. But the Popular Front never achieved its revolution or its single party (and neither did its opponents). What I once called, apropos of Spain, the 'lyrical illusion,' doesn't lead to a genuine political structure. It's as true of the Radicals as it is of the communists, only for different reasons, that they only join a Popular Front in order to destroy it."

"Do you think so?" His tone was perhaps ironic.

"I think that not only liberalism but the parliamentary game itself is doomed in any country where the parties are in coalition with a strong communist party. Parliamentary government implies playing the game according to the rules—as is shown by the most successful of all, the British. The communists use the game for their own ends, but they don't play it. And it only requires one player to ignore the rules for the nature of the entire game to be changed. If the Socialist party, the Radical party, and all the others are parties, then the communists are something else.

"Furthermore, the traditional right was bound up with Vichy, so we're going to see a left continually being outbid by the communists, and no recognized right. And yet it isn't only the Resistance, it's the country as a whole which has no wish to revert to old-style parliamentarianism. Because they sense that we are going through the most violent metamorphosis the West has known since the fall of the Roman Empire. And they don't want to face it under the guidance of M. Herriot. Then again, the end of the Third Republic is identified with defeat, although it didn't put up such a bad fight in the 1914-18 war . . ."

He raised his forefinger in an admonitory gesture: "It wasn't the Republic that won that war, it was France. When war was declared, then at the Marne, and after Clemenceau took over, party rivalries and bickering were put in cold storage."

"Didn't Clemenceau stand for Republican France?"

"I have reestablished the Republic. But it must be able to create a new France. The idea of the nation is quite a different matter from nationalism, I realize that. So do the communists, in their fashion. That was why they were so keen on the idea of militias. They know in their bones that a state that cannot guarantee the defense of the nation is doomed. Neither the two French Empires, nor the German Empire, nor the Russian Empire was able to survive defeat. Therein lies the basic legitimacy of the state. You are right when you say that communism enabled Russia to rebuild its army. . ."

"And to find its soul again."

I realized that I had interrupted him, for sometimes he would allow long pauses between his sentences while he pursued his train of thought.

". . . And Asia can only find its soul again, as you say, by recovering its nationhoods. Perhaps the French monarchy died at Rossbach. Please go on."

"Churchill writes somewhere that Clemenceau seemed to him one of the men of the Revolution."

He half-closed his eyes, with an expression of confidential irony which I often notice on his face when history is under discussion:

"They talked a lot, and very well. That counts for something. They created the concept of the nation in arms, against mercenary armies. It all fell apart when the other nations started playing the same game. But that was against Napoleon."

"Do you think Mirabeau would have saved the monarchy?"

"He died at the right time. I think he would have been a great disappointment—to himself as well."

Compared to the Roman gallery of the guillotined, this individualist who was ready to betray the Revolution for the sake of the Queen's eyes and the King's money, and who died slowly and nobly after the two women in his bed had left, seemed like a great adventurer. He lacked the mysterious charisma with which the nation or the people invested all the others up to the Ninth Thermidor. I had read what General de Gaulle had written about Hoche, and it was Hoche that he now thought of, perhaps because he too had died by poison:

"Hoche is an impressive figure. Wherever he was posted, he proved worthy of his office. And then in the Vendée, persuading people to sit round a table and talk instead of killing each other. But at the time he was poisoned he was having his troubles."

I looked at him interrogatively. He gave an ironic smile: "Dictatorship . . ."

"When he was released from the Conciergerie," I said, "he had to stand aside in the corridor to let a new prisoner pass: it was Saint-Just."

"Ah! The same ones keep turning up."

Saint-Just in the corridor, Josephine in the bedchamber, I thought. He raised his forefinger in the same gesture as before: "Make no mistake: France no longer wants Revolution. The time is past."

I was struck by the neutrality of his tone—he might have been talking about the Roman Empire. Our intellectuals were passionately living out a political mythology, and the armies of communism and fascism were still face to face. For the first time, I realized how trifling the supreme values of others, even of many people who were not his opponents, tended to seem to him. A short time before, in response to the revelations of the Minister of Food about the black market, with which Paris was obsessed, he had absentmindedly remarked: "Frenchmen will have to make up their minds that there are more important things to worry about than smoked herrings." It was not just Marie Antoinette all over again. "The time is past" was said in the tone in which a mystic might speak of the flesh. But mystics do not believe in history.

"The slogan of *Combat*," I said, "is still 'From Resistance to Revolution.'"

"And what's the circulation of *Combat?*

"I have announced that all the sources of power and credit will be nationalized in the course of this year. Not for the sake of the left, but for the sake of France. The right is in no hurry to support the state, and the left is in too much of a hurry. I was interested in what M. Palewski told me about your views on publicity and propaganda. What is the feeling among the intellectuals? I don't mean just about propaganda, but—in general."

"There are those whom the Resistance led toward historical romanticism, and the present time must be the height of their expectations. And there are those whom it led, or who led themselves, toward revolutionary romanticism, which consists in confusing political action with theater. I don't mean those who are ready to fight to create Soviets: it's not the actors I'm talking about but the spectators. Ever since the eighteenth century France has had its 'tender souls'—in which women of letters have always played a fairly constant role."

"But not as nurses."

"Literature is full of tender souls for whom the proletariat are noble savages. But it isn't easy to understand how Diderot could possibly have believed that Catherine the Great had anything to do with Liberty."

"Voltaire composed epigrams about the Battle of Rossbach. But it's a pity."

"The situation of the serious intellectuals is difficult. Writers have often carried weight in French politics, from Voltaire to Victor Hugo. They played an important role in the Dreyfus case. They thought they could play a similar role at the time of the Popular Front, but instead of influencing events they were made use of. It was all very cleverly worked out, on the communist side, by Willy Münzenberg—who has since died. But in spite of all their talk about action, which Montesquieu would have disclaimed, what have these intellectuals done since 1936? Drawn up petitions.

"Then there are the professional philosophers. For them, Lenin and Stalin are merely disciples of Marx. They remind me of a rabbi I once met in Isfahan who asked me if I could tell him, since I'd been to Russia, whether it was true that the communists too had a *Book*. They looked for the theory behind the action, but a particular kind of theory: Marx, but not Richelieu. For them, *Richelieu had no politics.* I told M. Palewski that at the present moment *you are not getting through to them.* They are hardly aware of the contradictory nature of their position, because it is never put to the test of action. But they have a vague inkling of it, as the MLN Congress showed. And then, the real Resistance lost two-thirds of its friends and family."

"I know," he said sadly, "I . . ."

I had the feeling that he was about to add: I know you lost some of your family too, but the sentence stayed on his lips, and he stood up.

"What struck you most when you came back to Paris?"

"The lies."

The aide had opened the door, and the General showed me out. "Thank you," he said.

As I walked along the street after descending the monumental staircase, dreamily confusing the ushers with the suits of armor, I wondered what it was that had surprised me about him. Through newsreels I had grown familiar with his physical appearance and even the rhythm of his speech, which was very similar in public and in private. But on the screen he was always doing the talking; I had just met a man who asked questions, and for me, his strength lay first and foremost in his silence.

Not that I had been cross-examined. He has too much regard for intellectual good manners for that. What had struck me was an inner *remoteness*, which I have only come across since in one other man,

Mao Tse-tung. He still wore a uniform. But the aloofness of generals like de Lattre and Leclerc did not spring from themselves, but from their rank. I often used to wonder, when I met military men, what they might be in civilian life. Sometimes I used to feel that de Lattre might have been an ambassador, sometimes a cardinal. In civilian life, General de Gaulle would always have been General de Gaulle.

His silence was an interrogation. I might have been reminded of Gide, had it not been for a sort of Chinese curiosity in Gide's silence. In Algiers he had asked General de Gaulle in his best deferential inquisitor's manner, "Will you permit me, General, to ask one question. When did you decide to *disobey?*" The General had replied with a vague gesture, and probably thought of the famous remark about Admiral Jellicoe: "He has all Nelson's qualities except disobedience." Gide had spoken to me about the "ceremonious nobility" with which De Gaulle had received him—at a luncheon, it is true. It was not an impression of ceremoniousness that stayed in my mind but this remoteness, all the more curious because it appeared not only between himself and his interlocutor but between what he said and what he was. I had already come across this intense presence that has nothing to do with words—not in military men, or politicians, or artists, but in distinguished men of religion, whose affably commonplace words seem to bear no relation to their inner life. It was this that had reminded me of the mystics when he had spoken of revolution.

He established with the person he was talking to a very powerful contact, which seeemed inexplicable when one had left him. A contact that was above all due to a feeling of having come up against a total personality—the opposite feeling from that which makes people say it is impossible to judge a man on the basis of a single conversation. What he had said to me had the added weight that historic responsibility gives to quite simple statements. (As in Stalin's reply to Hearst in 1933, when asked, "How can there be a war between Germany and the Soviet Union when they have no common frontiers?"—"There will be.") In spite of his courtesy, I always had the feeling that I was giving an account of myself. We had not touched on the modernization of education, nor specified the area in which I might possibly be of service. I had seen a general officer who respected ideas and saluted them imperceptibly in passing; a man before whom all felt responsible because he was responsible for the destiny of France; and finally a haunted figure, whose mind was obsessed with that destiny which he had yet to discover and affirm. In the case of a priest one might define it as the person, the priesthood, the transcendental. The transcendental as con-

ceived by the founders of the militant Orders. I glanced up casually
before crossing a street—Rue St. Dominique.

I was trying to get to the bottom of a complex impression: the man
lived up to his myth, but *in what sense?* Valéry lived up to his, because
he spoke with the rigor and penetration of M. Teste—slang and fantasy
to boot. Einstein was worthy of Einstein by virtue of that simplicity, as
of a rumpled Franciscan, which in fact the Franciscans lack. Great
painters are alike only when they talk about painting. The only figure
whom General de Gaulle then called to my mind, by way of antithesis
rather than resemblance, in the way that Ingres brings to mind Dela-
croix, was Trotsky.

Some days later I was asked to join the General's staff as technical
adviser. It was then that work began on plans for the modernization of
education, and that Stoetzel received the first million francs for the
purpose of organizing effective opinion polls. The gods were on our
side: the last poll, which was to do with the constitutional referendum,
was accurate to within three points in a thousand. Between April and
August, Roosevelt, Mussolini, and Hitler had died, Churchill had gone,
Germany had surrendered, and the atomic bomb had exploded at
Hiroshima. On October 21, the elections returned 302 communist and
socialist members to the Assembly. The General, unanimously elected
head of the government, formed his Ministry, in which I became Minister of Information. An instructive job: my chief task was to prevent
each party from grabbing all the bedclothes. Thorez observed the rules
of the game, putting the Communist party at the service of national
reconstruction. But at the same time the party was infiltrating furiously;
Marcel Paul's* reports were blatantly false. And in this tripartite government, false communist statements gave rise to false statements on
the part of the socialists and the MRP. After Cabinet meetings, the
General would make renewed efforts to convince this or that minister.
But his mediation, which he regarded as indispensable to the working
of the state, could not go on being permanently exercised between rival
fictions, and I doubted whether he would put up with this contest in
duplicity for long. He seemed to be discovering something which he
must always have known, but which the war, the Resistance, and perhaps his familiarity with British democracy had obscured: that our
democracy is a struggle between parties in which France plays a sub-

*Communist Minister of Industrial Production 1945-46. (Tr.)

ordinate role. He had been disconcerted by the refusal, first of Herriot and then of Léon Blum, to join the government as Ministers of State, in order to contribute toward the country's recovery, on the grounds that their first duty was to their parties. All the more so because he knew, at least in the second case, that party allegiance stemmed from something more than the desire to be the boss.

When Herriot attacked him, the main cause of his bitterness was the certainty that the parliamentary "game" was about to start up again. Did he think that France would soon have to recall him? We all thought so. Some days before his resignation Léon Blum and I were his guests at his villa in Neuilly. After dinner, the three of us were sitting around a little table, and he said to Léon Blum, half-seriously, half-ironically, "Well, convince him!"

The question at issue was how much confidence could be placed in communist cooperation with the government.

"How can you expect true communists not to take us for another Kerensky or Pilsudski government?" I asked. "It's simply a question of who shoots first: it's no longer a state, it's a Western gunfight. Remember the Popular Front."

"But the Popular Front worked."

Léon Blum turned his long delicate face toward us, and pressing his hands together, repeated firmly, in a frail and slightly disillusioned voice that contrasted with the General's deep tones, "It worked."

"Yes," the General answered bitterly.

He was probably thinking, "And then what happened?" For Léon Blum, in spite of his moral courage, which was considerable, politics was the art of conciliation. The Matignon agreements* had been a *tour de force*. His was not the surface conciliation that accompanies joint enterprises—the General himself is competent enough in this respect—but a conciliation in depth, a sort of conversion of the opposition. (Men are readily responsive to the skills in which they are especially gifted.) I think Léon Blum valued conciliation to the same extent General de Gaulle valued inflexibility.

"It worked," I said, "because the Soviet Union was weak. With the Red Army and the Stalin of today . . ."

"The Americans might not be too anxious to see the Russians in Paris . . ."

*Agreements concluded between employers and workers in 1936 through the mediation of Léon Blum's Popular Front government after a wave of strikes and disturbances. The Hôtel Matignon is the office of the French Prime Minister. (Tr.)

"If they called themselves the French Communist party, and there was no *coup d'état*, would the Americans lift a hand? But what I meant to say was this. During its revolutionary phase the Popular Front achieved some real reforms, and . . ."

"For one thing," Léon Blum said with a smile, "it tried to rearm France . . ."

"True. But when the revolutionary phase came to an end, we were back with the same old traditional parliament—which the present tripartite coalition is hoping to get back to in its turn and is only prevented from doing by the presence of General de Gaulle. Now what happened to all your defense efforts when war was declared? Our governments had tried to conciliate both Hitler's supporters and his opponents, both the advocates of armored divisions and their opponents. With the result that we put half a soldier in half a tank to fight half a battle."

"As you know," he replied, smiling more broadly, "I do not consider the parliamentary system the best possible form of democratic government."

I was aware of this. And no doubt what he had written on this subject had helped to create a rapport between him and General de Gaulle.

"The truth of the matter is," he went on, "that you think compromise belongs to the politics of the nineteenth century. Maybe. But then again, perhaps life itself is a compromise. Only—Stalin didn't put half-soldiers into half-tanks, but he did put a lot of people into coffins. When I was in the government, I often wondered whether compromise might not be the price of freedom."

"There's no question that the basic problem of the Liberation is how to reconcile real state authority with real civil liberty. Easier said than done."

"Up to a point, the Anglo-Saxons have managed it."

"But the Communist party doesn't count either in Britain or the United States."

Mme. de Gaulle brought coffee, and I went to join her. The General had said nothing. A little later, the two men were standing at the other end of the room while their two wives looked on with a slightly bewildered air. The General knew from reading his articles in Le Populaire that everything his interlocutor had just said in fits and starts was based on the belief—not the idea, the belief—that there could be no France without democracy, no political democracy without social democracy, and no social democracy without international democracy. Léon Blum held socialism to be the highest form of democracy: whence the need to reconcile his call for collectivism with his firm belief in individual liberty. He was imbued with a faith in man as profound as the communist faith and indeed he justified it by paraphrasing Spinoza: "Any action of which we ourselves are the cause, inasmuch as it comes from our idea of what is human, I would ascribe to religion."

He seemed to put his maturity at the service of his youth. And if he was ever taken in, it was only by the unpredictable. He too was a man with a vocation—patently so at this time, when he still bore the marks of his imprisonment. But his vocation drew him closer to the men he knew, whereas the General's drew him closer to men he did not know. The latter, in spite of the courtesy with which he always dispensed hospitality, seemed to be enclosed in a benevolent shell. Was he conscious of the absurdity of the Riom trials?* He was certainly conscious of the reforms which his interlocutor had enacted, of what he had done; and of the lucidity of some of his political analyses, colored without being distorted by his socialist beliefs. I think their association had developed from a mutual awareness of each other's qualities, a common tendency to look on politics as a mainspring of history. But the chips were already down. A few days before the elections, the General had suggested to Léon Blum that he should succeed him if he was forced to resign. "I cannot," Blum told him, "because of my health, and what is more I will not, because I drag too much hatred along in my wake."

The General knew that the French people had accepted defeat. He knew that they had accepted Pétain. And I believe he also knew, after the euphoria of the Liberation, that for millions of men he was their alibi. In the Resistance France recognized what she should have been rather than what she had been. And yet the General's real dialogue was always with her—whether she was called the Republic, the people, or the nation. "A statesman is always alone on one side, with the rest of the world on the other," Napoleon said. "Alone with France," General de Gaulle would doubtless have thought. Solitary great men often have a profound relationship with the masses, living or dead, for whom they fight. But would the nation forgive him for what it owed him unless he completed the alibi by disappearing from the scene (if only by becoming just "another politician")? Just as England had abandoned Churchill, as France had let the Radical Party Congress abandon Clemenceau. All the same, a one-party system having been ruled out,

*Trials of leaders of the Third Republic organized by the Vichy Government in 1941. (Tr.)

his return over the heads of the parties could only take place in the name of the nation. The first referendum held the seeds of the election of the President of the Republic by universal suffrage, the accession of the people to the role of supreme arbiters between the President and the Assembly, to which Léon Blum was passionately opposed. Perhaps the departure of the General was itself, among other things, a secret referendum.

After ministerial meetings I used to stay behind with him to draw up the official communiqué. One day, as we were going down the imitation marble staircase of the Hôtel Matignon, he said to me:

"What do you think you'll do at the Ministry of Information now?"

"Make a ministry of it, General. It will be finished in six weeks."

"I shall have gone by then."

It was then that I guessed, for no apparent reason, that General de Gaulle had never summoned me. This was confirmed to me some years later. We had been the characters in a curious intrigue, which he probably suspected before I did. I imagine that when his supposed request was transmitted to me, he must also have been given one from me, which was no less apocryphal.* This would explain the strangeness of our first meeting.

*As regards my offer to join the Free French Air Force, twenty years later—this year—I received a letter from M. Bénédite, director of the Guilde Internationale du Disque, which contained the following paragraph:

"We met several times at the Bureau du Centre in Marseilles, and we even dined together one evening with Victor Serge, with whom I was staying at the time. Knowing that Varian Fry was in a position to get messages through to England, you gave him a letter addressed to General de Gaulle; Fry entrusted the letter to my wife, who was his secretary, and unfortunately she was arrested by the police during the demonstrations in the Canebière at the spot where Alexander of Yugoslavia and Barthou were assassinated. My wife swallowed your letter in the police van so that it would not be found in the event of her being searched. I have no recollection of how contact was finally made between yourself and General de Gaulle after the unfortunate destruction of your letter, but I imagine some other means was found."

3

1958 / 1965. I was to see him again at Marly, at Colombey, at the Rue de Solférino in the days of the RPF,* then during the period we called the crossing of the desert. People say that he always knew he would return to power. Was he sure that he would return in time? I remember, some time before Dienbienphu, being with some friends in a châlet in the Valais next door to a group of tourists out of Labiche who were looking at Mont Blanc through an enormous spyglass. Elisabeth de Miribel asked me how I thought the General would come back. "Through a conspiracy of the military in Indochina," I answered. "They will think they're using him but will get their fingers burnt." It was not the Indochina army, and when my prophecy proved almost right I was visiting Venice, absolutely certain that nothing was going to happen.

"He's fishing in the lagoon," Bidault was to observe in his Machiavellian way, referring to a remark (of Delbecque's?) which had been credited to me: "One doesn't go to the edge of the Rubicon to fish."

It was not until I returned to Paris that I discovered how serious things were.

At one of the last Cabinet meetings M. Pleven had said: "We no longer represent anything but shadows. Let us not deceive ourselves. The Minister for Algeria cannot cross the Mediterranean. The Minister of Defense no longer has an army. The Minister of the Interior no longer has a police force." Many veterans of Indochina and former paratroopers were members of the Paris police force, which had been on strike since March.

The only alternative was the formation of militias. The Prime Minister, M. Pflimlin, was opposed to this. He thought it would involve an even graver threat of civil war than an appeal to General de Gaulle. In any case the Ministers were thinking in terms of setting up Committees for the Defense of the Republic rather than of arming militia groups which would be taken over by the communists—assuming any such groups could be formed at all. For the trade-union view was, "The masses can be spurred to action over wages, but not in support of the parliamentary system. The workers who remember that their liberties were restored in 1944, and many of whom have relatives in Algeria, prefer De Gaulle to the colonels." When the communists had talked

*The Rassemblement du Peuple Français—the political movement created by General de Gaulle in 1947, a year after his resignation as head of government. (Tr.)

about mobilizing, the militants had rejoined their cells, but had gone off the same morning leaving the hard core of the faithful to play cards. On the Sunday, there were 35,000 cars on the Autoroute de l'Ouest— three thousand more than the previous year.

The revolution in Algiers was equally confused. No one in Paris had much idea what was meant by the word integration. Soustelle had said it was the opposite of disintegration. Oh, yes? The myth of a France stretching from Dunkirk to Tamanrasset was born of a study carried out by the psychological warfare service of the army, then at the height of its glory. For the activist military, the SAS officers and even many of the paratroopers, the word meant fraternization. That the psychological warfare service organized it, if only by transporting Muslims in army trucks, seems more than likely; but they had not foreseen that "Night of August 4,"* and were incapable of renewing it. The "day of the miracle," May 16, surprised those who had planned it, and who wrote: "This surge of hope can only be compared to what we experienced in Paris just after the Liberation." It surprised the Muslims, who found themselves in the arms of the *pieds-noirs*† and the *pieds-noirs*, who found themselves in the arms of the Muslims. It disconcerted the communists, who decided not to believe it; and even the FLN, for there was not a single incident in Algiers during the period of fraternization. The paratroop captains proclaimed, "We shall base our movement on ten million Algerian Frenchmen—Europeans and Muslims alike." But when all the excitement had died down, the condition of the Muslims had not changed. The Committees of Public Safety decreed that the miserable wages of the agricultural workers should be increased; the settlers made them work from five A.M. until noon and paid them half a day's wage at the new rate—less than they were getting before the increase. The army grew more and more enraged, having expected the Algerian movement to produce a sort of technological French Revolution, a consulate of Saint-Just and Mao Tse-tung combined—and being united only by the desire for some kind of political action, by hatred of a regime which was incapable of either waging war or making peace. The civilians were suspicious of fraternization. In their political groups, which were nationalist but antimetropolitan, "French Algeria"

---

*La nuit du 4 août, 1789, when the Constituent Assembly voted for the abolition of feudal rights. The occasion symbolizes the voluntary renunciation of their privileges by the privileged, and was invoked in May 1958 to describe the short-lived outburst of fraternal rejoicing between Muslims and Europeans in Algiers. (Tr.)

†"Black feet"—slang term for French Algerians. (Tr.)

meant on occasion "Algerian France." The dyed-in-the-wool reactionaries declared for integration once they were convinced the Muslims
would get the vote and realized that nine million Muslims could out-
vote a million *pieds-noirs* but not twenty million Frenchmen. In Corsica, the acting mayor of Bastia, a socialist, had walked out of the town
hall, which the paratroops had taken over, singing the *Marseillaise*. The
paratroops had accompanied him, also singing it, and the crowd in the
square outside had joined in too, not knowing whether they were singing in support of the mayor, the paratroops, or both. On June 1 the
envoy of the Committees of Public Safety, who had expected to find
Paris in a state of siege, was flabbergasted to find people playing
*pétanque** on the Esplanade des Invalides. One of the most famous
American reporters assured me that General Massu had voluntarily sub-
mitted to torture so as to have the right to order it himself. The only
thing that emerged clearly from this chaos was that a muddled but
resolute movement had aircraft and fighting men at its disposal against
a government without either an army or a police force. Pflimlin's representative, Salan, had started the cry of "Vive De Gaulle," and it was
no longer expected of the General that he should stop the paratroops
but that he should prevent civil war—which looked as though it was
about to begin, like the Civil War in Spain, like the October Revolution, with the moviehouses open and the sightseers strolling in the
streets.

Two days after my return, he summoned me to the Hôtel Lapérouse.

At five o'clock, perhaps because he regarded our meeting as a moment of relaxation. He ordered whisky and tea to be brought up. We
were in the drawing room of the suite that was always kept ready for
him when he came to Paris: reproduction Louis Seize, together with
the calm which General de Gaulle has always imposed on his surroundings. The tea went back in the direction of the hubbub that rose
from the hall and filled the staircase, echoing the country's chaos.

The gist of what he said was: "The main question is whether the
French people want to rebuild France or whether they want to go back
to sleep. I cannot do it without them. And we must insure the continuity of our institutions until I call on the people to choose new ones.
For the moment, they don't want the colonels. So our task is to rebuild
the state, to stabilize the currency, and to finish with colonialism."

---

*Provençal variant of the game of *boules* — the French version of
bowling. (Tr.)

Once again, I recognized that ternary rhythm which is as natural to him as uncertainty is to other men.

"Creating a state that works means creating a constitution that works. Thus, universal suffrage must be the source of all power; executive and legislative power must be really separate; the government must be responsible to parliament.

"It will not be easy to stabilize the currency, but it will be less difficult than people say, if the state can provide a basis of firmness and continuity—that is, if it really is a state.

"As for the colonial question . . . I shall have to tell everyone concerned with the Empire that colonies are finished. Let us come together and create a Community, with a common defense, a common foreign policy, and a common economic policy.

"For the rest, we shall provide them with aid. It stands to reason that the poor countries will want to associate themselves with the rich, who will be less keen. We shall see. Let them create states—if they can.

"And if they agree.

"Those that don't can go. We won't stand in their way. And we'll build the French Community with the rest."

This project had been in his mind since his speech at Brazzaville in 1942. But now it was more than a pious hope. While the pathetic marchers trudged from the Place de la Bastille to the Place de la Nation, aping the Popular Front which had been guilty of no Suez adventures or Algerian wars and had brought more social justice than the Fourth Republic ever had, France was on the point of telling all its former colonies: "If you really want independence, take it!"

He had not mentioned Algeria, but he seemed to be circling the problem. First of all it was essential that the French army in Algeria should be the army of a France that was offering seventeen countries their freedom, not the army of a colonial empire. After the declaration of investiture, he was to leave for Algiers. Once again, the road to Algiers would pass through Brazzaville.

Where was this road leading? A caricature can be a good likeness, but the caricatures of the General produced by his adversaries—Roosevelt included—had always seemed to me to be quite unlike him. His present opponents took him for a reactionary, forgetting the social reforms which France owed to him, the only major reforms since the Popular Front. They took him for a paratroop leader; but Algiers would hardly be enraptured by the government he was forming, and he would no more be the tool of the Committees of Public Safety than he had been the tool of the Resistance groups. He was returning to power on a wave of disorder? It was less grave than that of 1944. His opponents believed that he would exercise power in accordance with his own preferences, hoping for the end of the Algerian conflict to bring about the recovery of France. I wondered whether he did not in fact hope for the recovery of France to bring about the end of the war. For the time being, he wanted to find things out for himself, and perhaps to test his power.

He scarcely mentioned social problems. The way he put off raising them, whereas he had clearly applied himself with some care to the problems of the currency, the Empire, and above all the state, seemed to me significant. He was fighting against the clock, but not in this domain. And perhaps he was not displeased to see the communists and the various eddies in the political undertow straying so far from what he felt to be the essential problems and the basic feeling of the country. A few days later he would say to me, "Don't forget that we didn't bring about a revolution." I have never seen him so completely monolithic, except at the time of the Algiers barricades. He had come out of retreat, for that is what the meditation of the past is, especially for a man whose memories are an epic: a week before, he had been correcting the proofs of his memoirs. He had emerged from the deep solitude he always bore within himself for the purpose of negotiations, but also for the sake of France's destiny which had haunted him for so many years. In his imperturbable dialogue with this shade, nothing had changed. At this time, when the men who called most passionately for him were avowed fascists, and those who attacked him most violently avowed communists, when France seemed doomed to a clash between totalitarian parties, he thought only of rebuilding the state. However, before leaving him, I spoke about the youth of France. "If I can see a new young generation before I die," he said, "it will be . . ." Perhaps his tone signified ". . . it will be as momentous as the Liberation." But he left the sentence in midair, like his gesture.

Having taken my leave, I remembered one winter's day on the edge of the Colombey wood. As far as the eye could reach, beyond the cemetery where his daughter is buried, not a single village was to be seen. He had stretched out his arm, as he had just done in the little drawing room, toward the melancholy downs of the plateau of Langres and the Argonne: "Before the great invasions, all that was full of people . . ."

As I drove away I thought of our first meeting.

His mustache, now gray, was scarcely visible, and the line of his mouth was continued by two deep furrows down to the jaw. Balthus had once asked me whether I had noticed his resemblance to Poussin's self-portrait. Now it had come true. And perhaps history brings with it its own physiognomy. His had become tinged, over the years, with an apparent benevolence, but it had retained its gravity. It seemed not so much to express his deepest feelings as to enclose them. Its habitual expression was one of courtesy—and sometimes humor. At these times his eyes would simultaneously light up and grow smaller, and his heavy gaze would be momentarily replaced by the twinkle of Babar the Elephant.

To know a man nowadays is above all to know the element of irrational in him, the part he is unable to control, which he would like to erase from his own image of himself. In this sense, I do not know General de Gaulle. "One must get to know men in order to influence them." Poor fools! One does not influence men by knowing them, but by constraint, confidence, or love. Nevertheless, a long acquaintance with the General had made me familiar with certain of his mental processes, and his relationship to the symbolic figure whom he refers to in his *Memoirs* as De Gaulle—or, more precisely, that person whose memoirs he wrote—those memoirs wherein Charles never appears.

Perhaps the remoteness which had so intrigued me at our first meeting arose in part from a characteristic which Stendhal noted apropos of Napoleon. "He directed the course of the conversation . . . And never a question, never an unconsidered supposition . . ."

But as soon as the Emperor abandoned his official role (and sometimes even when he was still engaged in it), there appeared the irascible or the play-acting Napoleon, the husband of Josephine, the lover of practical jokes. The entire Court knew this person. For General de Gaulle's colleagues, the private man was not at all a man who spoke about his private life, he was simply a man who did not talk about affairs of state. He would not allow himself a moment's impulsiveness or abandon, but was perfectly prepared, at receptions or at other occasions chosen by him, to indulge in superficial conversation. This he did with a good grace, but it was a matter of courtesy, and courtesy was part of his persona. Napoleon used to terrify women; De Gaulle they found distant and "charming" (in other words attentive) because he remained De Gaulle even when he was speaking to them about their children. And in the lives of the men who made our country's history, it is rare not to find women other than their wives. All this was of a piece with the Grand Master of the Knights Templars who had received me some years back at the War Ministry, for benevolence of that sort comes from the calling, not the other way round. To everyone, his family excepted no doubt, he seemed to be a courteous reflection of his legendary self.

One day it will be realized that men are distinguishable as much by the forms their memories take as by their characters. The depths vary, as do the nets they use and the quarry they hunt. But the deepest memories are not necessarily expressed in conversation, and this man who was famous for his memory and whose past had for eighteen years belonged to history, seemed to carry on his innermost dialogue not with the past but with the future. I have only twice heard him speak of himself—both times on the occasion of someone's death. Nor have I heard him speak much about others: a few sentences about Churchill and Stalin ("He was an Asiatic despot, and quite consciously so"), half a line on Roosevelt ("A patrician democrat"). The portraits he drew in conversation, like those in his Memoirs, were portrait busts. He thought of the great men of history in terms of their achievements, and of all men, perhaps, in terms of what he judged them capable of achieving. The scope of the conversations in which I participated, whenever he digressed from the matter in hand, was confined to ideas or history. Life beat around him like a storm-tossed sea, intruding only in a certain tone of rueful experience. His inner monologue never came to the surface; his scheme of references and comparisons (how meaningful they can be!) was historical, often literary when he was being ironical, never religious. At the time of his audience with the Pope, he was supposed to have said, "Now, your Holiness, shall we talk about France?" Yet the very distinctive tone of his portrait of Stalin in the War Memoirs springs from the memory of the dictator saying to him: "In the long run, death is the only victor."

He has written that this character without a Christian name in the Memoirs was born of the acclamations which greeted his return and which did not seem to him to be addressed to himself. But this book is not a book of memoirs either in the sense of Rousseau's Confessions or in the Saint-Simon sense. The part of his personality that the author has excluded (starting with Charles) is no less significant than what he has elected to record. Like the Commentaries, or the Anabasis, in which Caesar and Xenophon refer to themselves in the third person, the book is an account of a historic exploit by the man who accomplished it. Its hero is the anonymous hero of Au Fil de l'Epée. People have wondered at the prophetic character of this book, which prophesies a person rather than events—the portrait of an imaginary Plutarchian hero created out of the values which will create the destiny of this real historical hero—and resembles him for that reason. The dichotomy probably applies to most of the great men of history, and to most great artists; Napoleon is not Bonaparte, Titian is not Count Tiziano Vecelli, and Hugo, when he thought of the character he had first called Olympio, certainly called him Victor Hugo. The statues of the future have already, willy-nilly, taken possession of the men who are worthy of statues. Charles is modeled by life, and De Gaulle by destiny, as Victor is modeled by life, and Hugo by genius. But the creation—whether destiny or genius—is called into being by something which antedates it and which, like life, is subject to accident; the masterpiece is a guarantee of genius, but genius does not guarantee the masterpiece. No doubt most human beings are split in this way, but only within themselves. Yet it remains true that the creation of a persona is less rare than it might seem; the split is common among the great religious figures, and particularly striking in the case of film stars, who are dispossessed not only of their personalities but also of their faces, which undergo a metamorphosis on the screen. Of course these ephemeral Venuses can only be embodied in the roles they are given to play. And it is not the role which makes the historical personality, but the vocation.

All vocations arouse hatred—hence antimilitarism and anticlericalism —in a way that professions do not. The swindler does not provoke the same feelings as does the cowardly officer, the simoniac priest or the corrupt judge, because these men in uniform, when they are false to their vocation, become usurpers. Everyone knows that combat is linked with character; what is less well known is that character implies a particular manner of action, which the vocation chooses just as it chooses the combat.

General de Gaulle, who was only incidentally a military man, conceived of action in terms of the soldierly spirit, in the sense that one might talk of the priestly or the juridical spirit. But between fiction and satire, d'Artagnan and Croquebol,* the French had reached the point where they no longer even recognized this spirit. To think of Alexander, Caesar, Frederick the Great, Napoleon as "sots with swords" (as Anatole France put it) is at best frivolous. Thanks to Courteline, and in spite of Verdun, until the middle of this century the army meant the barrack square. The cultivated regular officer, the professor at the Staff College, was a much more common figure in Germany, through the traditions of Frederick the Great and the Prussian General Staff.

*Character in Les Gaîtés de l'escadron (1886), a popular comic novel about army life by Georges Courteline. (Tr.)

From the complex instrument that was the army, the only thing the Frenchman remembered was the discipline. Yet discipline is not a matter of course: Bonaparte in Italy, and Pétain at Verdun, had to begin by restoring it. And if in Russia and China the military vocation soon became reidentified with the national vocation, neither the Foreign Legion nor the mercenary regiments of our century are national units.

I believe that the military spirit influenced General de Gaulle in a profound but limited way. First, because when he entered it the army was committed to fight, and then because this spirit seemed to him to suggest methods of government superior to civilian methods. The organization of action is the primary task of the statesman, as it was of Alexander and Caesar.

The most effective methods in this field have been those of the army and the Church, which were taken up by the totalitarian parties and even, to a lesser extent, by the great capitalist and communist societies. But Napoleon did not make his marshals responsible for governing France; he created the strongest civil administration France has ever known. In 1958, as in 1944, General de Gaulle wanted to create an apparatus that would serve France in peace as a modern army would have served her in war.

Various other characteristics of his thinking had been derived from his military background. First, a conception of government as a weapon in the struggle to develop France. Although he has never treated the country as a barracks or an army, he treated the members of the Provisional Government, and then his Ministers, as a general staff, and later on, particularly, his closest associate—whether he was known as the Head of the Secretariat or Prime Minister—as a Chief of General Staff.

Another military characteristic is his conviction that decisions cannot be put off. Partly because speed is of the essence in decision-making, because the hare won't come past a second time, but mainly because a historic decision is inseparable from the moment when it is taken. Hence his exchange with General Juin:

"If you had waited," Juin said, "we might have had a better chance."

"Yes. But France would not. The future lasts a long time."

For this flair for the quick decision was not inconsistent with predictions which only the distant future would confirm: the appeal of June 18, his affirmation of the strength of the Red Army at the time when it was defeated; and later on, his immediate alignment with the United States over the sending of Soviet missiles to Cuba was to be followed by his long-term opposition to the United States over Southeast Asia.

He has always tried to get time on his side, or rather to put himself on the side of time, insofar as time is important to the success of his plans (not so much the soldier here as the farmer). He hoped that the next Republic would provide him with the sort of continuity of action which up to then had only appertained—inadequately—to the National Plan. To the military mind continuity, including that demanded by the war industries, is part of preparation: and the word is the means of expressing orders—a means of action. General de Gaulle organized action on the basis of a "grand design," which was variable since it was limited by the possible, which is also variable. He aimed to accomplish this design by every means at his disposal. He was aware of the influence which his symbolic persona could exercise both at home and abroad; but he cared a great deal about being right, about telling the French people what had to be *done for France*. There was nothing charismatic about his speeches and press-conferences. His strength lay—and still lies—in his authority, not in projecting an attractive image. "Ourselves and the enemy," thinks the military leader. "Ourselves and the destiny of the world," thinks the statesman. General de Gaulle owes his mental attitude to the latter and most of his methods to the former. No doubt he would willingly have subscribed to Marshal Foch's famous, "What is the basic issue?" At Cabinet meetings, at committee meetings of the RPF, as well as during interviews, I had been surprised to hear him summarize the ideas that had just been expounded to him. I soon realized that he was subjecting them to a filtering process. He seemed to be summing up the chapter headings of these statements, whereas in fact he was summing up that part of their content that he accepted, and he would issue his instructions on the basis of the modified design. Debate was reserved for major topics. The traditional give and take in the discussion of affairs of state was foreign to him. He would listen to what was said to him without interruption, perhaps ask a few questions, and then give his decision or issue whatever instructions were necessary. With some people, after listening to what they had to say, he would remark in a tone that was rather more confident than confiding: "Well, I'll tell you what I think." This could happen over really important questions, or with heads of state. The person concerned would have to shift for himself in Washington, or London, or Moscow; perhaps the following day, in Algiers or at the atomic testing grounds.

I believe that the hope aroused by his decision of June 1940 had always, for him, remained tinged with tragedy. Destiny had appeared again, and an atmosphere of battle stations reigned in the hotel which was his temporary headquarters. Perhaps the General had once thought of France as a "fairy-tale princess"; at all events I was persuaded that

he was less attached to the France of Austerlitz than to the moribund
France of 1940, or the sleepwalking France whose Assembly he was to
face again the following day. On the other side of the door I was to
find nothing but exultation. But as I took my leave of him, I remembered an Arab saying he had once quoted to me, "If your enemy insults
you, go and sit outside your door: you will see his corpse pass by."

Night sessions of the Assembly always have an unreal air, because of
the underwater glow which the high window diffuses like the light on a
snowy day over the *School of Athens* tapestry and the three rostrums
in the shape of a pyramid—president, speaker, stenographers—with their
Empire bas-reliefs like huge cameos. The crimson hemicycle was full to
overflowing. The public galleries too. The previous day, Bidault had
told the deputies: "Only he stands between you and the Seine. He is
the last umbrella against the locusts." Calm had not yet superseded
menace, but neither had turmoil. Historic sessions of the Third Republic, Barrès speaking, the surge of deputies toward the rostrum,
Clemenceau face to face with Jaurès, the victory proclamation of 1918
. . . These deputies on their benches, these spectators massed between
the tall columns, seemed suspended in time, as if the ancient film of
the National Assembly had been stopped on a single frame. The "ministerial declaration" of that afternoon had merged into amendments
and *explications de vote*, in the same aquarial light and the same
atmosphere of unreality engendered by the fact that no one spoke out
of any firm conviction. The General had said, "The state in a process
of headlong decline. The unity of France directly threatened. Algeria
immersed in a sea of trials and emotions. Corsica in the grip of the
contagion. In the metropolis, movements and countermovements hourly
growing stronger and more vehement. The army, having come through
long and bloody trials with merit, led astray by the dereliction of the
civil power. Our international position battered and breached even in
the very heart of our alliances. That is the situation of the country
today. At a time when so many opportunities are open to us, France is
threatened with collapse and perhaps civil war." The arguments of the
opposing sides were as familiar as was the gist of the General's analysis.
I was surrounded not by indifference but by an intense, diffused attentiveness, a waiting for the unforeseeable. Jacques Duclos* defended
democracy, which was laughable, but Mendès-France defended the

*Leader of the Communist party. (Tr.)

principles which had governed his life. Everyone claimed to represent
the people, the state, France, and yet everyone knew that the people
would not defend them. They were afraid that the colonels might become more powerful than De Gaulle (they were aware, as I was, of the
watchword, "Vive De Gaulle—and after Neguib, Nasser"); but the
colonels were more powerful than the Assembly. And how could anybody seriously label as fascist a government whose Ministers included
the ex-Premiers Guy Mollet, Pflimlin, and Pinay? Fascism means a
party, the masses, a leader. Algiers did not yet have a party, and Paris
had too many. The wings of history beat against the melancholy dome
above an Assembly in which the last smiles of contemptuous parliamentary irony faded from the friendly, haggard faces. The exhausted
spectators watched the omens mock. When, at the end of his final intervention, the General said that if the confidence of the Assembly
enabled him to renew our institutions by means of universal suffrage
"the man who now speaks to you will consider himself honored for
the rest of his life," an outburst of applause marked the end of the
drama, and MM. Mitterand and Pineau delivered their lines after the
curtain had gone down.

It was what the communists were to describe as "Operation Seduc-
tion, after Operation Sedition," forgetting that General de Gaulle is
not alone in being graceful when he is the winner. At the end of the
session, the theater (the House of Commons is a room, but the National Assembly is an auditorium) emptied noiselessly. As I left, I
passed an old woman in overalls and slippers brandishing a broom, and
felt as if I were seeing the figure which, at the time of Fleurus,*
became the symbol of the Republic.

It was not difficult to foresee the reaction of the Algiers activists to
a government in which Guy Mollet was Minister of State and Jacques
Soustelle had no place. Guy Mollet and Pierre Pflimlin, with the help
of other parliamentary Ministers, had carried on an exhausting liaison
operation with the Assemblies and had arrived at about nine in the
morning, unshaven, for the last meeting at the Hôtel Lapérouse. That
night, in accordance with custom, the General presented his Government to the President of the Republic. The feeble lights of the Elysée
Palace gave it the same air of unreality that I had found in the Chamber. And while President Coty, loquacious and cheerful, chatted away
affably to Mlle. Sid Cara, a somewhat overawed Minister, a Shake-

*Famous victory of the French revolutionary armies under General
Jourdan in 1794. (Tr.)

spearean flash of lightning blasted one of the big trees in the park, and
for a second the figure of General de Gaulle loomed out of the half-
light, surrounded by Ministers looking as though they had been turned
to stone.

Stabilization seemed easy, like war according to Napoleon. The Constitution, on the other hand, was the subject of innumerable Cabinet
meetings, which often continued into the night. "Are you enjoying
yourself?" the General asked me one day on the way out. "Yes, quite."
I did not believe that the twentieth century, or France, was capable
of producing a Constitution surrounded by the Roman respect which
characterizes that of the United States; and I believed that a Constitution which made the referendum a method of government would
be made for the people, and not the people for the Constitution. The
discussions concerning the "social" clauses began with a debate between
Guy Mollet and Antoine Pinay which rapidly became tense. All this
would pass, like the night session of the Chamber, of a piece with its
stopped clock, and like the sudden appearance of the Ministers in the
bluish snapshot of the lightning. But I followed attentively the play of
these rival forces, so different from the intoxications of revolution, and
the way General de Gaulle mediated between them. It was this that I
was "enjoying." And that he too was enjoying, perhaps—on the fringe
of his unrelenting efforts to construct, out of these bits of woods, the
pedestal on which he was hoping to reestablish his country. From my
seat in the Cabinet room I could see the rose garden full of June roses,
like those of the fall of France. (In 1945 I had seen only rain and
snow there.) On September 4 the General expounded the new Constitution in a speech in the Place de la République. Balloons rose above
the crowd, carrying streamers whose rippling message affirmed that
fascism "would not pass." And some days later M. le Trocquer, the
President of the Assembly, assured the Vietnamese delegation that
General de Gaulle would not get a quarter of the votes in the referendum.

4

1958/1965. The referendum meant that our overseas departments would either join the Community or become independent. The prefects were pessimistic. Aimé Césaire, member of parliament for Martinique and mayor of Fort-de-France, had not yet committed himself. General de Gaulle could not leave France at that time and gave me the task of representing him.

"Why go to Guiana," I asked him, "since the prefect says it's lost?"

"It is the last French territory in America. And besides, you must go there because it's heartrending."

It was the first time I had heard him use this word, and I was soon to understand why he had used it.

First, Guadeloupe. I arrived one morning at the subprefecture in Pointe-à-Pitre; a house with balconies around a little banana tree garden, slatted swing doors, fans on the ceiling: the world of Gorée, of the old Gold and Ivory Coasts, as if the slavetrade had brought the old colonial houses over with the slaves. I had brought a few colleagues, among them Trémaud, who was soon to become secretary general of the overseas departments. He was a high-ranking civil servant, liberal and intelligent, whose wife had been killed by a bomb delivered in a parcel when he was prefect of Strasbourg. We listened at once to people's complaints, went to place wreaths on monuments, attended meetings of the municipal council, talked to opposition leaders. What they expected from the central government was often unreasonable, but when I went through the poor quarters of the town—and there are few that are not poor—I realized that they had some right to be unreasonable. In the lower strata there was a lot of speechifying and not much action; at the top a lot of promises and no action at all. The most impressive man I talked to was the dockers' leader, a syndicalist and probably a communist. The prefect, no doubt a good prefect and certainly a good man, had been asking in vain for something to be done. Setting all this in order would be anything but easy, but it was long overdue. Nowhere could so much loyalty have been offered to France in vain. As for the referendum, the people of the Antilles wanted to vote No to indicate their discontent, and Yes to remain French. One might as well have talked about the independence of the Lozère.

That evening I was to make a speech, and the population assembled in the central square, with madras head-scarves at the windows and clusters of children dangling in the trees. Behind the bandstand cavorted merry horses rough hewn out of wood a hundred years ago. What was called politics here (not one elected representative in the Antilles was a Gaullist) played no part. Only two factors came into play, the call of France and the confidence inspired by the General. It was the first time I had addressed a black audience, and I felt its quivering stillness accord with the rhythm of the speech as its dancing accords with its music.

We were to sleep in the old governor's palace on the other side of the island. By the time the procession (motorcyclists, prefect, and so on) moved off, night had fallen. We passed through blind villages, their palm trees black against the luminous night and a sickle moon against the curving leaves of the banana trees. The radio was only just beginning to broadcast the speeches. From village to village, windows were lighting up, and from doors that opened as we passed came scraps of speech sometimes accompanied by applause from the shanties. Now my own words were being broadcast, sounding oddly unnatural in my ears, because they seemed to arrive at the same time as we did, and because one never recognizes one's own voice on the radio:

". . . the man who, during our country's terrible sleep, kept its honor alive like an imperishable dream . . ."

Shops, shanties.

Unintelligible phrases.

Blacks in Indian file.

A village. I could hear whole sentences, for in nearly every house the radios were tuned in to the speech.

"In the face of one of the greatest disasters in our history, while the endless exodus of peasant carts still cluttered our roads against a background of flames, one voice was raised in the night to proclaim against all odds . . ."

Forest, palms, silence. The smell of flowers in the night.

A township. White-eyed shadows waved their arms in the beam of our headlights. The police were arranging a barrier of trucks across the road to make way for a little house on a horse-drawn platform.

"France was in grave danger, the French Union was falling apart. General de Gaulle put a stop to civil war, passed the Constitution from which the French Community will be born, restored confidence, secured governmental stability. In less than four months, he has given back to the Republic the lineaments of hope in the eyes of France, and in a few weeks, the lineaments of pride in the eyes of the world . . ."

The horse-drawn house was past, and the road was clear.

"Without giving up a single fundamental freedom. Not even that of . . ."

Petit-Bourg, Goyave, Capesterre, Bananier, Trois-Rivières . . . Once again, the forest. The roar of invisible waterfalls.

Pursued by the radio, we passed through the last village to the sound of cheering. And we finally reached the house which had belonged to a governor of the isles; cascades of bougainvillaeas in the headlights, and the rasping of the nocturnal crickets over which there came the saddest of all creole songs:

> Adieu madras, adieu foulards,
> Adieu rob'soie et colliers-choux,
> Doudou à moi il est parti
> Hélas, hélas, c'est pour toujours . . .

It was written by a governor in the days of Louis XV, abandoned by his mulatto mistress into whose mouth he put his grief. Beautiful beguine singers, who had been awaiting our arrival in the vast corridors, continued the lament:

> Bonjour, monsieur le Gouverneur . . .

and in the dining room the purple and black-clad bishop awaited us, alone at the head of a horseshoe table set for thirty people. Behind him, through all the open french windows, the Caribbean shimmered in the moonlight.

Martinique was no less surprising. To get to St. Pierre, the old capital, you go over a mountain where the Amazonian lianas give way to fir trees; then you reach a town said to have been destroyed by an evil spell. All the roofs have caved in; everything is abandoned, but nothing has been destroyed. Deserted streets, doorless and windowless, stretch to the foot of Mount Pelée. No ashes or lava, but leprous stone stairways rise up into the listless sky. In what was once the main street, a phantom curator guided me through a phantom museum. Here you could see lava, encrusted on absurd and humble objects. It suggested a Pompeii in which the antique lamp has been replaced by a peppermill, the Roman street by a street as blind as those which align the dingy shacks and patches of empty lots around factories on the outskirts of towns. These objects, eaten away like treetrunks thrown up by the sea, seemed like the playthings of the spirits of the volcano; above them, queen of their maleficent court, a desert rose held sway.

There were some postcards of the Tascher de la Pagerie Museum. Another house of the isles, and ruins. I had seen old fortunetellers whispering in the ears of "young ladies." Was it here that the young Rose, who was not yet known as Josephine, held out her hand to the palmist? "More than a queen . . ." The words faded into the desolation, carried off by the ocean wind.

Every village brought me flowers, which I laid beneath the bust of the Republic. Often there was no Republic, but a plaster figure of Schoelcher.* Here the old enemy of slavery had also become a symbol of freedom.

At Fort-de-France, I was to speak after Aimé Césaire. He had greeted me at the town hall with the words, "In your person I salute the great French nation to which we are passionately attached." The main square was magnificent, immense, and full to overflowing—as if for a solemn festival. The bright dresses fell into line in the evening peace which descended over the sea. Césaire was winding up his introductory speech: "May you be the ambassador of rediscovered hope!"

I began by reading General de Gaulle's message: "In bringing you my salutations, André Malraux will tell you how well I remember you, and the magnificent welcome you gave me in 1956. All France remembers the glorious part you played in her victories in the two world wars."

My speech went much the same as the one in Guadeloupe. And the same contact was established—but more powerfully, because now I recognized it, because I was thinking of the listening villages ("Don't forget," one of the organizers had told me, "that here we're broadcasting live, and that it is customary to sing the *Marseillaise* at the end"). The square was so big I had difficulty in making out where it ended in the fading light of evening. As my voice rose, the crowd, in which not a sound could be heard, sensed that the speech was nearing its end.

"The mother country, which in time past chose the Antilles over Canada, which saw the people of the Antilles falling by my side at the Battle of Strasbourg, will not abandon the Antilles. And I believe, with General de Gaulle, that today as yesterday Martinique wishes to remain French as I myself wish to remain French.

"I call on you to witness, as this day draws to its close, you, my former companions in battle who will perhaps be my companions in eternity!

*Victor Schoelcher: leading French opponent of slavery (1804–1893). (Tr.)

Veterans of the First World War, veterans of the Antilles battalion who fought alongside my comrades in the Dordogne, you will answer yes, as those who fell would have answered yes!"

Over the heads of the crowd submerged in the evening twilight, floodlights lit up tall treetrunks and walls plastered over with posters saying No.

"Those of you who escaped from the island as early as 1940—seamen of our Free Naval Forces, and you, veterans of the Pacific battalion that suffered such grievous losses when we won the second victory of the Rhine together—you will answer yes as those who fell would have answered!

"Men and women, you will answer yes, as you did two years ago, to the man who said that your unforgettable welcome had erased so much forgetfulness for him!"

Night had now fallen, and out of the darkness rose the clamor of a stadium saluting victory.

"When the radio began broadcasting the *Marseillaise* on the anniversary of the Republic, those who heard it in the houses of France rose to their feet. Now we are going to sing it together. When you hear us, Frenchmen of Alsace and Royan, stand up in all your villages where the men of Martinique fell! Stand up, people of Martinique, in your houses on the plains and in the hills!"

There were about thirty rows of chairs in front of the platform, and I could sense that all the listeners had stood up. Those who had not been seated were beginning a *Marseillaise* as slow as the *Internationale* I once heard in Moscow while a profusion of red velvet flags gradually emerged from behind the cathedral of St. Basil. But the *Internationale*, slowed down, becomes a singsong, whereas the *Marseillaise* seemed to quiver with restrained momentum:

Entendez-vous, dans nos cam-pa-gnes . . .

Until there burst forth

Aux armes, citoyens!

It was the roar of black freedom, the roar of Toussaint L'Ouverture's soldiers and of the eternal Jacquerie—inextricably bound up with revolutionary hope and physical brotherhood. I had experienced it only once, almost fifteen years before, and in a prison. Césaire and I came down from the platform into the crowd which in the darkness we could only make out by its swaying movement, dazzled as we were by the floodlights whose beams crisscrossed over the rostrum, the trees, and the No posters. The first verse took up its solemn development again: "*Allons enfants de la patrie . . .*" No one moved from his place, everyone was punctuating the battle song with a slow stamping which accompanied it like a muffled tom-tom and bound it to the earth as the songs of paddlers are bound to the river.

L'étenda-ard sanglant est levé!

I had never heard a choir of twenty thousand voices, nor this stamping which seemed to bear witness to the earth: European dances glide over the earth, they do not drum upon it. Césaire and I walked side by side down the avenue which divided the square, and the square emptied behind us, one part of the crowd trying to cross it diagonally so as to meet us as we passed, another following behind us. One could sense this dark ferment underneath the floodlights by the strains of the *Marseillaise* and the cries that swirled about it. When we reached the lamp-lit street running along the square, the song was at once overlaid by the unbroken "*Vive De Gaulle, vive Césaire, Viv'-De-Gol! viv'-Cézer*" which unrolled from the invisible immensity of the sea to the center of the town. The windows seemed jammed with cotton head-scarves; in front of us a swarming throng walked backward clapping their hands in time to the swelling chorus into the midst of which we plunged and which faded behind us into the rhythmic clamor of the multitude. "It's an enormous *videh*," Césaire said to me. (The *videh* is the festival marking the death of Carnival, which is burned in effigy: in it the entire island dances around figures disguised as devils.) Perhaps . . . What I was surrounded by was the age-old festival in which humanity finds release from itself; the ceremony of the lion-men which I had glimpsed in Africa, the painted men of Chad putting ten thousand spectators into a trance on the boundless square of Fort Lamy. Césaire, who was waving amicably as we went by, knew that though we had unleashed this frenzy, we were not its heroes. It was addressed to a supernatural personage who was to General de Gaulle what the Republic is to its President: the intermediary between human life and the world of the unknown, between present misery and future happiness, and above all between solitude and fraternity. I had seen enough frenzy in Europe not to be surprised at finding it elsewhere; but in Europe I had never come across this transition from political excitement to preternatural intoxication, this rhythmic fury which had seemed to me, in the square, to be bearing witness to the earth. It was

dance, but not the recreational dance of Europe or the ritual ballet of
Asia: it was possession. *"Viv' Cézer! Viv' De Gol!"* We made our way
with difficulty to the prefecture. And while the champagne glasses
clinked among the bowings and scrapings of the Europeans, the rhyth-
mical clamor of hope seemed to fill the island to catch the passing
seafarers unawares, like the voice of the ancient gods.

So Guiana augured well. The plane had hugged the Caribbean coast
like a bus, flying over the forest which stretches down to the Amazon.
It passed over Devil's Island and circled the airfield. I had often read
reports about Cayenne and the famous prison colony, which no longer
exists. I was expecting an inferno of dust and desolation, but what I
saw were new colonial houses, far less modest than the shanties of
Martinique, and a fine sand-colored avenue. In front of the wooden
airport building, little girls in traditional costume were waiting with
nosegays like those of India and, like them, sprinkled with droplets of
water. Behind them, local beauties on a float of flowers with an archway that might have been intended to represent either a triumphal arch
or an enormous basket handle.

The prefect welcomed me in a sumptuous Cadillac. Until then,
government officials, like the Ministers in Paris, had only had Citroëns
at their disposal. We talked about arrangements for the speech I was
to make a few hours later. Or rather, I talked organization, microphones, police precautions, the political situation, and he answered
protocol. Perhaps there might be "a few troublemakers" during the
speech. The best thing would be to ignore them. Immediately afterward, he was giving a great banquet: the entire colony would be invited
to the prefecture. "I am most anxious, Minister, that you should agree
to receive the religious authorities first of all. I have arranged a little
cocktail party in a room apart. Unfortunately, the bishop is still in
France, and the chief Protestant pastor—who is a member of my administration, as it happens—is on a mission to St. Laurent-du-Maroni;
of course that doesn't matter so much. At any rate we'll have an assort-
ment of ecclesiastics, and the Worshipful Master of the Lodge. And I
thought I had better ask the rabbi." There were serious problems about
the refreshments. Faintly flabbergasted, I gazed at the pretty colonial
houses and the tumbledown shacks among the parallel strips of fields;
a bandstand and an art nouveau figure of the Republic; a sign reading
Grocer, *gold bought and sold;* and perpendicular streets full of jazz and
drunkards. We crossed the Place Félix Eboué, which contains the only
real monument in Cayenne, and where the speeches were to be made.

Its two-hundred-year-old palm trees, planted by the Jesuits, are among the most beautiful in the world. It is not a real square, for one can hardly distinguish the houses by which it is vaguely delineated; it is a gigantic colonnade of royal palms in a country of disheveled coconut trees bent by the wind. The scarves and the pastel head-scarves, like those of Martinique, were beginning their twilight ballet.

The prefecture, a convent whose portals had been replaced by slatted swing doors, was located in another square. The leaders of the opposition had asked to meet me. I sent a message to say that I would see them before my speech if they cared to call at the prefecture. The prefect seemed reproachful: I was probably upsetting his cocktail arrangements.

My colleagues had found out enough on the way from the airport to be able to tell me that only one of the opposition leaders mattered: he was a half-caste called Catayée, who was running in the coming elections, a hysterical and powerful orator—and a Companion of the Liberation.*

He had not expected to see me alone, nor to hear me address him formally as "My dear Companion." For him, the prefecture was the palace of the enemy, and the prefect was Evil personified. Not that he seemed naïve; rather he was ready to attack or to retreat, a hunted prophet such as are always thrown up at the start of revolutions; a Lumumba—but Lumumba had not been heard of yet.

"You've founded a clinic for unmarried mothers, haven't you?"

"They're all unmarried mothers. I take the worst cases."

"You were a doctor?"

"No, I was a patient. But they're sure to close down my hospital."

"I don't think so."

"They'll say my doctors aren't all as well qualified as they might be. They'll invent stories about abortions. Sometimes they won't have to invent them. Here, you can imagine!"

"I don't think your hospital will be closed down."

"You don't know them!"

"No, but I will. And your hospital will not be closed down."

"Do you think he knows what goes on here, le grand Charles?"

"At least he'll know what you tell me. That's the very reason I'm listening to you."

He looked at me, stood up, and started to walk up and down, his hands behind his back.

*Compagnon de la Libération: honor created by General de Gaulle in 1944 and awarded for services in the Resistance. (Tr.)

"I asked to meet you because I thought you wouldn't see me. But just now I'm beginning to wonder if you don't know the administration as well as I do. Not in detail, naturally . . ."

"Change it!"

"What with?"

"They say you intend to run in the next general election. In a country like this, a deputy can do a lot."

"You're telling me to run?"

"Either you think there is a Guianese nation and that it must develop in its own way—in which case you must vote No, and I don't think it will stand alone for long without falling into terrible poverty; but you can rest assured that it won't remain alone, there'll be plenty of bidders—or else you think that Guiana is French, like the Antilles, and that it will develop with the help of France—in which case you must vote Yes, and work from the inside. Césaire is no tool of the government."

He was disturbed, not by my arguments but by the feelings they aroused in him.

"In other words, you would see my placards with some such inscription as: 'France, yes; prefect, no'?"

"I don't know your prefect, but that would be the way forty per cent of Frenchmen would think. And it would make more sense than 'Down with France,' signed 'A Companion of the Liberation.' "

"Why?"

"Because the first placard is what you really think. Not the second."

The usher had poked his nose in two or three times. Catayée held out his hand. "I'll have to think about it. All the same, this is the first time I've been spoken to here as I was in France."

He left. Neither the *Internationale* nor the proletariat formed part of his vocabulary. Whatever his label, he was a distant brother of the Communards. Trémaud came to inform me, confidentially, that things looked bad. Then I received a few supernumeraries. And we set off for the Place Félix Eboué.

The stands had been set up in the middle of the southern half of the square; approaching from the side, it took us several minutes to reach them. Girls in dazzling dresses and head-scarves smiled at us as we went by, but whereas in the Antilles I had encountered a few scattered "Vive De Gaulle's," here I met with nothing but silence. And there was something eerie about our motorcycle escort and the big car gliding noiselessly through a multicolored crowd which closed up behind us in the darkness.

The stands—rows of notables in tiers—encircled the speaker's rostrum, which was a sort of booth. Behind, there were floodlights which lit up the crowd for a distance of some fifty yards, beyond which it disappeared from view as it had a few moments earlier past the beam of our headlights. (We were lit up, presumably, by floodlights pointing the other way.) On the platform, I was introduced against a vague murmuring. Here and there I spotted little placards bearing the words "Vive la France," carried by the little girls in costume who had brought me bouquets at the airport. This parish-hall setting accorded oddly with the uneasy tension of the crowd.

I went to the rostrum.

My arguments were the same as in the Antilles. During the first pause, a few small groups applauded, lost in the enormous silence. I assumed they had been organized. Some of them were in the dark, but others were visible in the floodlights. As I went on, they grew thicker, though still lost in the vastness which was now no longer silent, but talkative: the loudspeakers were out of order, except for those beneath which a few hundred people tried to huddle—lost among ten thousand. I began to bellow, very slowly, as I used to do before the introduction of microphones, but I was above the level of the crowd, and in any case no speech can be heard from three hundred yards away. Then, right under the lights, No placards began to rise above people's heads, over the Yes placards; and two banners slowly unfurled, twenty yards long, held at each end by poles: DOWN WITH—the startled crowd moved out of the way—FASCISM.

Then DOWN WITH DE GAULLE.

Then DOWN WITH FRANCE.

I still had enough voice left to shout: "If it's independence you want, you can have it on the twenty-eighth. And who gave you the chance before De Gaulle?"

There was applause as far as my voice carried, and the crowd moved away from the men holding the poles. Beyond, a jamboree was beginning. From the right, in the distance, came the noise of shouting: demonstrators were trying to outflank the police in order to attack the platforms. Then I heard shouts close by, and the space around my booth was suddenly empty. A glittering object whistled past my left ear, crashed into the back of the booth, and fell at my feet. I picked it up and raised it above my head while I went on with my speech. It was a weapon I had never seen before: a piece of wood about fifteen inches long, with an enormous nail sticking out of it. More of them arrived. If the throwers came nearer, it would be easy for them to take aim and hit me. As I went on with my speech, I surveyed the security precautions: between the throwers and myself, the little girls who had brought me bouquets; to the right, some boy scouts. The latter drew nearer, followed by a gesticulating black mass that hesitated as if in fear of the light. The placard carriers remained motionless. And so did the nail throwers. No doubt there were not many of them. One of my colleagues came up to me: "The prefect advises you to withdraw." "Does he now?" More nails arrived. In the hubbub that had replaced the silence, nobody could hear me, but the crowd was no longer listening, it was watching. "Catayée has a powerful microphone," my colleague said, "and offers to bring it to you." "No." The microphone would have made no difference. The whole sound system was laughable. Part of this tide of assailants ebbing and flowing at the edge of the floodlit area, but about to break, was probably made up of Catayée's men: he had not had time to cancel his orders. I had no intention of putting myself under his protection. The gesticulating mass was gradually encroaching on the floodlit area, while the DOWN WITH FRANCE banners remained as stationary as the unheeding advertisements around a football stadium. These were not the gestures of political activism, of militants standing shoulder to shoulder, but of murderous drunkenness. I remembered the first novel I had ever read: *Georges*, by Alexandre Dumas. The rebel slaves of the Ile-de-France are about to give battle to the royal troops when the planters roll barrels of arrack down the street toward them, and everything ends in a drunken orgy and a massacre. Screams and yells had replaced the slogans. The *videh* of Martinique was building up, and it would not be Carnival who was to be killed. One of the little girls still bravely holding her VIVE LA FRANCE placard was grabbed by the waist and sent spinning into the shadow behind her. Three others followed her. Then a wild-looking procession came into view and paused, dazzled by the light. In front, an injured man dragged by four others (presumably on a blanket), bloodstained, his arms and legs dangling; behind him, with the galvanic movements of crazed drunkenness and bloodlust, a hundred maniacs armed with nail-studded planks. They advanced toward me as I went on speaking, then veered toward the stands where a number of women were sitting. They seemed about to exhibit this twitching body as a kind of *Pietà*, when all at once their lunging advance was brought to a halt. The men carrying the body let it fall. In front of the platform a company of marines led by Trémaud were taking up positions on the double, their carbines at the ready.

There was an unnatural silence at the center of the noisy babble of those who were too low down to see what was happening. In front of the platform, the marines standing stock-still, spaced out at two-yard intervals (I knew that Trémaud would not give the order to fire without warning); all the women on their feet; a large gap in which the injured man, abandoned, stirred vaguely, and the hundred frenzied men retreating step by step like an animal being headed off, baffled and dejected-looking, up to the shadow's edge where the crowd parted to let them through. Neither the VIVE LA FRANCE placards—apart from those of the four children—nor the DOWN WITH DE GAULLE banners had stirred. Everything seemed to be entering eternity as the procession retreated into the night.

After finishing my speech, I got up again to shout hoarsely that the following morning I would go and pay my respects at the war memorial, and that I would speak at the town hall. (Those who heard me could tell the others.) An ambulance siren provided me with a sinister accompaniment. Stretcher bearers walked toward the injured man. All the marines had now arrived to join their comrades and were guarding the stands. The placards were being lowered, the banners rolled up. The crowd was thinning. The boles of the royal palm trees reached upward to the starry sky, like the pillars of Baalbek.

At the prefecture, the minor clerics were awaiting us. What a pity the others were absent! Never mind, monsieur le Préfet, another time. They appeared to be excellent people. But it seemed to me difficult to speak to missionaries and to a Worshipful Master at the same time. So I said nothing. But I asked Trémaud, "Will you take all but one of our men with you, and start the inquiry at once?" "I've already summoned the chief of police. There are a certain number of injured. It isn't over yet."

But not a sound could be heard through the open windows. The prefect was explaining details of protocol that meant nothing to me. Cayenne was appreciably smaller than New York, and I thought it should be a simple matter for him to introduce the guests with whom it was desirable for me to exchange a few words. However, there we were—my wife in a huge armchair, the prefect and I standing on either side of her, and a master of ceremonies announcing with the utmost pomp: "Captain Durand, Madame Durand, Councillor Dupont, Madame Dupont."

"Where did you find him?"

"Oh, at the prison, Minister, naturally. He's a convict. But of course, an 'ordinary passionnel' . . ."

An hour later I learned that he had slit his wife's throat. But as the prefect was saying, what style! It went on. "Monsieur the Clerk of the Court, Madame Masson; Monsieur the Member of Parliament."

A slight nuance of tone. Was it in honor of parliament, or of celibacy? I regretted the absence of the bishop—I would have liked to hear the master of ceremonies announce him. Then, "Monsieur the President of the IFAT."

What was that? From the tone, he was only a minor president.

"Monsieur the Secretary General of the BAFOG; Monsieur the Subprefect of St. Laurent-du-Maroni."

A glorious title, announced as such. This "ordinary *passionnel*" pleased me more and more. Perhaps he had developed his style not from having obeyed, but from having commanded. A Russian ex-prince, a bit of a cutthroat? To think I had once been a novelist! Suppose I were to ask the prefect to invite a dozen convicts to lunch next day? I had been told that one of them was an expert on butterflies. And all at once I realized what had not struck me before, because of the arm-chair—for the wife of the President of the Republic obviously does not remain seated during the introduction of the guests. We were in the process of aping the receptions at the Elysée—amid the shouting, which had started up again, and the wounded, and the "ordinary *passionnel*" to whom I was determined to send the works of Proust—and Guiana no doubt lost.

Cayenne high society is not inexhaustible. At last we went through to the drawing room. A cold buffet, people whom I questioned about Guiana and who answered with what General de Gaulle ought to do. And then, had I ever seen a manatee? Did I think they were the sirens of antiquity? A jeweler in the main street sold gold nuggets "which made very pretty pendants." An occasional outburst of shouting was still audible through the open windows, but I could hear no shots. The colleague who had stayed behind came and told me, "There have been quite a few scuffles, and Trémaud thinks we should act tonight." "Come to my room and bring him with you." I shook a few hands, took my leave of the prefect, and joined my colleagues in my room.

"Luckily," Trémaud told me, "the police are reliable. I think we'll have to give protection to the head of the Sûreté, who is determined to help us. We're in Clochemerle and a gangster film at the same time. On the one hand the prefect, who is a Radical of the kind you don't come across in France any more . . ."

"Export only!"

"In his opinion ninety per cent of the population will vote against us, so what we are doing constitutes provocation. Yet he has his own candidate for the forthcoming elections. He is on bad terms with the deputy, who's more or less a Gaullist, and at daggers drawn with Catayée, who is thought to be mad, but who exists. Anyway, the prefect made no security arrangements. Because he told Paris that Guiana was lost? To show that the deputy is powerless? To have an excuse for

taking steps against Catayée? Maybe out of stupidity! His boy scouts
and his little girls were just like the reception at the airport. The American car was hired especially for you."

"Say it with flowers!"

"The others thought they wouldn't have any opposition. They didn't
expect the marines. They all cooperated to a man: they were enraged
when they saw the little girls being manhandled. But I had to go and
fetch them myself, because the local authorities wouldn't lift a finger.
The men with the banners belong to Catayée, who is all over me at
the moment.

"He didn't know the sound system wasn't working. The prefect
should have had it tested in the morning and taken the necessary steps
—and Catayée wanted to prove that the prefect is an incompetent. As
for voting against France, we shall see. On the whole, he's a bit bothered
about that."

"I think so too."

"With a proper sound system you'd have had some rowdyism, and
an enthusiastic *Marseillaise* at the end. But this is where the plot
thickens: the people with the banners were Catayée's men, plus a few
vague communists, et cetera. But not the nail throwers."

"Had you come across this weapon before?"

"Never. But it was no joke. Anyhow, before the speech, somebody
brought casks of rum to the places in the square where there were
demonstrators known for their violence, then broached the casks and
beat it."

"Who's somebody?"

"I don't know. We'll probably never know. But it isn't only a question of politics, in spite of the number of injured. The police tell me
that the communists sent in men from British Guiana and the British
looked the other way. I've had some of them arrested, which is legal
because they entered the country clandestinely, and easy because they
were completely drunk. They are no more communist than Catayée,
and the British have nothing to do with this business. They're known
smugglers. So, Clochemerle develops into a rivalry between gangsters
doubtless connected with political rivalries. As to the bungling of the
arrangements, I can only tell you this: the anti-French tracts were
printed on the press at the prefecture; the first little girl who was sent
flying (she was caught by people behind her) is the daughter of the
headmaster of the lycée and the man who did it is one of the teachers."

"You're certain the handbills were printed on the press at the prefecture?"

"Absolutely."

"I have the right to replace the prefect provisionally, have I not?"

"He's expecting it. You represent the government."

"When you leave here, tell him he is under house arrest pending a decision from the Minister of the Interior. I shall be in Paris the day after tomorrow. Tonight, you'll take his place. How many 'trouble-makers' do you want arrested?"

"Apart from two or three, they already have been."

"Well done. For as short a time as possible, except for dangerous brutes like that teacher. We simply need to show people that the joke's over. As for the drunkenness, the people who supplied the barrels are of more interest to us than the drinkers. What's the general feeling in the town?"

"Furious with everybody. They had come to listen to you, and they were prevented from hearing what you had to say."

"My fame must end at the gates of Cayenne!"

"No, because the inscription on the monument to Governor Eboué is by you."

"A good deed is never wasted. So, let's say no more about the prefect until after the referendum. Send him on holiday. Who will take his place, at least until his successor is appointed? You would supervise, as long as it's necessary, of course. What's the secretary general like?"

"He's a good man. He's André Philip's son."

"Let's go and see him. But we'll have to ask for his agreement—because he'll be risking his neck after all. He will come with me to the war memorial and the town hall."

"If not, I'll be prefect."

"Thank you. Better to have a local authority, as you know. Either they will have thought better of it by the morning, which is to say that they won't attempt in broad daylight what they tried to do in the dark, and the disturbances will calm down, provided we take the necessary steps—you know all that better than I do. Or else it's really serious—which I don't believe—and there's no possible way of protecting us during the *Marseillaise* at the war memorial. Good luck with the rest of the inquiry, and good night."

They went back to work. The window was open, the bed covered with its cubical mosquito net. Outside, a dense crowd still flowed noiselessly by, like a procession of black deaf-mutes. In the distance, the occasional outburst of shouting was soon drowned in a frenzy of jazz. Beyond the houses, the royal palm trees that had sheltered missionaries and convicts rose up into the night, the most absurd night of my life.

Twelve miles away began the elemental forest, alive like the mountains
or the ocean, with its parrots head to tail and rivers full of carnivorous
fish, stretching to the foot of the high plateaus. President Kubitschek
had told me in Brasilia: ". . . then we flung the two great roads across
the forest, and sometimes we found colonies of men who had not
changed since the Stone Age." And, much closer, the Maroni River
and the beautiful Place Félix Eboué, which had previously been the
terrible Place des Palmistes where the mygale-spiders used to sting the
sleeping convicts to death.

I was waiting for sleep to come. There was a picture album on the
bedside table. It started with the entrance grill of the prison. I expected
Bastille-like bars, but found instead the arabesques of a provincial
doctor's house, surmounted by a lantern festooned with bougainvillaea.
Then the derelict church, where rank weeds and brambles grew beneath
the frescoes painted by condemned men, in which the Apostles wore
convict dress. In the cells, where insects scuttled between the graffiti,
the leg-irons, the holes for the straps that held the prisoners' bodies.
Then the bush "railway," pulled by men; the tombs (of warders), out
of place in this disused hell; and in the midst of the thorny luxuriance,
a tiny square of tamped-down earth where no plants grew but which
was surrounded by purple bougainvillaeas like those over the entrance:
the site of the guillotine.

From the garage of the prefecture rose the otherworldly tremolo of
an Indian flute. The convict settlement was no more, the fury of the
abortive revolt, recalled by the length of wood bristling with nails that
lay on the table, had died down. There remained the unearthly warbling
of the flute, the silent nocturnal procession in the square, and the departure of the last guests from that reception out of the *Tales of
Hoffmann*, shown out by the genteel cutthroat.

The morning began well. In Cayenne, what makes the prefect is the
uniform. The secretary general was eight inches taller than the prefect
—and the latter's uniform was the only one available. The gold-braided
hat looked like a little mushroom on the top of his head. He would
have to carry it. But he could hardly do the same with the trousers,
which only reached his shoes by means of a pair of curiously elongated
braces. There remained the tunic, a real necessity because of the in-
signia. The collar could be left open because of the heat; but the sleeves
were still a good four inches short, and the whole thing was more suggestive of the sailor with a pompom in cartoons than of a high dignitary
of the Republic. Chaplin as prefect. The secretary general put up with

the charade good-humoredly. We made our way to the war memorial. The splendid limousine had vanished.

No sooner were we outside than I realized how much the previous night's adventure had depended on the darkness. People looked at us in a friendly way; these were ordinary tradespeople, not throwers of nails. The war memorial lay in a narrow square where no one could have fired at me from a distance of more than ten yards, and so in full view. In any case, the crowd was sparse and well behaved. During the Last Post, a shadow with sleeves too short stretched alongside mine in front of the statue.

The ceremony over, we went on to the town hall. There, the crowd filled the street, in which loudspeakers had been installed. The entire municipal council drank my health. The mayor made a cordial speech, and ended it by shouting, "Vive la France!" I replied from the balcony (this time it came over loud and clear) in accordance with the traditions of 1848. I took up the themes of the previous day, which were partly those of Martinique, and which were punctuated with bursts of applause—as if the daytime population were anxious to disavow the night's demonstration. Without raising my voice, I told them of my interview with General de Gaulle: "He said to me: 'You must go to Guiana, because France must help Guiana.' And he added: 'You must go there because it is heartrending.'" A somber burst of approbation filled the street, like the acclamations in Martinique. The mayor came down with me, and we went to the prefecture arm in arm. The new prefect and Catayée followed us. The *videh* formed behind us, as it had in Fort-de-France; thousands of men, and a few women, arms linked, in immense improvised farandoles. When we arrived, for several minutes a great roar of YES beat against the prefecture—where the secretary general was at last able to put on his own clothes again.

He accompanied us to the airport in civilian clothes. No more little girls, no more flower floats with triumphal arches or even basket handles. "*Adieu madras, adieu foulards . . .*" A few coconut trees, some sinister birds, and the dust swirling around the little airport where one was surprised that anyone ever expected a plane.

We broke our flight at Martinique, where our friends, who had heard the news of the previous night but not of the morning, awaited us anxiously. They need not have worried. Guiana and the Antilles were to vote eighty per cent "yes," Catayée to become deputy, and the prefect secretary general. I had not had time to see the nugget merchant, or even the street where his shop was to be found. Could he have been the grocer whose sign I had seen?

5

1958/1965. It was after this excursion into the picturesque that General de Gaulle requested me to visit the heads of some of the Asian states with whom our relations were no more than formal—first of all Nehru.

I was familiar with the situation in India, having recently entertained Jayaprakash Narayan, the Bombay socialist leader. And my friend the writer Raja Rao, India's greatest expert on France, had also just been in Paris. Our ambassador was less pessimistic than the prefects of the Antilles.

He was waiting for me at the airport, at two in the morning, with the Secretary of State for Foreign Affairs, whose white sari shone in the landing lights. Her name was Lakshmi. A Western Secretary of State might well be called Mary, like the Virgin, but the goddesses of other religions provide more food for dreams. Count Ostrorog, a descendant of the Mogul conquerors, and an illegitimate son of Pierre Loti according to Quai d'Orsay gossip, was that rare specimen, a man worthy of what the title Ambassador to India conjures up for poets. An imaginary camera would travel from his delicately gnarled fingers, kneading an affectionate and willing India, to his distinguished pirate's face. This descendant of the lords of the steppes, hidalgo, Roman cardinal and exemplarily French, was the ambassador of an age-old Mediterranean culture to a young India—a curious thought, knowing what India is. At one of the dinners at the Capitol—the new name for the former palace of the viceroys, which was now that of the government—during an austere prime-ministerial speech, Ostrorog's hands seemed to be caressing the boot of Italy like a dancing girl's leg . . .

When we reached the Capitol that night (I was the guest of the government), I could only make out the dark mass of the building, the corridors, a big portrait of Gandhi in a *dhoti*, and the chief of protocol surrounded by a staff of servants worthy of viceregal days—one to open each door. Having dismissed these Ali Baba personages, we discussed the details of my mission. The minister responsible for culture was to receive me at eight o'clock.

The newspapers were already there when I woke up. Afro-Asian week was beginning. The ministers' welcome was what it always is: cautious and tactful. They were waiting for my interview with Nehru.

I finally saw the Capitol, and was now seeing New Delhi. I had retained no clear memory of it; in 1929 I was more interested in India than in England. But the departure of the British gave this soulless architecture a sort of soul. Gandhi and Clemenceau have both been credited with the remark, "It will make a splendid ruin." It had not made a ruin, any more than it had made a conquered palace, like the Kremlin. New Delhi is not a town, it is an "administrative capital," but its colossal vistas of red sandstone, with Sikh guards presenting arms in the solitude, did not open on to administrations—not even Parliament—they opened on to the vanished Empire.

Palaces, ministries, propylaea. The entire British Empire bears the stamp of English greatness, with the tone that Victorian Gothic gives to the Thames. Here, as at the Khyber Pass, the grandeur was Roman; the dream of Caesar at Alexandria, a powerful mass set out according to the vast Hellenistic theater. Mingled with another dream, that of an Anglo-Indian marriage to rival the Indo-Muslim. The Capitol was patently a rival to the Great Mosque at Delhi, one of the biggest in all Islam; and to Fatehpur Sikri, the Red Fort, and all that Mogul architecture which was the America of Persia. Islam was still there. And England? More than might appear? But it was not her presence that animated the imperial avenues of red sandstone down which I drove to the Parliament building: it was the courage with which she had abandoned them. In this land which has built so many illustrious tombs, the only achievement that rivals those of Alexander's successors became truly great, in spite of the mediocrity of its architecture, when it was transformed into the tomb of the Empire.

I was calling on Nehru in his office in the Parliament building. This meant a transition from the majesty of the Capitol to municipal corridors and waiting rooms for minor petitioners. But, as in the Capitol, innumerable pictures of Gandhi decorated the walls.

Gandhi was still present throughout India, in his achievements, his example, his image. For Europe, he was simply a liberator with clean hands; a symbol of saintliness, with the quaintness that goes with so many saints: an obstinate nun with a big toothless smile, dressed in a humble plebeian garment worn like the uniform of freedom. Although India was beginning to see in him the last avatar of Vishnu, certain outstanding phases of his life were still precisely remembered: the sermon in 1920 under a huge banyan tree, then the crowd on the banks of the Sabarmati; the Amritsar massacre; the fingers of his left hand held up to show the crowd the four main duties of India; the weird pyre made up of European clothes, collars, braces thrown away by people who thenceforth would wear only the khadi—the precursor of his own funeral pyre in front of which the *Bhagavad-Gita* would be recited. And civil disobedience, and the noncooperation movement which began on the day Tilak died. And above all, the Salt March.

On March 2, 1930, Gandhi had informed the Viceroy that civil disobedience would begin nine days later. On the twelfth he set off toward the sea, followed by seventy disciples. The peasants put out flags, spread branches over the roads, knelt as the pilgrims passed by. Three hundred village headmen resigned from their posts. The original seventy had grown to several thousand when Gandhi collected some salt left behind by the waves, thus infringing the salt tax laws. Tropical heat makes salt indispensable to working men and animals—but everyone knew that because of his own illness Gandhi had not touched it for six years. At a single stroke he had roused the whole of India.

All along the coast, fishermen began collecting salt; the peasants followed suit, and the police began to make mass arrests. The resisters let themselves be arrested, but would not surrender their salt. In Bombay sixty thousand people gathered in front of the House of Congress, on whose terrace saline sand was processed. The salt which Gandhi had collected was sold for 1,600 rupees. When Nehru was sentenced to six months in prison, India answered with *hartals*. In Patna a crowd flung themselves on the ground in front of the government cavalry and stopped it. In Karachi fifty thousand Indians watched salt being collected while the police stood by, helpless. Nevertheless, soon there were a hundred thousand people in prison. On the night of May 4-5, Gandhi was arrested in a village among his disciples.

At Dharasana, north of Bombay, crowds marched on the government salt depot, which was guarded by four hundred policemen. One after the other, as they approached the factory, they were struck down; others silently replaced them, and fell in their turn. Stretcher bearers removed the bleeding bodies. The factory went on working, a temporary hospital had to be opened, and all India became aware of its servitude. Soon, Churchill was to speak of "this seditious *fakir*, half-naked in the palace of the Viceroy!"

Now the Viceroy was gone, and the legend of Gandhi, which for the West had become one of noble passivity, remained a fighting legend here. A fight, above all, with words. When he had announced that he would give up eating if the rights of the Untouchables were not recognized, it was not a matter of "fasting" but of starving to death. This self-inflicted torture which challenged India's most powerful taboo was no less irrational than the taboo itself, and the Hindus had followed it like a slow crucifixion. In these multitudes, of whom ninety-five per cent did not own a radio, everyone knew when Gandhi began to be in danger of death. And everyone knew that his ultimate aim was the purification of India, that independence was not the primary consideration. He wanted his teachings to reach the most humble, even when he said, "Swaraj will not come through the victory of the few, but only when all have become capable of resisting injustice." And they had all prayed aloud when they heard that the cartridge-case had fallen from the murdered Mahatma's shawl, and that everything had come to an end at last with a dark red bullet glowing in his white ashes. Nevertheless, Gandhi was still present in this Parliament as he was in the Capitol. Vinoba Bhave, whose only weapons were his words, had just been given five million acres of land (not the best, of course) for the peasants. In a world from which the shadows of Stalin and Hitler had not yet faded, India could boast of having freed herself from England without a single English casualty. In spite of all the poverty, the word democracy took on an almost religious meaning here. Bandoeng had shown Nehru's authority—as had the uneasiness roused by his silence in the face of the Russian action in Budapest. But the policies of India were no more fashioned in the Congress or in Parliament than the policies of Hitler's Germany were fashioned in the Reichstag: the policies of India were the legacy of the little man in a loincloth who had taken it into his head to lead millions of Indians off to glean salt from the Indian Ocean as a protest against the salt tax, and to find freedom there.

I was shown into an office where the press and about fifty agitated photographers were waiting for the usher who would come to fetch me. Suddenly they all turned: another door had opened to reveal not the usher but Nehru.

He knew that he was under attack from the Delhi press for receiving me. For good reasons: Indochina and Algeria. And for puerile reasons: a number of journalists, taking their cue from certain London weeklies, had the perspicacity to see General de Gaulle as a successor to Hitler. And also for another reason of which I was not aware, although Nehru was: the majority of the Delhi papers would be hostile to him whatever he did. The journalists now stood aside to make way for him, murmuring his first name as the crowd were said to have done when he came to the place where the murdered Gandhi lay. He embraced me and said (the occasion was being televised), as if we had met a month before, though it was more than twenty years since we had met, "I'm glad to see you again. The last time was after you were wounded in Spain. You were just out of the hospital and I was just out of jail."

I admired the skill with which, for the time being, he had disarmed this herd; and I admired the human quality, which no skill could have contrived. He took my arm, and we went into his office.

I remember only the table, of a rare wood which, after reflecting the last of the television lights, now reflected only the rose that lay between us—the same as the one he always wore—and his face. When people read this, perhaps that face will no longer be as familiar as it is today: history will only have preserved the mask. It was a Roman face with a slight heaviness about the lower lip which gave his apparently "posed" smile the seductiveness which a suggestion of innocence imparts to a great man. No one was taken in by it, any more than he was. But beyond the set mask of the photographs, there was that smile linked with a dreaming expression which suggested blue eyes (they were brown) in harmony with his nearly gray complexion.

He had had something of the look of a maquis leader when I knew him, especially with the forage cap he used to wear before 1940. Now he evinced a benevolently ironic worldweariness, which overlay his toughness without entirely concealing it. (When his mother was insulted while taking food to prisoners, he had renounced all visits for a period of seven months at the prison of Dehra Dun. Gandhi used to say: "He is courage itself.") Time had not so much aged his face as somehow given him a slightly different one—as it can happen to men who early in life resemble their mothers and come to resemble their fathers as they grow older. And in his voice, his bearing, there appeared (or reappeared?) beneath the patrician intellectual the English gentleman's ease and self-possession which he had doubtless learned to emulate in his youth.

He read General de Gaulle's letter outlining my credentials, put it on the table, and said with a broad smile, "So now you're a Minister."

The phrase did not in the least mean "you're a member of the French government." In a slightly Balzackian, and especially Hindu, sense, it meant "so this is your latest incarnation."

"Mallarmé used to tell this story," I answered. "One night he was listening to the cats talking in the gutter. One inquisitive black cat asked his, a venerable tom, 'And what do you do?' The reply was: 'At the moment, I'm pretending to be the cat at the Mallarmés'.' "

Nehru smiled even more broadly, and nodded. His hand gestures, once so expansive, were now turned inward toward his body, the fingers almost closed. And it was in these chilly gestures, which gave his authority a charm such as I have never since encountered, that I saw the only real difference between the old Nehru and the man I was talking to now. For authority is a state of being, which remains constant. I explained to him briefly how I envisaged the exhibition of Indian art that we wished to put on in Paris. He gave his assent and asked me what we suggested in exchange. I proposed Romanesque sculpture, or a historical exhibition on the subject of the Revolution.

"For us," he said, "France means the Revolution. When Vivekananda discovered it, he spent a whole day shouting 'Vive la République!' to his friends. Did you know that Les Misérables is one of the most famous foreign books in India?"

I had already come across this French presence, and was to come across it again later on many occasions. Soviet Russia has not erased it. In the underdeveloped countries, the machine brings qualified technicians rather than an industrial proletariat. And wherever revolution is called for not by the proletariat but by the nation, the message of the French Revolution, the exaltation of the fight for justice proclaimed from Saint-Just to Jaurès, by way of Michelet and above all Victor Hugo, has retained a prestige at least as great as that of Marxism. I saw piles of copies of Les Misérables between Bakunin and the theoretical writings of Tolstoy on the Ramblas in Barcelona during the Civil War.

"Romanesque sculpture?" he went on. "Practically no one here really admires our own sculpture from the classical period. It exercises a magical force on the masses, up to a certain point; so do roadside idols. The members of Parliament respect Ellora but don't go there."

"The relationship of politicians to art is always fairly complicated; but after all, yours at least know the Bhagavad-Gita."

"In the same way as English MP's know the Bible."

He was creating India while surrounded by a Saturn's Ring of hostile politicians. When I said how surprised I was at the Delhi papers' strange image of the French government, he answered, "Oh! and of the Indian government too!"—with a gesture of hope and resignation, an ironic inshallah.

I suggested to him that in this respect General de Gaulle's position was not very different from his own. He was intrigued by the idea, but I doubt if he was convinced.

The memory—or the presence—of totalitarian parties remained so powerful that in French eyes Nehru resembled Stalin more than Roosevelt; but for Nehru, in spite of himself, General de Gaulle probably resembled Mussolini rather than Churchill. Nevertheless, too intelligent and too well informed to believe that the General was a fascist leader, or "that he must soon be taken over by the party of M. Soustelle," he followed the progress of events in France with attention. He had not intervened in Indochina or in Algeria, because he considered that a nation should win its independence without foreign help. He did not take the Fourth Republic seriously: one of its prime ministers had prudently entertained him in a restaurant in the Bois de Boulogne, because it was spring. But he had a close-up view of the decline of Britain, which he had known for so long as the strongest power in the world; and he observed the decline of Europe, without forgetting that he had seen the rebirth of Germany and Russia. Then again, concerned as he was with Africa, he found it hard to reconcile the creation of the French Community with the Algerian war. The word Algeria came up in the course of the conversation and I could see from his slight gesture of withdrawal that as my host he was apologetic about having pronounced it. I merely said, "It will be General de Gaulle who brings peace to Algeria."

He looked at me, puzzled or incredulous.

I had thought about what was called at the time "the peace of the brave," and about the fraternization of which to this day I cannot determine the degree of sincerity or sham. But for me as for him, neither the maintenance of the French Community nor the independence of our former African colonies, if that was what succeeded the Community, was consonant with the endless pursuit of the Algerian war.

"What part do the communists play in it, in your opinion?" he asked.

"A big part in Paris, a small one in Algiers. But do you think there is still such a thing as a communist policy?"

He gave me a questioning look.

"What I mean is this. In the old days Great Britain used to have a global policy after her fashion. Not so the United States. She has become the most powerful nation in the world without wishing to. Which was not the case either with Alexander, or Caesar, or Tamerlane, or Napoleon: their hegemonies were the result of their conquests. This is perhaps why the United States makes war so well and peace so badly."

I remembered seeing John Foster Dulles, the American Secretary of State, drive through the gates of the Hôtel Matignon in an enormous car, like a Roman proconsul entering some city of the East. The following day, the General had said to me, "Either there is a West, with a common policy toward the rest of the world, or else . . . But there will be no West." And there had been none.

"The present global policy of the Americans," I went on, "is based on anticommunism; in other words, it is determined by Russian policy.

This applies even to something as impressive as the Marshall Plan. On the other hand, we have experience of a Russian global policy, the policy of harnessing the forces of the International to the service of the Soviet Union. But since Stalin's death that particular policy seems to have had its day. At least that is what's suggested by Algeria, and Africa in general—and even Bandoeng. Today it's mostly the intellectuals who put political problems in terms of communism."

"What is their attitude toward it?"

"In France, communism means the Communist party, such as you have always known it for better or worse. Many intellectuals are torn between social justice and the nation, rather than between communism and capitalism. In the Resistance, I chose France, and I am not the only one.

"In the United States, things seem to me quite different. For my American friends, after the Hiss trial and the Oppenheimer affair, communism was a *plot:* the communists were secret agents of the Russians—who were fighting for the proletariat: only the proletariat was the trade unions, who were not communists."

He smiled again. "Everyone believes in other people's communists. But everyone approaches God by way of his own gods, is the Indian saying."

A quip?

"My remark surprises you? From what I know of Europe, I'm surprised at your surprise. Approaching God by way of one's own gods—surely the West does nothing else but that, in the realm of the mind, in admiring at the same time Plato, Spinoza, Hegel, Spencer—not to mention the people who admire Nietzsche—or Marx—and Jesus at the same time?"

He returned to the subject of communism. Like General de Gaulle, he no longer regarded it as of fundamental importance. "Here, the communists are mainly occupied with polemics," he said. And, "One of our states, Kerala, is communist: all the same, the members of the Central Committee are Brahmans." I knew that he did not share the anticommunism of Gandhi, who had said, "Russia has a dictator who dreams of peace and thinks he can reach it across a sea of blood." But he had also said, "The intellectuals are appalled by my ideas and my methods." Nehru saw and admired the Russian Revolution as a war of liberation against Tsarism, which he identified with colonialism. Since he did not feel threatened either by the Indian Communist party or the Red Army, he thought of Russia from a distance; since he did not believe in an armed conflict between the Soviet Union and the

United States, he was not perhaps averse to a cold war in which the
two great adversaries competed for Indian favors. For me, the history
of the last forty years had meant the rise of communism and the super-
session of Europe by the United States. For him, it had meant decolonization, and above all the liberation of Asia. His state socialism
had nothing in common either with the Soviets or with capitalism,
"which is not lacking in violence either, in its own way." The West
(and perhaps Russia) judged India in terms of the cold war, and talked
about a Third World and neutralism. But for Nehru there was *his*
world, which was not to be defined in terms of the two others: the
world of the countries at once newly liberated and underdeveloped,
which must first and foremost change their civilization. By Westernizing
themselves? "To a certain extent; but in two hundred years science
and machines have produced a very different civilization from the one
that existed at the time of the French Revolution and the American
War of Independence; the India they will produce in a hundred years'
time will not be much like the present one, but perhaps it won't be
much like Europe either." For the West, the Soviet Union was the
symbol of a past revolution, and sometimes, perhaps, a future one; for
Nehru, it was primarily a symbol of planning. "Nothing since the discovery of nonviolence has struck me as forcibly as the development of
Soviet Central Asia. And perhaps Europeans do not realize that in Asia
today, industrialization is as powerful a myth as independence was."
    They would have to use Russian techniques and American capital
according to circumstances. Without too many illusions, however, for
though foreign aid was indispensable to India's development, that development itself could only come from India's own efforts, "otherwise
we run the risk of a colonialism of the mind; and in any case I don't
believe that every Indian is particularly anxious to possess a refrigerator
and a car." What refrigerators? The tragedy that had India by the
throat was hunger. Would communist planning prove more effective
against famine than liberal capitalism?
    I realized why his words had shaken what we called the Third World.
In this domain, like Gandhi, he was revealing the obvious. He made
some reference to the Round Table Conference, Gandhi huddled in
his blanket among dignitaries as gilded as the painted nymphs on
the ceiling, "at the time when the Aga Khan was making a show of
support for Independence, and when the parlor socialists, in London
and in India, were calling Gandhi a superreactionary." Beside this
tiny shadow, Stalin remained colossal but seemed like an interloper.
Khrushchev and Bulganin had come to the Capitol as heads of state

like any others. Nehru's English upbringing was not Marxist, and his Indian upbringing drove him to fight against caste rather than class; for the Untouchables, who despite the Constitution were dying on the lawns of the Capitol, rather than for the proletariat.

But the maintenance of true independence, and the industrialization of India, could only be founded on a state. And Nehru was conscious of the fragility of the one he was fashioning. He held that all revolution was inseparable from an ethical drive, a desire for justice; in the West this had come from individuals and was founded on reason and equality before the law, which they held to be the supreme values. It was not so in India. There individualism, and even the individual, played only a minor role. The fundamental reality is caste. The Indian is not an individual who finds himself a member of a caste in the sense in which one can say that a European is an individual who belongs to a nation: he is a member of his caste as a true Christian is baptized before being an individual. In the past the Hindu ethic was never profoundly altered by secular men, nor even by the Brahmans, but only by the ascetics; because the ascetic is outside caste, and because he is dedicated to the gods. Apart from self-denial, the fundamental ethic of India is devotion to caste, which is inseparable from religion: there is no conception of a lay ethic. Gandhi, in the eyes of the West, India's political leader, was in Indian eyes, and no doubt his own, a traditional great ascetic.

The liberation struggle had not called in question the nature of Indian society. The communists accused the Congress party of being a bourgeois party. When had it ever claimed to be proletarian? Its objective, independence, was national not social. It had fought for all Indians. But the objective once gained, social justice became a major problem. And caste consciousness was stronger than class consciousness. The political apparatus did not constitute an order like the Communist party: members of Parliament were only partially emancipated from their caste. The parliamentary ideal derived from an ideal image of the British Parliament, and had no connection with the Indian past; the agnostic Nehru strove in vain to make it Indian. To create a modern India, he was obliged to rely directly on his people by associating the humblest Indian with an epic (he simply called it "a great enterprise"). "India must be activated, but by herself, not by government orders." But immemorial India saw social injustice as part of the cosmic order, and the cosmic order must of necessity mean justice. Had Gandhi, though determined to destroy untouchability, been equally determined to destroy the castes? His struggle against untouchability

had been enough to have him assassinated, not by a communist, but
by one of those traditionalists who put the assassin's picture up on
their walls, and who still played a role in the army which the Minister of
War did not take lightly. Long live the eternal order, with kchatriya*
armored divisions and air force, its Brahman administrators, and the
corpse of Nehru after the corpse of Gandhi!

This was what even his socialist opponents called the second great
problem of India.

"Obviously I have never envisioned a Congress whose members were
ascetics. But after all," he added sadly, "how can our political personnel
compare with that of a totalitarian party, or of British democracy? So,
I have to strengthen the state. The great historic figures of our time
have been linked with a struggle; more often than not with the seizure
of power by a victorious party. Even Gandhi's name remains linked
with the struggle for the liberation of India."

When the struggle was for independence or for revolution, of whatever sort, it carried within itself the seeds of its own metamorphosis.
I remembered Trotsky once talking to me about Thermidor. But in
this banal office surrounded by glory and by famine, I was aware that
the enigmatic force which transformed the leather-jacketed people's
commissars into gilt-edged marshals far exceeded the miserable gains
of the winning side, and swept along the conquerors whom it found
in its path as the Ganges sweeps along its flotsam. Lenin had ended
his life still wearing the cap shown in all his photographs in Soviet
embassies—but he had written, "There is no instance of a revolution
which did not end up by increasing the power of the state." And
Stalin's cap was a field marshal's cap. Thermidor was studied by the
revolutionaries in the spirit of the bourgeoisie itself, and they defined
it as a return. None of the pitfalls encountered by the Indian government would bring back the power of England. What was holding back
the permanent revolution and the time of equality was not the past
but the future, the seeds which independence and revolution carry in
themselves.

"I must sustain the feelings that we brought to life, in order to create
a state in a country whose national consciousness is primarily religious
and where the word state, whether applied to the Mogul Empire or
the British Raj, has always stood for administration. I once wrote,
'shaped for independence, our organization is in the process of becoming electoral.' "

Poor elections! What I sensed behind these friendly and clearheaded

*The warrior caste.

observations was the inescapable necessity which Lenin, Mao, and Mussolini had come up against, and which was not only the power of a single party: the imperative of the state, which alone could insure India's survival and its destiny, the state, which had perhaps haunted Alexander and had certainly haunted Caesar and Charlemagne and Napoleon. But before the advent of Islam (and even then), had India ever been a state?

"Don't forget that Europe continually calls 'nonviolence' what we call 'nonviolent resistance.' When was India ever a state before the Moguls? Not under the Guptas, I imagine? And to what extent," he added sadly, "could a state be founded on nonviolent action? But in any case, was it really a state that we wanted to build?"

He pitied India. He knew its misery. But he wanted to see it committed to a unique destiny, dedicated to becoming the conscience of the world. And it was no doubt because he knew that I loved this India that he had not forgotten our former meetings.

"General de Gaulle," I said, "thinks that a state which does not sooner or later found its legitimacy on the *defense* of the nation is doomed to disappear."

"Yes. If they want to bomb India, well, let them. You can destroy an army, a government, perhaps a regime: you cannot destroy a people."

Who were "they"? The West? But he added, "Every time China becomes China again, she becomes imperialist."

In speech after speech he had reminded his listeners that although the peoples of India did not claim to be superior to others, they knew themselves to be different. The difference to which he had dedicated his life, the supreme value that India had brought to the world, was nonviolent action, by virtue of which the liberation of India could rank with the great revolutions of history. He knew better than I did why Gandhi had translated the *Bhagavad-Gita*; he knew better than I why he himself had called the Buddha "India's greatest son." Despite the horrors of the separation of Hindustan and Pakistan, despite Kashmir, nonviolence retained its luster. Here, the word democracy did not yet make people smile. Europe confused the passionate ideology inherited from Gandhi with passivity, but Nehru still believed what he had once written: "It has been said that nonviolent action was an illusion; here, it has been the only *real* means of political action. Even in politics, an evil action has evil consequences. That, I believe, is a law of Nature as precise as any law of physics or chemistry."

I remembered Ramakrishna: "God cannot appear where there is hate, or shame, or fear." But I also remembered Gandhi: "It is better to fight than to be afraid."

Just as Stalin had claimed to be creating the Soviet Union on the same basis as Lenin had created the Revolution, so Nehru was compelled to give at least the appearance of creating India on the same basis as Gandhi had won independence. Everything, in particular the unity of this federal state, rested on a foundation of preaching, but this in its turn was based less on a British rationalism to which Nehru readily subscribed than on the expression of the deepest feelings of India. Hence their effectiveness, which surprised the West. When I met Nehru for the first time in Paris around 1935, I had asked him, "What connection do you see between nonviolence and reincarnation?" He had paused to reflect; he still retained from his imprisonment a grave deliberation of mind, very different from the suggestion of playfulness beneath the smiling seriousness of the head of state. He was well aware that *ahimsa*, the nonviolence of India, could only be confused with a method for gaining independence at the risk of a bad reincarnation; he saw it as a powerful myth, not a theory. He remembered our talk: "Tolstoy is supposed to have asked Gandhi the same question."

"What was Gandhi's answer? The same as yours?"

"What was my answer?"

"Roughly, 'Reincarnation had to be the fertilizer.' "

The struggle against poverty combined with indifference to the standard of living, the refusal to choose between the communist and capitalist nations, or to justify the means by the end, did not spring from nineteenth-century liberalism but from thousands of years of Hindu thought. Hadn't Gandhi been Nehru's guru? Bandoeng had given India a moral rather than a political authority.

"Were you not struck," he asked me, half-smiling, half-serious, "by that saying in the *Bhagavad-Gita*: 'He who really does what he should will obtain what he wants'?"

I was deeply interested in what he said, for the element of irony was superficial. Any head of state or head of government must reckon sooner or later with "reasons of state," and he masks it either with the values of the man he is talking to or with the traditional values of his people, which are often his own values. I have heard Russian communists appeal to Orthodox values, and Chinese communists appeal to Confucian values scarcely without a change of terminology. And I have heard everybody use the vocabulary of democracy. But here, the ethic was really fundamental.

"What has been your greatest difficulty since independence?" I asked him.

His reply was instantaneous, although up to this point he had often spoken of India as if he were groping in the dark: "Creating a just state by just means, I think."

And, after a brief pause, "Perhaps, too, creating a secular state in a religious country. Especially when its religion is not founded on a book of revelation."

I was face to face simultaneously with eternal India and with an India akin to what is represented in our memory by the France of the Year II or the United States of Washington: the end of an exemplary period of history. "One day men will have lived according to their hearts." At this hour, at the other end of the earth, Western intellectuals were fitting India into their little Marxist or democratic pigeonholes. And Nehru was attempting one of the most profound metamorphoses in the world, in this weakly federal country against which Pakistan was building up its strength—in this capital where the Untouchables squatted on the English lawns, and where at night the cars skirted the skeletal sacred cows asleep on the asphalt of the triumphal avenues. I imagined Stalin hearing, "Building a just state by just means," and his successors, great and small; and Hitler before them. And above all Mao Tse-tung, an Asian like Nehru, a liberator like Nehru, who would have considered that the poverty of the Indian peasants was the sole reality; that the castes could be crushed as he had crushed the moneylenders and landowners of China; that a communist army of ten million men would joyfully transform into people's communes the kingdoms of Prince Siddhartha and the last maharajahs —and that the fleet of wooden gods would one day float down the Ganges with the ashes of Benares.

"In some ways," Nehru went on, "it's impossible to judge what is most difficult. For Gandhi, it was to overcome the hardness of heart of cultivated people. The leaders of the independence struggle were men with a vocation. And now India must struggle against herself. But each year is a little better than the last. For how many years?

"I shall never see Kailas again." Kailas is the mountain of the sacred texts, the Sinai of India. It is also one of the most beautiful mountains in the Himalayas. In his youth, he had loved High Kashmir, and dreamed of an expedition. In prison, he had planned one down to the last detail: the beaten earth of prisonyards was the ideal context for the most beautiful lake of Tibet and the most beautiful mountain of Kashmir. Then the burden of power had revived the dream, and he had written, "Perhaps the weight of India will be so heavy that old age will come without my setting eyes on the lake and the mountain of my dreams."

He was looking absently at the cover of a children's newspaper on his desk, which I had leafed through in the Capitol while having breakfast. It contained an interview with Nehru in which he said, "I sometimes forget that it's a long time since I was a child."

He raised his eyes again: "You were in prison too, weren't you, during the war? We hardly ever meet anyone nowadays who hasn't been in prison."

He had spent thirteen years there. I remembered passages in his memoirs (written in fact during one of his spells inside) where he noted his discovery of the color of clouds, or his joy on hearing a dog bark for the first time in seven months, or his taste for travelbooks and, during the hot season, for atlases where there were glaciers to be seen.

"I remember the squirrel that used to come and sit on your lap," I said, "and that would run away as soon as he caught your eye. At Derah Dun, wasn't it?"

"At Lucknow. There were also little squirrels that used to fall out of the branches. Their mothers would rush down, roll them up into a ball, and carry them off."

I did not know that a squirrel could be rolled into a ball, but the Indian ones haven't the same tufted tails that ours have.

"Gandhi," he went on, "used to say that without humor he would have been unable to live."

I knew that on several occasions Nehru had left an official procession and disappeared into the crowd, leaving the explanations to the authorities. His tone of voice ruled out pretense: he meant what he said, like the few great statesmen I have met, and like most of the painters.

He came back to prison memories: "After all these years, do you know what the word prison evokes for me? A ramshackle building with rows of identical windows, and the struggle going on outside; a blade of grass sprouting from the beaten earth just outside the fence, and looking so surprised at being there. And you?"

"Tortured men being taken away under a big arcade with Gestapo men playing leapfrog."

And off we went on the subject of prisons. His own (he did not stop smiling during this part of the conversation) made me think of Chirico's vast yellow buildings casting their shadows over deserted streets. English prisons, "administrative" prisons, which one was allowed out of to go and see one's dying father, and where special trains brought to Gandhi and Nehru the leaders of the Independence struggle, prisoners like themselves. All the same, a nothingness, cut off from life, but limited in time. No torture. And in this geometry of stone and dead hours, the passing of an animal, the slow growth of a branch over a wall. My own memories intrigued him: our prisons were alike in our isolation from the continuing struggle, "and yet, what a difference!" The ambassador was beginning to feel ashamed that he had never even been taken to a police station, but was not unpleased to see the usher's head popping in and out in vain.

"Tomorrow," Nehru said, "we shall learn from the newspapers what we said to each other."

"You know that the day before a Catholic marriage the bride and bridegroom go to confession. My mother went into the confessional and came out after a few minutes. Then my father went in. Five, ten, fifteen minutes! What terrible sins could take so long to enumerate? When my father came out and they left the church, she ventured a timid question. 'Confession,' my father said, 'oh no, but the priest used to be the chaplain of my squadron, and we had a chat.' "

"Even if they believe we 'had a chat,' " Nehru replied, "the papers will still enumerate the sins."

He stood up and said, "See you this evening." The ambassador had passed on to me his invitation to the official dinner.

Dinners at the Capitol were no less haunted than the avenues of New Delhi by the shadow of the Empire. In the gardens, the geometrical sandstone paths seemed to bring the flowers in the flowerbeds sharply to attention. Nehru, dressed in his familiar smoke-gray tunic and white forage cap, greeted some hundred guests in an enormous reception room under a naïve ceiling painting illustrating a Persian tale. "Wouldn't you like to go and see our sacred caves?" he asked me. "I should like to know what you think of the work of our archaeological service." Was he seeking to please me? He went off again with little rapid steps among the overdressed groups of guests, and I remembered his speech to the multitude massed in front of the Red Fort on Independence Day: "For a long time we have had a rendezvous with fate, and now, here it is!"

I thought of our conversation that afternoon, of the blade of grass emerging from the ground with an air of astonishment, of the almost tame animals. For him, as for me, prison had been a wall cutting us off from events, and for him, behind this wall, there had been—for thirteen years—the destiny of India. This evening, he was in the world

—and even in the theater. Surrounded by respect, not like a parliamentary leader, but like a dictator, although for different reasons. I knew that he had asked himself whether he would be able to hold to nonviolence if he saw his mother being beaten by the police; that his father had spent a night on concrete so as to know what it was like to sleep in prison; that his dying wife had said to him, "Never give your word to abandon the struggle." I thought of the letter from his father which, following him round the world, had reached him five years after the latter's death. But this personal life portrayed him far less than the indirect influence he had had on the world, and the direct influence he had on his country. Even more than his speech at the Red Fort, I remembered his defense at the Gorakhpur trial (on November 3, 1940, the day of my first escape). "It is not me you are seeking to judge and condemn, but the hundreds of millions of my people, and that is a heavy task, even for a proud Empire." Even more profoundly than before, the feeling I had experienced in the Parliament building came back to me now: Nehru was the nation's guru, as Gandhi had been.

Waiting for a diplomatic corps dinner is not calculated to evoke the great images of history. And India herself repels them, because their romance is not hers. There is no coronation of Napoleon, no cruiser Aurora with its guns' great fingers seeking out the target of the Winter Palace, in the world of the Bhagavad-Gita. Nehru's life offered little for the picture album. The legend seemed linked to Gandhi, from the Salt March to the assassination. And even then it remained remote, blurred by the slow-movingness, the dreams, and the immensity of India. Its multitudes were present, not like the crowds of the October Revolution, but like the stars in the Indian night. I had seen Gandhi's portrait everywhere, and now Nehru going from group to group, but of all that they had done there remained only a profound and confused epic. Five hundred million men had lived under foreign rule; in a single generation, the moral action of a few men had freed them, not by a series of battles but by a concatenation of symbols which were already being submerged in the swamps of independence; and yet the awareness, the steadfastness given to these multitudes surrounded Nehru as an immense cemetery surrounds the tombs of conquerors. In any case, the conversations of the diplomatic corps showed that it was not all over yet. When I had asked Nehru what he had found most difficult, he had answered straight off, as if to avert another reply—which would probably have been Pakistan. Not that he feared a Pakistani attack, as the European newspapers were suggesting; but because nonviolence was far more dangerously challenged by Partition than it had been by the British. Gandhi had once declared, "I am fighting against three opponents: the British, the Indians, myself." For him, only the purification of India would bring ultimate victory. On the one hand, this endless preaching, and on the other, this murder hunt from village to village—so many Hindu houses burned, so many Muslim houses looted, and the Sikhs waiting for the Muslim refugee trains in Amritsar station, their sabers across their knees, as the Muslims waited for the Hindu refugees in the stations of Bengal; this inexhaustible Sermon on the Mount preached to so many murdered men right up to the funeral pyre. A few hours earlier Nehru had said to me, before talking of the "better years," "And now India must struggle against itself." The successor of the grinning old prophet was building India with his back turned to the demons of blood as it was now turned to the red fireplace. After what Gandhi had called India's *danse macabre*, one of humanity's greatest adventures was under way, groping toward the establishment of a nation of four hundred million souls on the basis of faith in the ineluctable power of forgiveness.

We went into dinner between two lines of Bengal Lancers. And in the dining room, where immense portraits of the British viceroys still covered the walls, a file of serving men in white dolmans and red turbans, as numerous as the guests, stretched back to the deep-set entrance hall, where the perspective of sloping lances receded into the distance. When I had taken the elevator down from my room, the young elevator boy had asked me to sign his autograph album. I had flourished my pen with a grandiose gesture, and then stopped, gaping at the signatures of half a score of kings. Were there still so many? This chapter of Proust had now developed into a tale by Voltaire.

When had I ever been so conscious of being present at a spectacle where the guests would disappear at dawn? It was the atmosphere of provisional governments, of the twists and turns of fate. There was nothing of that sense of famous palaces occupied by revolutionaries turned bourgeois, but neither was there a sense of this being the government of India. Even if the dawn were slow in coming, it would come one day with men daubed with white ash, with hordes of the Untouchables brandishing their torches—or with eternal Islam which thinks that "shame comes into the house with the plough." Nehru made a banal reply to a banal speech by a Scandinavian Minister for Foreign Affairs, and I asked myself again, when had I had this feeling of being present at a doomed spectacle, with this feeling of having been there before. It was at the Hôtel de Beauharnais, now the Ministry of Cooperation, with its façade supported by Bonaparte's caryatids.

The leaders of Central Africa had come for the handing over of the flags of the Community, and were slowly climbing the front steps. The parliamentary crowd stood aside to let them pass in their tenebrous robes preceded by their sorcerer musicians walking backward singing of the glory of their race.

After dinner, Nehru took me down a spiral staircase with a few of his more important guests to a small underground theater, where classical dances followed one another while an orchestra played "music which it is suitable to play in the evening." When everyone was seated, he leaned toward me and said, "For you, prison was an accident; for us, an end. When one of our men was arrested, Gandhi would send him a telegram of congratulation. At that time, he used to say, 'Freedom must often be sought behind prison walls, sometimes on the scaffold, never in council chambers, law courts, or schools.' "

Stately figures slowly unwound their sinuous convolutions to melodies of an ageless nostalgia.

The dances over, he left us all at the Capitol and went home.

6

1944 / 1965. "Freedom must be sought behind prison walls," Gandhi and Nehru had said. Mine had not quite been prisons, or had not been prisons for long. There had been the camp in 1940, from which I had escaped easily, in spite of my shoes being too small: a vast meadow turned into a compound, the pink glow of dawn, carts on the road on the other side of the barbed wire, bloodstained tins of food, shacks built of squat beams, drainpipes and branches, in which soldiers sat, hunched up like Peruvian mummies, writing letters that would never be sent.

1944 had been more serious. My comrades, arrested by the German security forces, usually the Gestapo, had gone to their deaths by way of the familiar channels; whereas I had been captured in uniform by the tanks of the *Das Reich* division.

My prisons begin with a field. I regained consciousness on a stretcher laid on the grass and held by two German soldiers. Under my legs, the canvas was soaked with blood. They had put together a makeshift dressing over my trousers. The British officer's body had disappeared. In the car were the still bodies of my two comrades. A German was removing the pennant. My stretcher bearers set off for Gramat, escorted by an NCO. It seemed far.

I had gone to arbitrate a dispute between a Buckmaster* maquis and an FTP† maquis. On the way back—twenty minutes earlier—we had been dozing as we approached Gramat, with our Cross of Lorraine pennant flapping in the warm breeze. A sudden volley of firing, the rear window shattered, and the car slewed round and plunged into a ditch. The driver had been killed instantaneously by a bullet in the head as he put his foot down hard on the brake. The escort lay slumped over our weapons. The British officer jumped into the road to the right and fell, both hands red with blood clutched to his stomach. I jumped to the left and ran, my legs numb after three hours' driving. A machine gun was firing at me; the car shielded me from another. A bullet cut through the kneestrap of my right legging which flapped loose, still attached by the footstrap. I had to stop to rip it off. A bullet in the right leg. The pain very slight. Only the blood told me I had been hit. Then a terrible wrench in the left leg.

---

* Colonel Maurice Buckmaster, head of the French Section of SOE (Special Operations Executive), the British organization responsible for planning resistance in occupied Europe. (Tr.)

† *Francs-tireurs et Partisans*: Communist-led resistance network. (Tr.)

The two men, who were carrying me like a parcel, did not look at all unpleasant. There would be others. It was extraordinarily absurd. How could the Germans be in Gramat?

Everything was going to end here, God knew how, at the end of this road above which the radiant July sky seemed to be fixed in eternity, while the peasants watched me as I went by, their hands crossed on their spadehandles, and the women made the sign of the cross as at a funeral procession. I would not see our victory. What was, that would ever be, the meaning of this life? But I was drawn on by a grim curiosity about what lay in store for me.

From the first houses onward, the street was lined with tanks. The French watched me go by with anguish, the Germans with surprise. My porters went into the office of a garage. An NCO questioned the one who was escorting me. Then, "Your papers!"

They were in the pocket of my tunic, and I reached them without difficulty. I held out the wallet and said: "They're false."

Without taking the wallet, he translated. The two NCO's stared at me like a couple of hypnotized hens. The stretcher bearers set off again. This time we went into a small barn. The stretcher was put down on its folding legs. The Germans left. A key turned in the lock. There was a sentry outside the narrow window. I tried to sit up on the stretcher. My left leg was giving me hardly any pain. I felt very dazed. I must have lost a lot of blood, for it was still flowing, in spite of the handkerchiefs knotted round my thighs.

The silhouette of the sentry presented arms. The key turned. And an officer who looked like Buster Keaton came in.

"How sad for your poor family! You are a Catholic, are you not?"

"Yes."

It was not the occasion for a lecture on agnosticism.

"I am the Catholic chaplain."

He looked at the bloodstained handkerchiefs. "How sad for your poor family!"

"The Passion can't have been very pleasant for Christ's family, Father. Not that I'm Christ."

He looked at me, more stupefied than I was. But in his case it was stupidity. "You have children?" he asked.

"Unfortunately. Am I to be tried or not?"

"I don't know. But if you have need of the consolations of religion, you can call for me."

He opened the door, a black shape against the still dazzling sky.

Then, by way of valediction, "All the same, how very sad for your poor family."

A queer sort of chaplain, or a queer sort of religion. A bogus priest would at least have asked questions.

An NCO beckoned me outside. The yard was full of soldiers. I was able to take a few steps. He made me face the wall, hands leaning against the stones above my head. I heard a command: "Achtung," and turned round. I was facing a firing squad.

"Slope arms! Present arms!"

It is customary to present arms to those who are about to be executed. A recent dream came back to me. I was in the cabin of a liner, and the porthole had just been ripped away; water was pouring in; faced with the irremediable fact that my life was over, that it would never be other than what it had been, I burst into an endless peal of laughter (my brother Roland died shortly afterward in the sinking of the Cap-Arcona). I had had several brushes with violent death.

"Take aim!"

I stared at the heads bent over the rifle sights.

"At ease!"

The soldiers put their rifles under their arms and sauntered off with disappointed smiles.

After all, why could they not have fired round me? No one else would have been endangered: I was standing against the wall. Why had I not really believed in death? I had seen it in a much more threatening form on the Gramat road. I had neither the feeling, which I know well, that someone was going to shoot at me, nor that of imminent separation from life. I remember once telling Saint-Exupéry, who had asked me what I thought of courage, that it seemed to me a curious and banal consequence of the feeling of invulnerability. Saint-Ex had concurred, though not without surprise. The comedy in which I had just taken part had not touched this feeling in me. Were its aura, its ceremonial, directly associated with death? Perhaps we believe in death only when a companion falls at our side? I went back to my barn, where I was now beginning to feel at home, and lay down again. A second lieutenant came in with two soldiers who picked up the stretcher. We went out. The second lieutenant was not a young officer: over forty, big, erect, red-faced, and rugged-faced, his head shaven. Soon he was walking in front of the stretcher, and I could see only his back.

We were going to the first aid post. A nurse looked at me with hatred. The medical officer and the orderlies, who had seen others like me, dressed my wound with care. The stretcher moved off again. We went down into a cellar. I knew what cellars were used for. "It will be a hard day," Damiens* used to say. No. We came up again, went on for about half a mile—and Gramat is not a big town. Tanks everywhere. The inhabitants withdrew before the stretcher. We reached a somewhat isolated farm and went into the storage shed. A harrow, rakes, wooden pitchforks. I had seen these ageless storage sheds during the 1940 campaign, but it had not struck me then how much these implements, particularly the harrow, look like instruments of torture. The procession moved off again, stopping twice more in similar places. I had the impression that we were in search of a suitable torture chamber. Evidently the soldiers were assembled, for none were to be seen. Solitude, a town inhabited by sleeping tanks, houses furnished with pitchforks, and harrows to hang corpses on. Five minutes later, my porters stopped.

"Kommandantur," said the second lieutenant.

It was the Hôtel de France. The maquis had its postbox here. The Germans had just evacuated the reception office, but the manageress was at the paydesk. White hair, regular features, whalebone collar: a boarding-school headmistress. I had seen her twice before.

"Do you know him?" the German asked, on the off chance.

"Me? No," she answered absently, almost without looking at me.

"And you?" he asked me.

"The maquis don't put up at hotels, unfortunately!"

The office connected with the little hall through a swingdoor. The second lieutenant sat down behind the desk. The stretcher bearers put me down on the black and white tiles without unfolding the supports of the stretcher. A soldier came in, notebook in hand, examined me with more curiosity than hostility, and sat down on the officer's left. The street was narrow, and the lamps were already lit. The clerk, with his protruding chin and forehead, looked like a haricot bean; the interrogator like a sparrow—nose in the air, little round mouth. He did not seem very German, except for his close-cropped red hair, completely shorn above his ears, which stuck out from his head. They had both made themselves comfortable.

"Your papers?"

I stood up, took one step forward, and held out my wallet. I lay down again at once: I was beginning to feel faint. Nevertheless, my head was clear, for the game had begun.

* Robert François Damiens was tortured to death for attempted regicide after stabbing Louis XV with a penknife in 1757. (Tr.)

"I told your colleague that those papers are false."

The old sparrow looked at them carefully. Identity card, car license, other trivia in the name of Berger. A thousand or so francs in notes. A photograph of my wife and son. He made them into a little pile, which he put next to the wallet.

"You speak German?"

"No."

"Your name, Christian name, rank?"

"Lieutenant Colonel Malraux, André, alias Colonel Berger. I am the military chief of this region."

He threw a puzzled glance at my officer's tunic, which had no badges of rank. What moral did he hope to draw from that? I had been captured in a car that flew a tricolor flag with the Cross of Lorraine.

"What organization?"

"De Gaulle."

"You . . . have some prisoners, have you not?"

He had a North German accent, hard, not at all "Teutonic." His interrogation was menacing, but not aggressive.

"In the unit directly under my command, about a hundred."

What a strange game fate was playing! It was the custom, God knows why, to have prisoners taken by the maquis tried by court-martial. I had been present at a trial of this kind in an FTP maquis, with maquis leaders pretending to be judges, an indictment that was acceptable because hate always looks like hate, and a parody of a defense by a kind of clerk who was working off ten years of frustrated ambition by playing the lawyer. In a low, cool room in a château by the Lot, with goats bleating outside in the heat, and yellow flowers. It was to preside over a court-martial the day before that I had put on again the uniform I was wearing. We had already set free some twenty Alsatians —for there were many Alsatians among the troops facing us, as there were in our own maquis groups from which the Alsace-Lorraine brigade would be born. One of our lieutenants, a schoolteacher from the Colmar region, had offered to undertake the defense of the German prisoners, and had said, in French and then in German, "None of these men belongs to the SS or the Gestapo. They are soldiers, and you cannot shoot soldiers for having been called up and for carrying out the orders they have been given." There were many of our men at the end of the room, and I could sense the anxiety of our Alsatians. It was decided that the prisoners should be handed over to the first allied unit we came across.

"How are they treated?"

The clerk, who was taking everything down in shorthand, put down his pencil.

"They spend their time playing prisoner's base and eat the same food as our own men. For them, the war is over."

The old sparrow wondered if I was making fun of him, but decided that I was not.

"They had been expecting savages in rags," I told him, "and they came across soldiers in uniform."

"Parachuted?"

"No. The French maquis."

"Where are they?"

"Who, the prisoners?"

"It's the same thing!"

"Still, there are more maquisards than prisoners."

"Where are they?"

"I have no idea, fortunately. Let's get this straight. They were in the Siorac woods. For at least two hours my men have known that I'm in your hands. For an hour and a half my successor has been in command, and he is a regular staff officer. By now, not a single soldier, ours or yours, will be left in the camp."

He pondered. "What is your civilian profession?"

"Professor, and writer. I have lectured in your universities. At Marburg, Leipzig, Berlin."

"Professor" sounded serious.

"You obviously speak German. But that is of no importance."

"My first book, *Die Eroberer*, was translated by Max Claus."

It was alleged (falsely as it later transpired) that Max Claus, having become a Nazi, was some sort of undersecretary of state with Goebbels. My interrogator was growing more and more puzzled. He started playing cat and mouse. After ten minutes:

"Lieutenant," I said, "I think we are wasting each other's time. Usually you interrogate prisoners who say they are innocent, or who really are, and you have to make them confess. I have nothing to confess: I have been your opponent since the day of the Armistice."

"But it was Marshal Pétain who signed the Armistice!"

"It certainly wasn't me. So I'm not officially a combatant. So you can have me shot—after you've weighed the consequences. I may tell you that my deputy commanded the Legion in Morocco, and I commanded . . . elsewhere, and we are not playing at soldiers. We have more than one assembly point. We never make contact except on out-of-the-way roads, covered by four lookout men. The German forces have never taken a single one of my men prisoner. I am here because you have just carried out a very brilliant maneuver, and I went and threw myself in front of your machine guns like an idiot. But in capturing me you set off the alarm system; up to a hundred kilometers north of here all the command posts have been evacuated. In order to find out the extent of our forces—or the way we treat our prisoners, if it comes to that—you have only to ask the Milice. And you could have my men tortured—if you captured any of them—without getting anything out of them, because they know nothing: our entire organization is based on the assumption that no human being can know what he will do under torture."

"The Wehrmacht does not use torture."

"Furthermore, a unit like yours, if the whole division is grouped together, has other fish to fry."

He asked me where our former command posts were, and I reeled off a list of châteaus abandoned by collaborators, or clearings where he would find listening posts and the remains of fires. No question of mentioning the woods of dwarf oaks, which the Germans thought unusable. As for the identity of the leaders of the other maquis groups, the Gestapo and the Milice knew their pseudonyms as well as I did, and I was as little aware of their real names as they were. (At least in certain cases.) The old sparrow had certainly received orders to treat me as a prisoner-of-war. But it was obvious that all this was just a beginning. We continued to talk about the maquis. I exaggerated our numbers. It turned into a conversation.

Eventually the two Germans left—perhaps to dine? A sentry guarded me, on the other side of the swingdoor: I could only see him up to the knees. Sometimes he chatted: a lot of Germans passed through the little hall. I would have liked to think, but it was only the interrogation that had kept my faculties alert: I sank back, exhausted.

Nine o'clock in the evening. (There was a large wallclock hanging above the desk.) Two other Germans arrived with papers, no doubt a summary of my interrogation. They asked me the questions I had already been asked and I gave the same answers. To crosscheck? No matter. The two Germans left.

Three quarters of an hour later, there was a great clicking of heels outside. The swingdoors, usually pushed open breezily, parted gently, and a colonel came in and sat behind the desk. No secretary. He looked like his predecessors. No, it was because I was not used to looking up at people from ground level. But his hair was white.

"What are you hoping for?" he asked me.

"From our military activities, or from . . . my own fate?"

"From your military activities."

"To slow you up, of course."

He nodded, as if in agreement, or as if to say, "That's what I thought." Then, "Why do you destroy things we can quickly repair?"

"It's part of the plan."

(It was also, on occasion, because we could not do any better.)

"You didn't fight in the last war?"

"I was too young. My identity card is false, but the date of birth is correct—1901."

"You fought in this one?"

"Yes."

"In what branch?"

"Tanks."

(And what tanks! But that was none of his business. I had envied his, then.) He glanced through my papers absently, as if to give his hands something to do.

"Your maquis has antitank weapons?"

"Yes."

The Gestapo could not be unaware that London had been dropping bazookas by parachute for over a month. Therefore he knew this, or more precisely, was afraid of it. For in wooded country tanks can only be covered by infantry. German armored divisions had motorized infantry at their disposal, but if it stayed in its trucks it could not protect the tanks against the bazookas, and if it protected the tanks by patrolling both sides of the road, the latter would be reduced to walking speed. My interrogator did not seem surprised, or even very interested. Curious, rather. Had he simply wanted to see an officer of this mysterious maquis that was all round him? Was he rediscovering the French army, the "pigheads" of Verdun?

He put back the little pile of papers beside the empty wallet, got up and came round to the front of the desk. As he passed in front of me, he picked up my wallet from the desk and handed it to me. I could feel at once that it was no longer empty. The colonel left. The sentry outside clicked his heels. The German had put back the photograph of my wife and son in one of the wallet pockets.

No one came after him. Finished for the night? The hotel was dropping off to sleep. The electric light in the office was still on. I thought I would be unable to sleep. I was wrong. Sleep overcame me as it used to do in Spain, when a meal followed an air battle: dead asleep, as we say dead-drunk.

Dawn. Daylight. A slamming of doors upstairs and the clatter of swingdoors on the ground floor. Sounds of water. The crop-headed sparrow came back and sat down behind the desk without saying a word. Boots clumping on the stairs, and the hubbub of a hotel, of a barrack room, and above all of departure. Why does the German language, when shouted, always sound as if it is expressing anger? The voices went back and forth:

"Matâme! Have you any butter?"

"No!"

"Any chocolate?"

"No!"

"Matâme! Have you any bread?"

"Only in exchange for coupons."

Then they stopped asking. The manageress must have left the pay-desk. An interval. Boots going upstairs, accompanied by a clink of messtins. Then from the upper floors came a strange clamor which grew louder as it came nearer: the noise children make when the Christmas tree is uncovered before their eyes. The swingdoors parted, pushed by a tray on which were set a steaming bowl of coffee and some huge slices of bread and butter. Behind it came the manageress. Her white hair was very carefully done; she had put on a black dress, as if to go to Mass, but was wearing a white apron because she had come from the kitchen. She looked at the bloodstained tiles (my wounds had bled during the night), came toward me, knelt down—first one leg, then the other. It is not easy for an elderly woman to kneel down while carrying a tray. She placed it on my chest, got up again, went toward the swingdoor, turned round—two big red stains on the white apron, where she had knelt—and said, in the tone which she must often have used forty years earlier to say, "I'll trouble you not to pinch your brothers' bread and butter," but with an almost imperceptible hint of solemnity now: "It's for the wounded French officer!" Then she went back upstairs to the sound of boots shuffling.

My sparrow was staring at me with his beak open. To snatch bread from a wounded man would have been ridiculous, but how provoking it all was!

"Let's share it," I said.

He got up, went out and came back with a glass. Took one of my pieces of bread and put it on the desk. Took the bowl to pour half the coffee into his glass—and burned himself. Put the glass on the desk, took hold of the bowl again with his handkerchief, and poured, measuring carefully. Then gave me the bowl back. On the white tiles there were now two sets of bloody footprints, big ones to and from the desk, and small ones to and from the door.

Around eight o'clock, we left. The manageress was back.

"Thank you, Madame. You were admirable: the personification of France."

She stopped writing. Her features remained immobile, and her gaze followed me until the hotel door closed.

I was taken to the sick bay, where my dressings were changed. I would now be able to stand up, and perhaps take a few steps. No need. I was shut into an armored van—an ambulance, perhaps. To the rear, a double door, bolted from the outside. Four partitions. I was alone. Lying down, I could see, through a little barred window in the door, a line of trucks, and the countryside flashing by. Would the maquis attack? I hardly thought so, for though the area was fairly mountainous, it was not wooded. To my knowledge there were no maquis units of any importance this side of the Garonne. No doubt the German armored division was engaged on some punitive expedition: above the road and its riverbends our villages burned beneath long, slanting trails of smoke.

When the column halted, I was allowed to get out.

At Figeac (where Roger Martin du Gard lived), a peasant brought me a walking stick and disappeared.

Every French glance told me that I was a condemned man. I did not think so—at least, not yet. I assumed I was destined for another interrogation, or a trial. But something was bound to happen.

At Villefranche-de-Rouergue, where I recognized the almost Spanish church I had used as a setting for some episodes in *L'Espoir*, the column halted for the night. I was put up at the convent. As soon as I was in bed, the Mother Superior brought me some coffee. She was no more than forty years old, and she was beautiful. As she went by, she smiled at the soldier who was guarding me, an inaccessible smile.

I had sometimes wondered what the Gospel would mean to one in the face of death.

"Mother Superior, could you lend me the Gospel according to St. John?"

"Oh, of course!"

She brought a Bible, and went out again. I searched for the text of St. John, but the book fell open at the marker that she must have just put there. I might have been killed many times, in Asia, in Spain, at home; the idea that I could have stayed behind, instead of attending a court-martial, or an execution at the edge of a ditch, seemed to me laughable. Even that night, dying seemed banal to me. What interested me was death.

But it was not in the face of death that I had encountered St. John. It was at Ephesus, and above all in the Byzantine and Slav world which had venerated his tomb no less than Christ's. Through him, my memory retained a fairly complex image of Jesus: convincing and near, like that of St. Francis of Assisi, yet curiously hazy in this text where John refers to himself only as "He whom Jesus loved." I remembered the sellers of doves driven from the Temple, and certain phrases which made the Gospel a sort of incantation: ". . . for his hour was not yet come . . . ," "Can a devil open the eyes of the blind?" and the dark tone of "Father, deliver me from this hour . . . ," and the words spoken to Judas, "That thou doest, do quickly." I remembered the story of the woman taken in adultery, which is so often related as a judgment, whereas Christ in fact turns neither to the accusers nor to the woman, and says, "He that is without sin among you . . . ," while continuing to draw figures in the sand. I discovered again, "For God so loved the world, that he gave his only begotten Son, that whosoever believeth in him should not perish, but have everlasting life. For God sent not his Son into the world to condemn the world; but that the world through him might be saved." I had not believed in the burlesque firing squad at Gramat, but I would probably meet one soon that would not be burlesque. On the road, I might have received the bullets in the head, like the driver, instead of in the legs. I felt strongly that all faith dissolves life into the eternal, and I was cut off from the eternal. My life was one of those human adventures which Shakespeare justifies by calling dreams and which are not dreams. A human destiny coming to an end in front of a dozen rifles, among so many other destinies as ephemeral as the earth. What was about to befall me was of passionate concern to a worthless part of myself, like the urge to escape from the water when one is drowning. But I did not seek the meaning of the world in a thrashing of the limbs. The genius of Christianity is to have proclaimed that the path to the deepest mystery is the path of love. A love which is not confined to men's feelings, but transcends them like the soul of the world, more powerful than death and more powerful than justice: "For God did not send his son into the world to judge the world, but to save it." Alone in face of death, I encountered that immemorial compassion which had enveloped so many despairs as the Day of Judgment would roll back so many sepulchers: "Lord, help us in the hour of our death . . ." But faith means belief; I had a great respect for the Christian message which had pervaded this earth in which I would doubtless soon be lying, but I did not believe in it. The memory of St. John is more powerful against misfortune than his presence is against death. In what oriental text had I read, "The meaning of the world is as inaccessible to man as the behavior of the chariots of kings to the scorpions they crush"? It was all as though my supreme value was Truth—and yet what did Truth matter to me, that night?

My past, my biographical life, was of no importance. I did not think of my childhood. I did not think of my family. I thought of the atheist peasant women who saluted my wounds with the sign of the cross, of the stick brought to me by the frightened peasant, of the coffee from the manageress of the Hôtel de France and from the Mother Superior. All that remained in my memory was fraternity. In this convent silence probably filled with prayers for me, and broken by the distant clattering of a tank on the move, what lived as profoundly in my mind as the approach of death—even when I thought of the scorpions of Babylon— was the despairing caress that closes the eyes of the dead.

At Albi (we were still going south, and villages were still burning), I lay on a settee in a big room, probably in the town hall. The sentry, who did not belong to the tank command but to a regiment billeted in the town, came and sat by me, and pulled two photographs from his pocket: Marshal Pétain and—to my stupefaction—General de Gaulle. Placing his finger on the one of Pétain, he said: "Very good!" Then, reprovingly, with his finger on the one of De Gaulle: "Terrorist!" He looked at me. I was waiting for him to continue. Raising his finger to call for my attention, he said: "Tomorrow," and lowered it first on to De Gaulle, "Perhaps: very good?"—then on to Pétain, "Perhaps terrorist?" Then he made a gesture that meant "You never know," shrugged his shoulders, and went back to his post.

At Revel, on the ground floor of a deserted villa, I had a small garden at my disposal. Leaning on the stick, I was able to walk a little. With the evening meal (I was given the same food as the soldiers—so indeed were the officers), I found by the side of my plate a cigarette and one match.

The following day, an officer and two soldiers came to fetch me. I sat in the back of the car, next to the officer. On the way out of the town, he blindfolded me. I did not feel threatened; indeed I felt the blindfold as a sort of protection. When the officer took it off, we were entering the grounds of a rather ugly château. In front of it were a dozen or so officers' cars: obviously a court-martial.

The mock execution had not been convincing; this squad of cars was. This idiotic château—the last?—took on the intensity of things that are touched by fate. Some days before he killed himself, my father had said that death inspired in him an intense curiosity. I felt curiosity, not about death but about the court-martial—perhaps for the simple reason that this was what still separated me from death. Surprised to see my step quicken, my guards followed. The french windows at the top of the steps opened on to a hall beyond which, in a big ballroom, a score of officers were dancing with "gray mice."*

It was not a court-martial; it was a dance.

First floor. A long corridor, a double door. The officer went in, clicked his heels, gave the Hitler salute, and went out again. I was standing inside the door, which he had closed behind him. A huge room lit by three big windows opened on to a park and a little lake. Behind the Louis XV desk gleaming with ormolu bronze, a general. Iron Cross with oak leaves. I had difficulty in making out his features against the light; he was wearing dark glasses, and the light shone on his white hair. He went to a little table surrounded with chairs, sat down, and gestured to me to sit down too. On the table was a silver box. He held it out to me.

"No thanks. I no longer smoke."

He lit a cigarette. The sudden glow revealed a strange physiognomy, which was again lost against the daylight.

"I would like to hear from you why you do not recognize the Armistice. Marshal Pétain is a great soldier, the victor of Verdun, as you say. France pledged her word. And it was not we who declared war on you."

"A nation does not pledge its word to die by proxy. Allow me to make a hypothesis: Marshal von Hindenburg is President of the German Republic, a world war breaks out, Germany is beaten as we were, and the Marshal surrenders. The Führer—who of course is not Chancellor—launches an appeal from Rome to the German combatants to continue the war. Who speaks for Germany? And whose side are you on?"

---

* *Souris grises:* popular term for gray-uniformed female auxiliaries of the German Occupation forces. (Tr.)

"Why is De Gaulle in London?"

"The heads of state are in London, except for one, who is in Vichy. General de Gaulle is not the commander of a French Legion under the Allies."

"What is the point of your activities? You know very well that for every soldier you kill we will shoot three hostages."

"Each man who is shot sends three soldiers to the maquis. But in my opinion, that is not the question. Since you are interested, I'll tell you what I think. There are all sorts in the maquis."

"Especially the people who are afraid of the forced labor service."

"Indeed, even people who refuse to serve Germany. But you know very well that every struggle presupposes a soul. Ours escapes you. You believe we are fighting to conquer."

He raised his head. The glasses hid his eyes, which must have been showing surprise.

"The volunteers of the Free French Forces, the men of the Resistance, are only a handful compared with the Wehrmacht. It is for that reason that they exist. In 1940 France suffered one of the most appalling defeats in her history. Those who are fighting you are guarantors of her survival. Victors, vanquished, shot, or tortured."

"The Wehrmacht does not use torture. But I think I understand you. In a way, I pity you. You, the Gaullists, you are a bit like a French SS. You will be the ones to suffer most. If we end up losing the war, you will have another government of Jews and Freemasons, at the beck and call of England. And it will be gobbled up by the communists."

"If you lose the war, I believe that what will happen will be nothing like what either of us can foresee. In 1920, everyone believed that the decisive fact of the 1914-18 war was the collapse of German military power. We know today that the decisive fact was the Russian Revolution. This time, it may be the end of Europe as master of the world. For twenty years, fifty years, things will go badly for France, badly for Germany. Then there will be a new France, a new Germany—and perhaps, once again, war."

He stood up. I thought that he was going to his desk, but he walked up and down aimlessly, gazing at the carpet. In front of the middle window, his face came into the light. I realized what had disturbed me when the match had illuminated it: below the dark blotches of the glasses, the very high cheekbones gave his face the appearance of a puppet's mask.

"You really believe what you just said about Germany?"

"Sooner or later we will become your adversaries again. But whatever the outcome of the struggle, whatever the regimes, I don't know many French intellectuals who would be prepared to repudiate Hölderlin and Nietzsche, Bach and even Wagner."

"Do you know Soviet Russia?"

"Yes, Germany cannot be torn away from Europe."

"I beg your pardon?"

"They cannot tear Germany away from Europe, or from the world."

"They'll try. The brutes of the East, and the salesmen of cars and canned food who have never been able to wage war, and England led by that Shakespearean drunkard."

He had turned toward me. The dark glasses still hid his eyes. Other German generals were planning the attempt on Hitler's life. I did not know about it then. Perhaps he did.

He rang.

The strains of the dance music invaded the room, snaking around this baffled figure of Death in the uniform of a German general. Through the window, a small lake for rowboats, with its deserted cabins. My escorting officer had just come in, and beckoned me to follow him.

I was back with my Revel carnation beds; my cigarette, my match. The next day, another armored car came to pick me up. Beside me, on the backseat, a soldier with a submachine gun. We were no longer going south, but east. After a few hours we entered Toulouse. Night was falling. The Place Wilson, the Café Lafayette where I had sat so often during the Spanish Civil War. One day, in the little square, I was fiddling with my revolver—the barrel pointing downward—in my overcoat pocket. Inadvertently I had pulled the trigger. The noise did not attract anyone's attention, and I had got off with a reddish-brown hole in my overcoat. I was whistling for joy, for I had just seen the copies of Les Thibault* in the bookshop windows with the band of the Nobel Prize round them.

I was hustled into one of the houses in the square, up to the mezzanine floor. The room—a bourgeois drawing room—had only a semi-circular fanlight for a window.

There were bars on the inside. Outside, couples were strolling round the little square or sitting outside the cafés: an ordinary evening scene,

---

* Roger Martin du Gard's masterpiece. He was awarded the Nobel Prize for Literature in 1937. (Tr.)

except for the German uniforms. My sister-in-law (my brother had been arrested more than a month ago) lived in the Rue Alsace-Lorraine, a hundred yards from the square. A German major ordered ham and eggs to be brought for me, and a bottle of Bordeaux. Did they regard me as a prisoner of note? It could not be anything to do with Vichy, since no Frenchman had interrogated me. I remembered a piece of advice: never empty a bottle, for the Gestapo use them to hit you with and empty bottles make the most painful bludgeons. I had not yet reached that stage. The dialogue was hardly an interrogation at all, with the usual: "Marshal Pétain signed the Armistice," and "The Wehrmacht does not use torture." We talked about Verdun, and the major said, "At that time, I was a prisoner of the French." The armored car drove us into a district with wide avenues, skirted the huge War Memorial, and stopped outside a luxury hotel. A hall empty of furniture except for a desk behind which two NCO's were at work. The major handed them my papers, which had been passed on by each of my jailers successively. One of the NCO's said, "Thirty-four" (a room number?). His colleague and the major escorted me. There was an elevator, but we went up by the stairs, which were covered with a thick carpet with gleaming copper rods. I had difficulty in climbing, but the two Germans kept in step with me. In the corridor were military guards, with no weapons except holstered revolvers. Second floor. Room 34. A guard opened the door, closed it again, and the carpet in the corridor muffled the footsteps of the three Germans as they went away.

It was a large bathroom converted into a bedroom. In one corner was a bed, with white sheets and a blanket. In the other, a cupboard. No bell. No handle on the door. I banged on it with my fist. The guard came, and gave me a dirty look.

"Bathroom?"

He escorted me to a room in which there were a dozen stand-up ceramic urinals, like those in cafés. He stood behind me. We went back. He started yelling at me. He was probably telling me that I should not have banged on the door. How long was he going to go on? I looked at him and shouted, as loud as he, "I may be here to be shot, but certainly not to be shouted at by you! That's enough!"

As stupefied as if I had turned into a rabbit before his eyes, he fell silent and closed the door of my room again with ominous deliberation.

It might have been a nursing home, only the nurse had just been braying at me. I opened the cupboard. On one of the shelves, a few bits and pieces, some pencils and a ruler with one end carefully whittled down. The warder had not opened the door with a key, but with a lever handle. I examined the lock. The bolt was engaged, but the door was only locked because the handle had been removed. Through the square hole in which the warder had engaged his lever handle, I could see the light in the corridor as through a keyhole.

The end of the ruler fitted the hole. There was enough leverage to open the door. This I did cautiously. The warder was in the corridor, a little farther down, with his back turned. I closed the door noiselessly, and put the ruler back in the cupboard.

I was unable to run. Or to walk on tiptoe—though I could have left my shoes off. An escape cannot succeed without taking some risk that confounds the enemy, and this one would be as good as any. But it was strange that the ruler should be in the cupboard. Had my predecessor carved it and then been summoned before he could use it? You do not leave a prisoner his knife. He may be able to make a makeshift blade (so they say) but this ruler was very neatly carved. And didn't they examine the cupboards? "Shot while trying to escape . . ." What was this prison where they seemed to confine themselves to registering the prisoners?

I supposed that the major represented the authority to which the armored division had handed me over. This authority had judged me worthy of a boardinghouse which was certainly bizarre, but which did not suggest the waiting room before the firing squad. The room had no window. If the decision they had taken was not to have me shot— or at least, not immediately—it must certainly have been to interrogate me in Paris. I would have to find out whether the ruler would be useful, and if the day in this worthy establishment was like the night. I started to undress. The door opened. It was the soldier who had accompanied the major, this time with an NCO. I got dressed again. On the ground floor, the latter picked up my papers. Once more, the armored car.

A district some way off, a tower, a very long wall; the car turned left with a grinding of brakes and went through an archway. It was a prison. The traditional registration. They only took my watch, and they gave me a receipt! They shut me in a room with about twenty prisoners brought in that day. Everyone was suspicious of everyone else, but the mythomania of news swapping reigned supreme. It was the same sort of thing I remembered from the camp at Sens: "Pétain has been killed by Weygand, right in the middle of a Cabinet meeting!" "No, you've got it wrong! Pétain and Weygand have both been arrested by Mandel!" Tonight it was: "The Normandy front has caved in, and Chartres has been captured by paratroops."

The following day, around ten o'clock, we were divided up. The carpeted passages were succeeded by huge prison corridors with grilled doors. I was expecting a cell, but I was pushed into a room—two big barred windows obscured by some boxes piled up on the outside, allowing only a vertical light to penetrate. A dozen or so prisoners, in civilian clothes, watched me come in without leaving their mattresses, except one, a redhead with a broad smile, who shook my hand warmly:

"I'm the room leader. Welcome, on behalf of the boys. My name is André."

"Mine too. Thank you."

"When were you captured?"

"Last week."

He looked at my plain uniform: "You're a maquis leader?"

"Yes."

"You're lucky they didn't clobber you."

"Not yet. Maybe it's the uniform. And then, we've got a fair number of prisoners ourselves."

"Really."

From one mattress after another prisoners rose and slowly converged, as in the theater.

"How's it going, the landing? The latest arrival here was three weeks back. Sure, there's the telephone, but all you hear is a load of cock-and-bull stories."

"You can communicate?"

"You bet! We'll show you. But after the Fritzes have brought the grub."

Here it was. Horrible, to put it mildly. The piece of bread was enough to keep you going.

The clanking of tins in the corridor had stopped. André went to the window, and said in a fairly loud voice, without shouting, "Hullo! Hullo! Hullo!" General silence. The neighboring cell answered, "Hullo." André went into the corner, sat down on the ground and knocked three times on the dividing wall. Answering knocks came from the other side. The other prisoners stood between him and the spyhole in the door. In the same tone of voice he said, "Everything all right?"

Two of our number, ears flattened against the wall, transmitted the replies.

"Yes, and you?"

"Yes. We've got a colonel, from De Gaulle's outfit. Arrested on July 23. He says Caen and St.-Lô were taken. And that the Allied air forces made daylight parachute drops. Since then, he knows nothing."

"Reliable information?"

"Yes."

("Don't worry," André told me, "here all the information is supposed to be reliable!")

"Good. We'll pass it on."

Same game with the left-hand wall. Behind me, the corridor; in front, the ·vindows. The free mattress was next to André's, which allowed us, after the "telephone," to talk quietly. The others were dozing. They had no more stories to tell each other.

"Do you think there are any stool pigeons here?"

"Don't talk too much about yourself, that's all."

I caught his meaning. A stool pigeon would not be able to report anything much except improbable escape preparations or extravagant boasts. St. Michel was a halfway house. The oldest inhabitant had been there only three months. Every month, a convoy left for Germany. Whence a disquieting atmosphere of station waiting room, lottery, fortress, not of prison camp. We were not forced to do any work. The warders were private soldiers, indifferent to us in spite of their occasional urge to bellow. They were not "after" us, André said. They knew about the "transmissions," for every room picked up the latest rumors as a wireless receiver picks up soundwaves. Even in Fresnes* they never stopped. But nothing mattered, provided the consignment was complete, and all the prisoners present. To be sent to Germany, for us, would only mean being set free much later. But at six o'clock we would hear two soldiers and an official walk down the corridor. Usually they would open one or two doors, and take away one or two prisoners.

It was for the Gestapo.

When six o'clock sounded from the churches, the silence of the grave would descend on our corridor.

A few of these prisoners had come back. There was one in our room. He described the bath torture with the black humor of prisons.

"It's not that it hurts all that much, but it keeps starting all over again, after a while you don't know what's happening. And then they're shouting and knocking you round, so if you're not careful you'd end up answering them. Got to be very careful—the fourth time it's really rough. And the tub is disgusting—full of puke and all that. I thought they were going to drown me like a rat!"

He burst into fits of laughter, and slapped his thighs.

"Like a rat!

* Prison in the suburbs of Paris which was taken over by the Germans and transformed into a camp for political detainees. (Tr.)

"And talking about rats, there was a mouse there too—but she just bangs on a typewriter. And you know what she said to me the third time round, the bitch: 'Oh stop, that's enough, I can't stand that!' She figured I was putting it on, the cow! How do you like that? If we get out of here, she'd better not get into my clutches."

Stories like that made up the folklore of St. Michel. Before my arrival, an officer had gone round the prison checking everybody's names. The prisoners stood up, all except the man who had been tortured, who could not get up. When he gave his name, the officer consulted his list and said, "Ter-ro-rist." One of the other prisoners, who had since been known as the Professor (and who had left for Germany), took a step forward, raised a philological forefinger, and said respectfully, "Not terro-rist, tou-rist," and stepped back into line. The officer went on with his check, and as he was leaving, glared round the room and shouted with angry contempt, "Tourists, the lot of you!"

The door slammed and the laughter burst forth.

The main object was not to be a member of the next convoy. Those who had been designated for the last one had been sent back to their cells "with their belongings." But the prisoners had no control over the selection. They tried hard not to attract attention, for they might be picked at random. It was for this reason that André had told me not to talk about myself. In spite of this, everyone—except for the few who had been arrested for black-marketing—described the circumstances of his arrest. This was the boring and inexhaustible subject, thanks to which I discovered that the hotel near the War Memorial where I had spent a few hours before being transferred to the prison was the headquarters of the Gestapo in Toulouse. The baths there were strictly for interrogations. But usually there were no beds. The yelling guard who had been so amazed when I told him to go to hell was probably one of the torturers. I was struck by the sinister humor of it, like coming on the dance in the château. Also by the feeling of having had a brush with fate—a feeling all the more intense because the atmosphere of this prison, since the departure of the last convoy had been postponed, was one of impotent waiting upon fate: new convoy or Gestapo.

The days passed by, formless as always in prisons, sometimes interrupted by the distribution of parcels from the Red Cross or from the Marshal, and every evening, at six o'clock, by the boots in the corridor that heralded torture. Until one morning, a long, drawn-out rumbling, faint and muffled, could be heard in the distance. Nobody moved. A few prisoners put their ears against the wall: stone conducts ground noises better than air does. An hour went by. Two hours. The halfhearted games, the daydreams, the blankness took over again.

A second rumble, fainter than the first. It was not the sound of artillery. Sabotage by the maquis? But the noise of a bridge being blown up is the same as that of an aircraft dropping a bomb. An Allied air raid, with no answering antiaircraft fire? Nothing like what we had heard in 1940, but rather an instant from one of those interminable static battles of long ago, transmitted through the earth—the rumble of Verdun that none of us had heard.

This inexplicable rumbling that had nothing in common with our own dynamitings was in fact the Allied advance—although the second had been farther away than the first. No shouts in the street. No shots. What was happening was happening a long way off. The life of the prison had not changed.

But it was about to change.

At two o'clock, one of the rounds stopped in a few cells. Then our door opened. A German in mufti said, "Malraux, six o'clock."

It was the Gestapo interrogation.

I realized that I had thought they had forgotten me.

I tried to find out from my companions precisely what they knew. The warmth of fellowship that had surrounded me ever since the door had shut was that of a wake. Even on the part of the black marketeers. Most of my comrades called the military police who had beaten them up the Gestapo. The prisoner who had undergone the bath treatment knew what he was talking about. But the Germans had interrogated him to force him to tell them where his group's transmitters were. He had been tortured on two occasions, with three days in between. When a member of the group was captured, the transmitters were moved. He had held out the first time, and the second time had given the address of a house that was now empty.

What I was trying, in vain, to get clear was what kind of terrain I would be fighting on. "What the boys say is no help," said André, "it's never the same way twice." An interrogation about the maquis? I had been under arrest too long. A confrontation? Using me as bait? We had foreseen this. The Montignac maquis had caves where the Germans would never be able to pursue them. It had been agreed that if one of us scratched his nose as he approached, it would mean that the Germans were behind him; our men would shoot him in the head before making off, so that he should not be tortured again. And I had two old comrades from Spain there.

But the Gestapo had probably got hold of my complete dossier. Better informed than the press, they would thus know that I had never been a member of the Communist party or of the International Brigade, but also that I had been one of the presidents of the World Committee against fascism, and of the League against anti-Semitism, and that I had commanded the international air force in the service of the Spanish Republic, before the communists decided what they were going to do. They had enough against me to have me shot ten times over. Why interrogate me? No one anticipates torture cheerfully. I thought of how much I had written about it, and now it seemed like a premonition.

Six o'clock. The prisoners had gathered round the door. When it opened, they were standing on either side of it, and they all shook hands with me.

The same civilian as in the morning. The same two guards. We went down. I thought we were going back to the hotel, but we turned in the opposite direction from the street, into a courtyard surrounded by arcades. German guards were playing leapfrog. One of them mistimed his jump, fell over, and yelled at me as I went by. We stopped outside a smallish doorway, like the entrance to the office of a French barracks. Before the two guards had knocked, it opened to reveal two soldiers carrying a poor fellow with a Jewish cast of features: face swollen, a trickle of blood at the corner of his mouth, and short movements of his short arms, as if to protect himself still.

We went into a kind of guardroom. A fantastic din: a soldier was hammering on a piece of sheet iron which he was holding by a chain in his left hand. This racket drowned the screams.

A haggard woman prisoner was convulsively trying to introduce a spoonful of tea between the teeth of a prisoner whose features had been beaten into an unrecognizable pulp and who must have fainted. She was spilling the tea almost as if she were throwing it away, then starting again. They handcuffed my hands behind my back. We went into the next room. There were doors open to right and left to reveal two men with their hands tied to their feet being battered by booted feet and a kind of bludgeon that I could not make out. In spite of the din, it seemed to me that I could hear the dull thud of blows on the naked bodies. I had already averted my eyes, from shame more than fear, perhaps. A man with curly blond hair, seated behind a desk, looked at me expressionlessly. I was expecting first of all an interrogation about my identity.

"Don't give me a lot of stupid answers; Galitzina is working for us now!"

What was he driving at? It could be a good thing that he was on the wrong tack. The important thing was to keep a clear head in spite of the atmosphere, the uproar, and the feeling of having only one arm.

"You spent eighteen months in Soviet Russia?"

"I haven't spent more than three months outside France for ten years. That can easily be checked through the passport office."

"You spent a year in our country?"

He was obliged to shout, as I was.

"Never more than a fortnight. I gave the dates and whereabouts of my lectures in your universities to the military police when they interrogated me."

Working himself into a rage (a false one), he stood up and yelled: "So you're innocent?"

"Of what? I started off by stating, without any pressure, that I'm the military chief of this region."

He sat down again, flung the blotter at my face with full force, missed, and did not pursue the matter. Something was puzzling him. He was examining my uniform without stripes or decorations, and my single legging.

"You said, 'for ten years'?"

"Yes."

"And you are thirty-three?"

"Forty-two."

The barber had come to our cell the previous day. A thick beard is ageless; but after being shaved the day before it was obvious that I was more than thirty-three years old.

He rang. The man hammering on the sheet iron stopped. The screams, now plaintive moans, grew fainter. Had the demonstration gone on long enough? All the same, I felt in greater danger than under the machine gun fire on the Gramat road, or in front of the fake firing squad. He had resumed his normal voice, and almost lost his accent.

"You claim you are not the son of Fernand Malraux and of Berthe Lamy, deceased?"

"Yes, I am."

"From what illness did your father die?"

"He killed himself."

He leafed through the dossier.

"Date?"

"1930 or 1931. But there can't be any mistake: in my family, he is the only Fernand."

He looked at me as if to say aggressively, "Well then, explain to me what's going on!" I thought of that gesture of my outspread hands which would have meant, "I've no more idea than you have." But they were handcuffed behind my back. However, I was beginning to guess what had happened.

Thirty-three was my brother Roland's age. He had spent a year in Germany before Hitler and eighteen months in the Soviet Union. The self-styled Princess Galitzine was his mistress. It was his dossier that Paris had sent. Roland was in their hands. And if they had not yet located my dossier, it was because I always forget that my name is not André. I have never been called anything else, but officially my name is Georges. So the armored division had probably not passed on the complete interrogation report: it had merely sent for the dossier of André Malraux which the registry office had been unable to find because it does not exist. Among the Malraux dossiers (in the Dunkirk region I have fifty-two cousins, of whom about thirty are called Malraux), it had picked out the most suspect. But there was something else in the dossier, for they had not started by hitting me, and my interrogator was not being insolently overfamiliar.

"You stated that our prisoners were well treated?"

So the interrogation report sent on by the armored division was more thorough than I had thought.

"Since then, you must have been able to check that through police informers."

"No need. We've got them back."

I did not believe it.

"You really are Berger, are you not?"

"Yes."

"So you admit you are guilty."

"From your point of view, there's no question about it."

Behind me, the civilian was taking notes. The interrogator was still leafing through the dossier.

"We'll have to start all over again!"

Then, like a dog pointing, he looked at me and shouted, in the tone of a man indignant in face of so much stupidity: "But what in God's name can have induced you to get yourself involved in all that?"

A moment's hesitation.

"My convictions."

"Your convictions," he spat back. "We'll see about that!"

He left his desk and went into the next room. Whatever happened, I had just done, following the example of many others, what was probably the bravest thing I would ever do in my life.

At least five minutes. Now it was all going to begin, or end.

* * * *

A buzzer sounded.

The civilian rejoined his colleague in the next room, came back almost at once, told the guards to take me away, and went out again. We followed the route by which we had come. Under the arcades, the warders were still playing.

I began to reconstruct the room in which I had been interrogated, and which I thought I had not looked at. On the wall, over a filing cabinet, there was one of the *Pernod Pontarlier* posters that used to hang in every café. Insects scurried about. The bound man whom the torturer on the right had been kicking to his feet was fair-haired and covered with blood. The features of my curly-headed interrogator— close-set eyes, small nose, small mouth—were inscribed within a circle much smaller than his face.

The stairs. The room full of prisoners. Handshakes. General stupefaction.

"Match postponed," I said. "They had the wrong dossier."

The wall telephone. Congratulations from the neighboring cells. We learned that Nantes and Orleans had fallen, and that the German troops in Corrèze had surrendered. If it was true, they had surrendered to my successor, which would explain a great deal. My companions were hoping for information about what they called the air raids. They had heard a rumbling less distant than the first two. During the night, we heard three more—perhaps because of the silence.

The following morning, there were explosions so close and so violent that we thought Toulouse was being bombed. But there was no sound of aircraft. André made a hole in one of the overturned awnings which blocked our windows; through it we could see only a patch of sky streaked with smoke. Long-range guns? Where could the front be? Some of the explosions were not shell bursts. "Hullo! Hullo! The Fritzes are blowing up their stuff." What stuff? German depots or French buildings, they were going up in accordance with a German plan, not an Allied advance, which explained why the explosions sometimes sounded nearer, sometimes farther away. Listening, waiting, guessing— that was the life of the prison.

Obviously what was happening was the thing most of us had been hoping for since our arrival: the front had caved in, and the troops occupying Southern France were falling back on Paris.

A clatter of doors opening one after another. A warder shouted as he went by, "Everybody below with your belongings!" and ran to the next door. In theory, "with your belongings" meant leaving for Germany. When I had been captured, most of the main railway lines had been cut. Would they transport us by truck through the maquis in the Massif Central? They took us into the big room where I had spent my first night. Were all the prisoners assembled? There were more than five hundred of us, with our shabby bundles and convicts' pallor. Nearly all sitting on the ground. The eternal squatting of the defeated. Wild rumors appeared and disappeared like a game of who's got the button. After three hours' waiting, we were sent back to our cells.

Too late for Germany? Now they would have to abandon us or shoot us. It does not take many machine guns to kill a thousand men.

No evening meal. A few prisoners banged on the doors furiously. Guards fired a few random shots in the corridor. Silence.

All night long, troops passed by. One of the main roads ran along the front of the prison. In the morning, no breakfast. But around ten o'clock the rumble of trucks was succeeded by the hurried clatter of tanks. Either there was fighting to the north of Toulouse (but we heard neither guns nor bombers) or the Germans were evacuating the town.

And suddenly we all looked at each other, words and gestures suspended in midair: in the prison yard, women's voices were yelling the Marseillaise. It was not the solemn chant of prisoners on their way to the extermination camp; it was the roar that perhaps was heard when the women of Paris marched on Versailles. There could be no doubt about it, the Germans had gone. Had the women found some keys? Men were running in the corridor shouting, "Out! Out!" On the ground floor, a colossal wooden gong sounded slowly, then developed into a rapid tattoo. Suddenly we got it. In each room there was only one piece of furniture—a table, thick and heavy as in all the old prisons, perhaps dating from the Second Empire. All of us together took hold of ours, placed it upright against the door, and stepped back to the windows. André counted, "One, Two, Three!" The room shook with a great reverberating clang. The door seemed to bend like a bow, although our efforts had been badly coordinated, some plaster fell; André picked up a piece, made a cross on the door, and said: "We all aim at that!" The noise of battering rams rose from the ground floor. We stepped back to the windows. "One, Two, Three!" The door bent as if it would burst. We withdrew again. We were very weak, but hysterically excited. The battering rams resounded on all sides, and we heard a few cracking noises. For weeks we had been living on sound and threats. The messages through the wall, the footsteps of torture, this house of silence being eaten away by cautious noises like a wooden beam by worms; and ourselves, listening. We had not yet stopped living by ear, enveloped as we were in this eruption of shouting punctuated by the deep thundercrashes of the battering rams. The entire prison reverberated. Above this tom-tom of death (for the Germans might come back) the *Marseillaise* took on a prophetic meaning: the "day of glory" was our liberation from this prison; the "tyranny" we knew; "do you hear in our fields" the tanks that might be approaching; "To arms!" seemed to be the signal for the battering rams. In the cells there were only scattered phrases from the hymn: you do not break down a door to the rhythm of a song. But the battering rams, whose thudding seemed rapid because of their numbers, accompanied the roar from outside like a charge of gigantic subterranean drums. At the fifth blow, our door burst open.

We had to dislodge the table from it. In the corridor to the right, prisoners were pouring out of several cells through doors shattered or wrenched from their hinges; to the left, from the staircase, brandishing their fists and chanting in response to the battering rams, there emerged the ageless insurrectionary crowd, as seen by women's magazines, for the women who were intermingled with the tattered prisoners were elegant, or were trying to be. A man at their head waving a bunch of skeleton keys started to open the doors that had not yet been broken down. Now the singing was only going on above us, but everywhere freedom was beating its impassioned gong. We went down against the stream, and reached the yard in time to hear a few cries of pain and the gate of the prison slamming shut with a great clang above the receding noise of tanks and machine guns. A dozen prisoners came back covered with blood or holding their stomachs before collapsing. Above us, the distant *Marseillaise* and the battering rams; below, an unreal silence. Outside, shouts. Except for the fallen wounded, everyone had taken refuge in the big assembly room: three or four hundred.

"Berger in command! Berger! Berger!"

The cry must have come from the occupants of the cells next to ours; everyone wanted to escape from this chaotic freedom, to act in concert: they were unarmed, and there were German tanks on the other side of the gate. I was the only prisoner in uniform, which gave me a bizarre authority. "Go on," said André. "Jump to it!"

I climbed on to a packing case.

"Form up!"

They sorted themselves into rows.

"Doctors, step forward!"

Four.

"Are there any medical orderlies?"

One came up. We would have to choose at random among the prisoners.

"The first ten men, you will be at the doctors' disposal to look after the wounded—existing ones and any subsequent ones!"

"What shall I do with them?" one of the doctors asked.

"Whatever you like. Move!"

"The next eight men!"

They were close by me, but I went on shouting what we were going to do. There were observation towers at all four corners of the walls.

"Two men to each tower. One stays up there, one reports back at once and remains the liaison man."

André picked out the men and the towers. I sent him in person to one of those overlooking the road.

Not a sound apart from the cries of the wounded. If there had been German troops there, they would have tried to break down the gate; if there had been a single tank, it *would* have broken it down. For a few minutes at least, nothing would happen. At the far end, prisoners were arriving, and others were leaving.

"Officers and maquis leaders!"

Three.

"Those of you who know your way around St. Michel!"

Some prisoners had been used for fatigue-duties a few weeks earlier. About twenty came up.

"Those who know where the arms were kept!"

Two men with mustaches.

"There's probably nothing left, but run and have a look!"

"Those who know where the ladders are!"

Nobody.

"Those who know where the picks or hammers were!"

Five. Not so bad.

"Run and look!"

I called over a man who had been wounded in the arm, with the cell-mate who was putting a tourniquet on him.

"What happened?"

"We went dashing out, there were some tanks, they machine-gunned us."

"And then?"

"Those who were able came back."

"And the tanks?"

"Don't know . . . "

Back to shouting:

"All the wounded who can walk, over here!"

Here they were. The second doctor would try to treat them.

"The tanks that opened fire on you, did they stay in position or move off?"

Many of them did not know. Four or five said they had left. One, that they had stayed. I remembered the clatter receding.

I called one of the women, who was fairly calm. "How did you get in?"

"As soon as the first Fritzes left, a lot of women started keeping watch, because their husbands were inside. When they saw the soldiers from St. Michel leave, a few of them wandered in looking dumb, with some excuse ready. The gate wasn't even locked. There was no one around. The first ones yelled, and we all came in."

"There were no tanks, of course?"

"Nothing. That's why the first ones came out without looking."

One of the mustaches came back.

"We couldn't find any weapons, but we found some grenades."

"How many?"

"About fifty."

"Try one out where you can. Then take four men with you and bring the rest to either side of the archway over the entrance."

André was back: "Paris is liberated! From my tower, I talked to a neighbor who saw everything. He figures the Fritzes have left the prison, and it's the last we'll see of them. But they haven't finished evacuating Toulouse, and we're on one of the evacuation routes. Some tanks that were leaving recognized the prison, realized what was obviously happening, and took a few pot shots."

"Send two more liaison men."

The man from the other tower on the roadway came and confirmed André's news.

Again, I shouted out what we were going to try to do, went to the prison gate, and had it opened. The road was empty. Three bodies crushed by the tanks had left a gory mess.

"There's some sand in the yard," I told one of the officers who accompanied me. "Get that blood covered up. Don't leave anything that might attract the Germans' attention. If the tower signals their arrival, get back inside without hurrying, as if you're returning from some routine fatigue duty."

On the opposite side of the road were poor houses and small shops where people used to buy foodbaskets for the prisoners; behind them, little gardens.

I sent twenty or so of the men around me to open all the doors.

"Then slip away through the back, and leave everything you can open."

They crossed over. The men who were scattering sand hurried along with them. All the prisoners formed up into groups of twenty. There was a whistle from the tower. No need: we could already hear the tanks. We fastened the enormous bolts on the gate.

Either the tanks would ignore the prison, and after they had gone by the prisoners could leave in groups. Or else they would break open the gate. But the archway was too narrow for them to approach at an angle, so they would have to maneuver; there would be little room for them to reverse, even if they knocked in one or two shop fronts. We would have a few minutes' grace. Once inside the archway, they would be vulnerable to grenades, while we would be protected by the right angle of the wall. If they got through they would massacre us; but they still had to get through. If our grenades set the first tank ablaze, the passage would be obstructed; those behind would not waste time on a siege. Two ex-NCO's from an antitank unit and two stalwarts who were used to grenades joined me. The German grenades—with handles—which the man with the mustache had just set down on both sides of the black hole of the archway, were easier to manipulate than our own. Not a sound could now be heard except the clatter of the approaching tank (a fairly light one). Once more, in this prison, to live was to listen. The tank could not maneuver without slowing down, and it was not slowing down. Perhaps we were saved. Our watchers were crouched down in the towers. Like a line of angry ants, bullets whined over the top of the gate. The tank was already past the prison.

It was the same with the next two. They gave us a farewell burst, just for the hell of it. But it was over, out of indifference or on orders. Nine more tanks came by, past the prison and past all the houses. The last took away the noise with it.

I ran to the left-hand tower. The tank was just going into the bend of the road. The treads had taken up the blood and the sand; there were no stains left in front of the prison. "Open the gate!" The first prisoners went out almost as if they were going for a stroll; but the frenzy of freedom sent the others shooting out from the porch like sinister schoolboys. If more tanks arrived, the massacre would begin again.

No more tanks were to come.

TEMPTATION

THE

OF THE

WEST

1

1958 / 1965. Before the sacred caves, I had wanted to revisit Benares, and also to see the great temples of the South. But to reach the holy city of Shiva I had to go through Sarnath, where the Buddha preached in the Deer Park. Along a road that was reminiscent of the royal highways on which Asoka, twenty-three centuries before, had proclaimed, "I have planted these trees to protect both men and beasts from the sun," I rediscovered the deserted temples, the reed cottages crumbling beneath their wooden tiles, and the peasants loaded with votive garlands sitting in circles beneath the shade of the banyan trees. A few camels, looking homesick for Islam, meandered past a sanctuary to Shiva.

Since 1929 I have had frequent encounters with Buddhism, from Ceylon to Japan. Colombo is one of the calmest places on earth. Its inhabitants wander imperturbably among the scarlet poincianas, the purple bougainvillaeas, and the shrubs dominated by pink acacias. The asphalt avenues with their very occasional cars are graced, in the evening, by processions of saris whose colors are those of the pastel drawings by the English spinsters buried in the nearby cemeteries. Beside the Victorian commemorative monuments, neat and proud as ironclads overgrown with orchids, a Sinhalese musician plays, watching the remains of the British Empire gently rusting under the thorns.

In Burma (who now remembers the road to Mandalay?) I have seen the thousands of gladioli bending over with the women at prayer, bowing to the Buddha like ears of corn bent over by the wind. In Japan I saw the temple of Nara when its walls were covered with the most famous frescoes in Asia—a bloodred Buddha, princes with tiaras and lotus hands—which, when I saw them again, were white as a blind man's eyes around the temple's charred pillars.

All that was still India.

"At that time, on the borders of Nepal, Prince Siddhartha was born at Kapilavastu . . . " For me, the India of this figure who touches so lightly upon history but who brews so many dreams means necklets of damp tuberoses over royal jewels. Yet I have never seen those tiaras or those necklets; and the tuberoses—whose perfume is the perfume of the marshlands of paradise—I have seen only round the necks of visitors: they are the flowers of the garlands of welcome. But the tiaras of Ajanta, the Greco-Buddhist torsos, always bring to my mind that great legendary life. And Sarnath evoked first and foremost the phrase which answers to the solemn words inscribed on the gates of the great religions. "In the beginning was the Word," St. John relates; and the disciples of the Buddha, "Sorrowful is all life." At Sarnath, Prince Siddhartha is already Sakyamuni. At the moment when he enters into meditation, the King of the Cobras, who has spread his hood to protect him from the sun, says to him, "Above thy head, a flock of blue jays is wheeling in the sky, from left to right." It is the portent of the Enlightenment. Then the demon intervenes (fables are always intermingled with the great myths) with his flowered arrows and his devilish legions, their gray skin spotted with red. "And at the hour when day breaks and the drum is beaten, when the stars announced the fourth watch, he attained enlightenment." From then on his life is dedicated to the preaching of the Truth, until death comes. "Set a bed between these two trees, its head toward the north . . ." The trees blossom with flowers, which fall and cover his body.

And the funeral pyre will burst into flames of its own accord.

The brief flames of this pyre, which have burned through the centuries, were those I had seen in Benares. The gardens on whose paths the prince will encounter life, the women sleeping on mattresses of flowers with fleshy petals, the genie who opens the gate of the city, the friendly trees, the prophetic birds, the peacocks which greet him by spreading their tails, the prince who becomes an ascetic and the horse "shaken with sobs" which returns to the palace without a rider—all this is India. The earth-colored robe was the one worn by criminals on their way to the scaffold, and the one which the Rajput horsemen put on when they set out for certain death. Deliverance is one of the peaks of Hindu thought, and the successive buddhas will become incarnations of the uncreated Buddha who is one with the supreme Wisdom.

But the Deer Park is now no more than an exhibition of neatly swept ruins which belong to archaeology like the Sphinx and like all the past which our century has rescued; beyond, there stretches a banal and incongruous garden, with its lawns for vice-regal parties. A few red-brown animals were passing by in the distance. The road did not follow them. I shall never see the gazelles of Sarnath.

The Franciscan gentleness of the bonzes, in this land of Brahmans; nosegays glistening with cool drops of water in the furnace of noon. But in front of this pathetic temple with its Esperanto architecture, its laughable Japanese frescoes, the fragile prelate who gave me his blessing in Pali was indistinguishable from the ascetics who blessed Prince Siddhartha.

Yet the Buddha was much more present in Benares, although it was already dedicated to Shiva when he came there twenty-five hundred years ago. Since 1929 the mosque of Aurangzeb had lost its two imperious minarets, like threatening arms raised above the town. But the Ganges was still a haunted and funereal Grand Canal. The temples, half covered by the waters, had sunk a little more between the boats; the children still dived off them. The monkeys still scurried along the ledges of the palaces. The town was still the color of hemp and clay, in spite of the white blotch of the hospital and the huge advertisements. Under arched roofs, the same colossal flights of steps climbed toward the temples now forsaken by the clouds of the epics: the monsoon season was over.

At this hour, Benares was the Ganges. A sparrow hawk followed our boat among the fires of the funeral pyres, constantly replenished, and the piles of wood for the cremations. Amid the swirling of the river, hemp-colored like the city, a silent voice within me was quoting: "Here are the sacred waters of the Ganges, which sanctify the gaping mouths of the dead." The great prayer of India, which the West must have known at the time when the first peals of bells awoke the faithful in the Merovingian dawn, rose from this multitude which for so many years had been greeting the same river and the same sun with the same hymns—and with the same cremations casually incinerating what the West calls life.

> Worn-out garments are shed by the body:
> Worn-out bodies are shed by the dweller
> Within the body . . .*

The voice of the faithful who had just purified themselves would have been no less penetrating without temples, without palaces, without amulets, without a city—on the curve, peopled with funeral pyres, of a vast, slow-moving river of Africa.

In 1914 my class had been taken to the fields of the Marne, a few days after the battle. At lunchtime, bread was handed round to us, which we dropped, terror-stricken, because the wind covered it with a light sprinkling of ash from the dead piled up a little farther off. Here, a housewife leaned out of her window in the smoke of the corpses,

* Translations of passages from the *Bhagavad-Gita* here and following are from the English version by Christopher Isherwood and Swami Prabhavanda (London, Phoenix House), to whom thanks and acknowledgment are due. (Tr.)

which the crowd watched floating by as the first inhabitants of Benares
watched the calm flight of migratory birds. "A garment cast off . . ."
An elder son lit his father's funeral pyre, the family gossiped and
smoked, the lean dogs trotted by, nose to the ground, in front of the
lines of patient vultures—in front of the big pyres of the rich, the little
pyres of the poor and of children, and the ascetics, as numerous as
ever. The slope was so steep that the dead seemed to descend standing.
The holy city surrendered itself to the continuation of life with an
absentminded submission. Far more than the crosses in our cemeteries,
these pyres, this crowd that climbed slowly back up from the river,
chanting the names of the supreme God, evoked the files of men
marching slowly toward the sound of the guns, along the Via Sacra
of Verdun, along the road to Stalingrad. Europe's surrender to fate is
war.

Here, it is detachment from life, expressed by the ascetic and the
pyre. That is why the Buddha is at home here: "Escape the Wheel!"
The rivals of Benares are the cities of another life, while she is the city
of another death. The capital of transmigration? But whatever transmigrates, transmigrates from soul to soul as much as from body to
body. The tradition, rigorous and unbroken, is already precise in the
Milindapanha, which recounts the dialogues between the Buddhist
Nagasena and King Menander, in some court of Gandhara, where the
eagles swoop down from the Pamirs like seagulls from the ocean, and
"where one might find in abundance everything that men eat, chew,
suck, drink, or savor."

"A man goes up with a torch to the upper story of his house and
eats his meal there. The torch sets fire to the straw of the roof, the
straw to the house, the house to the village. The villagers seize the man:
'Why have you burned the village?' 'I did not burn the village. One
fire gave the light by which I ate, another burned the village.'

"The fire which burned the village came out of the first."

No doubt he who is reborn is other than he who dies, but he proceeds from him: it cannot then be said that he is freed from previous
sins.

No doubt every civilization is haunted, visibly or invisibly, by what
it thinks about death. The truth of death, domain of the unverifiable,
can only be the subject of a revelation. But this revelation is the relationship between India and the world, in its totality. "The changeless
flame of the torch which never ceases to change as it consumes itself,"
says Buddhism; and Brahmanism, "The ever-changing waters of the
changeless Ganges." The Jains pour powdered sugar on the roadway
to feed the ants, and the legend shows us a Brahman child (who is

Vishnu) being received by Indra and bursting out laughing at the sight of a procession of ants. "Why do you laugh, mysterious being in the guise of a child?" "Each of these ants was once an Indra, and it takes twenty-eight kingships of Indras to complete a day and a night of Brahma." Obviously we are dealing with a religious time like the Christian eternity, but opposed to eternity as transmigration is opposed to resurrection. A cosmic cycle is more than four million years; a day of Brahma, four billion, and a cycle of Brahma more than three hundred billion; whatever the number, Hinduism was ready to give it a multiplier. But this Hindu time, animated by the birth, the life and the death of its cycles, enters into an endless dialectic with the essence of the world, which will never be reborn in the same likeness—in spite of its ineluctable return to its eternal origin. The cosmic cycles make us think of light-years, but we do not live in light-years, whereas the Hindu does live in cosmic cycles. It is not Shiva but Vishnu, God of Life, who says, "The privileged expressions of my maya are the ages of the world. My name is Death-of-the-Universe." The professors at the Sanskrit University told me the story of the ascetic Narada, which I once transcribed, was studied at their university (sacred trees, rooms in English Gothic style, professors in yellow robes) in the Matsya Purana, but that it was also told by nurses.

In the solitude of the forest, Narada meditates, his gaze fixed on a little shining leaf. The leaf begins to tremble; soon the great tree, motionless in its luxuriant splendor above the sleeping peacocks, is quivering all over as when the monsoon passes: it is Vishnu.

"Choose between your desires," says the rustling of the leaves in the silence.

"What desire could I have, except to know the secret of your maya?"

"So be it; but go and fetch me some water."

The tree is shimmering in the heat.

The ascetic reaches the first hamlet and calls out. The animals are asleep. A young girl opens a door. "Her voice was as a golden noose slipped round the neck of the stranger." Yet the occupants treat him as a member of the family whose return has been long awaited. He has always been one of them. He has forgotten the water. He will marry the girl, and they all expected him to marry her.

He has also married the earth, the crushing sun on the paths of beaten earth where a cow passes by, the warm ricefields, the well which is worked by walking on its horizontal beam, the twilight over the palm roofs, the pink flame of the little dung fires in the night. He has known the town through which the endless road passes, in which there are acrobats, a usurer, and a little temple with infantile gods. He has discovered the helpful beasts and plants, evening falling on the exhausted body, the depth of the calm after the harvest, the seasons which return as the buffalo returns from the waterhole at the end of the day. And the smile of the thin children in the years of famine. With the death of his father-in-law, he has become the head of the family.

One night during the twelfth year, the periodic floods drown the livestock and carry away the houses. Supporting his wife, leading two of his children and carrying the third, he flees through the avalanche of primordial mud. The child he is carrying slips from his shoulder. He lets go of the two others and of his wife to pick it up again: they are carried away. No sooner is he upright again, in the darkness filled with the roar of the sticky flood, than he is felled by an uprooted tree. The thick torrent flings him onto a rock; when he regains consciousness, he is surrounded by nothing but a sea of mud through which there drift the corpses of trees full of monkeys.

He weeps in the fading wind. "My children, my children."

"My child," echoes the voice of the wind become suddenly grave, "where is the water? I have been waiting more than half an hour."

Vishnu awaits him in the motionless incandescence of the forest, beside the great quivering tree.

The legend also belongs to Christianity, where it has taken another form. In one of those monasteries buried in the medieval forest, a monk asks what are the tasks of the elect in heaven. "None: they contemplate the Lord." "For all eternity? That must be long . . ." The Superior does not answer. The monk goes back to clearing the forest. Above his head, a marvelous bird comes and perches. Soon it flies away, but to a tree not very far off, for it flies badly. The monk follows it. The bird flies off again, and the monk finds it so beautiful and so mysterious that he follows again. The chase continues until evening. The bird disappears, and the monk hurries to get back to his monastery before nightfall. He hardly recognizes it: the buildings are much larger, the older friars are dead, the Superior has become an old man. "If it takes only a bird to make twenty years seem to you like a few hours, what must the eternity of the elect be like?"

Beneath the edifying anecdote we perceive the other world, the godly time of the Christian eternity. But the illusory time which the monk experienced is a time as magic as the bird. It does not call in question the life of men. The monk was under a spell—the ascetic too. But the spell undergone by the ascetic calls life into question, because his earthly existence is, even in his own eyes, of the same nature as his maya existence. From the text of the Purana to the tales of nurses, the return to the "real" itself belongs to a cycle of appearance—and even Vishnu himself only belongs to a superior cycle. It is not because it was a dream that Narada's second existence is of no consequence, it is because it was as real as the first. To be sure, maya is not limited to the rule of time, but all that is subject to time is maya.

Subterranean, indestructible maya, which conjured up not so much this carnival of death, these straw parasols hanging like shields on the walls of the palaces, as the soul of this swarming multitude dedicated to its pyres and its ritual baths. In spite of its fifteen hundred temples, the sacred city has left not a single statue in my memory. For me its supreme maya was a body burning in the century of the decline of Europe—a century among so many others, and among so many other declines—under the eyes of an ascetic whom these ephemeral flames directed toward the supreme Truth, and who recited the Rig Veda:

> Flames, carry this body gently in your arms,
> Make it perfect and luminous, bear it to the place
> Where the forefathers no longer know grief or death . . .

For me, on that day, the supreme maya was the only thing which for India eludes death: the supreme Truth, the uncreated Spirit—Hinduism.

The two most powerful expressions of metamorphosis, the soul of religious India, are the death-struggle and twilight; whence the significance which night takes on there. I came back through the darkness of the narrow side streets in an opaque silence. The flights of steps had lost their mammoth proportions. The porches were no longer visible, the steps barely so. Against the night sky, less dark than the streets, birds were sleeping in rows. In the distance someone was chanting the lines of the Gita which define the divine:

> I am the beginning the middle and the end in creation,
> And in the living, I am consciousness;
> I am the love-god, begetter of children;
> Among rivers, I am the Ganges,
> Among purifiers I am the wind;
> I am Time without end . . .

The voice rose:

> . . . *And I am Death* . . .

There were red gleams at the temple entrances, in front of the holes dug in the walls for the idols, and on the gilt flames fastened to the heads of ascetics carved in stone. A poor seller of little gods was shutting up his stall. These were the lanes of Kapilavastu at the time when Prince Siddhartha left the palace behind him. The throng of lepers had left these passages, empty as aviaries where there are no birds. But the pyres still burned, with their pole carriers busy pushing the corpses with the parted toes, and a chattering murmur which harmonized with the imperceptible crackling of the flames. The steps changed direction, passed under an archway. Below me, a corpse blazing in the middle of a circle of silent, motionless men made their shadows revolve like a wheel of the law. The chanting voice could still be heard:

> . . . *I am Death that snatches all,*
> *And the source of all that shall be born;*
> *I am beautiful speech, memory, steadfastness and forgiveness,*
> *And the silence of things secret* . . .

I thought of the ring of dead walnuts, back there in Alsace, around a gnarled trunk—like this ring of the living around a body which seemed to be burning reluctantly. "Among rivers, I am the Ganges . . ." The invisible current carried along occasional blue and red gleams in the darkness.

For hundreds of miles, I had met with no other art but that of the little gods of fabric and painted wood which are to be found cluttering up the towers of modern temples. These towers, with the aid of polychromy, have much more sway over the mustached Ramayana of millions of men than over the Absolute of the sacred caves. But around this divine pullulation there was the majesty of the trees—and the tameness of the animals, the nudity of the children who smiled so sadly, the grave old men, and the Panathenaeas of saris in the skimming light of the rising sun. Across this India which does not believe in life, what was sacred was life, with its despairing nobility; and what was not, was this divine circus. But it is inexplicably in harmony with the monsoon that sweeps over it, with the sexual symbols which Victorian England judged indecent and which we know to be related to the figures of the sacred darkness; just as the petrified gesticulations of the gods of the first little temple I had seen on my previous visit to India were in harmony with the odor of aromatic herbs that impregnated the steam rising after a tropical downpour.

Superstition goes deeper than religion, Paul Valéry used to say. The force of his sally lies in its identification of superstition with magic. Of course, magic was present everywhere, as it must have been in our own Middle Ages. Is it not present at Lourdes or Fatima? This climbing plant clung to all the roadside sanctuaries, as the fantastic ivy of the colocynths clung to their wooden tiles. And these clay horses beside the sacred pools, a hibiscus bloom between their ears, were truly the humble and faithful disciples of the divine horses rearing up along the columns of Madurai. Nehru had told me: "Even illiterate women know our national epics, and tell them to the children as bedtime stories." The Ramayana of potter's clay bore witness to the immense Golden Legend that covered India, and I knew that children were put to sleep with lullabies inspired by the Bhagavad-Gita: "Child, you are yourself when you sleep, and when you dream and even when you are awake; look at the world going by." I remembered the simplest prayer, the equivalent of our Ave Maria: "Lead me from the unreal to the real, from darkness to light, from death to immortality."

The temple of Madurai is much bigger than a cathedral. Its towers of a dazzling blue against the blue sky dominate the town, looming up at every turning in the narrow streets; its immensity is present like that of the sea in the streets of port towns. It is as though peasant piety had raised these towers of Babel covered with a vegetation of gods as it raised the towers of Chartres. As I entered this barbaric Angkor, a Brahman, naked to the waist, had marked my forehead with crimson powder and the warm humidity had begun, in a narthex piled with avalanches of bouquets like those of the florists in our cemeteries on All Souls' Day; curcuma for castemarks, devotional bric-a-brac, basil, sandalwood, and camphor which are lit in front of sanctuaries and whose burning scent came and mingled with that of the flowers; chrysanthemums (here, at this time of year!), garlands of frangipani such as I had seen round Khrushchev's neck, whose scent will remind me of India for the rest of my life; and that beautiful leper-woman who held out one of these garlands to me with a poignant smile. In the frame of the porch, when I turned round, all the tall carts with roofs of dried palm leaves, shafts sticking up in the shimmering glare, were lined up as in the encampments of the great migrations.

Madurai was the sky reflected in the dark waters of the ritual pools full of green scum, three white flowers in front of an invisible deity, a black Kali covered with bloodstained linen, the smell of corruption overlaid by that of tuberoses, the oily black gleam of arcades polished by the sweat of men and the passage of beasts, the walkers silhouetted against dazzling apertures or plunged in the depths of darkness: I realized then that our cathedrals are peopled by *motionless* Christians. I was making my way through the endless arcades of a cathedral without a nave, whose nine towers loomed up unexpectedly, riddled with swallows beneath the eagles' solemn flight. This architecture, so rigorously controlled, its plans determined by geomancers, appeared as an epic chaos: on its towers, in its cavernous aisles, the statues had no more significance than the walkers. Springy monkeys accompanied us one moment, left us the next. As I passed in front of a bloodstained Durga, a black cat came down from her shoulder and walked slowly away into the shadows beneath the rearing cavalcade of divine horses, as if he were the secret of the universe.

Everything which belonged to the half-light belonged to the music of the shades, while the jumble of gods on the towers seemed to belong to the desperate piety which stretched from village to village. If one focused hard on the highest tower, where the supernatural glitters above the motionless coconut palms, one could make out Krishna and his cow, Rama and his monkey, the Pandavas and their elephants. And even the sacred elephants, who have wings and who converse with the clouds; and Indra beside the tree-that-fulfills-desires; and the nagas who live under the sea in palaces of luminous coral; and the serpent-princesses "famous for their dancing, their intelligence, and their charm," from whom several dynasties of the South are descended. In the spiritual world of India, the serpent sometimes plays a naïvely epic role, like everything that has to do with the gigantic; but it is he who supports the Buddha at the moment of Enlightenment, and spreads his murderous hood to protect him. One of the sacred texts most charged with darkness is surely the one depicting Krishna's half brother, his soul advancing in colossal undulations: ". . . and the serpents sang his praises . . ." Nehru was right to talk of stories. The musical dream of legend made up for the powerful unreality of life. Krishna and Rama were not only more real than Akbar, they were as real as Gandhi, in this religion whose images are of heroes and gods, but rarely of kings. Our Romanesque world, too, portrays only what carries the reflection of the divine legend. The little clay elephants on sale at the entrance to the temple represented the solemn Ganesha of Madurai, elephant-headed god of wisdom, one foot on his rat; but the young girl who sold them sang, "And when Ganesha rode on his rat/The moon laughed among the clouds." And in a few million years, Ganesha will ride away on his rat once more, once more the moon will laugh when it has risen once more from the ocean into the starless night. The Vishnu with the head of a boar who carries the goddess of earth tells her in his eternal sad voice, in face of the endless cycle of rebirths, "Each time that I carry you thus. . ."

Only the Brahmans had access to the sanctuary in whose shadows dimly glowed the goddess-with-the-fish-eyes to whom it is dedicated—covered with rubies as if with scales, carrying a fan of yak's hair, with her fish-eyes made of diamonds—much closer in spirit to a village idol covered with divine jewels than to the depths of this supernatural bazaar.

A procession emerged slowly from the shadows. Both men and women were obviously in costume, and the dignity of their costume made them look awkward. But the first couple had the stateliness of the dancers of the epics, and the sari is undoubtedly the most beautiful dress in the world. The procession advanced toward me, hands joined together with fingers extended in the moving salute so rare in Hindu art and so common in that of the Buddhists: I was preceded by an escort. "It is a marriage," Raja Rao told me. I walked toward the couple; not knowing a word of Tamil, I wished them good luck in Sanskrit (a fairly elementary orientalism). Whereupon they both prostrated themselves. Utterly taken aback, I went to raise the woman to her feet; my Indian neighbor stopped me, and we moved off again, after some friendly words, toward the merry-go-round of gods teeming in the shadows. "They take you for Vishnu," said Raja Rao, "and with good reason." He explained later. Parents who have arranged a marriage between a boy and a girl have saved for years to take them on their wedding day to the Great Temple, which will bring them good fortune. There they meet a vizier from a distant country, a country that has never sent a vizier to Madurai: strange enough. He goes toward them: very strange. He wishes them good luck: viziers do not wish good luck to peasants. In Sanskrit (the couple does not know Sanskrit, but one of the priests has said, etc. . . .): absolutely unreal. Therefore, there is no vizier. These words of good fortune have been sent by the gods: so they prostrate themselves.

Was I, after all, really a vizier? This unreality was contagious. Primarily because its action was not artistic. This frenzy of winged horses and of gods had the unreality of a festival. The fantastic paper animals, made for the last processions, lay rotting in corners. Europe believes that whatever does not imitate its reality represents a dream. These figures no more imitated a dream than those on the Royal Portal of Chartres imitate the kings of France. Beneath its towers, inextricably cluttered with scenes of its Passion and of its Golden Legend, the entire temple is infested with statues: there, too, as on the towers, rearing horses, divine animals, and personages have for centuries been carrying on their frantic, petrified dance. The faithful were the world according to the maya of men; the temple, the world according to the maya of the gods. And yoga means union.

I imagined such temples looming over Benares: none mingles animal, human, and divine figures so strikingly in its motionless dance. It is the dance of the universe, and the soul of the temple is the dance of Shiva. But the word dance suggests to us the opposite of what it means in India, which knows nothing of the ballroom. The dance of the gods is a solemnization of gesture, as sacred music is a solemnization of the word. Initially Shiva danced his victory over the enemies he had just exterminated; but he also dances the Dance of Death, which the Hindus see in the flames of the pyres and which he resumes in the darkness which will forever follow the end of each age of humanity. One more world has disappeared, the pyres of the Ganges have been extinguished for millennia, and in the cosmic night, Shiva solemnly raises his multiple arms to dance the return to the eternal origin. It is through this image that the Hindu strives for the communion of the spirit which transcends its successive souls, with the Uncreated Being which transcends the gods and the ages of the world:

> Since, Shiva, thou lovest the Place of Burning,
> I have made my heart a Place of Burning,
> So that there thou mayest dance thy eternal dance . . .

As in Benares, I came back by night. The crowd was no more religious than it had been in the afternoon, but less busy-weary as the recumbent cattle on whose flanks the turtledoves cooed. Lit up by lamps, without its pools and towers, the temple became more fantastic and less sacred. Before the most venerated statue of Shiva, a group of pilgrims was praying aloud:

> I am here before thee to adore thee,
> O my god who art only myself . . .

It was still—in the opposite sense—the identity of the divine in man and in the universe which the afternoon prayer had expressed. The gravity of the latter seemed to have been replaced (was it an illusion of the darkness?) by a kind of hypnosis. But the Brahmans thrust all these sleepwalkers aside: it was the hour of the marriage of Shiva and Parvati. The subdued murmuring was drowned by the snarl of long medieval trumpets; then, as if the music were plunging deeper into time, the breathy percussion of the tambourines throbbing to the rhythm of the cosmic events ushered in the reed flute. The Brahmans carried Shiva in a black and silver palanquin which scattered the listless and wretched animals through the few sleeping figures. The cortege stopped before the statue of Parvati. Huge bats zigzagged overhead with ratlike squeaks. Illuminated by night lights, the stone lingams succeeded one another into the depths of the shadows. The plaintive reed took up again the yearning amorous melody which became modulated out on the huge ramparts and then fell silent. The marriage of Shiva and Parvati called forth silence and stars. Gently, over the dark towers, the Vedic night descended.

Soon I was to see it descend over Ellora. (It seemed that I was being drawn into a pilgrimage to Shiva: Benares, Madurai, Ellora, then Elephanta.) As in Egypt, as at Angkor, the ruins had been cleared of vegetation, which in the past had been powerfully wedded to the divinities of destruction. But these caves combine the effect of the mountain and of the crypt. The Kailas temples were not built; they were hewn out of the mountain. They are literally buried in the earth —and we have never seen a network of cathedrals at the bottom of a crevasse, without story levels, without towers, their ribbed vaults suggesting the thoracic cages of legendary monsters; whence, then, did this nagging memory of a cathedral come? From the sense of infinite space. The upper floors, buried in a crevasse on the Kailas side, from the other side overlook the immensity of the plain; although the plan of the temples is the work of geomancers, Ellora as a whole preserves the mystery of the original grottoes, the geological accident of a chaos pierced with openings. The darkest parts reminded me of Lascaux. Beyond a gallery where the half-light leads a jungle of figures toward the void, the sunlight poured down on a combat of monsters in diadems and gods in tiaras, whose multiple arms are tangled in a cataract of jewelry. The memory of the confusion at Madurai emphasized the

extent to which this statuary is controlled. The figures of the sacred
rivers, the *Ganga*, the *Jumna*, seem as if sculpted by the men who
fashioned the amphoras of the divine epics. The isolated flying genies
are written in flame. And in spite of Shiva, in spite of the terrible
mother-goddesses, this flame is not the flame of burning corpses. The
monsters and heroes of Ellora blaze on a pyre of red gladioli.

The greatest sculptors of these caves were seeking to grasp the un-
graspable better than or in a different way from their predecessors. "O
Lord, thou who takest on the forms imagined by thy faithful." But
the faithful do not invent the forms of the gods: they recognize them.
The prayer which applied here was more disturbing, and it is in fact
owed to a sculptor: "O Lord of all the gods, teach me *in dreams* how
to execute the works that are in my mind!" Not that Ellora is any more
oneiric than a lot of other temples, but what reigns there, and what
the Hindu prayer invokes is the immemorial world of archetypes and
of symbols, which pursues its nocturnal life through generations of
sleepers; just as the mind, for those who call upon these gods, pursues
its life through their own selves. Temples, statues, bas-reliefs are part
of the mountain, like an efflorescence of the divine. Hindu, Buddhist,
Jain, they evoke an unseen world which they do not seek to imitate
since its successive representations are all equally legitimate. The dialogue of the immutable Nirvana with the dances of the gods is self-
evident; the dance of Shiva which I contemplate is said to be that of
the Atman at the moment when death delivers it from the body, the
mind and the soul. And this dance, even in a museum, would not
belong to the world of art alone; its perfection, here, does not pertain
to art but to the enigmatically convincing realm of myth, of wild
things, of orchids. A work of the gods. Nowhere had I been so over-
whelmingly aware of how much all sacred art presupposes that those
to whom it is addressed take for granted the existence of a secret of
the world which art passes on without unveiling, and which it makes
them share. I was in the nocturnal garden of the great dreams of India.

The real night was coming. A dull green shadow was gathering in
the ravines of Kailas. I remembered Nehru and his Tibetan mountain:
"I shall never see Kailas again." In the cleft in the rock that forms the
entrance to the temple, the sun still glowed red on the wild mimosa
and the vast, dusty plain, as if reflected in the sea. We reached the
Buddhist caves, with their rows of ascetics "like motionless flames
sheltered from the wind"; then the Jain caves, and their Roman mas-
siveness. But Ellora was Shiva.

We were making our way toward the temple of Mahalinga—symbol of Shiva, and one of the eight sacred lingams of India. It was already completely dark. There was no temple, but a vast terrace, which one reached by way of a flight of steps that might have led to some ruined palace. The lingam was somewhere in the gloom. The muffled boom of the ritual conch rose up, followed by murmured hymns, and by a distant music. No doubt the temple was a little farther on, and as at Madurai, it was the hour of the marriage of Shiva and Parvati. The true place of worship was this void, these flagstones of the Ramayana appearing in the lantern's gleam, in the silence of a forest without beasts.

And yet, in the darkness haunted by royal and divine cosmogonies, there had never been a Creation. For the Fall, the Redemption, the Last Judgment that Christianity reveals, the world is a backdrop; for Brahmanism, man is an episode. Not only because of transmigration, but because the fabled cycles that divide the successive returns from the shades have the gods and the elements for heroes. India experiences the infinite as Job experiences the majesty of Jehovah. And the Kailas, and this empty terrace where for so long men had been talking of the gods, and these nocturnal hymns, were all communing with Being across the infinite as if they were worshiping the infinite—which happens upon man as it goes by. In the temple of Chidambaram, in the place where the god of the sanctuary ought to be, the Brahmans show you an empty circular space: "Here is Shiva dancing." In the center burns camphor, whose flame leaves no ashes.

At Ellora, maya finds its most profound expression, because there it seems to antedate the religions as the rock antedates the figures which those religions have each in their turn hewn out of it. And in Gandhi's eyes, as in those of the ascetics who greeted Prince Siddhartha in the forest, and in those of the Vedic poets who signed their hymns with the names of the gods, the favored means toward deliverance was detachment. The obstacle to Deliverance is not the vain spectacle of things, but the attachment we bear to them. Desire is the demon in a great many religions. And for Christianity, ever since the original sin, the demon has been in man; for India, attachment is in man in the shape of a metaphysical demon, not so much concupiscence as life itself, the enslavement of man, blind to the essence which transcends him, and by his blindness delivered over to the world of illusion. If all the gods were dead, maya would still exist, because the Hindu carries it within himself as the Christian carries sin. The irresistible agent of maya is not divine action, it is the human condition.

The hymns had stopped. The music of night began.

For centuries, India has distinguished the music of morning from the music of night, as we distinguish dance music from funeral music. As in the time of the great pilgrimages, and as in the time when the Kailas was buried beneath the jungle, at the appointed hour ephemeral man has sung the ephemeral stars. A light approached. Bearers of the camphor that is burned as an offering, some Brahmans were bringing flowers of welcome.

The town from which one reaches Ellora is Aurangabad, a Muslim city dominated by the tomb of Aurangzeb's wife, a rugged Taj Mahal amid rosebushes that have gone back to nature, which reminded me of the archaeological museum at Autun, a kitchen-garden with Celtic steles and Romanesque statues growing among the artichokes.

The town from which one reached Elephanta is Bombay.

Like Calcutta, Bombay, which was born in the nineteenth century, is not at all a modernized Indian town: it is a town as Anglo-Indian as Agra, Lahore, and Aurangabad are Indo-Muslim. The Red Fort, from whose gigantic gateway a woebegone camel emerged, the domes of marble and confectionery surrounded by woods full of squirrels, the Victorian Gothic buildings (inspired by what cathedrals?) bristling with outsize dentists' advertisements designed in the form of Sanskrit invocations, the dusty coconut palms overgrown with a jumble of old tires—all this blurred into a single derisory backdrop as soon as one entered the sacred caves. Their link with the bowels of the earth suggested an entire subterranean India, secretly watching over the India of the villages, the animals, the processions of urn-carrying women, the majestic trees, while the towns, chimerical and theatrical, made ready to return to dust. The caves of Ellora reign over the bare and unprepossessing plain which they overlook, while those of Elephanta seem hidden away in their island where the gulf shone with a Hellenic radiance, under the gulls of the Arabian Sea. But they are all united in their sacred darkness. As soon as one entered Elephanta, the glittering ocean was borne away, like the towns, like the India of the British Raj, the India of the Moguls, the India of Nehru—all perishable offerings to the famous Majesty, the gigantic triple head of Shiva.

Photographs, and even the cinema, give no idea of the scale. These heads, fifteen to twenty feet high, are smaller than those of the Bayon at Angkor; but, colossal in comparison to the figures around them, they fill the cave as the Pantocrator fills the Byzantine cathedrals of Sicily. Like the Pantocrator, this Shiva stops below the shoulders without becoming a bust. Hence its disturbing aspect of severed head and divine apparition. It is not simply a question of its being "one of the most beautiful statues in India," whatever meaning one may assign to the word "beautiful."

Here, recognizable at first glance, is a masterpiece of sculpture. A full face and two monumental profiles, whose planes (notably those of the eyes) are worthy of the very highest works of art in spite of a seductiveness which has more to do with the jewelry than with the faces.

But then there is Shiva, the cavernous gloom, the sense of the Sacred. This figure belongs, like those of Moissac, to the domain of the great symbols, and what this symbol expresses, it alone can express. This face with its eyes closed on the flow of time as on a funeral chant is to the dancing Shiva of Ellora what the latter is to the Dances of Death of the South, and even to the fabulous figures of Madurai.

Finally, as with many of the works which make up the treasury of humanity's imaginary museum, there is the conjunction of the artistic effect of the work, its religious effect and another, unforeseeable, effect. The effect of the Pharaoh Zoser arises from the fact that the weathering of the stone has turned it into a death's head, that of the Winged Victory from the fact that fate has devised the perfect mythical creature which men have looked for in vain in the angels: wings being the arms of birds, the Victory is perfect only without arms. The famous line that runs from the point of the breast to the tip of the wing was born of this amputation. The perfection (in this sense) of Shiva demanded the sacred gloom, the absence of a body, even a dancing one, the two profiles still embedded in the mountain, the mask with closed eyes—but above all the unique creation by which the Shiva of Elephanta is also the symbol of India.

In the neighboring cave, they were chanting verses from the Bhaga-vad-Gita. It is familiar to all Hindus. It was recited during Gandhi's funeral wake, and during the fourteen hours of the cremation. Mysteriously in harmony with the subterranean temple, with the colossal Shiva, it seemed the very voice of this sanctuary to which it owed nothing.

Then, standing in their great chariot drawn by white horses,
Krishna and Arjuna sounded their sacred conches . . .
And Arjuna, filled with deep compassion, spoke despairingly . . .

The two legendary armies of India are face to face. The old king whom Arjuna is fighting against is blind. His charioteer has the magical power of knowing what is happening on the battlefield. He hears the

194 ::   ANTI-MEMOIRS

dialogue begin, in the midst of the enemy army, in the chariot with the white horses, between Prince Arjuna and his charioteer, who is Krishna and will become the supreme Deity. The *Gita* is divine speech reported by magic to a blind Priam enclosed in his darkness.

Arjuna looks at those who are to die, and Krishna reminds him that if the greatness of man is to free himself from fate, it is not for the warrior to free himself from courage. It is the fratricidal combat of the epics, and for us the Trojan sadness of Arjuna seems like the desolate echo of the voice of Antigone:

> *Krishna, I see such omens of evil!*
> *What can we hope from this killing of kinsmen?*
> *What do I want with victory, empire,*
> *Or their enjoyment?*
> *How can I care for power or pleasure,*
> *My own life, even?*

The chanting voice was answered by another, as Krishna answers Arjuna in the poem.

> *Your words are wise, Arjuna, but your sorrow is for nothing.*
> *The truly wise mourn neither for the living or the dead.*
> *There never was a time when I did not exist, nor you,*
>   *nor any of these kings.*
> *Nor is there any future in which we shall cease to be . . .*

This chant began the Revelation which my companions knew by heart, accompanied in the darkness by the distant surge of the ocean and streaked with the cries of gulls: the song of the Deity who transcends, animates, and destroys worlds, and of the spirit which transmigrates through bodies and souls, the Atman:

> *Know this Atman, unborn, undying,*
> *Never ceasing, never beginning,*
> *Deathless, birthless, unchanging for ever.*
> *How can it die the death of the body?*
> *Worn-out garments are shed by the body:*
> *Worn-out bodies are shed by the dweller*
> *Within the body . . .*

I had heard this last stanza at Benares. Here it had shed its funereal overtones; and what followed took on among these unseeing gods an even greater solemnity than among the funeral pyres:

> There is a day, also, and night in the universe:
> The wise know this, declaring the day of Brahma
> A thousand ages in span
> And the night a thousand ages.
> Day dawns, and all those lives that lay hidden asleep
> Come forth and show themselves, mortally manifest:
> Night falls, and all are dissolved
> Into the sleeping germ of life . . .
> And all creatures exist within me:
> As the vast air, wandering worldwide,
> Remains within the ether always,
> So these, my wandering creatures,
> Are always within me . . .
> . . . I am Being and non-Being, immortality and death . . .

One of my companions answered the distant chant with one of the most celebrated verses of the poem, and his voice reached across the enormous pillars, muffled and yet carried by the low roof of the caves:

> Who can kill immortality? . . .

For the chanting priests, was this response rising out of the silence as mysteriously natural as my wish for the poor couple at Madurai had been? They had fallen silent. At Benares, I had reread the *Gita*. From its subterranean depths, from all that it owes to an earlier Brahmanism, there emerged dimly, like the figures in these caves, the divine sermon of love which Brahmanism scorned, and above all the cosmic stoicism to which the poem owes its fame. In the inexorable march of constellations which is the return to the source, man is united with God when he discovers his identity with Him and when he observes the Law, which is caste duty. Action is necessary, because the divine scheme must be fulfilled: it is not you who are about to kill your kinsmen, says Krishna to Arjuna, it is I. And action is purified of life if man is sufficiently in communion with God to offer it up to him as a sacrifice.

..... *Because they understood this, the ancient seekers for*
   liberation
Could safely engage in action . . . .
There is nothing, in all the three worlds,
Which I do not already possess;
Nothing I have yet to acquire.
But I go on working, nevertheless . . .
Realize that pleasure and pain, gain and loss, victory
And defeat, are all one and the same: then go into battle . . .

For my companions, this famous moment was an eternal moment.
Yet the sculptures all around me in the shadow, and the Gita itself,
expressed not so much the sacred stoicism of the last verses as the
communion with God into which the metaphysical austerity had transformed itself: the mystique which Brahmanism, like Buddhism, Christianity, and Islam, had discovered. Even if the verses of communion
had not been recited in another cave, the metamorphosis of faith would
have been present here as palpably as it is in St. Peter's in Rome when
one remembers our cathedrals there. India is obsessed by the image of
the ever-changing waters of the changeless rivers, and the successive
souls of its religion passed before Shiva as did its ancient armies before
the sacrificial pyres. The Old Testament of the Upanishads had become
the New Testament of the Gita. In the depths of time, there was the
hymn to Kali:

   Thou, Mother of Blessings,
   Thou, terrible Night, Night of delusion, Night of death,
   We greet thee.

And, well after Elephanta, the parable of prayer:

"*I pray in vain,*" said the daughter of the disciple to the Master.
"*What do you love best in the world?*" "*My brother's little child.*"
"*Retire and meditate on him alone, and you will see that he is Krishna.*
Only love can cure the blind."

The meditation of the colossal heads of the Majesty on eternity and
time, twin prisoners of the Sacred, also seemed like a meditation on
the destiny which guides religions from veneration to love as it guides
mortals from birth to death—but beneath which there remained an
inviolable permanence. If the Bhagavad-Gita is present in so many holy

places, it is because it expresses this; like the *Majesty*, it is India. Gandhi had tried to translate it. The greatest of the Renouncers of modern times regarded action carried out in the spirit of surrender to his God as the supreme form of renunciation. "My devotion to my people is one of the aspects of the discipline I impose upon myself in order to liberate my soul. I have no need to seek refuge in a cave: I carry my cave inside myself."

> *Certain is death for all who shall be born,*
> *And certain is birth for all who have died . . .*

Night falls on the dead of the final combat, after the seventeen-day battle. The few survivors have withdrawn into the forest to die there as ascetics. The patient birds of prey are waiting, and among the fallen swords glittering in the moonlight, monkeys like those which accompanied me at Madurai touch the eyes of the dead with puzzled fingers.

Girls were passing by outside, each with a red flower in her hand. The gulls of Oman still wheeled across the sparkling gulf. A motorboat took us back. Bombay, a crazy bazaar that thinks itself a town, rose little by little above the water, and we made our way toward the enormous archway of the Gateway to the East. Once it watched over the English steamships like a marine temple over a war fleet. Today, ours was the only boat to berth there—back from the India of eternity. On the waterfront, atomic reactors glittered.

We were to return to Delhi overnight. For the evening, the former bungalow of the governor at the tip of the peninsula had been put at my disposal. It was a sad place, like all the uninhabited houses on the shores of the gulf. The garden, still more uninhabited in spite of a few silent gardeners, seemed like a cemetery of Indian army officers. And the Indian army was as remote as Akbar's horsemen.

The passion which Asia, vanished civilizations, and ethnography have long inspired in me arose from an essential wonderment at the forms which man has been able to assume, but also from the light which every strange civilization threw on my own, that quality of the unusual or the arbitrary which it revealed in one or other of its aspects. I had just relived one of the most profound and complex experiences of my youth. More so than my first encounter with pre-Hispanic America, because England did not destroy the priests and warriors of India and because temples are still built there to the ancient gods. More so than Islam and Japan, because India is less Westernized, because it spreads more widely the nocturnal wings of man; more so than Africa because of its elaboration, its continuity. Remote from ourselves in dream and in time, India belongs to the Ancient Orient of our soul. The last rajahs are not pharaohs, but the Brahmans of Benares evoke the priests of Isis, the fakirs were there in Alexander's time, and the peacocks in the derelict palaces of Amber had called to my mind the Chaldean multitude, astounded by the ambassadors from the kingdoms of India "whose birds could spread their tails." And this other Egypt, whose people and beliefs had changed little since the time of Ramses, was perhaps the last religious civilization, certainly the last great polytheism. What is Zeus, compared with Shiva? The only god of antiquity whose language is worthy of India is the god without temples—Fate.

What did I really know of this civilization? Its arts, its thought, its history. No more than I knew of the great dead civilizations—except that I had heard its music and had met a few gurus, which was not without importance in a land whose religious thinking expresses a Truth which is not to be understood but lived. "Believe nothing that you have not first experienced." I was not presumptuous enough to "know" (on the way through) a way of thought that had survived seventeen conquests and two millennia; I merely sought to grasp something of its haunting message.

Man can experience the presence of universal Being in all beings, and of all beings in universal Being; he discovers then the identity of all appearances, whether they be pleasure and pain, life and death, outside himself and within Being; he can reach that essence in himself which transcends his transmigrated souls, and experience its identity with the essence of a world of endless returning, which he escapes through his ineffable communion with it. But there is something at once bewitching and bewitched in Indian thought, which has to do with the feeling it gives us of climbing a sacred mountain whose summit constantly recedes; of going forth in darkness by the light of the torch which it carries. We know this feeling through some of our saints and philosophers; but it is in India alone that Being, conquered from universal appearance and metamorphosis, does not part company with them, but often becomes inseparable from them "like the two sides of a medal," to point the way to an inexhaustible Absolute which even transcends Being itself.

Of course, the word "being" is not a satisfactory rendering of the "uncreated" Brahman, the supreme Deity—to which the wise man gains access through what is deepest in his soul, and not through the mind. The gods are merely different means of reaching it, and "each man approaches God through his own gods." It is *It* that the Buddha seeks to destroy in his earliest teachings, when he gives as the final end of ecstasy what he magnificently calls "the peace of the abyss."

Superstitions swarmed like mayflies around this peak of thought, which animated all the temples I had seen, as well as Benares. But how inadequately it illuminated the vast nation that surrounded me! I had met men of the Brahman caste, but no priests; intellectuals, artists, diplomats—and their wives; a few great figures, and many politicians, a race unknown at the beginning of the century. Not a single tradesman, not a single peasant. Alone in this melancholy garden of an enormous city looking out over the most religious and surely the most affectionate country in the world, I could recall only an immense and silent multitude—as silent as its friendly animals. A Hindu rather than an Indian crowd: its fields resembled French fields, but its dreams did not resemble French dreams. But what I evoked by way of contrast (more precisely, what was evoked in me) was not a Christian crowd; it was the crowd of the Paris *métro*, and more especially the one I had known best, that of the war. The spirituality of India made me think fleetingly of the Glières chaplain, but the Hindu multitudes, for whom death gives a meaning to life, made me think with bitterness of the men of our own land for whom death has no meaning: the shadowy figures who for centuries had laid a scarlet hibiscus at the foot of a dark god or of a tree reminiscent of a divine benediction, brothers of the peasants in whom I perceived only the sad smile that had perhaps greeted Semiramis, the little tradesmen, brothers of so many other little tradesmen, spoke to me of all our own men without caste whom I had seen in the face of death.

Beyond the garden where the sound of the waves was inaudible, the gulf still glittered; the gulls of Oman would wheel back and forth until nightfall. I went inside the deserted bungalow of the last governor of Bombay, to reread what I wrote in 1940 about my comrades who fought and died in vain.

2

1940. A road that is always the same, bordered by trees that are always the same, and the stones of Flanders always as hard under the tracks of our tanks. The boredom of convoys on the roads across the plain. Our last road of boredom; from now on, it would be either excitement or fear: we were moving up to the front. Our attention burned with the faint glimmer of a night-light in the stupefying heat, the din of the engines and the hammering of the tracks which seemed to be pounding on our heads as much as on the road. I knew what our faces looked like when we got out of the tanks after a long stretch, the flaccid features and fluttering eyes of men who have been bludgeoned, clowns' faces under our lansquenet helmets.

Around us, the boundless Flemish night. Behind us, nine months of barracks and billets; the time it takes to make a man.

Nine months earlier, I was in a hotel in Quercy. The maids could not keep away from the radio. They were old women. One morning, I had passed two of them on the stairs, pattering up to their rooms with tears streaming down their long-suffering faces. That was how I learned that the German army had entered Poland.

In the afternoon, I had seen the call-up notices in Beaulieu. The church of Beaulieu has one of the finest of all Romanesque tympanums, the only one in which, behind the arms of Christ stretched out to embrace the world, the sculptor has depicted the arms of the cross like a prophetic shadow. A tropical downpour had flooded the village. In front of the church there is a statue of the Virgin; as they had done every year for five hundred years to celebrate the wine harvest, the peasants had fastened one of the finest bunches of grapes to the Infant's hand. In the deserted square, the peeling notices were beginning to droop; the raindrops on the bunch of grapes slid from grape to grape and plopped lightly into the middle of a puddle, one after the other, in the silence.

Our tanks drove on toward the German lines. There were four of us in ours. Nothing to do but follow this road through the night and draw closer to the war. Was it tonight that we were to die?

I had seen them leave by the thousands, at the beginning of September, anonymous men like my three comrades: five million men had reported to barracks without a word.

In the square at Moulins, the loudspeakers had announced the first skirmishes. Night was falling. Two or three thousand conscripts listened, awkward in their new uniforms because they were new, or in their old ones because they were dirty: not one of them said a word. Along every road, the men had set out to report for duty and the heavyhearted women had led the horses off to be requisitioned, with the resignation of peasants in the face of natural disaster: they were advancing to meet the scourge. It was in much the same spirit that my three companions were now driving through the night along this dismal road toward the German tanks and guns.

Bonneau, the mechanic, was sure to be away from his post. (In all the tanks driving one after another along the nocturnal road, there was not a single mechanic who had not left his engines: to hell with regulations!) Since none of us could hear him, he was probably talking to himself, his monologue drowned by the pounding of the tracks.

When he arrived at the squadron under police escort, unshaven, leather-jacketed, he looked so tough that the captain had put him under the orders of a professional boxer. This man reacted to the assignment of Bonneau with a slight nervous panic. I have seldom seen true courage among devotees of pugilism.

In any case there were no fisticuffs. Simply, at the outset, a certain uneasiness. Bonneau had arrived dressed like a pimp, accustomed to inspiring either contempt or fear, and the more eager to inspire fear the more he met with contempt. But soldiers are not given to contempt, and when Bonneau stuck out his jaw and asked, "What d'you mean by looking at me like that?" the only answer he got was a vague, "Me? Wasn't even looking at you at all."

He claimed to have killed a man in a brawl, which was probably a lie because he would have been assigned to a disciplinary squad. But the word soon got round that his record contained three convictions for assault. The working class are much less susceptible than the bourgeoisie to the romance of murder: in their eyes, the murderer is only a particular species, like the wolf. What interested them was whether Bonneau really belonged to the species, whether "all that stuff was genuine or phony."

The only one who believed in this romance was he himself. Stories about jail, stories about pimping, remarks about "wanting to let his beard grow" so as to be given permission not to shave and thereby preserve a real bruiser's look, and the back-street accent, and the songs of indignation during the latrine duties to which he was more or less permanently condemned. The child of misfortune. When the whole squadron was crowded together on the stairs waiting for the issue of boots, we suddenly heard *Le Légionnaire*, then a monologue beginning: "I had a great broad once—I really went for her. Those bastards killed her." One gathered it was something to do with a hospital in which "they" were at the same time the doctors and all law-abiders; and his wary roommates, though digging each other in the ribs like schoolboys at the class joker, devised complicated schemes to make sure that he was never allowed to be barrack-room orderly. They were learning something of the folklore of the low-class music hall: the victim of society because of drink or sex; the refractory member of the disciplinary squad; the outlaw fighting singlehanded against an entire police force in some Fort Chabrol;* the Bonnot† (and ours was certainly not unaware that his own name was almost identical) who shoots the commissioner of police through the arm; but above all the gallant, soulful pimp, tough but straight, faithful to friends and murdering for love, who escapes from the penal colony and ends his saturnine existence among the alligators of the Maroni River. For Bonneau's hell, whether its damned were heroic or pathetic, had only one circle, and that was a circle of victims.

When he had brought in an injured chaffinch and claimed that he was going to rear it, fear of him had grown; in the eyes of my companions, all murderers were primarily madmen.

The stricter the lights-out regulations, the more ingenious was the camouflage in each barrack-room. The NCO's removed the bulbs, but when the time came, other bulbs would be produced from under pillows. One evening, when two plugs failed to work, Bonneau claimed that he "knew about electricity," fought a clandestine battle against the building's wiring system, and did so well that he blew all the fuses in his own barrack-room and in four others. Growls could be heard in the darkness: "How did we get stuck with a jerk like that!" "Just what we need—that kind of nut." "I'm an electrician, but I wouldn't fiddle with that unless I was told, and now this bastard . . ." From the way the door of the first barrack-room slammed, everybody realized it was Bonneau coming back: silence fell at once. Then a muffled squabble began and a voice stood out, very precise, calm and harsh, and not the

---

* Nickname given to the headquarters in the rue de Chabrol in Paris of a right-wing extremist group whose leader, Jules Guérin, held out there against the police for over a month in 1899. (Tr.)

† Joseph Bonnot was the leader of an anarchist gang who indulged in some fairly spectacular mayhem (bank robberies accompanied by indiscriminate shootings) before being rounded up in 1912. The *bande à Bonnot* has something of the same legendary reputation as Bonnie and Clyde. (Tr.)

voice of the boxer corporal: "Look, Bonneau, we're beginning to get a bit fed up with you. I don't give a shit for tough guys. But if they're going to mess up my bulb, they better look out. And if you don't like it, here's my face." (A face loomed up, brightly lit by a flashlight.) "Now if you want to look for me tomorrow morning you won't have any trouble finding me."

It was the first time I had heard Pradé speak.

And Bonneau began to explain in the darkness that it "wasn't his fault," that "the current . . . that the fuses, etc. . . ." I was expecting everyone to say that he was afraid, but the general impression was that "he had taken it pretty well, that he was okay, that he didn't keep on when he knew he was in the wrong . . ." So he was not so mad after all. The squadron was almost ready to adopt him; but the barrack-room remained without light.

A tank driver who had been a bus driver in civilian life started to sing *Le P'tit Quinquin*. There were a good many soldiers from French Flanders there, but it was not nostalgia that gave the music its power, it was the slow tempo. He made a dirge out of it, and just as he reproduced the true funereal rhythm, he also reproduced the appropriate nasal timbre, as though in this darkness a miserable voice was enough to give a song of misery its full meaning. And the soldiers asked for verse after verse, just as they asked for glass after glass in the canteen, determined to get drunk as a protest against this war which to them was like a prison.

Tired of this inglorious music, the singer began the great aria from *Tosca*. An embarrassed silence followed the final howls; the driver muttered angrily, "All right then, if it doesn't please you gentlemen!" and went back to bed, and to the sadness of the first song was added the uneasy feeling of a bond of sympathy having been broken. Bonneau was forgotten. Each of them sank into his own individual dejection. Which of them was the first to take his wife's photograph out of his wallet, to gaze at it by the clandestine glow of a torch? Five minutes later, pictures were being passed around among little groups, four or five forage caps round a dim light, amateur snapshots dropping from thick fingers onto the straw amid shouts of abuse. None of them in fact gave a damn about the others' wives, and only looked at them in order to be able to show their own. And yet, in this intimate light, they seemed like shared secrets, their dresses suddenly suggesting the husbands' lives much better than their own photographs in civilian clothes would have done. Pradé's was a housewife carved out of solid wood, her hair parted down the middle and combed flat. Bonneau alone had photographs of four women, each of them more of a whore than the last. And little beetroot-nosed Léonard—the radioman in our tank—shy and rather reluctant, finally produced a postcard of a gorgeous girl in a dazzling feathered dress. There were a few words written at the bottom. And the roommates, heads glued together under Léonard's nose, which was lit up fantastically from below, bent over the flashlight and deciphered, "To my darling little Louis," and the signature of a star of the music halls.

Léonard had been a fireman at the Casino de Paris. Every night with undiminished admiration he would watch the star come off stage, flushed with applause. He had never spoken to her. His face was not unattractive in spite of his extraordinary nose: soft spaniel eyes and the poignancy that sometimes characterizes an expression completely devoid of conceit. Had the dancer been touched by this untiring devotion? Had it been a whim on her part? One very successful night, "when you could still hear the cheering even on the way upstairs," she had taken him to her dressing room and slept with him. "Then, the best part of it was . . . when we were in bed, she suddenly sees my uniform on the chair, and she says to me, like she was going to jump out of her skin, 'Hey, you're not a policeman, are you?' 'Of course not, I'm a fireman.' 'Because if you were . . .' That's a good one, isn't it? She used to see me every night and she didn't even recognize the fireman's uniform. We're soldiers too. Of course I was younger in those days."

Each of them had his own dream, Marlene Dietrich, or Mistinguett, or the Duchess of Windsor; but it remained a dream. And they did not look on this pal of theirs to whom the fairies had spoken—the simpleton of the barrack-room—merely as a lucky dog, but as a man of destiny: the little frizzled head with the red nose was to them proof of the mysterious side of love; what fascinated them about the actress's whim, without their knowing it, was Isolde's love potion.

"Well then, what happened afterward?" they asked in chorus, and their fingers trembled as they handled the photograph once more.

"She never gave another sign, so then I realized . . ."

He spoke without bitterness, even without resignation; he was in agreement. To the general approval. Their heredity had not made my companions offhand about happiness.

Not surprisingly, the greatest success after Léonard's postcard were Bonneau's four photographs. The latter was decidedly becoming one of the boys. And gradually, seeing him bend down during a march to pick up an old knife and put it in his knapsack, and then start a fresh lecture, "A tool like that could be dangerous," invariably ending up with, "It'll come in handy," they had realized that this fire-eater was only a ragpicker man; and you know where you are with them. Then again, time had brought out another person, a respecter of priests: "My old lady didn't teach me much, but she did teach me to have some respect for those people! Why did the state take everything they had away from them? Robbery, that's what I call it. It's the Rothschilds, the bankers, that bunch, who did it; it's always the poor that get robbed!" He sported the Ruhr Occupation Medal, worshiped Captain de Mortemart ("who I was in the Hussars with in Strasbourg, not like these fat-heads here, but someone who knew how to command, who could take off his stripes and tell a guy to step outside"), and was quite ready, if he were made a corporal, to think of himself as a model soldier, kindhearted and hardheaded, yet without abandoning his righteous indignation. A member of the employers' federation, and a respecter of respectability. "Now then, Bonneau," the lieutenant had said, "you're not as bad as you like to make out." "Me, sir? I'm not bad! It's the others who've made me like that." And with his thick lips thrust out, his black eyebrows lifted, it seemed as if his "holy terror's" mask had been suddenly snatched off to reveal an incurably infantile soul.

He bore no grudge against Pradé for what he had said. We were members of the same tank crew and often went to the canteen together; as soon as Bonneau started holding forth, Pradé would shrug his shoulders, look at him, and remain silent. Bonneau would begin to stutter, realizing that he was face to face with a different species—one that never daydreams.

One day we were together like this over a bottle of red wine after coming out of a lecture to which we had been sent in columns of four to learn from a likable young lieutenant why it was necessary to dismember Germany. Pradé, as inscrutable as the orientals whose flat features and slanting eyes he shared, said without looking at me, with his Lorrainer's accent and slow delivery:

"It's about what you were asking the boys—what they thought of the youngster with the stripes and that speech of his. If you ask Pradé, he figures that talking to soldiers is one thing and talking to French citizens is another. As a soldier, I'm prepared to listen to anything; I've heard it all before. But if someone addresses me as a citizen, then it's not the same thing. It's not the same thing at all!" Whenever he spoke, he seemed to be furiously answering some invisible liar. "In that case, I don't like people trying to force me to think. Or telling me a load of garbage. I know those Fritzes. When they came to our town in '15 everyone was in the cellars. They banged on the doors with their rifle-butts; I was a kid, and I was sent to open up. I was shaking like this. Some of them belted us, some of them gave us bread. It's the same all over."

He repeated, his toothless jaw jutting out, still furious with the imaginary liar, "It's the same all over!"

And he added in the same tone of voice, "And *they* don't take the trouble to talk about citizens!"

Often I felt that the soldiers I was living with were of another age. Listening to Pradé, I seemed to hear the ancient voice of republican dignity, a voice that had scarcely changed for a hundred years. He had taken me into his confidence, and told me that one of his brothers, a hothead, had come back from the International Brigade in Spain. "And when you come back from there, take it from Pradé, it's no use looking for a job." But one day he came looking for me and said, still in the same slow voice and that accent that seemed as though he were emphasizing everything with his fist, "The captain's orderly's leaving. Being an orderly in the army isn't such a bad job." I waited. Whenever he came looking for me like this, starting off with some general state-ment, it was to ask for help or advice. He went on, "There's nothing worse than an officer."

"So why put yourself in his clutches, especially doing a servant's job?"

"Who isn't a servant here? I can tell you that if you're an orderly you have more to do with the wife than with the boss himself. A steady man who does his job—who does his job, mind you—a man like that can manage to get some peace. With an officer and everyone else there is between him and us, you never get any peace. A woman's only a woman—anyway she doesn't wear stripes!"

Reluctant to use the word "dignity," I beat about the bush; but he used it at once: "If a man's got dignity, then he'll have it wherever he is; otherwise I say he hasn't got any at all."

His son was the only positive element in this dismal and degrading adventure called life. When he asked me if I thought it would be a long war, it was not because he wanted to know how long he would be in the army: "The youngster's eleven—a little older than I was in the last one. That's what stopped me getting an education. They managed to send me to catechism class all right, but not to school. He's a brainy kid, really brainy. He'd have got a scholarship. But what's happened to all the scholarships, with this war on? If he was to go on with his studies I'd have to work, and the only work I'm doing is hacking around with a gun. And afterward, if he misses two years, there'll be nothing we can do, it'll be too late. He's the first one in the family who could have had an education. There's no getting away from it, at that age a kid's got to have some guidance. I could still give it to him. After the certificate, I couldn't manage, but now I could, except for spelling. I learned arithmetic on purpose. I can help him all right. But what can the wife do? She comes from a big family."

And in the peremptory tone he often adopted, tinged with melancholy this time: "She's not very smart."

It was he who was driving. And although our tanks were fairly recent, the intercom did not operate between the tank commander and the driver; we were connected by two strings attached to his arms, which I held in my hands.

In spite of the din of the tracks, we suddenly seemed to have plunged into silence: the tanks had just turned off the road. Like a boat released from a sandbank, or an aircraft taking off, we were entering our own element; our muscles, tensed by the vibration of the armor-plating, by the ceaseless pounding of the tracks on the road, now relaxed in harmony with the peaceful moonlight.

We rolled on like that for a minute, set free, through orchards in blossom and banks of mist. In the smell of castor oil and burning rubber I nervously held on to my strings, ready to stop the tank in order to fire: it was pitching too much, even in these apparently smooth fields, for it to be possible to take aim on the move. Since we had left the road, and the occasional shapes we could now make out might be potential targets, we were all the more conscious of the way we were swaying like an angular galley. Clouds hid the moon. We were entering the cornfields.

This was the moment when the war would begin.

There is no word to describe the sensation of advancing on the enemy, and yet it is as specific and as powerful as sexual desire or pain. The whole world becomes an undifferentiated menace. We were steering by compass, and could only distinguish what was outlined against the sky: telegraph poles, roofs, treetops; the orchards, scarcely more distinct than the mists, had disappeared, the darkness seemed to gather at ground level in these cornfields which alternately swayed or jolted us; if a track should break, we would be dead men or prisoners. I knew how intensely Pradé's slanting eyes were watching his dashboard, and I could feel the strings tickling my hand every other second, as if about to warn me with a jerk. And we were not yet in contact. The war awaited us a little farther on, perhaps behind that rising ground bristling with concrete telegraph poles, phosphorescent in the moonlight which had just come out again.

The dim outlines of the nocturnal plain, the banks of mist looming up again a dazzling white, rose and fell with each forward heave of the tank. Against the harsh, shuddering movement, against the frenzied vibrations when we hit a patch of hard ground between cornfields, our bodies were hunched up as in a car at the moment of an accident; I was clinging to the turret not so much with my hands as with the muscles of my back. If the furious vibrations cracked one of the gas feedlines, the tank would be left waiting for the shells while spinning round on itself like an epileptic cat. But the tracks still crunched over the fields and the stones, and through the slits in the turret, beyond what I could see of the young corn, the mist and the orchards, I watched the horizon, as yet unstreaked by a single gun flash, rise and fall against the night sky.

The German positions were ahead of us. From the front, we were only vulnerable through the viewfinder and the shield of the gun. We had faith in our armor. The enemy was not the Germans, it was a broken track, a mine, or a tank trap.

Especially the last. We did not talk about mines any more than we talked about death; one was either blown up or not—it was not a subject for conversation. Tank traps were: we had heard stories from the last war—and in training we had seen modern tank traps, sloping inward at the bottom to prevent the tank from lifting its nose, their four antitank guns automatically set off by the impact. There was not one of us who had not imagined himself caught in the crossfire of four antitank guns at the moment when they were about to open up. And the range of traps was vast, from this instant death-dealer to the hastily camouflaged pit where the falling tank only set off a signal for a heavy gun trained on it from a distance—down to a simple ditch.

Nothing remained of the old harmony between man and earth: these cornfields through which we were lurching in the night were no longer cornfields but camouflage; the earth no longer bred crops, but traps and mines; and it seemed as though the tank was crawling of its own accord toward some self-laid trap, as though the species of the future had tonight embarked on their own battle, independently of the human adventure.

On a low hill a few purple flashes appeared at last in quick succession: the German heavy artillery. Had their brief flicker been merged with the moonlight, or had the barrage just begun? It stretched mainly from our right to our left, as far as our swaying turrets let us see, like a huge match being struck along the horizon. But near us there was not a single explosion. Our engines drowned all noise: we must have left the cornfields, for the angry clang of the tracks had begun to hammer at us again. I signaled a halt for a moment.

Out of the sudden overwhelming silence rose the thudding of the German gunfire, which was carried away on the wind. And the same wind brought to my ears, still faintly echoing with our own uproar, beneath the sporadic shell bursts behind us and the quick clatter of the tracks of our immediate neighbors, a deep forest murmur, a rustling of great curtains of poplars: the advance of the invisible French tanks through the depths of the night.

The firing stopped. Behind us, then in front, an occasional shell still exploded, and as the crimson flash faded, an expectant silence rose again, filled with the dim rumble of our tanks advancing.

We moved off again, forcing the pace to catch up with our invisible group. The hammering of the tracks had begun again and once more we were deafened, Pradé and I glued once more to the armor-plating and the control levers, our eyes painfully on the lookout for a gush of stones and earth followed by a fiery explosion which we would not hear. Pools of stars between enormous clouds drifted on the wind toward the German lines.

Nothing seems slower than moving into battle. To our left, in the May mist, the other two tanks of our group were advancing; beyond them, other groups; still farther beyond, and to the rear, all the sections were moving into position in the moonlight. Léonard and Bonneau, blind against the armor-plating, knew it as well as Pradé glued to his periscope and myself glued to my viewing slits; I could feel it in my very bones, as I could feel the grip of the tracks in the rich soil— the parallel thrust of the tanks through the night. Ahead of us, other tanks were advancing against us through the same clear night; men equally tense, equally absorbed. To my left, the bows of our tanks rose and fell dimly against the lighter background of the cornfields. Behind them came the half-tracks, and the serried masses of the French infantry. The peasants whom I had seen silently marching off to the army along every road in France at the beginning of September were now converging on this squadron of tanks gliding ominously across the Flemish plain. Ah, might victory rest with those who went to war without any love for it!

Suddenly every nearby shape disappeared, except for the treetops; at ground level nothing was visible; our accompanying tanks were enveloped in darkness. A cloud must have blotted out the moon, which was now too high in the sky for me to see it through the viewing slits. And once again we thought of the mines toward which this movement of oiled gears was leading us through the springy cornfields, and the friendly shadows round us vanished. Cut off from everything that was not Pradé, Léonard, Bonneau, myself: a single crew—alone.

The hand of Léonard, the radio man, appeared between my hip and the turret, and deposited a piece of paper beside the compass. I switched on the light and my eyes, half-blinded by the glare, eventually deciphered, letter by letter through the scarlet suns: "Tank B-21 encountered tank trap."

Pradé switched off the light. Through the gaps in the clouds, the moonlight came and went across the stretch of plain. Our tanks loomed up a little behind us: we had overtaken them. Then, a hundred yards ahead, a melodramatic burst of shells, whose impact could be felt through the vibration of our armor-plating. The smoke, which for a moment looked red, curled in the wind and drifted, black and opaque, in the moonlight.

More explosions. Not very numerous. It was not even a barrage. Our squadron advanced faster, but not yet at full throttle. What was the point of this scattered bombardment? Were the Germans short of artillery? I switched my eyes back to the dimly luminous compass, and pulled one of the strings, correcting Pradé's steering: the tank was drifting off course on a surface which had become hard and uneven. Suddenly we were sliding forward in panic, sucked in by the earth.

It is not true that one sees the whole of one's past life on the point of death.

Below me, someone was yelling, "Bonneau?"

Léonard, his arms flung round my legs, shouted, "Pradé! Pradé!"

Through my thighs, I could hear his high-pitched yells like the cries of a bird in the cataclysmic silence which had overwhelmed us as soon as Pradé, sensing our fall, had jammed on the brakes.

The tank trap.

The sound of the engine starting up again drowned our voices.

Pradé drove the sloping tank forward.

"Reverse! Reverse!"

I pulled the right-hand string with all my strength: it broke. The shells I had seen falling intermittently were from the artillery trained on the pinpointed antitank ditches. The earth was ringing with the noise of living tanks advancing all around our dead one.

Pradé had only been getting a run-up, and was now in reverse. How many seconds before the shell? We had drawn our heads into our shoulders, at the limits of our endurance. Tilting alarmingly forward, its tail in the air like a Japanese fish, the tank backed out, buried its rear at an angle in the wall of the ditch, vibrating from end to end like an ax quivering in a treetrunk. It slipped, fell back again. Was it blood or sweat running down my nose? We had fallen slantwise. Bonneau, who was still yelling, tried to open the side door, managed to do so, then shut it again. Now it opened practically underneath the tank. One of the tracks was thrashing the empty air; Pradé heaved the tank around on the other one, and it fell head first again, as though it were crashing into a second ditch. My helmet clanged against the turret, and I felt as if my head was swelling and swelling, although anticipation of a shell still drove it into my shoulders like a nail. If the bottom of the ditch was soft, we were bogged down, and the shell could take its time. No, the tank moved forward, reversed, started off again. A modern tank trap wedges a tank in, and the intersecting antitank guns should have fired already; so we must have fallen into a pinpointed ditch. If the wall in front was vertical or sloping, perhaps we might get out (but before that, the shell); if we were in a crater, we would never get out, never get out, never get out. This invisible wall must be quite close. Bonneau, hysterical with fright, kept opening and shutting the door with all his strength, and in spite of the din of the engine in this hole, the armor-plating was ringing like a bell. Why had the shell not come? Léonard let go of my legs and started kicking them furiously. He wanted to open the door of my turret. The shell would burst in the pit; one cannot get out of a pit; to rush out of the tank would be even more idiotic than to stay paralyzed inside it, between one madman trying to break one's legs and another, crazy with fear both of getting out and of staying inside, beating out a sinister tattoo of delirium by continually slamming the door. I left the turret and bent down to move toward Pradé, who suddenly switched on the lights. Now the shell would not come; they don't kill you in the light, they only kill you in the dark.

While I was stooping to get into the interior of the tank, Léonard had slipped into the turret in my place; at last he pushed open the door, then stopped, his mouth open; he did not jump out, but crouched down suddenly and turned toward me without saying a word; terror left his head still but his shoulders were shaking against the black background of the door opening on to the pit. The tracks were not gripping. We were in a crater. On hands and knees I made my way toward Pradé, pushing Bonneau out of the way as he sat there still yelling and slamming the side door. As I went by, I shouted, "Shut up!"

"Me? I didn't say anything," he replied in his ordinary voice, which I recognized in spite of the roar of the engine. He was looking at me with the restless eyes and trembling features of a child who expects a slap in the face. He got up, banging his helmet against the roof of the tank, and fell back on to his knees. His movie villain's face had taken on a sort of horrifying innocence in the face of death.

"I didn't say anything," he repeated (at the same time, like me, like all of us, he was listening for, waiting for the shell); then, slamming the door again, he fixed his eyes on mine and, with his hands outstretched and his helmet squashed down over his forehead by the blow, lurching from the jolt of the skidding tracks, he yelled and yelled, without taking his eyes off me.

I reached Pradé and was able to raise myself a little. We were in the front of the tank, the nose of which was in the air, and gradually my body rose as if this tank lit up in the pit were offering it up as a sacrifice to death. Were we going to fall back again? I was wedged firm at last. The tracks were still slipping; my oily hands covered with blood clawed the air like a burrowing animal, as though I myself were the tank.

The tracks gripped!

Would we get out before the shell? My three companions had become my oldest friends. Like an explosion, a door banged again. It was possible that the German gunners had not seen the signal of the tank crashing because a relief had taken over, or because the lookout was dozing, or . . . Nonsense! But even more nonsensical to hope that there were tank traps without guns trained on them. The tracks were still gripping.

Pradé switched off the lights.

"What the hell are you up to?"

In spite of my longing to get out, I felt the silence round us like a breastplate: as long as we heard nothing whistling overhead, we had another few seconds to live. When would that door stop banging? I listened with the same lunatic concentration with which I had hitherto been looking, and through the gong-beat of the door could hear only the rumble of our waves of tanks reverberating from the pit and the armor-plating, going past us and into the distance. With my helmet glued to Pradé's, I yelled into the hole of his earpiece: "Get her up!" With his legs in the air, wedged into the motionless, rearing tank by his seat, Pradé turned toward me: like Bonneau's, his old face, in spite of the helmet, had taken on a sort of innocence: with his slanting eyes and his three teeth he gave the ghost of a smile, the patient smile of a dying man, "The lad's had it for sure this time. The tracks are starting to slip again."

Through his words I tried to listen for the faint, incipient whistle of a shell: "If we keep on like this, we'll tip over backward."

The whistling. Our necks disappeared. Pradé lifted his legs from the pedals in the attitude of a frog, to protect his stomach. The shell exploded in front of us, very close.

No more light. Curled up, we waited for the next shell—not the whistle or the explosion but the distant sound of the gun firing—the very voice of death. And Pradé's oriental face emerged dimly from the darkness, gradually becoming more distinct, with the leaden solemnity of the faces of the dead; a mysterious glow, murky and very faint, filled the tank. As if death had given us a sign. Pradé's motionless face, curiously disembodied, divorced by terror from every vestige of life, loomed up more and more clearly from the shadows. I was no longer even listening: death was already in the tank. Pradé turned his head, caught sight of me, and jerked back his hunched-in neck, released even from the tension of the shell by an unearthly terror, hitting his head hard against the side of the tank. And the clang of the helmet on the armor-plating, dispelling the terrifying presence, at last made me notice the glass of the periscope: the rearing tank was looking up at the sky, in which the moon had just come out, and what was now lighting up our faces, seemingly drained of life, was the mirror reflecting the moon-filled sky, vast and once more studded with stars.

The door banged again. A hand gripped my back. I wanted to shake it off, but I was dangling in midair.

"We can get out, boys! We can get out!" yelled Léonard's childish voice. It was he who was shaking my back. He had got out of the tank during our maneuvering. He clambered into the now vertical passageway as though he were climbing a scaffolding.

"There's piles of rubble. It's some sort of ditch. At least twenty or thirty yards long. With rubble in it."

Pradé immediately put the tank into reverse. Léonard and I rolled over, thrown flat on our faces. The tank was horizontal once more.

I got up, jumped through the side door which Léonard had left open, while the tank, still reversing, came to a stop on my left, with only the rectangle of the open door illuminated in the darkness in which tank and ditch were indistinguishable: Pradé had managed to light up again.

Up there, on the surface of the earth, our armored formation was still advancing, sounding fainter than when we had heard it from inside our armor-plating. The shells seemed to start slowly, then accelerate in order to reach us; every whistle seemed to be aimed toward our ditch. A shell burst in front of us, very close, in the same place as the first. By the flash of the explosion I made out that the wall we had been attacking was on a slope. If only we could get out before being blown up. I did not dare switch on my flashlight. In any case, I had left it behind in the tank.

"We could have a try," said Pradé, close beside me in the darkness.

He too was glued to the side of the pit: outside our armor-plating we felt naked. From the clay wall oozed a smell of mushrooms; memories of childhood. Pradé lit a match: its light only reached about six feet. Another shell whistled toward us, modulating from high to low pitch as it hurtled down. With our shoulders pressed into the clay, hypnotized by the patch of sky which would be replaced by the glittering red flash, we waited once more. One can never get used to dying. The match was extraordinarily still, its flame guttering. How vulnerable and soft a human body is! We were spreadeagled against the side of our pauper's grave: myself, Léonard, Bonneau, Pradé—a single cross. Our patch of sky disappeared, went out; clods of earth tumbled down on to our helmets and shoulders.

The waves of tanks were still passing, up there, but in the opposite direction. In retreat? Would we get out of here only to fall upon the German armored columns?

I had already begun to believe that we would get out.

Bonneau's light appeared. He was no longer yelling. All four of us moved forward, still clinging to the clay. There was a corner of my mind that nothing distracted, that nothing would distract from the thought of the shells. The camouflage stretched well beyond the hole the tank had made as it fell through. Part of the pit wall had collapsed to a gentle slope. We climbed it until we bumped our heads on the treetrunks which covered the pit.

We would never reach the gap; prisoners do not escape through the ceiling. The two nearest beams would have to be shifted. Crouched underneath them, we tested them with our shoulders, petrified into Peruvian mummies at every shell burst; but since we had been able to take some sort of action, action had become a substitute for fear. If we could do nothing with the beams, perhaps the tank could move them. It stood there behind us silent, darker than the pit; from its half-open door came a beam of light across which a nocturnal insect flitted.

We rushed toward it without taking cover, looking on it now as a fortress. Pradé maneuvered it into position in front of the caved-in gap. Loose earth had piled up there. Above us, the waves continued to roll back toward the French lines. Meanwhile we were beginning to get bogged down. Pradé fixed the emergency beam under the tracks; the tank lifted itself, groped forward: the tracks gripped like claws. The tank climbed farther up, jammed, slipped again, stuck fast, wedged into the ceiling of treetrunks. If it did not give, our efforts would jam us farther and farther in; within a minute or two the body of the tank would be glued to the earth and the tracks would be turning in the void.

The emergency beam was now unusable.

"Let's get some stones!"

Pradé did not answer.

Engine racing, the mass of steel churned into the treetrunks; with the furious strength of a dying bull, the tank hurled me against the turret in a resounding clatter of trunks showering on to the armor; there were shouts behind me, a helmet clanged, and suddenly we were gliding away like a boat. Pulling myself up, I roughly pushed aside Pradé's head, which was glued to the periscope, and switched off the lights: in the mirror, stretching to infinity, the open plain.

We were advancing at full speed between the shell bursts, each man huddled at his post, thinking only of the next tank trap. And yet the darkness, which was no longer the sepulcher of the pit, the living darkness seemed to me like a prodigious gift, like an immense germination.

By the time we reached the village the Germans had evacuated it. We got out of the tank. Chaos everywhere. We moved with a strange, swaying motion that I was beginning to recognize, the movement of utter fatigue, when soldiers march with their heads down and their mouths hanging open, and can no longer see clearly. Leaving our tank roughly camouflaged (like all the others), we flopped down into the straw in a barn. In the beam of my light, which I switched on for a moment, I saw Pradé, lying down, take a fistful of straw and clutch it as though it were life itself.

"This time it wasn't our turn," I said.

No doubt he was thinking that the youngster had been reprieved. "The war's not over yet," he answered with his bitter smile. He let go of the straw and closed his eyes.

The morning was as pure as if war did not exist. Pradé had awakened me when he got up at daybreak; of all of us, he had always been the first to rise: "I'll have plenty of time to lie down when I'm dead."

I went to look for a pump. The cold water not only woke me from the night's sleep, but also from the pit. A few yards away, Pradé stood looking straight in front of him. He shook his head.

"If someone told me I'd look at chickens one day and be surprised, I wouldn't have believed him!"

The hens that had not yet been stolen were roaming about, apparently unaware of the war, but their beady eyes followed us with sly suspicion. It was them that Pradé was watching; I watched their mechanical pecking too, the sharp thrust of the head as if released by a spring, and their warmth seemed to permeate my hands as though I were holding them, the warmth of new laid eggs—the warmth of life: the beasts were alive on this strange planet. We walked through the quiet morning, devoid of peasants. Barbary ducks, magpies—and mosquitoes. In front of me were two watering cans with mushroom-shaped sprinklers, like the ones I loved to play with as a child; and suddenly it seemed to me that man had emerged from the depths of time simply in order to invent the watering can. Beyond the hens, peacefully or furtively enjoying their freedom, an Angora rabbit with an overweight backside was trying to run like a hare; hayricks gleamed in the morning light, spiders' webs sparkled with dew. For a long time I stared in a slight daze at a ridiculous flower, born of humanity as the disordered flowers around it were born of the earth: a broom. At the sudden, lithe movement of a cat scampering away, I felt astounded that this wriggling fur could really exist. (All the cats were running away, moreover. Whereas the mongrel dogs stayed put, as they had probably done when our tanks came.) What was it inside me, then, that marveled that on this well-ordered earth the dogs should still behave like dogs, the cats like cats? Some gray doves flew off, leaving the tomcat below them clutching the air at the height of its fruitless leap; they described a silent arc in the luminous blue sky, then cut it short and, suddenly white, flew off in another direction. I was prepared to see them come back and run after the cat which would fly away in turn. The days when animals could speak, the queer poetry of the oldest tales—one brings them back with one from the other side of life.

As at the time when I had first encountered Asia, I heard the drone of centuries buried almost as deep as the shadows of the previous night: these barns bursting with grain and straw, these barns with their beams hidden under piles of husks, full of harrows, rakes, wagon shafts, wheelbarrows, these barns in which everything was wood, straw or leather (everything metal had been requisitioned), surrounded by the dead fires of refugees and soldiers, were the barns of Gothic times; our tanks at the end of the street were filling up with water, monsters kneeling at the wells of the Bible. O life, how old you are!

And how stubborn! In every farmyard, wood had been gathered for the winter. Soldiers getting up lit their first fires with it. Everywhere were tidy vegetable plots. There was nothing here that did not bear man's imprint. Wooden clothespins bobbed up and down in the wind like swallows on telegraph wires. The washing that hung from them was not yet dry: threadbare stockings, working gloves, blue overalls; in the midst of this desolation, this disaster, the towels bore initials.

We ourselves, and the Germans facing us, were no longer good for anything but manipulating our murderous pieces of machinery; but the old race of men which we had driven off and which had left behind its tools, its washing and its initialed towels, seemed to me to have risen, across the millennia, from the shadows of the night just past— slowly, laden like misers with all the paraphernalia it had now abandoned in our path, the wheelbarrows and harrows, the biblical plows, the dog kennels and rabbit hutches, the empty ovens.

My legs could still feel Léonard's arms clutching them. Would I remember forever that childish expression on Pradé's face, Bonneau's look of amazement as he stopped in the middle of a yell to say, "Me? I'm not shouting!" These ghosts flitting past the barns in the sunlight shimmering on the tips of the young branches only added to their luster.

Perhaps pain is always strongest; perhaps the joy granted to the only animal that knows it is not eternal is poisoned from the start. But that morning I was all nascency. I still felt within me the irruption of the terrestrial night as we emerged from the pit, that germination in the deepened shadow of constellations in the gaps of the scudding clouds; and just as I had seen that rumbling, teeming night rise up out of the pit, so now from that night had risen the miraculous revelation of day.

The world might have been as simple as the sky and the sea. And looking at these shapes in front of me which were only the shapes of an abandoned, condemned village, looking at these barns of Paradise, these clothespins, these dead fires and these wells, these scattered dog roses and voracious brambles which in a year's time would perhaps have overrun everything, these animals, these trees, these houses, I felt as if I were in the presence of an inexplicable gift—an apparition. All this might not have been as it was. How all these unique shapes harmonized with the earth! There were other worlds—the world of crystals, of the deeps of the sea. With its trees branching out like veins, the universe was as full and as mysterious as a young body. The door of the farmhouse I was now walking past had been left open by its fleeing occupants: I caught a glimpse of a half-ransacked room. Ah! The shepherds of Israel did not bring gifts to the Child, they only told him that on the night when he came doors swung open on the life that had been revealed to me, this morning for the first time, as powerful as the darkness and as powerful as death.

Two very old peasants were sitting on a bench, the man's jacket still smeared with the cobwebs from his cellar. Pradé went up to them, smiling through his three teeth: "Well then, granddad, getting some sun?"

By his accent the old man recognized a fellow peasant; he looked at him with an absentminded friendliness, as though he was at the same time looking into the distance. The woman's hair hung down in a tight little gray plait. It was she who answered, "What else is there to do? You, you're young; when you're old, there's nothing left but wear and tear."

Attuned to the cosmos like a stone. Yet she smiled, with a slow, lingering, reflective smile. Beyond the turrets of the tanks, glistening with dew like the bushes that camouflaged them, she seemed to be looking at death in the distance, with indulgence and even—what was that mysterious flicker, that sharp shadow in the corner of the eyelids? —with irony.

Open doors, washing, barns, traces of men, biblical dawn in which the centuries jostled one another—the whole dazzling mystery of the morning deepened into the mystery that lurked on those worn lips. Let but the mystery of man reappear in an enigmatic smile, and the resurrection of the earth became nothing more than a shimmering backdrop.

I knew now the meaning of the ancient myths about the living being snatched from the dead. I scarcely remembered death; what I bore within me was the discovery of a very simple secret, incommunicable and sacred.

Thus it was, perhaps, that God looked at the first man.

Why that morning of 1940, with its dahlias crushed by the tanks? It was a return to earth, like the one I had experienced after battling with the hurricane in the airplane on the way home from Sheba—but that night I did not give it a single thought. The weirdness of towns, shops with dogs lying on a furrier's skins, and that enormous red glove-maker's sign suspended over Bône like the hand of an unknown deity, did not begin to approach the depth of peasant life, which was attuned to death as day is to night.

And did my memory cling to the morning or to the night? Why this battle among so many others? It was the only one I had fought in which my companions were not volunteers. For a volunteer, battle seems to express the very meaning of his life; waiting for a shell to fall in a tank trap seems a piercing denial that life has any meaning. Unless the fatality of war becomes fraternity.

We learned the next day how we had been saved. Our tanks had run into a line of tank traps on which the German guns, which were at fairly long range, were not all accurately trained. The shells intended for us had exploded outside the pit and caved in one of its walls.

The great hum of release which rises from tropical cities at nightfall was reaching me across the gulf from Bombay. What I had known or guessed about the lives of Pradé, Bonneau, and Léonard was what I did not know about the men who surrounded me in India. Was the foreign vizier encountered by the newlyweds at Madurai the equivalent of the music-hall star in Léonard's life? That sinister night followed by that dew-drenched morning (I would have died on the Flemish soil from which my family came) and then, soon afterward, Dunkirk in flames—the cycle of blood, rebirth and death was that of Vishnu and of Shiva. But what might a Hindu Pradé be? And even if no such person existed, if the dreams of the Ramayana were all that might correspond to Léonard's romance and all the romance of the cinema, to the photographs of wives being passed round from hand to hand in the little circles of torchlight, the real dialogue would not have been between the Bhagavad-Gita and the Gospel, between Elephanta and

Chartres, but between the Majesty in the shadow of the cave and
Pradé's face, pale, phosphorescent, transfigured by the moon reflected
through the periscope like the glimmer of death—between the civilizations for which death has a meaning, and the men for whom life has
none.

In spite of the elementary sentiments. "He's a smart kid, he could
make something of himself," Pradé used to say; and, the day after the
battle: "This time the youngster came out of it all right." And the
ascetic Narada cried, "My children!" in the dying wind, before Vishnu
said to him: "I have been waiting more than half an hour."

But how these feelings paled before the unity of the world after a
season in hell: before the certitude that the world—much more than
men—could not be otherwise. A conviction reinforced here by this
religion intoxicated with the unreal, whose imprisoned maya would go
on forever bringing back the same men, the same dreams and the same
gods in its eternal cycles.

According to the song I had heard at Madurai, the brave elephant-
god Ganesha "will come back riding on his rat, and the moon will
laugh through the clouds," as on my airplane in Spain, my tank in
1940, the snow of Alsace in 1944, and on serene landscapes since time
immemorial. "Here are the sacred waters of the Ganges, which sanctify
the gaping mouths of the dead"; here is the moon over our Flanders
field, over Stalingrad, over Verdun, over all the other nameless battle-
fields with their Pradés eaten away and blackened like burned logs,
the moon over famine-stricken fields or over trees adrift in the vastness
of flooding rivers. For centuries yet, the prayer of India will say, "Lead
us from the unreal to the real, from darkness to light, from death to
immortality," while the West, where forgiveness has been reduced to
either rancor or forgetfulness, will chant, "Forgive us our trespasses as
we forgive those that trespass against us." The prayer of India will
also say: "Since, Shiva, thou lovest the place of burning, I have made
my heart a place of burning, so that there thou mayst dance thy eternal
dance." But no god danced in the hearts of my tank companions.

I thought of other battles and other barracks, of the Spanish republican monk I described in L'Espoir. I had listened to him one night
among a group of militiamen and soldiers of the International Brigade,
as he related, with the wild eloquence of popular improvisers, the story
of the last incarnation of Christ in the most desolate region of Spain,
Los Hurdes.

"The angel looked for the best of the region's women, and then
appeared to her. She answered: 'Oh, not worth trying: the child would

come before its time, seeing I won't have anything to eat. In my street, there's only one peasant who's eaten meat in the last four months; he killed his cat.'

"So the angel went to another woman's house. When Christ was born, there were only rats round the cradle. A bit small for keeping the child warm, and not much in the way of company.

"The descendants of the Three Kings weren't there—because they'd become government officials. So, for the first time in history, from every country, those that were near and those that were thousands of miles away, those where it was hot and those where it was freezing cold, everybody who was brave and poor set off with guns.

"And they knew in their hearts that Christ was alive among the poor and the humiliated in our country. And from every country, with their guns if they had any and with their hands if they hadn't, they came and slept one after another on the soil of Spain.

"They spoke every language, and there were even Chinese shoelace peddlers among them.

"And when they'd all done enough killing—and when the last file of the poor had set off on their march . . .

". . . a star that no one had ever seen rose above them . . ."

I thought, too, of the dawn rising over a cemetery in Corrèze surrounded by woods white with hoarfrost. The Germans had shot some maquisards, and the inhabitants were to bury them in the morning. A company had occupied the cemetery, submachine guns at the ready. In that region, the women do not follow the hearse, they wait for it beside the family grave. At daybreak, on each of the tombs on the hillside like the scattered stones of ancient amphitheaters, a woman in black could be seen standing, and not praying.

Might little Léonard have gone into that cemetery? Yes. Might he have joined the maquis? Perhaps. And Pradé? What did he hold sacred, except the "youngster"? Hardly even his desires, for he was almost devoid of them. How many Pradés I had known, secluded in their caverns of nothingness! Atheist about everything, even perhaps about themselves. And it was this stony multitude whose silence answered the colossal Majesty. What became of the mysterious metamorphosis of the sacred into love that I had felt so profoundly in the cave, compared to the metamorphosis of the sacred into nothingness? This hardened multitude, for whom life had no meaning—for knowledge and truth and suchlike fribbles meant little to them: they'd sooner starve than swallow that sort of stuff—had vanished from the earth since the time of the Roman Empire. Russia, resurrected from her prehistoric darkness, and the primitive and implacable communism which was rising with the slow deliberation of an aurochs on the other side of Tibet, were the heirs of a time-honored fraternity, and had nothing in common with this sinister solitude. "And all creatures exist within me—as within a great wind that moves ceaselessly in space. I am Being and non-Being, immortality and death . . ." murmured the immense profile buried in the granite; and the Flemish peasant woman with the gray plaits had answered, "When you're old, there's nothing left but wear and tear." And beneath the moon which had lit up our tank like a funeral lamp, the Chinese face of Pradé with its three teeth had answered nothing— beneath that gleam which had guided the monkeys round the body of the old blind king on the battlefield of the *Bhagavad-Gita*.

3

1948/1965. Nehru did not live in the Capitol. His house, which was like a large villa on the Côte d'Azur, had, I believe, been put at his disposal recently. Gifts lay around here and there—two enormous carved elephant's tusks, a Romanesque Virgin presented by France. The charm of the place came from his daughter, and from himself. He moved among his temporary furniture like a Siamese cat— but also like the muse of history through the columns of newspapers, for he belonged too much to history not to seem more at home in the Capitol than in this villa.

Before lunch, I talked to him about a speech he had made the day before in front of four or five hundred thousand listeners. He answered by referring to Gandhi. But Europe, after the orators of the totalitarian regimes, had found it hard to grasp that Gandhi could convince multitudes without raising his voice. His influence seemed to me closer to that of the great preachers than to that of political orators; on the terrace at Vézelay, it was obvious that most of those who listened to St. Bernard had been unable to hear him. Nevertheless, they had taken up the Cross.

"Here," Nehru replied, "the crowds come to see a guru, even if he doesn't speak: they expect some vague blessing from him. They used to come to see Gandhi. Up to a point they knew what he was going to say to them: crowds often know what you're going to say to them. But he revealed to them what was in themselves. And above all, what they could *do*. You spoke of a crusade. The freedom struggle, as he conceived and led it, did to a certain extent resemble a crusade; the Salt March was exactly like one. In order to shape the future, Gandhi appealed to very ancient feelings. And then there was his genius for symbols: the spinning wheel, salt. What he proclaimed surprised people by its obviousness."

"To reveal the obvious is one of the marks of the prophet."

"Long before he became famous, Gokhale had said of him that he had the power to make heroes out of clay. He gave people confidence in themselves, and used to say, 'You become what you admire.' His listeners of course became volunteers in the independence struggle, but also something else. Civil disobedience and the struggle against untouchability had the same root. He called it religious. That was why his political activity disconcerted people. Don't forget his saying: parliamentary work is the last of a nation's activities. And then, if he showed the masses what was in themselves, he was only telling them what they expected of him. He had been a nonconformist subject, but he was no more conformist as a Hindu, a nationalist, a pacifist or a revolutionary."

"He was killed by an enemy, but mourned by everybody?"

"The photograph of his murderer is still to be found in too many houses. We are not yet done with the reactionaries."

He had said to me in the Parliament building, "Tanks and planes for the kchatriyas, legislation and administration for the Brahmans."

"And then," he added, "many others."

He took a book from a shelf behind him, and handed it to me. It was *Gandhi*, by Tagore's communist nephew.

"Look at the dedication."

I knew it: "To the masses of India, that they may annihilate Gandhism which enslaves them to priestly intrigue, to feudal autocracy, to native capitalism, and holds them by trickery under the yoke of British imperialism."

Sadly he quoted Vivekananda's saying about his master: "He was content to live that great life—and left it to others to explain it."

Certain of Nehru's speeches, especially during the independence struggle, were those of a traditional orator in their calculated persuasiveness and their eloquence. But many of his speeches to the masses were like long monologues, and he spoke them in an almost conversational tone.

"When my eyes meet the eyes of these thousands," he said, "it seems to me that we recognize each other. Occasionally I attack sentiments to which this crowd is very attached. It accepts me. But what is the person it accepts behind my name, or my photograph, or my silhouette?

"And yet, I have to do everything I can to carry people with me."

He had given a tired smile as he made this last remark. I thought at the time that I would never forget it—and I do indeed remember that characterless room, with the Romanesque Virgin on a low table.

"How far away the independence struggle seems!" he said.

While he was in prison, a fifteen-year-old boy called Azad had been sentenced to be flogged—and at each savage stroke had cried "Long live Gandhi!" until he lost consciousness. (I was unclear whether Nehru had been present at the flogging, or whether it had been described to him.) Some years later Azad, who had become a terrorist leader in the northern provinces, came to ask him whether, in the event of an agreement with the British, the terrorists would be abandoned by Congress. He no longer believed in the efficacy of terrorism, but violence seemed to him inevitable. A fortnight later, tracked down by the police in a park in Allahabad—Nehru's hometown—during the discussions between Gandhi and the Viceroy, he had fought back until he was killed.

"Destruction, agitation, noncooperation are not normal activities, even without terrorism. Once I used to think that only our sons would have a chance to be builders. Our grandsons, perhaps."

He seemed to have forgotten that terrorism had changed targets and that since Gandhi's death he himself had become the target.

"The Resistance wasn't a normal activity either," I said, "and among the youngest survivors many are beginning to pay dearly for it."

One of the photographs on the low table, next to the Virgin, was of a Ceylonese Buddha—doubtless the one of which Nehru had written that it comforted him in his prison cell. I remembered the speech in which he had called the Buddha "India's greatest son." We went in to lunch.

"The speech you made on the occasion of the great Buddhist commemorations seemed to me to differ a good deal from what you've written about religion."

"I've always been struck by the personality of the Buddha. By that of Christ too. But especially the Buddha. Has my feeling about religion evolved? I have become more aware of the obscure need in human nature to which it responds. What I wrote before was a general opinion."

In his *Autobiography* he had stated that the spectacle of religion had nearly always filled him with horror; for him the word religion evoked blind belief, superstition, a domain linked to the defense of vested interests. Christianity had not fought against slavery. He had gone on to say that religion had almost lost its spirituality, in India as in the West; even Protestantism, which was probably the only religion that was still a living one. This statement had flabbergasted me.

Meanwhile he went on: "Look at our attachment to animals. You know that there are no sacred cows: all cows are sacred. And you've seen how they're treated! And the monkeys! Ah, if only they'd all go off to China one night! They weigh more heavily on India than poverty. You've seen the Temple of the Monkeys at Benares?"

I had seen it years before and had not forgotten it. Its living monkeys squatted against the sandstone ones, around a solitary Brahman who seemed to be officiating on their behalf. Their life, bordering on the human, had never seemed to me more disconcerting than in this temple where they were depicted on every wall—as if they had painted them-selves—and seemed on the point of being united with the Absolute through the monkey-god, had my arrival not disturbed their veneration. "Eventually they became much too numerous," Nehru went on. "The Brahmans decided to get rid of them. They discovered that our monkeys are afraid of the black Egyptian ones. Go back to the temple. You'll find only a dozen black monkeys in the aisles; the others have gone back to the forest."

The story sounded like a fable, but his tone was not ironic. I thought of the black monkeys who were now masters of the temple's solitude, like monkey-demons among the monkey-gods of stone. I reminded Nehru of the story narrated by the historians of Alexander the Great.

The Macedonian army, victorious over the East, victorious over the world, reaches Khyber, that legendary pass dotted with myrtles and mulberry trees. There are four chiefs in white cloaks, and Alexander in a red one. Neither the standards of Rome raised up against the gods, nor the bronze boars of the barbarians, nor the flags of Islam looming out of the gorges amid the fleeing jerboas and the indifferent eagles, but an army out of which I know only these four white-clad horsemen and this one red-clad horseman before a prostrate guide. The soldiers have entered the pass between the steep mountains, one of which seems to be swaying, on the point of toppling over on to their heads. Alexander motions the guide to stand up, and points at the quavering mountain: "Oh, it's nothing," answers the sad native, "it's only the monkeys." Alexander looks up at the menacing peak, alive with furtive bounding. And the army sets off again.

"In the great forest," Nehru said, "I used to hear them landing on the branches, and sometimes I would see them hanging by their tails. At dawn, a great wail would spread from valley to valley and fill the forest, like the cry of despair of the monkey army over the death of their king, Hanuman. The Buddhists explained, 'The Buddha promised them that if they behaved well, one morning they would become men. So every evening they hope—and every morning they weep.'"

The speech which Nehru had recently devoted to the Buddha had reminded me of the passage in which he alludes to a conversation we had in the past. "Eight or nine years ago, when I was in Paris, André Malraux asked me a strange question: What was it that enabled Hin-duism to expel a well-organized Buddhism from India without any seri-ous conflict, more than a thousand years ago? How had Hinduism managed, so to speak, to absorb a great and widespread popular re-ligion without the usual wars of religion? . . . It was obvious that for

Malraux the question was not a purely academic one. He blurted it out the very moment we met. It was a question after my own heart, or rather it was the kind of question I myself frequently asked. But I could not give a satisfactory answer either to him or to myself. For there are many answers and explanations, but they never seem to get to the heart of the problem."

His speech had replied indirectly to the same question.

It was a conversational speech, in the simplest tone, which began, "As you know, I busy myself in the field of politics . . ." but quickly came to the point of saying that politics should try to fight against the destruction which science brings in its wake, and against the violence which humanity carries within itself. Yet "we have been failing, for so many years, so many generations! There must be some other way than the one adopted by men of my kind and my profession."

"Men of good will meet each other, talk of a brave new world, a brave united world, of all nations being only one, of cooperation and friendship. This good will is vain, because it is cut off from the real action which must solve real problems. We cannot go on thinking in a dream world. On the other hand, if it is essential for us to have our feet on the ground, it is equally essential that our heads do not remain at ground level."

A noteworthy remark coming from the mouth of the most effective spokesman for political idealism the world has ever known.

"Humanity lacks some essential quality. What? A sort of spiritual element, which could curb the scientific power of modern man. It is now clear that science is incapable of ordering life. A life is ordered by values. Our own, but also that of nations—and perhaps that of humanity. You remember General Bradley's speech, in 1948, I believe: 'We have unraveled the mystery of the atom and rejected the Sermon on the Mount: we know the art of killing, not the art of living . . .' In this I become a Hindu again; in my youth I used to talk of spiritualizing politics. What is the highest value of the West today, in your opinion?"

"I wonder if we shouldn't leave the word values in the plural? The values of the West preserve life more and more, and control it less and less. I don't know about the communist republics. In the capitalist states, or the free world—whichever you prefer—individual liberty passes for the supreme value."

"But if, in a Paris street, you were to ask a passerby capable of giving you an answer what he most desired, what would he reply?"

"Power?" the ambassador suggested.

"Happiness?" I said. "But these are objects of desire, not supreme values. I believe that the civilization of the machine is the first civilization which has no supreme value for the majority of men. There are vestiges—plenty of them. But it is in the nature of a civilization of action that each man should be, as it were, possessed by action. Action as against contemplation; a human life, and sometimes the passing moment, as against eternity. It remains to be seen whether a civilization can exist only as a civilization of questioning or of the moment, and whether it can base its values for long on something other than a religion."

"I still don't know how Buddhism died," Nehru said, "but I think I have an inkling why. The genius of the Buddha has to do with the fact that he is a man. The originator of one of the most profound systems of thought in the history of humanity, an inflexible spirit and the most noble compassion. An accuser, vis-à-vis the teeming multitude of the gods. When he became deified, he merged with that multitude, which closed round him."

But this did not appear in the speech. Nor had Nehru retraced the legendary life, which he assumed his audience would know. I thought of the king's pathetic struggle (nearly always omitted from Western versions) to insure his son's happiness. Each of the four "encounters" brings out a more and more desperate affection. "Wishing to keep the prince ignorant of pain and of evil, the king has a wall built round the palace, pierced by a single door with heavy bars." When, for the first time, Prince Siddhartha wants to go through the town to see the gardens, the king has scented waters poured on the earth: "Line the avenues with many-colored lanterns, put urns of clear water at the crossroads!" Nevertheless, the prince discovers old age, and then, the second time he goes, disease. But the king transforms the palace into an enchanted place, "and the round of pleasure goes on there day and night, and the finest singer sings him the Song of the Forest." Then Siddhartha goes out for the third time, finds a motionless body, and his equerry tells him, "Prince, that is what is called a dead man."

I quoted the sentence, and Nehru answered with the one spoken by the king, who has just learned that Siddhartha wishes to leave the world after meeting the ascetic: "Abandon this decision, my son, for I must soon leave my kingdom and retire into the solitude of the forests, and you must succeed me."

I remembered how it went on, and Nehru had certainly not forgotten it: after putting on the earth-colored robe, the prince goes into the forest, and answers his father's envoy, "A gilded house in flames, such is kingship."

He had quoted, ". . . and you must succeed me."

And one day he had said to Ostrorog, no doubt in the same tone of voice, "Gandhi had a successor."

"Both of us admire the Buddha," I said, "but we don't pray to him. We don't believe in his divinity. In other words, it's as though our supreme value were Truth, and yet . . ."

I told him about Villefranche-de-Rouergue, and my fruitless reread-ing of St. John.

"It may be that Truth is my supreme value," he replied. "I don't know; but I can't do without it. You remember Gandhi's saying, 'I have said that God was truth, and now I say that truth is God.'"

"What did he mean by God, in that context? The Vedic *rita*?"

"He said something like 'God is not a person: God is the law.' He said, the immutable law."

"It's the same as Einstein's affirmation: 'The most extraordinary thing is that the world certainly has a meaning.' It remains to be established why that meaning should concern itself with men."

"Certainly. But Gandhi also used to say, 'I can only look for God in the heart of humanity.' And again, 'I am a seeker after Truth.' With us, the identity between the meaning of the world and the meaning of man—what you would call the soul of the world and the soul of man—is taken for granted. To the same extent, it seems to me, as Christianity assumes the existence of the soul, and its survival. But do you know that Narayana, who only died in about 1925, had had the images of the gods on the sacrificial stones in the temples replaced by mirrors?"

I did not know this. It struck me as a symbol on a par with the Dance of Death and Gandhi's march to the ocean. The sacrificial tables sunk in the walls were still present in my memory, with their idols barely visible beneath the tuberoses. The divine character of the Madurai statues, like that of the statues in our cathedrals, obviously came from their incorporations in the temple, where the stream of ephemeral men passed by. I imagined my newlyweds before the altar of Shiva, bemusedly contemplating, in the depths of the sacred gloom, their double image merged with the dance of the gods above the ava-lanche of flowers. "I adore thee, O God who art only the image of myself."

Although this sadly smiling head of state, more gentleman than

British, did not merge with India as Gandhi had done, he was India; although there remained an enigmatic distance between India and him, although he did not believe in the divinity of the Ganges, he carried the Ganges in his heart. He had the reputation of being an intellectual (and was), because he had written a great deal. But his speeches belonged to the realm of action; his memories, a few family memories aside, were memories of stubborn action. He admired originality of thought, and saluted it with a passing smile, as a lover of painting might have saluted a fine picture. But intellectuals enjoy such originality for its own sake; I believe that Nehru enjoyed it only when it was linked to action.

"I don't think I'm interested in religion in a fundamental way. Only in its relation to ethics."

"Only India," I said, citing a familiar thesis, "has made religious philosophy the essential and intelligible basis of its popular culture and of its national government."

"Gandhi's India is genuinely based on an ethic; perhaps more so, in some respects, than the West is based on Christian morality. But remember an odd saying of Gandhi's: 'India must eventually have a true religion.' "

The basis of the West was individualism; an individualism which was at the same time the crucifix and the atomic reactor. I had earlier come across the uneasiness of Buddhists in face of the crucifix ("Why do they worship a man being tortured?") and the ambivalence of India in face of the machine: Gandhi's spinning wheels revolved in houses a stone's throw from reactors as threatening as the last incarnation of Shiva. India has adopted Christ as it adopts all the other gods, and readily sees in him an avatar (avatar signifying descent, incarnation). But Christ took on a startling aspect here. One can see in original sin the source of a universal maya, and in heredity a karma in which the Westerner inherits the ills of his parents as the Hindu suffers the consequences of his past lives; but transmigration is always a suspended sentence, while the Christian plays out his fate once and for all. The atheist too. Europe has conceived of Indian transmigration as being similar to that which makes a Christian one of the elect or one of the damned, but the damned in this case do not even know that they were once men. In spite of sin, in spite of the devil, in spite of the absurd, in spite of the unconscious, the European thinks of himself as acting, in a world in which change is value, in which progress is conquest, in which destiny is history. The Hindu thinks of himself as acted upon, in a world of commemorations. The West regards as truth what the

Hindu regards as appearance (for if human life, in the age of Christendom, was doubtless an ordeal, it was certainly truth and not illusion), and the Westerner can regard knowledge of the laws of the universe as the supreme value, while for the Hindu the supreme value is accession to the divine Absolute. But the most profound difference is based on the fact that the fundamental reality for the West, Christian or atheist, is death, in whatever sense it may be interpreted—while the fundamental reality for India is the endlessness of life in the endlessness of time: "Who can kill immortality?"

On top of a bookshelf, there was a large drawing by Le Corbusier: the palace of Chandigarh, surmounted by the immense Hand of Peace, looking like a cross between an emblem and a giant weathervane; and a model of the Hand, in bronze, about eighteen inches long. Le Corbusier set great store by it. Nehru, not so much. Le Corbusier had taken me round Chandigarh and shown me the unfinished buildings which he had designed down to the wallpaper. In the main square, files of men and women were climbing the inclined planes, like the bowmen of Persepolis, with baskets of cement on their heads. "Here, the Assembly!" he had said to me briskly, waving his hand toward the distant Pamirs where a solitary goat was passing by. "And here" (he pointed to the roof of the law courts), "the Hand of Peace!"

I thought of the glovemaker's sign in Bône, the enormous hand I had seen watching over the town like the sign of life rediscovered; and I looked at the bronze hand with its lines of fate—perhaps the fate of India.

On the occasion of my departure, Nehru came to dine at our embassy. France was about to create a Ministry of Cultural Affairs; he was investigating the creation of a similar institution, and was anxious to know what we had in mind—in particular, how we conceived of the problems subsumed under so vague a word as culture, for they seemed to him very different "according to whether he thought of Shakespeare or the Ramayana." Ostrorog was the only ambassador in Delhi capable of providing a gastronome's dinner. I remember a pâté garnished with hibiscus, a conversation about Japan, and Nehru saying, "Japan has many reasons to be sad, and elephants are almost unknown there, I don't know why. So in order to revive the smiles of yesterday, I wanted to take an elephant with me. But I was prevented from doing so."

After dinner, Nehru, the ambassador, and I settled down together beneath the Persian carpet that hung on the wall. We indulged in some small talk. I said I had made a mild hit in the Cabinet by stating that I was the only Minister who knew that he had no idea what culture was. I said that Akbar, and even a pharaoh, would have been able to discuss affairs of state with Napoleon, but not with President Eisenhower; the kings of the Napoleonic era still ruled in a great agrarian civilization.

"In a sense," Nehru said, "colonialism was born when modern weapons enabled small European expeditionary forces to sweep away the armies of the most populous empires in the world—and it died when these empires found their own weapons, which were not only guns."

"During this time (our own lifetime) the West has moved from the buses of my youth to jet airplanes. During this time politics—true politics—has played the sort of role it had never played before, or even adumbrated, except during the few years of the French Revolution: communism is more important than a change of dynasty. As if the craving for justice had ended up by delivering men into the hands of the machine just as much as the craving for power, fascism after communism."

"I'm afraid the spinning wheel is *not* as strong as the machine," said Nehru sadly.

"But does the antithesis between the civilization of the machine and the agrarian civilizations seem to you to be an antithesis between materialism and spirituality, or one between action and transcendence? What the West, and above all the United States, calls action is at once *that which creates* and the fragmenting of life, which has probably never existed to such a degree; the stimulus-reflex of the Americans, the activation of man by his creation."

"Like the activation of the donkey by the carrot which it never eats," said the ambassador.

"Man eats the carrot," I said, "but it makes him hungry."

"The donkey, or Sisyphus. It's curious that the United States and Russia should have entered history together in the eighteenth century. In fact, in your speech about the Buddha, Mr. Nehru, you put the problem in the same perspective."

"Did I?" he asked, with an appropriate smile. The ambassador had the speech brought to him.

"It's true," said Nehru. And he handed it back, pointing out the passage: "In fact, we live two different lives: one, which people call the practical life or which is concerned with practical matters; the other, which we reserve for our moments of inner solitude. Thus we develop a dual personality as individuals, just as we do as communities or nations."

"Life estranged from religion," I went on, "seems to me roughly contemporaneous with the machine age. In the seventeenth century, old age was a preparation for eternal life. Every year, St. Simon used to retire to La Trappe. The new factor could be summed up as the legitimization of life through action—or more precisely, the intoxication which enables action to ignore the legitimization of life. It isn't that the response has changed, but that the question has disappeared."

"For how long?" Nehru asked.

"And there's another element, which the West no longer mentions because it has lost it: communion with the world. The Christian used to be linked to the seasons, the trees, the animals, because he was linked to all God's creation. Man in the urban civilizations is isolated, and it's perhaps for that reason that the question 'What are you doing on earth?' can take on such a meaning."

"It had in its way a great deal of meaning for primitive Buddhism," Nehru said.

"Although it may have changed character many times, it's probably as old as consciousness. But much less rational than it seems, because it probably finds its true character in death, old age, destiny. And in pain, in Evil in the widest sense of the word. So it's a question of knowing whether intoxication through action can silence the question death puts to man."

"If it doesn't succeed, do you think art can?"

"No, alas. But if art is to play the part we see it playing today, the question must be unanswerable. Let us not forget that culture is first and foremost a vast resurrection. One can teach people the place of Beethoven in the history of music, but one cannot teach them either to like him or to resuscitate him. To make a masterpiece loved is to give it its voice, to render it actual. Sometimes through interpretation, sometimes through other means."

"I can well imagine the interpretation of Mozart, the representation of Molière," said the ambassador. "But isn't the interpretation of Ellora bound to be a matter of teaching?"

"I think the interpretation of Ellora involves first of all making it plain that the sculptures of Ellora are not imitations of living creatures, do not refer to the world of living creatures, but to another world: for us, the world of sculpture; for India, the world of the divine—and for everyone, perhaps, the two combined. Something which can only be made tangible by juxtaposing statues or photographs of Ellora with statues or photographs of other sacred art: Romanesque, Sumerian, Egyptian, or whatever. Bringing the Ellora statues to life obviously doesn't mean animating them like puppets; it means freeing them from the world of imitation, of mere appearance, in order to admit them into the world of art, or readmit them into the world of the sacred."

I was also thinking of Egypt, which, viewed from Ellora, seemed like an austere and geometric India.

"All of which would be glaringly obvious if, in Europe, art hadn't been confused for so long with beauty. It seems simple, perhaps because the same word is used to describe the beauty of statues and the beauty of women. The world of art originated with us, out of the multiplicity of civilizations which we have discovered. And this makes it somewhat enigmatic. Moreover, beauty seemed to carry within itself its power to survive. In other words, it justified immortality. Yet that beauty was consigned to oblivion for a thousand years."

"Here it has always been among our imports," Nehru replied. "Except perhaps in literature—but is that the same thing?"

"To talk of beauty in connection with Shakespeare is at least as legitimate as it is apropos of Phidias, but it's not so obvious. So much so that it would not be all that paradoxical to say that beauty, today, is what has survived. India is still wrapped up in a very deep-rooted past, which gives it the continuity of a forest; but nearly all the objects which survive in the West survive only in the domain of knowledge. Flint implements teach us something; they do not move us, except as proofs of human intelligence. Whereas our Romanesque statues, and the statues in your sacred caves, do not belong only to the sphere of knowledge. They are of their time, of course: we can date them; but they are survivors. In the same way as the saint to whom people pray belongs at one and the same time to the age he lived in and to the present of those who pray to him. This is what I meant when I wrote that the domain of culture was the life of what ought to belong to death."

I did not know to what extent Nehru was artistically minded. He had a wide knowledge of the literature of India and of England, but made few references to it. It seemed to me that I had only heard him refer to Gandhi and to a few sacred texts. Did he like the plastic arts? The valuable works of art which surrounded us (Ostrorog was a collector) reminded me that I had seen no true works of art in the prime minister's villa. Was it the sculpture that he admired at Ellora, or the expression of India? He was familiar with music, for Hindu culture inculcates it as ours does literature. And he was fond of the dance. I reminded him of the evening at the Capitol, and added that Stalin had once said to me, "In art, I only like Shakespeare and the dance."

He smiled. "Perhaps it was not the same sort of dance. You see, the dance of the past, in Europe, always seems historical: tutus have always intrigued me. Whereas ours seems somehow to be divorced from time. In some respects, nothing here belongs absolutely to death. But what you say about the plastic arts being called in question is also true for us. The arts of Asia have been called in question by the art of Europe; yet we have never quite accepted it. Since the end of colonialism, it has become one art among others. But Europe invented museums, and museums have conquered Asia."

The ambassador's cat strutted across the room, and Nehru gave it a friendly wave, as if he were stroking its back from a distance.

"In Egypt," he said dreamily, "I used to wonder why Greek art never depicted cats. What is the animal of Greece, in your opinion?"

"Great-hearted horses," I replied, quoting Homer.

"And of India?"

"The elephant," the ambassador said.

I would have thought the monkey or the cow. But Nehru was casting his mind back.

"When I arrived in England, I was very interested by the Western idea of beauty. It seemed to me that it sought to conquer things, whereas ours wanted to release us from them. Later, I got to know a plastic art, which like our music, sought to come to terms with the world, Chinese painting. But tell me, if the resurrection you spoke of is not contingent on beauty, what is it contingent on?"

"I don't think it's contingent on anything. It is a fact. Art consists of the works that have been resuscitated; one of the objects of culture is the whole body of resurrections. Allow me one major reservation, however: the thing resuscitated is not the thing as it was when alive. It resembles it. It is its brother. The statues in your caves or those of our cathedrals are not what they were for the men who sculpted them. Greece for us is not what it was for itself, obviously. What is not so obvious is the fact that the metamorphosis by means of which the works and the spirit of dead civilizations reach us is not an accident, but the very law of the civilization which is beginning with us. The past of the world consists of all the cultures different from our own, and moreover themselves heterogeneous. They are being brought together for the first time in our own, through their metamorphosis."

"In the Soviet Union I have seen a communist past take shape, then a national one. To what extent does the West accept a capitalist past?"

"A religious past, rather. Nearly all our resurrections are religious, but their works do not reappear in the name of a religion. We are taking part in the most colossal resurrection the world has ever known. And

it goes hand in hand with cinema, television, all the forms of dis-
seminating works of the imagination. In assimilating rationalism and the
machine, the West lumped them together in opposition to what it
called fantasy. Whereas in fact, in Moscow as in Chicago or Rio or
Paris, our age is precisely the age of the industrialization of fantasy."

"A century ago," the ambassador said, "the audience for all the shows
in Paris put together did not amount to three thousand people in an
evening. Whereas the television audience in the Paris region probably
amounts to three million."

"Our civilization gives birth to as many dreams every week as to machines in a year. It has created some of the most inaccessible arts that humanity has known; but it is also the civilization in which Chaplin and
Garbo have shown that an artist can make the whole world laugh or
cry."

"Do you believe," Nehru asked, "that this imaginary world of the
West is more developed than the world of the *Ramayana* here?"

"I would dearly like to know. After all, the family gathering in front
of the television set has superseded the evening by the fireside. But it
seems to me that the make-believe of the *Ramayana*, as of our Golden
Legend, is didactic: its values are the highest values of India. That is not
so true of the Arabian Nights, in spite of the constant reference to Allah.
It is no longer true at all of the present-day make-believe of the Western
masses.

"We must realize that it is not a question of one type of romance as
against another, as the Golden Legend might have been set against the
World of Fable. It would appear as though a new cycle of blood, sex,
sentimentality, politics, or death had superseded the cycle of the Round
Table or the Arabian Nights. (The limits of fantasy are always fairly
narrow.) But the Western make-believe we are speaking of has no cycles:
it has instincts. The owners of the dream factories are not unaware of
this. And they are not here to help people, but to make money."

"The devil in retirement becomes a general manager," said Ostrorog.
"His products have always sold well."

"And yet we are the managers of the biggest dream factory in the
world," Nehru said in an undertone, as though by way of parenthesis.
It struck me that his role as guru of an entire people was indeed inseparable from the radio. But he looked at me as if he were asking me to
continue, without taking any notice of what he had just said. So I
went on:

"If this civilization, which satisfies the instincts of the masses in a
way they have never been satisfied before, is at the same time the civili-

zation of artistic resurrection, this is surely not by accident. For the resuscitated works, which would once have been called immortal images, alone seem powerful enough to withstand the powers of sex and death. If the nations did not invoke these works—and through emotion, not through knowledge alone—what would happen? Within fifty years our civilization, which wants to be and believes itself to be—and which is —the civilization of knowledge, would become more enslaved to instincts and to elementary dreams than almost any civilization the world has ever known. It is there, I think, that the problem of culture forces itself on our attention."

"I think so too," said Nehru. "Or at least . . . But haven't the Western governments put the question in terms of leisure?"

"In our country, the first Ministry of Sports and Leisure was created by the Popular Front—in other words, about twenty years ago. But if there is no culture without leisure there is certainly leisure without culture. Beginning, precisely, with sport. Nevertheless, with the exception of sport and games, what does leisure mean, if not the world of the imagination? There, our gods are dead, and our demons very much alive and kicking. Obviously culture cannot replace the gods, but it can reveal the heritage of the nobility of the world."

I remembered the philosopher Alain* thirty years ago, with his solid block of a head and his white hair, sitting in the car which he could not get out of because of illness, and saying to me with a kind of astonishment, "When all's said and done, it is the purest and best in man which rules through reverence and admiration—and it has never existed."

"What do you think, Mr. Prime Minister?" the ambassador asked.

Nehru had folded his hands. Through the open french windows came the scented darkness of a beautiful garden, in which a few large blooms stood out dimly. It was the darkness of the empty terrace where I had heard the music for the nocturnal deities—the darkness of palaces, of poverty, and of the gods.

"I'm a little puzzled. Our problems are of a different sort. There is illiteracy, and after all one of the things that gives me most pleasure, when I travel around India, is to see new schools everywhere full of children."

I remembered General de Gaulle: "If, before I die, I have the good

* Pseudonym of Emile Chartier (1868–1951), moralist, essayist, teacher, who might be described as the philosopher of French radicalism. His writings had a profound influence on the post-World War I generation. (Tr.)

fortune to see a new young generation." On the way back to Delhi, I had watched a disorderly march of the Congress Party Youth, with the same distress with which I had watched the Youth of the Popular Front marching past when I had crossed France to meet Trotsky at Royan. I had asked Nehru what he thought of them and to my astonishment he had answered, "I suspect that youth can only be organized politically by totalitarian states." Neither the United States nor Britain had created youth movements. "And then," he had added with some scorn, "the Western myth of youth is foreign to us.

"India is only to a certain extent an underdeveloped country, since it builds atomic reactors. What should we retain or revive from its past, for the betterment of its future? Our conquests have been of the spirit rather than of the sword; and with us even the scholar has always been more respected than the rich man. Much has been written about the clash between our culture and Christianity. The real clash begins with Independence, between Hinduism and the machine. The West will be the stronger, because science will eventually conquer famine. Europeans do not know what famine is—at any rate, not in the way we do. The West also brings socialism, cooperation in the service of the community. That is not all that far from the old Brahman ideal of 'service.'

"So we are heading toward a kind of marriage with the West. Independence makes it easier than British domination. Science may not be opposed to religious metaphysics, and scientists are often ascetics. But how are we to harmonize a civilization of the machine with what was a civilization of the soul? What is it that drives Europe to this mechanical frenzy? In the endless time which is still the time of this country, why should anyone be in such a hurry to arrive? And then, listening to you, I was thinking: all that has to do with Man. Even the demons and gods you were speaking of. The intensity of Western civilization arises from death. In the cosmic adventure which the universe represents here, death gives no intensity to life. Which is why it is difficult for us to prevent people from allowing themselves to die. For India—sometimes it's also true for me—the divine may perhaps be in man, but man should be in the divine. One of our gurus said, 'God is in all men, but not all men are in God,' and that is why they suffer."

"Didn't Ramakrishna also say, 'Since you seek God, seek him in man'?" the ambassador asked.

"Every time I have really sought in man," I said, "I have found misery there."

Nehru put his hands on his knees, and looked at me attentively. "It was a disciple of Ramakrishna who said that half mankind was born to seek after pain."

The scent of India was wafted in on the night air. We fell silent. Then he resumed, as if wishing to return to the beginning of the discussion.

"Here, it's difficult to speak generally about art. Our people have remained, in their way, fundamentally artistic, without knowing it. Not our bourgeoisie; not our towns. You've seen them. The villages are the true India, Gandhi used to say, the India I live for."

"Your towns are no worse than the suburbs of Tokyo and Paris," said the ambassador. "Yet the Japanese, and my countrymen, are considered artistic peoples."

"When I was in prison, I was quite determined that one day a liberated India would destroy the color prints and the pianolas. Well! India is liberated, and the pianolas are still here. To link the cultural activity of the state with what you call the dream factories seems to me to be right. Not forgetting that here your twelfth century and your twentieth century coexist. In other words, it's a question of making the past of India present, as nobly as possible, for the greatest possible number of Indians. It isn't easy but it isn't insurmountable. Perhaps I should like to advance with India toward the whole of the world's past, but I would want to be sure of not losing her on the way. And our towns are not very encouraging."

"The Soviet Union has created its own world past. Fanatically. And when it became Christendom, the whole of Europe changed its past."

"True enough. And my country has a great power of assimilation. You remember Tagore's saying, 'India, alas, is only a name—an idol-name: she does not exist.' For me, she exists only too palpably. But we still speak of her as of a queen out of the *Ramayana*, when in fact she is a beggar woman, like all those old grannies you have seen by the roadside."

Why should his agnosticism have cut him off from Shankara, since mine did not cut me off from St. Augustine? But were the women at the roadside India, or simply the eternal *Pietà*—the sisters of my women in black standing at dawn in the cemetery in Corrèze, of the anticlerical peasant women who had greeted my blood dripping on to the road with the sign of the cross? With the same smile as when he had spoken during dinner about the elephant he wanted to take to Japan, Nehru added:

"Perhaps all our ministers should act like Europeans and die like Hindus. There's a story that has always stuck in my mind which illustrates the connection between religion and art. You know that Gandhi used to receive anyone who came to ask his help—which meant that he saw a fair number of eccentrics. One day, a man from the mountains came and said to us (but he was addressing Gandhi), 'The gods are about to die.' 'Why?' 'They only live as long as they are beautiful. In order to be beautiful, they need the feather of the red parrot.' He pulled out of his loincloth a pathetic home-made god with a halo of small feathers topped by a red one. 'For a long time it's been impossible to find these birds in our forests. They used to come from Brazil. Brazil has forbidden them to be sold abroad. The gods will die.' We waited for him to go on. 'But we have been told that if you were to ask our ambassador, he would send you the red feathers.' "

"The diplomatic bag has its uses," said Ostrorog. "What did Gandhi do?"

"He had the feathers sent."

He left late. Returning to the Capitol through the great deserted avenues where the headlights did not wake the sleeping cows, I thought of General de Gaulle once again. "All my life, I have held a certain idea of France." From Hitler to Mao Tse-tung, how many national vocations there had been, in this century which was to be that of the International! The ambassador accompanied me. He was going to call on two antique dealers, for Delhi is a town where people go to see clandestine statues after midnight.

"Has Nehru changed much?" he asked me.

"A good deal."

"Age?"

"No: tolerance."

"When I arrived, he was still a revolutionary, a liberator. You've written somewhere that all action is Manichean. In becoming an arbitrator, pulled by opposing forces, he has discovered what is a professional law in our department: the legitimacy of conflicting points of view. Today he would make an admirable ambassador. All the same, there's an iron fist inside that velvet glove: he won't yield an inch over Kashmir.

"I've been wondering for years about his relationship with Hinduism. Gandhi was really a Hindu. Not at all a gentleman, like Nehru. The Renouncers of the past must have had the same sort of gentle old face, which one wants to stroke or take on one's shoulder. One day he said to me, 'The outcome doesn't matter, it's the struggle that counts.' Neither he nor his companions realized that it was a transposition of the *Gita*."

"And yet he had translated it."

"He knew the feelings of the masses because he shared them. 'Without sacrifices,' he said to me, 'the world would fall apart.' He defended the Untouchables, though traditional Hinduism scarcely acknowledged them."

The car was traversing the broad avenues of the embassy quarter.

"The profundity of Gandhi and Tagore incorporates an element of childishness, a disconcerting autosuggestion. You've read what Gandhi wrote after his wife's death: 'She passed away on my lap. I am happy beyond all measure.' It was quite untrue. One had only to read the whole text to be certain of it. He was in despair. He seemed invulnerable because he hid away to grieve as animals do to die, and because his weakness never deflected his public actions. Einstein once said to me, 'He gathers a powerful multitude behind him through the irresistible example of a morally superior way of life.' That example will not always be irresistible, as Gandhi knew and Nehru knows. Their stubbornness has to be taken into account, comparable to the tenacity of the British in spite of the perpetual chaos you find in these countries. When they operated on Gandhi for acute appendicitis, it was so urgent that the English doctor did not want to wait until the following day. He operated at midnight. It was in Poona Prison. A hurricane had cut the electricity. They carried on the operation by the light of a nurse's flashlight. The battery was low, and the light went out. They continued with a hurricane-lamp.

"Nehru told you that everything hangs on his word; that's true. He told you there was no state; that's almost true. Nehru welcomed you as he did because he knows you admire what India stands for, and also because he's not all that confident of victory. He wants to channel the forces born of the freedom struggle into the development of this unfortunate land of starving people. On the whole he's succeeding. But if Gandhi and Nehru accepted Partition it was only because it was the price of Independence. They knew it was a cancer. Gandhi confided to Nehru, 'Even at the time of the Chowri murders I had never really had to face despair. Now I know I have failed to convince India. Violence reigns all around us. I am a spent bullet.' The India of today is living with its fifty million Muslims; a united India would have lived with all its Muslims: one may doubt it, but they believe it. And Nehru will undertake the most justifiable of wars with a very bad conscience. The strength of nonviolence lay in the fact that the enemy was a colonial empire. It remains to be seen what will happen if it encounters an Asian adversary. And the Asian adversary is waiting."

I remembered the photographs of what was delicately called the exchange of populations, at the time when the corpses were piled up on luggage trolleys. The pregnant women carried by the men, the little children in the arms of the big ones, the mattresses on people's heads, and that winding procession fifty miles long, from the oxcarts with huge wheels in the foreground to the tiny carts on the horizon; the wandering procession of death pursued by famine, malaria, and exhaustion; the camps overwhelmed by floods, the cholera hospitals strewn with the dead, the Untouchables fighting the vultures to salvage dead men's rags, the immense trail of the immense column, the children's graves and the faces that seemed to be dreaming—of nothing, like all starving people—the dead and the dying, either too young or too old, the endless procession under the banyan trees and the sky.

"You know the sort of feeling one has in Japan," Ostrorog went on, "in villages rebuilt after earthquakes, and which seem to be expecting another. Well, behind everything you see here, everything Nehru said to you the first day—this evening he was on holiday!—is a country on the alert. They're waiting for the first rumblings of the cataclysm."

"War?"

"The trial of nonviolence may well be an almost silent cataclysm. Nehru is more vulnerable than Gandhi, because this pandit is an agnostic."

"Does his relationship with Hinduism seem to you more complex than that of a man like Renan with Christianity?"

"If I think of him as an Indian, I'm struck by his Englishness. Beginning with his socialism—which is not at all an acquired veneer, a fancy dress. There is an English Nehru. But there's also the other."

"Isn't the problem the same for most of the heads of state of the French Community?"

(One of them had told me: "Don't forget that many of my colleagues, as well as being Protestants, Freemasons, or Catholics, are also witch doctors; and that if they weren't they wouldn't be in power.")

"And for most of the Muslim rulers. The Hellenic world was probably familiar with situations of this sort."

"Go back as far as Cleopatra, both Athena and Isis, with her Roman lovers," I said. "But I suspect that never before our time have the leaders of half the world been spiritually bilingual."

"Decolonization has changed the feeling of Europe, and even America, much less than people think: the West civilizes the colored races, brings them democracy, machines, and medicines; they abandon their Middle Ages, of which nothing remains, and become inferior versions to us. Second-class Westerners. There is only one civilization. And all the past was converging on it without knowing it. Read the American newspapers."

"That's also what the Russians think, though they would put it rather differently. But even if Nehru is spiritually bilingual, can India become so?"

"I've been asking myself that question ever since I was posted here. My counselor, who has just become ambassador in Kabul, used to ask it too. It's true that it's a question that Islam has faced me with ever since I was a child."

I remembered that the Ostrorog family owned a palace on the Bosphorus.

"Claudel," he went on, "who detested Hindu thought, told me when I was appointed, 'No interest whatsoever! People are everywhere and always the same!' "

"He said that to me too."

"Yet he was responsive to the old Japan, and even to the old China."

"He used to play at writing French haikus. But he also used to play at giving eggs to his friends and writing on the shell, 'With the author's compliments,' signed 'Ducky.' "

"Such are the little jokes of the diplomatic corps. Nevertheless I think that assertion of his was, partly at least, a reflection of what I might call the foreign service point of view. Our jobs take us from one end of the world to the other. And we can feel a profound difference between a Zen drawing and a Cézanne, but not between our colleagues. The diplomatic corps is a sort of International; you know those cocktail parties. Apart from a few conventions, diplomacy is the same everywhere. And I would have had to take more conventions into account with Stalin, and probably with Hitler, than here. Our experience is probably applicable to every form of action. The British had no trouble in organizing the Indian army. When the European businessmen were cooped up in the godowns of China, they used to talk of the Chinese as mysterious people, whereas the European banks in Hong Kong operate as normally as those of Casablanca."

In the wide avenue into which the car had just turned, a flock of Untouchables lay sleeping, or squatting around diffident fires.

"Claudel," I said, "in spite of those sledgehammer assertions of his, to borrow a phrase of Jules Renard's, did not in the least think himself 'the same' as a pagan. Nor did the Christians think so in the days of Christendom: St. Louis didn't think of himself as being 'the same' as Saladin. It was the Renaissance which decided that the great minds of Greece and Rome were the brothers of the great Christian minds.

The West does not believe that men have always been the same—
it thinks they are going to become the same. Because it mixes up its
civilization with its techniques, which are unprecedented.

"What do men have in common, in historical times? Instincts,
physiology, love? No. The deadly sins."

"Perhaps civilizations resemble each other in their vices, and differ
in their virtues?"

"Or resemble each other in what they know, and differ in what they
believe. Beliefs are not only religious. But there's something else, which
I cannot put a name to. The conquerors are the greatest figures of
history, and also powerful figures of fantasy. They exist everywhere,
their techniques are relatively similar, and they have made no small
contribution toward people's belief in the consistency of human nature.
As a counterpart to Plutarch's *Parallel Lives*, it would be extremely interesting to write a history of what humanity has lost, when what it
has lost has left some trace."

"You would begin with the history of the gods."

"I'm not very convinced by theories which see in our civilization
only the end product of one culture among others. Einstein used to say,
and I believe Oppenheimer says the same thing: there are more research-
ers alive now than during the whole of human history. Even if we are
experiencing the end of a Romano-Christian culture, or a Faustian one,
as Spengler put it, we are also experiencing the beginning of the greatest adventure mankind has known since the birth of historical cultures.
These have lasted for roughly six thousand years—a pretty short time,
compared with man's prehistory. All of them have been religious civilizations, if by religion we mean the link not only with the gods but
also with the dead; except our own, which is not even three centuries
old—and, for a rather vague period, that of Rome. (The paganism of
Caesar must have resembled the Christianity of Napoleon.) Not that
they are atheist civilizations. President Eisenhower would certainly
claim to be Protestant; Caesar probably believed in the augurers, and
undoubtedly in his ancestors. But our civilization is not *founded* on a
religion, is not even guided by a transcendental idea. The heads of the
two greatest world powers are neither the Lord's elect, nor Sovereign
Pontiffs, nor Sons of Heaven."

We passed the cupolas and minarets of the Great Mosque silhouetted
against the night sky.

"Islam is a city around a mosque; Christianity, a city around a cathedral; Benares, a city on the banks of a purifying river. But Bombay is
built around a port, not a church; the churches of New York have to

be searched out among the skyscrapers like crabs between rocks. What strikes me very forcibly here is that throughout the entire world what used to be called the soul seems to be dying out. Even among believers. Unless they live in monasteries or in forests—in places which modern civilization has not touched. I should have said to Nehru just now that since the end of the nineteenth century the word materialism has no longer meant the replacement of the soul by matter, but by mind. This time, it isn't the 'Enlightenment' that sets itself up against religion, it's atomic reactors."

"He would have agreed. Regretfully perhaps. Yet India could have its atom bomb if it wished, and it does not wish."

"Mao will. Each of the great African and Asian cultures touched by the Western spirit will sooner or later give it a different form, which obviously won't be the one it destroyed, but won't be what we see now either. It's a long way from Mao to Stalin, and it was a long way from Stalin to Marx."

"I had something of that feeling when I was stationed in Moscow. Here, whether we are dealing with Muslims or Hindus, thought has only one supreme object: God. Look at the Muslims' worst enemies, the Sikhs. They understand Islam very well. But the West is unintelligible to them. They regard us in the same way as our backwoods peasants regard the America of the gangster films: greed and frenzy. Even Nehru told me that when he arrived in England he was staggered to hear India being reproached for sacrificing animals to the gods, when the critics themselves were killing animals every day in order to eat them. My Hindu friends say that we are seeking God, without knowing it, up blind alleys. Your Brahmans at the Sanskrit University think the same, I imagine."

"Our research into the laws of the universe appears pointless to them. For them, the true Law is of another kind. The epic of Western research, man's struggle against the earth, which actuates the Soviet Union as well as the United States, baffles them. More, it is anathema to them. They say that no progress of the mind will answer the questions put by the soul."

"The West doesn't try to answer those questions, but to destroy them."

"It will not destroy suffering, or old age, or the pangs of death. You remember the Buddhist texts: 'Prince, that is what is called a dead man.'"

"It seems to me that a civilization can be defined at once by the basic questions it asks and by those it does not ask."

"It's true that India has for long been wedded to death. It is still a civilization of the soul. But when the soul fades, what appears in its place: action, or the calling in question of life by death?"

The car slowed down under the stately trees.

"Perhaps action first, death afterward."

I dropped Ostrorog off in front of a rectangle of light in the depths of which a Tibetan god the size of a man seemed to be waiting for him. The antique dealer was asleep somewhere in the darkness. I set off again for the Capitol. The sacred cows had grown less numerous, and the driver switched off the headlights. The car sped along in silence, and I felt as if I were plunging into the centuries—not through the Mogul streets of Delhi but through those of Kapilavistu, two hundred years before the advent of Alexander. The night of the Great Departure pervades Buddhism as that of the Nativity pervades Christianity: the forsaking of the palace, the forsaking of women, "the musical instruments scattered, the tuberoses withered," the forsaking of love (and the kiss so lightly bestowed on the princess's foot that she does not wake), the forsaking of the child. The genies who come down from the heavens to cloak the hooves of the horse which the prince mounts for the last time, so that no one may hear him depart into the great silence. An exhausted beggar regains his hovel; beneath high, windowless walls a candle stump surrounded by a few flowers burns before a god. Through the sleeping cattle, the horse crosses the town. "The genie of the city awaited him, and magically opened the Eastern Gate for him. The prince lifted his eyes toward the starry sky: it was the hour when the star Kvei was entering into conjunction with the moon; all the genies descended to accompany his departure, and strewed his path with invisible flowers."

Like him, I traveled in silence at the foot of high walls between the skinny sleeping cows, past the red and white gods illuminated by night lights; furtive shadows flitted through the darkness. The sentry posts of the Capitol, hollowed out of the rock, resembled the sacred caves, and the turbaned soldiers presenting arms as we passed by these dimly lit openings seemed to be waiting for the genie of the city to open a gate in a rampart from which the stars could be observed. When I entered my suite, I found the bedroom windows open. Beyond the gardens a string of lights, like those of an airfield, ringed the town. There was no sign of the glow or the vague murmur which rise from European cities; sleeping Delhi filled the room with an immense repose. This nocturnal silence might have reigned over the ice age, over the gardens of the palaces of Babylon, so like those which stretched before me; over the obsidian darkness in which the soldiers of Cortez heard the cries of their companions whose hearts were being ripped out to the beating of the Aztec gongs, over the immemorial Chinese darkness strewn with obliterated capitals—lotuses of Hangchow tinged blue in the moonlight, as the last emperors painted their last falcons; Tartar gateways whose somber red faded like a dying conflagration—over the horsemen asleep by their chargers on the eve of Arbela or of Austerlitz; over the restless night of the French Revolution and the polar night of the Russian Revolution. For fifty centuries diurnal humanity had been shaken by its battle convulsions, but quadrangular Peking slept at the foot of its drum tower which had heralded the day, and of its clock tower which had heralded the night, like Delhi below me; the pyres of Benares were reflected in the river as once the torches of Babylon were reflected, as the lights of vertical New York were reflected in the icy Hudson beneath the squalls of snow. Over the forest of the Casamance, the giant tree of the Queen rose toward the stars. For fifty centuries, the same silence filled with stray noises had enfolded generations of men reconciled by sleep to the nocturnal earth—recumbent, like the dead.

Low down on the horizon, a thin gray glow was beginning to spread: the dawn, with its lunar reflection on the very high clouds of the zenith, as if it were about to appear in the middle of the sky. The first dawn I experienced was that of August 4, 1914: the apparition, in a field in the Ardennes, of cattle asleep on their feet, suddenly scattered by a whirlwind of lancers. Next, the illuminated clockfaces on railway stations, enormous lemon-colored circles against the grayish sky; then, a variety of airfields with the grass flattened by the early morning wind; and at the time when I was flying in Spain, after the sinister nocturnal departure from fields marked out by the bluish flames of fire made of dried oranges, our binoculars leveled at the ground where the enemy lines were about to appear in the first glimmer of dawn . . . Even here, the day opposed its infinite multiplicity to the all-embracing unity of the night. And yet it was the day of India, the day revealed by every dawn as it had once been for me when it had risen above our tanks in a village in Flanders. Soon the torches would be brandished in the temple courtyards, the priests would be gathering the night flowers for the offerings, the first bells would start to ring. I thought of the destiny of which I had spoken that night to Nehru as of the inexorable progression of life toward death; the imperceptible coolness of the tropical dawn was mingling on my face with the eternal Hindu resurrection in which life and death were united as night and day are united: "Everything you spoke about was to do with Man." But for Man, death has no dawn.

The relations between India and France were about to change. Mrs. Pandit, Nehru's sister, ambassadress in London, was returning to India via Paris. She came to the Elysée, accompanied by the Indian ambassador to France, Serdar Pannikar, a little man with a goatee beard and pince-nez, anti-European, full of shrewd or chimerical ideas, who reminded one of a cross between Lenin and Tartarin. After a few words of welcome, General de Gaulle asked Mrs. Pandit for her views on Chinese foreign policy. Pannikar had represented India in Peking, and Mrs. Pandit, who is courtesy itself (and who was perhaps not displeased to remain an observer for a minute or two), turned toward him. He began a lecture on China which contributed nothing. Time passed. China led him to a parallel between the Sinn Feiners and the fellaghas. Time passed. When an aide came to announce the ambassador of the United States, neither Mrs. Pandit nor General de Gaulle had been able to get in a word.

I went down with her, Pannikar lingering in the aides' room.

"So there you are!" she said to me with a charming smile.

Pannikar soon went back to India. It was said that Nehru was not sorry to be rid of him. But having become more heedful of the importance of the Paris post, he appointed to it a good friend of France. The latter, some years later, was to leave the diplomatic service to take on, extremely courageously, the rectorship of the most dangerous university in India, to be badly wounded there, and to take up his functions again even before he had completely recovered. The gray-eyed ambassadress looked like a heroine from an Indian tale; slim and lithe as a Kashmir gazelle, one could imagine her as the inspiration for the Taj Mahal. Nehru came to Paris in 1960; together we inaugurated the exhibition of the Treasures of India at the Petit-Palais. The crowd cheered as he went by, which took him by surprise. He was the official guest of France in 1962. We lunched at Orly Airport when he went to London for the Commonwealth meeting. "The older I get, the more I judge people by their character, not by their ideas." But after the conflict with China he never came back again.

Back in Delhi once again. The Chinese attack has taken place, and the Pakistani threat is becoming more palpable. This morning, in accordance with custom, I went to place some flowers on Gandhi's funeral slab. For the people of India, he has become an avatar of Vishnu. I wanted to take another wreath to Nehru's slab. It has not yet been laid: its place is marked by a square of grass. The slabs are symbolic, since they cover no bodies. The man who, when I last came to Delhi, held India in the palm of his hand, is a square of lawn on which the blades of grass ripple in the warm wind, among the cut flowers thrown by hands joined in prayer.

On the way to lunch with Radakrishnan, who is now President of the Republic, I cross the great salon with the Persian-tale ceiling. It is empty like all the reception rooms of the Capitol at this hour.

India too.

Nehru's house, now a House of Remembrance, is a subsidiary of the Great Museum, which I do not yet know, and where I go to meet the curator, an elderly Englishwoman who speaks knowledgeably about her collections and affectionately about Nehru. We arrange to visit his house as soon as the museum closes, so as to be alone there.

The tour of the museum begins with the collections of popular art. I am reminded of the Singapore Aquarium, where every variety of fish swims to and fro, spiny, metallic, or multicolored. Most of the popular figures partake of the sea egg and the hogfish: divine musicians covered in scales, and all kinds of sirens or mermaids with the curves of sea-horses. In the heavy heat of the Indian afternoon, I think of the Flemish mist regularly penetrated by the call of the siren. But it is another memory besides that of the foghorn that the word siren has awakened in me. I am in James Ensor's studio in Ostend. Above the piano, the strident genius of the *Entry of Christ into Brussels* fills the wall with its male choirs grimacing around Jesus. On the piano, a stuffed mermaid. Ensor's gaze follows mine.

"I've seen them in China," I tell him.

"Alive?" he asks, with the humor that characterizes his engravings.

"They make them in the form of a little monkey from the waist up and a fish from the waist down."

"Mermaids do exist."

And, with professorial gravity, forefinger raised: "But they are not like that."

Thirty years later I saw that picture again, tarnished, at the exhibition of the Sources of the Twentieth Century; the color was inexorably flaking off, and in the morning the cleaning women were sweeping up the dust of a masterpiece.

What has happened to the feathered gods whose survival Gandhi insured through the diplomatic bag? The shaggy sirens of Delhi, too, have lost their brilliant colors, like the whole pullulating, puppet show *Ramayana*, rugged and naïve, which surrounds them, and which is to the art of India what superstitions are to faith.

And here is faith: on the ground floor, the great stone sculptures, some of them masterpieces. Since Elephanta, it is the first time I have seen an Indian museum. The statue which was alive is not dead, it is reincarnated. I think of Cairo, but the *Shiva* of Elephanta differs from any colossus of Thebes by the mere fact that men pray to it. I ask whether people come here, as in Cambodia and Mexico, to lay flowers before the gods. No. But in the temples, from the tumultuous populace of sculptures at Madurai around its fish-eyed goddess, to the *Mothers*, the *Kiss*, or the *Dance of Death* of Ellora and the *Majesty* of Elephanta, I have not seen one figure that does not guide man to the divine unknown.

Once again I experience that Western feeling which arises in front of the images of gods transformed into works of art. An inverse transmigration from that of men: like the bristling profusion of the little popular gods, these statues have not changed bodies but have changed souls.

It is time to leave. It is not yet evening, but it is the end of the day. The cars drive off amid the smells of modern Asia: Indian incense, Islamic camels and dust, Western petrol. I remember the newsreels of Nehru's funeral: the trees bowed down with men, a crowd as vast as India, bristling with umbrellas opened as protection from the sun—the crowd to which he had said at the Red Fort: "We have long had a rendezvous with destiny"; the procession of elephants and lancers beneath a bridge that bore a gigantic Coca-Cola advertisement, then the little vertical pyre whose thin black smoke mingled with the thick clumps of dust hanging in the Delhi heat, and the foreground of sobbing peasant women. "India is not a queen out of the *Ramayana*, she is a beggar woman like those old grannies you see by the roadside."

Here is the house. I imagine it is not the villa to which he had invited me, but it resembles it, all the more so because I recognize the furniture, the elephant tusks, the Romanesque Virgin sent by the French government. I do not see either the plan of Chandigarh or the bronze of the Hand of Peace.

Today there are numerous photographs on display. It is the family album, as meaningless as all family albums, save for one or two striking images: the child (he looks like his own grandson), a photograph taken after the first stroke, a blank look on the shattered features; the noble deathbed photograph, the face strangely white, which reminds me of the death of Ramakrishna: "We all thought it was ecstasy. And his disciples shouted: Victory!" It is not the house of a living man, nor yet a deserted house; it is a set for the film of history. Nevertheless the garden is haunted. It in no way suggests a familiar presence; it is very much a garden of death; but these trees were his trees, these flowers were his flowers, birds such as these must have sung here as they are singing now in the gathering dusk. I think of Shalamar, with its sudden great gaps in the immensity of the trees. And also of one of the oldest images of India, the ever-changing waves of the changeless Ganges, which he had taken up often in speeches and in his last will and testament as well:

My desire to have a handful of my ashes thrown into the Ganga at Allahabad has no religious significance, so far as I am concerned. I have no religious sentiment in the matter. I have been attached to the Ganga and the Jumna rivers in Allahabad ever since my childhood and, as I have grown older, this attachment has also grown. The Ganga, especially, is the river of India, beloved of her people, round which are intertwined her racial memories, her hopes and fears, her songs of triumph, her victories and her defeats. She has been a symbol of India's age-long culture and civilization, everchanging, ever-flowing, and ever the same Ganga. She reminds me of the snow-covered peaks and deep valleys of the Himalayas, which I have loved so much, and of the rich and vast plains below, where my life and work have been cast.

I do not wish to cut myself off from the past completely. I am proud of that great inheritance that has been, and is, ours, and I am conscious that I too, like all of us, am a link in that unbroken chain which goes back to the dawn of history in the immemorial past of India. That chain I would not break, for I treasure it and seek inspiration from it. And as witness of this desire of mine and as my last homage to India's cultural inheritance, I am making this request that a handful of my ashes be thrown into the Ganga at Allahabad to be carried to the great ocean that washes India's shore.

The major portion of my ashes should, however, be disposed of otherwise. I want these to be carried high up into the air in an aeroplane and scattered from that height over the fields where the peasants of India toil, so that they might mingle with the dust and soil of India and become an indistinguishable part of India.

Here is the shimmering red glow of evening, such as I had seen stretching across the plain as far as the eye could see as I emerged from the Ellora caves. Soon the birds will be hushed, and the nightflowers will open like those I used to see in the gardens of the Capitol, attended by a solitary lantern, a sleeping watchman, and an occasional distant cry. Here, the watchful caretaker stands beside a little commemorative slab, near the banyan tree beneath which Nehru used to work, in this garden of memory with no mortal remains and no grave. Of his private life, there remains nothing except the affection he bore his family, which merges into that which he bore toward India. Night is falling. I think of what he told me about the animals and the plants: of the tiny prison yard where he discovered the ants, of the cell where he lived with hundreds of wasps and hornets "in an atmosphere of mutual respect"; of the lizards which emerged from the rafters in the evening and chased each other about, waggling their tails; of the bats, and, higher up in the twilight, the flying foxes; of the brain fever bird which repeated its obsessive cry above the prison where a few snakes broke the monotony; of the mongooses which the prisoners used to rear; and the big monkey who came to rescue her little one from the prison yard, charging right into a crowd of armed guards, who were probably stunned with admiration; of the black monkeys which had driven the gray ones from the temple in Benares, and the elephant he wanted to take with him to make the Japanese smile; of his voice saying firmly, "To make a just state by just means," and a little ironically, "I don't think I shall see Kailas again." The summer twilight has changed from red to green, as it does over the Acropolis, and is beginning to blur the leaves. In the Himalayan prison, the spring used to make the buds spring out of the bare branches. "It was there I discovered that the color of the young mango leaves is remarkably like the autumn tints on the Kashmir hills." The wasps are asleep. A bat flits by at the bottom of the garden. There will be no more mongooses, no more squirrels rolling their young into a ball, no more monkeys or flying foxes. Night falls like a dirge over the almost invisible inscription: *With all his mind and all his heart, this man loved India and the Indian people. The latter, in return, was indulgent to him and loved him beyond all bounds and all reason.*

The motorcar horns of Delhi are silent. As I leave the house, the bare feet of the passing beggar children tread softly on the silence. The cry of the ravens rises from the depths of India. From ocean to ocean, around sacred trees which no longer protect them from the sun, motionless men are forming great rings, as around the glowing pyres of Benares—and as once, above Strasbourg, did the young shoots and the dead nuts of winter.

THE ROYAL WAY

1

Singapore. So I believed that shipwrecks no longer happened? At dawn, an inexplicable blow makes the *Cambodge* shudder like a billiard ball on the edge of the pocket. Every loose object falls. The boat does not stop. I go to the cabin window. An oil tanker, its bow crushed, is slowly pulling away from the side of our boat. No danger, unless we sink like a stone: we are in the straits, and I can see the coast. There is a hundred-foot hole in the hull, but the deck passengers, already awake, had seen the tanker coming and run astern.

Thanks to frogmen and pumps, we reach an emergency berth. Someone brings me a telegram from our ambassador in Vietnam, which advises me not to land at Saigon. (No matter, for the boat will not be resuming its voyage.) And a telegram from Paris, ruling out Japan and reverting to the mission to Mao Tse-tung which I was to undertake.

Meanwhile I am staying in our Consulate General.

In spite of its two million inhabitants, Singapore is no longer, as it was of old, a Chinese city. But the dying vestiges of what used to be China have taken refuge there. Soon the high-rise projects bristling with washing hung out on poles, not on balconies, will have replaced the streets built in the time of Governor Raffles, when shoals of junks used to invade the ports which are now silted up, when Macao echoed with the gold pieces of its gaming houses, and distant China with the clatter of the mah-jongg tiles painted with flowers and the winds. Today, July 14, there is the traditional reception. In addition to the French, the guests include our Malayan and Chinese friends, Belgians, Swiss, and other French-speakers. There are a few Indians from Pondichéry. An individual appears whom I recognize before he is announced, although I have not seen him for thirty years: it is the Baron de Clappique.* He no longer wears an eye-patch, but a monocle. In spite of his baldness, his friendly ferret's profile is unchanged. Once, he would have rushed up to me, arms waving like a windmill: "You here! Not a word! Away with you!" Age has calmed him down. The greetings over, he tells me: "I came because the newspapers announced that you were here. I'd love to have a chat with you, partly for old times' sake, but principally because I'm in the middle of making a tiny film about a character you were interested in at the time of *La Voie royale*: David de Mayrena, the king of the Sedangs. I've dug up

* The Baron de Clappique is one of the central characters in André Malraux's novel *La Condition humaine*. (Tr.)

quite a few documents which will interest you!" He himself would be enough to interest me. "You received some stamps of the Kingdom of Sedang, did you not? You see, I thought of you." I had wondered who on earth could have sent me these extremely rare stamps, some years before. The Baron lives at the Raffles Hotel, where I once lived, and where I shall go and see him after dinner. He is an antique dealer, but worked in Hollywood again after the war, and looks after most of the film companies who come to shoot exteriors in Malaysia. He arouses in the consul and his wife the same benevolent affection which he used to arouse in everyone. After the ceremony, he stays to dinner. He sits with his glass of whisky in his left hand, as he used to thirty years ago; and although he has already drunk a great deal, he is as lucid as he was thirty years ago.

He complains of being swamped with fake objets d'art manufactured by the Chinese and sold "like bananas, by inferior *farfelus*: there are no real soldiers of fortune left!"

India to the left, Siam to the north, China and Indonesia to the right . . .

"All the real *farfelus* are in Hong Kong, but the race is dying out."

"The European race," the consul says. "Although there are a few journalists staying near you in the Raffles who went and got themselves wounded in the guerrilla war in Borneo. But there can't be any shortage of *farfelus* among the communists who almost conquered Bali, or the anticommunists who shot them. Singapore will proclaim its independence one of these days. Sukarno isn't finished with his enemies yet, nor Thailand with China. Vietnam is not very peaceful, and there is guerrilla warfare in Sumatra. What more do you want?"

We talk about adventurers.

"What," asks our ambassador to Malaysia, former high commissioner in the New Hebrides, here for the July 14 celebrations, "does the slumber of Asia that Conrad and Kipling and others knew mean to the natives who have seen the fighting between the Americans and the Japanese, and who build imaginary radio-transmitters out of petrol cans and tap messages on them to make the magic airplanes come?"

The ambassador, Pierre Anthonioz, has seen Rajah Brooke's palace in Sarawak: only a pink pavilion remains. The adventurer is a nineteenth-century phenomenon which overlaps into the eighteenth century in India, and a little into the twentieth. The myth of Rimbaud is fading.

"Rimbaud," says Clappique. "Frightful fellow. Away with you! Forty thousand francs in gold in his belt. Comes back to get married. First of all, an adventurer is a bachelor! Secondly, he doesn't save up his sous to go back to Europe. A moneygrubbing adventurer is a nincompoop."

The old vocabulary has not disappeared.

"But a penniless adventurer can very well get himself repatriated by you. Do you still find them?"

"Do you know who was ambassador in Sweden when Rimbaud abandoned his circus and had himself repatriated?" asks Anthonioz. "Gobineau."

"A circus," says Clappique. "That's right. He should have stayed there. I told you, he was a bourgeois."

The dessert is *gula malacca*, rice with caramel and coconut milk. I remember eating it at the Raffles Hotel, in about 1922. I try to steer Clappique on to the subject of Mayrena, but he probably wants to talk to me about him when we are alone, for my remark does not start him off. The conversation becomes commonplace. We leave for the Street of Death, which the consul has told me about, and which I have never seen. I will join Clappique at the hotel.

As we arrive, the Street of Death is beginning its sleepwalking life. As everywhere in southern Asia, the neon lighting springs up around the market stalls. And shadows converge upon this long street lit by a more ancient glow, with its intersecting alleys where three dim lights tremble in the depths of eternal China. The last peddler vanishes down one of them, his bamboo on his shoulder, to the gradually receding sound of his clacker. The market blares with every kind of record, but here the music is of real voices and real instruments, for it is the music of death. Wreaths of white flowers, which would be reminiscent of the welcoming bouquets of India, tuberoses and frangipanis, if they were not so huge; families beginning a funeral feast in front of rows of coffins curved like boats, next to an artisan whose bow-shaped implement seems to be playing on his deep-toned lathe to draw from it weird napkin rings. A little farther on, hotels like the opium dens or 'tween-decks of yesterday, a few concentration camp arms dangling from superposed bunks. Around the circular tables of the almost empty Chinese cafés a few customers are sprawled, and at the square tables in the street sit a few old men who will soon repair to their squalid bunks; an asylum population, patient in the sickly glow, beneath a sky full of stars glimmering like funeral lights, gathered through thousands of death agonies in the funereal music from capitals now disemboweled, Loyang or Singanfu, when the emperor planted the first seeds. The old dragon, who lay down to die among his shadowy people, stripped of all the dazzle of his empires, is falling asleep under his last scales of hemp, sacks, and rags.

The Raffles has changed considerably, but its patio surrounded by rooms with swingdoors is still there. In the middle of the little garden there are drink tables. Clappique is waiting for me in front of a whisky, under a tall palm tree. At the next table, one of the American journalists wounded in Borneo is also drinking, his arm in a sling.

"Sit down. Pen-Wiper, come here!"

A charming tousled black cat leaves its wicker armchair and goes and sits in Clappique's lap.

"So Pen-Wiper and I have produced a tiny masterpiece on which I should like to have your opinion. It's called *The Devil's Kingdom*. There's nothing worse than a literary bore, but you shall see."

I have certainly not forgotten Mayrena, whose legend, still alive in the Indochina of the 1920's, is in part the source of my novel *La Voie royale*. Even so, it merely provided me with a background. Perken was the incarnation, in a type of outlaw still common when I wrote my book, of the negative hero. His march against the Stiengs, his deliberate defiance of torture, owe everything to his self-created image, to the most terrifying struggle against death. I knew fairly little about Mayrena, and would have liked to know more, but the old Indochina hands had created the legend with their dreams, and marred the telling of it with their own inadequacy.

"Is he still talked about in Indochina?"

"There's no longer an Indochina! No, he isn't talked about anymore. War and independence aren't very conducive to the prestige of adventure. His day of glory was at the time of his arrival in Paris, then immediately after his death, around 1890, then after 1918."

"After the war, yes. But why?"

"Because of another legend, that of Colonel Lawrence. Not a word!"

But the legend of Lawrence, especially as it was put about by Lowell Thomas at the beginning, is the dazzling legend of a Queen of Sheba army, with its Arab partisans deployed beneath flying banners among the jerboas of the desert, and imaginary battles in the defiles of rose-red Petra. The setting for Mayrena's is the boredom of Cochin-China, pith-helmets, drink time on the terrace of the *Continental* as the brief twilight descended on the carob trees and the victorias going up and down the Rue Catinat to the jingle of bells, and lights out in the barracks of the Senegalese riflemen.

There are two sources for the legend of the king of the Sedangs. The first is Indochinese: a sort of foreign legion officer, very daring, who had carved himself a kingdom in an untamed land; a Brooke who had failed at the end, without anyone really understanding why. The other source is Parisian: a disreputable hero, destined less for kingship than for assassination, redeemed by the feeling he inspired. The two different personae have one characteristic in common: the eloquence of an alcoholic or an oriental storyteller.

It all began with an exploration, reminiscent of Brazza. Accompanied by a small force of militia lent by the governor, and helped by the missionaries, Mayrena had negotiated a personal alliance with tribe after tribe, with the probable intention of handing them over to France.

He had acquired or conquered nearly all the territory of the Moïs, after defeating the Sadet of Fire, chief of their sorcerer-kings, in a saber fight, glimpsing and disregarding the gold he had come to seek, and creating a military order for his warriors who fought wild elephants with lances, at the time when the great Revolt of the Literati was drawing to a close.

I also knew the stories of the Moulin Rouge dancers who threw flowers to him, of his banishment from Indochina, and of his end in Malaysia, a hunter of birds of paradise.

I summarized all this to Clappique.

"Away with you! Pen-Wiper, you see the sort of thing ministers believe! It didn't quite happen like that. In fact it didn't happen like that at all! I've received a fair amount of reliable information, and I've tried to imagine the rest as convincingly as possible. Not that I care two hoots about truth, of course. But in a film, I think it's more interesting. A lot of details will have to be 'worked in' to what I'm going to read to you. I'll take care of that."

"It all starts with a bell: ting-a-ling, ting-a-ling! Not a word. Close-up of an oil lamp hanging from a dingy ceiling. Around it, a bunch of tiny lizards scuttling off in all directions. The camera pans through the garden, the house, and enters; but we'll leave out the camera directions.

"So, on either side of a table as fly-blown as the ceiling, with glasses of Pernod and everything else to match, Mayrena and his friend Mercurol, stripped to the waist, sit listening to the bell.

"Mercurol is a rumpled, seedy-looking fellow. The mustache and beard of a poor man's musketeer. Mayrena is a toothy Jupiter. Wavy hair, parting down the middle, straight nose, square-cut beard, you can see the sort of thing. Superb teeth, slightly prominent: a toothpaste smile. I said Jupiter, but a bumptious Jupiter. From the first shot onward, he's the boss.

"Bell rings again. A nebulous character in policeman's uniform.

"MAYRENA: They wouldn't dare arrest one of Saigon's top newspapermen.

"MERCUROL: There's no proof.

"Mayrena puts on a civilian jacket, picks up a revolver, and puts it in his pocket.

"He leaves the house, goes to the gate. The character raises a storm lantern which lights up his face and the badges on his collar. GG. It isn't a policeman, it's a courier from the Governor General.

"The lantern goes out. Tall vegetation against the sky. Yapping of an Annamese domestic quarrel from the depths of the night.

"THE COURIER: Monsieur Mayrena?

"MAYRENA: Baron de Mayrena, my good man.

"The courier lights up his lantern again and hands Mayrena a letter which he opens.

"MAYRENA: Tonight?

"THE COURIER: Lieutenant, all I can say is: now this minute."

Clappique still possesses that astonishing talent for imitation which used to dazzle me years ago. He reads without indicating the names of the characters. For Mayrena, he has developed a tone of voice as peculiar as his own—the tone of the last romantics?—inherited, apparently, from Don César de Bazan and from the crazy bombast of Frédérick Lemaître in Robert Macaire. In fact there is a suggestion of "Robert Macaire in Asia" in his Mayrena. But also an odd suggestion of fellow feeling. He reads the technical directions in a neutral tone:

Fade to Mayrena before the Governor. Vast official room, whitewashed and almost without furniture. Maps on the walls. On a table, two pith-helmets.

The window is wide open on to the night. Noises off: a one-stringed violin, the clatter of mah-jongg tiles, the padding of the rickshaw-coolies' bare feet, distant bells.

The Governor—a mulatto—walks up and down. A white scarf of Annamese silk round his neck.

"Well then, Mayrena, how goes it? Not too well? Never mind: police records are not my cup of tea. Let's talk about something else. How long have you known that the German mission had left for the Mekong?"

"Since the day before yesterday, sir."

"From whom?"

"My usual sources."

A firm reply. The Governor looks at him: "I suppose you mean Scheherazade, mainly."

"You know her name?"

"Incidentally, are you married?"

"Oh, here, you know . . ."

"Pity. Should get married. Much better that way. Incidentally, you're a believer, aren't you?"

"Of course."

"Good, good. What you suggested in your article, suppose you are asked to do it yourself. What do you do? Go on!"

And he flings the end of the Annamese scarf, which is dangling, round his neck again.

"If gold mining is to be developed in the Attopeu region and transportation has to go via Annam, we at once have four unsubdued tribes to deal with: Bahnars, Rongaos, Sedangs, and Jarais. These tribes can be pacified either by our army, or by the development company itself."

"Let's leave the army out of it: it isn't the government's policy to intervene in that region. As for the gold, I doubt if you'd find enough for your development to be profitable. That's your business."

"But, Governor, if there's to be no development, why try . . ."

"Because!"

Another flick of the muffler.

"You wrote that 'a determined man could succeed in organizing the hinterland and arranging transport, provided he could be sure of the neutrality of the administration.' You are. What do you do?"

"I contact one chief of a big village. To find just one wouldn't be difficult. I smother him with modest gifts. I organize a team of fighting men there, armed with rifles, either from the Annamese guards I bring with me, or else . . ."

"I don't want any official French presence beyond Kontum—get that into your head."

"Former guards could be used, or the local warriors could be taught to shoot: savages learn fast and are good marksmen. But rifles and ammunition would be needed. Then I arrange an alliance with the neighboring village, which has everything to gain and nothing to lose, since it has no guns. Then a dozen small villages; all small villages want protection."

"The Siamese are still a long way away."

"Are the Siamese interested? But the Jarais pillage and burn villages periodically, and carry off the prisoners as slaves. Up to the moment when we reach the Jarai country, it would be best to organize the confederation against the Jarais. I have studied Dupleix's and Cortez's expeditions, and the life of the Bishop of Adran. What else did they do but rely on one tribe against another, on two tribes against a third, with energy, the knowledge of a few dialects—and the help of God!—I think there are still some Cham tribes in that direction, and my . . . my lady friend is descended from the kings of My-Son, as you perhaps know, since you know of her existence. I shall do tribe by tribe what I shall have done village by village. And what risk is there for the government in an adventure where big sums would serve no purpose and it would always be easy to disown me?"

"You can count on that."

"Fifty French rifles, which I might even have bought in China . . ."

"Swiss or Belgian, German perhaps, certainly not French. And while we're on the subject, if there are any knocking about in your cellar at the moment, just see that they stay there."

The Governor looks at the map. "It might be a long job . . ."

"When Pizarro left for Peru, sir, he was fifty-three years old! There might be a way of going about it faster. Not all the Moïs are fetishists. Some of the Bahnars have been converted."

"You will get in touch with the Fathers as soon as the Resident at Qui Nhon has forwarded my final instructions to you."

"The bishop has a lot of influence. He is a saint out of the Middle Ages, an inspired figure. Will he agree to this collaboration? The missions are very poor: I could try to interest them in the gold . . ."

"My friend, get this well into your head: fifty per cent of *talapoins* are people who believe in anything, manipulated by a few others who believe in nothing; and fifty per cent are people who believe in nothing, manipulated by a few others who believe in anything. But whether here, in heaven or in hell, there's never been an instance of a missionary failing to obey a governor. There's no question about it. It only remains to be seen *how* they will obey. Go and see the bishop and give me a report on your visit. I want to know whether or not, in French territory, these missionary gentlemen are prepared to carry out the policy of France! It would interest me to know. At Qui Nhon, you can still rely on me. You cease to act in the name of France, whatever the excuse, from the Bahnar country onward. You go down toward the Mekong . . ."

"The placers are on the Mekong itself . . ."

"That's your affair. But be circumspect: you'll certainly come across Siamese officials there. Always stay within your rights. I'm going to put at your disposal an interpreter from the Sûreté to levy what you need; at Qui Nhon, a team of porters, an escort of Annamese guards which will accompany you as far as Kontum, and some money. Do you want anything else?"

"The gold-mining concession for the Jarai and Sedang country."

The Governor gives a slight shrug of the shoulders. "I'm not surprised! All right. Is that all?"

MAYRENA (after a silence, in a lower voice): You're putting your trust in me, and I won't let you down.

The Governor claps him on the shoulder, starts coughing, tightens his Annamese scarf and accompanies him to the door.

Mayrena gets out of a rickshaw in front of an ill-lit little bazaar. On the door: Mercurol and Co. He goes in.

Mercurol and the native servant advance to meet him.

MAYRENA: We leave for the gold by the first boat. My first job is to establish communications. Tickets on the house. Porters.

"I say, the administration's really thinking of us!"

"Of me."

"You said we were leaving . . ."

"I arranged all that . . ."

"Then it's all right, see. It comes to the same thing. It must be because of your article. I told you, remember. They're putting up the dough?"

"A little. Porters, military escort, letters for the Residents and the Fathers, concession for the goldfields. Signed, sealed, and delivered."

A big oil lamp, the only source of light, illuminates some life-size fairground target figures against a background of Chinese bric-à-brac. Mercurol sits down sadly on the counter. "We'll do the job, a real tough job: then when it's all fixed, just you wait, old man, they'll pull something dirty, they'll gyp us out of those mines."

He whistles. A mongoose emerges from the shadows and stretches out beside him.

"I'd have liked to do it in a nice economical way. I'd have done a bit of palmistry, or taken some photos, the natives would have fed us, or if you didn't like that idea we could have eaten Annamese style; it costs next to nothing, and I could always have found a way of paying the wogs enough to buy an occasional box of smokes, or a little bottle of Pernod. And then, see, that way they couldn't have cheated us. We could have ignored their lousy intrigues; just slipped in, without anyone knowing."

"So much for human nature!"

"I didn't say I wouldn't go, old man, I never said I wouldn't go. Well then, I'll make out a preliminary list of what we're taking."

He goes and sits at the cash desk:

"Pernod, quinine, underwear, boots, camp beds, canned food we'll deal with later, mosquito nets. Camera? No, we couldn't develop the film, pity. Beer, no. Brandy, yes. Paper, hot water bottles, scout knives. Hey, couldn't we take the camera anyway?"

"Only the bare minimum."

"Oh, I'm not all that keen on packing. So, we were saying: boot laces, soap, buttons. Books. Hey, by the way, if you don't mind, I wish you wouldn't give me my books back all dogeared. 'Cause I'd like to take that *History of the Adventurers in the Indies*, see, and if it's already dogeared . . . Powder, bullets, weapon grease."

"I'll take care of the flag and the pennons personally. As much ammunition as possible for the revolvers."

"Depends how much money we have. By the way, old man, we could do one little bit of business right away. We could take some junk for the Moïs, no? What I've got here, carefully chosen."

"Anything small, and the dummies, that's all. Above all, we mustn't be overloaded."

"Are we taking some equipment for the gold? I made inquiries at the importers' over a month ago now: they have to order from Singapore."

"No: once the deposits are located, I see it immediately on an industrial scale."

The little boat that plies between Cochin-China and Tonkin. Passengers pacing up and down the deck. A little to one side, Mayrena and another man, stretched out on cane chairs. Pernods.

The Governor General and one of his colleagues.

"Why are you saddling yourself with this wildman?"

"Because we don't settle the problem of the independent tribes with choirboys—or with blackskirts. And because he doesn't bore me as much as the others."

The camera follows Mercurol toward Mayrena who is leaning over the rails, surrounded by all the people who are not playing cards in the big saloon whose open windows can be seen to the right. Men and women in white: nocturnal pierrots. Against the background noise we hear, "Monsieur le Baron, call me Alphonsine!"

Four Chinese are playing mah-jongg on deck, squatting round a little opium lamp.

MAYRENA: What do you know about the Jarais? The names of the men they have killed! What awaits an explorer out there? When Cortez won his first victory (he was the conqueror of Mexico, ladies!) he nearly died of hunger: no sooner had the Indians concluded that his men were invulnerable and decided to honor them, than they wanted to feed them on children's hearts, copal and parrots' feathers."

"Children's hearts! Oh, monsieur le Baron, anything you like, but not children's hearts!"

"But the first gift of the Aztec emperor was a carved wheel in solid gold, and so many uncut emeralds that he had to build a little cart to carry them."

"He could have stuffed them up his . . . " Mercurol mutters. Then, aloud: "The emeralds were flawed. The Pizarro business was better: there, every soldier got a couple of hundred thousand francs. That's some pay."

"But, monsieur le Baron, we're always hearing about men: it's interesting for the ladies too, that kind of thing. Don't you know some stories about women?"

"These lands are full of them, madame. Think, gentlemen, of Timur's granddaughter. She was a granddaughter to him in the same way as that charming trollop De Lavallière was to Henri IV! But at least she was married—Muslim style. She had been captured by the Emir's troops with a Persian caravan and sold as a slave, and ended up as the slave of the Emperor's grandson. A shrimp of a fellow whose tastes were, h'm . . . You understand what I mean, gentlemen! and wrapped up in poetry when the imperial horses were trampling the Iron Gates!

"But the crown prince, who commanded the horsemen of the guard at the battle of Angora, was cut down by Bajazet's men. Our prince became heir to the Empire. I can just see old Timur, bowed down with sorrow, looking out of the corner of his eye at those shoulders incapable of bearing even a lance, and onto which he was about to toss the greatest empire in the world! The first thing he did was to have the girl arrested, judging no doubt, gentlemen, that an empire may occasionally survive the stupidity of a man, but the baseness of a woman, never!"

"Oh, monsieur le Baron, you're against us poor women too."

"I'm only referring to this one, madame. So there is Timur departing for the Chinese marches with that great army which was not to experience a retreat from Russia."

Vague gesture toward the coast; fires in the Annamite Chain, and in the very depths of the night, the marches toward which the army of Samarkand made its way five hundred years ago. The steady throb of the engines.

MERCUROL (between his teeth): And what about the broad, then?

MAYRENA: You know that Timur took to his deathbed as soon as he reached China. He died a few days later; the generals ordered a retreat. And, gentlemen, such was the terror he inspired that no one dared to announce his death: the lancers came back, foxtails on their lances, and the Imperial Guard escorted the closed litter in which the terrifying cadaver was decomposing, with the smell becoming more frightful every day—as if, in spite of the stench, the Emir might suddenly have been capable of waking up and chopping off a few more indiscreet heads, gentlemen!

WOMAN'S VOICE: But the woman?

"She was queen, madame—queen as no woman ever was—of the richest empire in the world, which she had made her plaything! Arrested on Timur's orders, and certain to be condemned to death, she threw herself at the feet of the Empress and confessed that she was pregnant. That sex, so gracious and so sorely tried, is lucky, gentlemen! What means could a man have found of gaining seven months' respite? Timur dead, no more sign of a child than the man in the moon, but the prince becomes emperor. Utterly incapable of assuming the reins of empire. Imperial couriers were dispatched to every province, with instructions to give the order in every capital to send their treasures to Samarkand. All these treasures were brought together, and so were the Persian musicians with their viols and their long-necked instruments."

Above the heads of his audience, Mayrena's long arm rises toward the deck lights.

"Each night, the former slave sat on one of the thrones before the great pool of Samarkand, the pool of turquoise mosaic in which the sacred fish of Timur swam. The musicians played under the stars of Asia which we see above our own heads, gentlemen! On great gold platters, the servants brought the treasures of the Empire to the motionless princess. And she took them and threw them to the fishes. Fistfuls of pearls trickled between her fingers like grains of rice between the fingers of our native servants when they take it out of the sacks."

"Jewels as well?"

"And jewels, madame, and precious stones from Kashgar to Vienna and from Rostov to Isfahan!"

One of the two NCO's stifles a burst of laughter. His companion, under his breath: "What are you laughing at, fathead: it's scientific fact."

"Oh, come off it: Rostoff and Cachart and Timur and his Samaritan capital! It's all a big joke to me!"

"The army came back by forced marches," Mayrena goes on, his beard turned toward the man who has dared to laugh. "The generals seized power. The prince having been deposed, his sublime strumpet was put in the pillory for two days, while the populace came to spit in those devilish eyes which had scorned treasures! She did not die until twenty years later, in a suburban house where she had become a washerwoman."

Silence. Engines.

"All the same," Alphonsine says at last, in an undertone, "the poor girl didn't have much luck, because after all her husband—all right, so he wasn't the soldier type: why didn't he have a good general? In a battle, you've got to have a winner as well as a loser, so you've got a fifty-fifty chance, at least."

Hubbub.

"About the treasures," Mayrena resumes, "I know nothing, but there was gold here during the great periods. More than two hundred and fifty miles of the Mekong in Middle Laos is lined with quartz. We have good reason to think that this quartz is gold-bearing, and perhaps France possesses an unsuspected California here, gentlemen!"

"It would be known . . ." says a shy voice.

"And how so, monsieur?"

"It would have been seen—the gold."

"Yes? Well then, watch this: I'll show you some. Mercurol, go and get the feather! Mister assistant-director of the Bank, it was probably like this when someone in a boat off the coast of California said: 'Gold has been found in the Sacramento Valley.' "

Mercurol returns, a heavy lantern in his left hand, a goose-feather in his right. He hands it to Mayrena who gives it to the schoolmistress. The feather passes from hand to hand.

"The Moïs," says Mayrena, "keep gold dust in the quills of these big feathers. You see, they stop them up with a little wooden plug."

He takes back the feather, pulls a large notebook out of his pocket, tears out one leaf, folds it in two and places it on the deck. Everybody is on all fours. The lantern is put down on a corner of the paper to keep it in place. Mayrena carefully removes the little wooden plug, and turns the feather upside down.

"Careful," says a voice, "the wind!"

"No, it's heavy."

The irregular grains flow into the beam of light, a few inches from the lantern.

(The camera revolves slowly and takes in, one after another, the fascinated faces.)

Mercurol goes off again with the feather, the gold in the folded sheet of paper, and the lamp.

A SERGEANT: Well, in that case the mandarins are going to take a bit of a bashing.

MAYRENA: The mandarins will only be disturbed by our passage; and not immediately. The gold is in tribal territory: the Sedang and Jarai country. Obviously, gentlemen, as long as we leave savages in control of the gold-bearing lands, we will only see it here in miserable quantities. The Indochina Company will take steps to avoid having to fear such catastrophes. Admirable troops, gentlemen, those soldiers of fortune scattered around the world; but not without dangers.

A dark junk passes the little steamer.

"Ooh, I say!" murmurs Alphonsine. "I almost thought there was gold in the sails!"

"This wealth must become the wealth of France! The gold of Peru and Mexico made Spain, the gold of the Pacific made the United States of America; will the Sedang gold avenge our great humiliation of seventeen years ago?"

In his cabin, Mayrena tips the gold back into the quill. Close-up of his anxious face.

*   *   *   *

A large crucifix rising to ceiling height. The camera, receding, brings into view the white parlor of the bishop of Qui Nhon, and Mayrena sitting facing the bishop. Black table and chairs.

"We will help you, monsieur, as it is proper for us to help any French explorer. All the more so if he is recommended to us."

"Your grace, at the present moment your missions have more power in the tribal areas than the French government itself: obviously this will not always be so. Even if we leave aside the possibility of a German take-over—and everything leads one to believe that we would be mistaken in leaving it aside!—a take-over by the French government will be subject to the vicissitudes of its policy. I have been given carte blanche by the Governor General. And he knows my feelings: I was brought up by the Fathers, and I am a firm believer. What do the missions want? To bring souls to God? I am entirely devoted to their cause, however much or however little help they may give me. And though the Republic may change faith with every ministry, a gentleman never does. Your Grace, I am gambling with my life. Help me or not, according as God dictates; what *I* ask of you . . ."

Close-up of the bishop listening, motionless: crisp gray hair and beard, snub nose.

". . . is instructions for your Fathers, and above all your prayers for us all."

"I have already told you, my son: it is proper for us to assist any French explorer. I will give you a letter for the mission. It is a heavy task you have chosen. Will you be able to overcome all those obstacles, so disturbing, so fearful even for those poor missionaries among the savages?"

"My friend Father Auger has spoken to me of Father Georges as a priest of truly medieval energy, Your Grace."

"Father Georges is a warrior-monk, it is true. You will judge of that when you see him: Providence, foreseeing that he would have to deal with simple men, has written his soul on his face, or rather in his eyebrows."

He looks out of the window: the China Sea, fishermen returning, Mayrena's boat receding.

"The Sedangs, and above all the Jarais, whom you are making toward, are assuredly the most cruel of all the pagans. Murder is honored among them: they only acknowledge an adolescent to be a man when he brings proof of his first murder. Before building their communal houses, they bury alive a slave crushed by the main beam."

"If the Confederation is established, believe me the Jarais will soon be dissuaded from taking Christians from the missions as slaves!"

"They live by slave-trading and pillage. Yes, it is as if the struggle our Fathers have undertaken were being waged against the devil himself, and that he were the true king of these tribes. And yet . . ."

The smooth sea has lost its sparkling depth, and has become opaque and milky. Evening is about to fall.

"Inside their villages, among themselves, and when they leave behind their blood-lust, they are honest and straightforward. They do not fight each other, except for their idols; theft is unknown among them. On this point they are more civilized than many of our own people, who have not the excuse of ignorance. They help each other instinctively. And if their women ao not even know what modesty is, they also know nothing of adultery.

"What a strange thing it is, and how moved and troubled I am when I listen to the stories of our Fathers about the nature of the savages—so similar, in its way, to that of all men. It is as though I were touching original sin with my hands, and the effort, so beautiful, so moving—so hard sometimes, alas!—which has been conducted on earth ever since the coming of the Redeemer.

"Perhaps you will indeed open these unfortunate lands to the influence of Our Lord. It is no criticism of the administration of this country to think that it will support your efforts with greater solicitude than it has shown toward ours."

"What I do may involve some violence."

The bishop makes no answer.

"It is a great thing, Your Grace, to suppress murder and misery wherever one goes. I shall pray to God this evening to thank him for the honor he has done me, and which I had never expected."

M. Chaminade, Resident at Binh-Dinh, has decided to give a special dinner party in two days' time: better not introduce just anybody to a man on a mission from Saigon on behalf of the Governor General. M. Chaminade, an extremely obliging little man with graying hair, is like a well-behaved Mercurol; Mme. Nathalie Chaminade has a pen name, "Thalie de Sombreuse." And Mayrena, puzzled, puts on a knowing look. He takes stock of the room: Annamese paintings, Cham statues, collections of insects and butterflies. Books. Mme. Chaminade wears a dress with a large floral design, and her hair in ringlets. An old

Ceres blighted by the menopause, the tropics and solitude: in this town where there are no white women, year by year her dress and make-up have brought her closer to her dreams—to the point of masquerade. It is obvious to Mayrena that his host looks upon him as his superior: which makes him angelic. He has talked about the bishop, but with caution; about the Governor General, in terms implying intimacy, which his mission makes plausible; he wonders how he can do M. Chaminade a favor with the powers that be, "since it is only through the concerted action of all Frenchmen, through friendly mutual assistance, that we shall accomplish the admirable task that each of us has set himself here, do you not think so, madame?" They have got to the point of talking about the massacre two years before of twenty-five thousand Annamese Christians by the rebels. "Your Father Georges," says Chaminade, "had a few rifles, two little fieldguns which must have created more noise than damage. Five hundred Moïs with their crossbows. Naturally he gave asylum to all the hunted missionaries who reached the mountains. He held out up there at Kontum, surrounded, for two years. No salt, no quinine, nothing. Two years. He's a very brave man, you know, oh, a very brave man. But still, you can be as close to the Fathers as you like, but you'll never be *one of them.*"

"Do you think they have enough influence over the chiefs to get them to join the Confederation I am to set up?"

"In the places where they're established, you know, they can do anything. Elsewhere, not much."

"What do you call established?"

"Oh, it's simple enough: if, in a village, one straw hut is converted into a church, they are powerful there. They hold the territory of the Bahnars. But the Sedangs and the Jarais are quite another matter. The missions can hold out against them, but not subdue them."

There exists another base of operations, but M. Chaminade prefers not to mention it. At the time of the inauguration of the French protectorate over Annam, three years earlier, the Residents received a confidential instruction to lose no opportunity of winning over the unsubdued mountains. Now Phim, the chief of Kong-Jeri, had been preparing for a long time a federation of the chiefs of the eastern region, those whose territories border on Annam. He was on the point of succeeding. He had been to Bangkok, and one day when he was at Qui Nhon he had seen the French naval squadron, which had inspired in him an unqualified respect for the power of France. His federation would extend over half the area between the frontier and the missions.

That is by no means negligible; and if the Resident has not yet mentioned it, it is because this success would contribute in the most effective manner toward his advancement. So Phim is not for Mayrena.
Father Georges "writes." Which leads the conversation on to literature. Mayrena begs Mme. Chaminade to read something. But Thalie
de Sombreuse knows her lines by heart. She stands up. The poem is
called *The Curse*: the Asians are doomed to misfortune and will be
defeated because they do not know love:

> *The Princes of Annam, who are the sons of Fire*
> *Know nothing of thy power, O burning mystery . . .*

Mayrena listens, eyes closed, beard nodding approval. Wine, brandy,
respect. He would approve of much worse. Thalie is not so bad when
she speaks the language of the gods. And those breasts: a white woman.

> *O love, O joy, O love, within thy veils are hid*
> *So many frenzied hearts beneath the virgin stars! . . .*

"The whole piece has a lyrical beauty about it," says Mayrena. "*Frenzied* in particular. *Frenzied hearts*. How strange it is to find poetry in
the furthest depths of the Far East!"

As at the priory, the long drawn-out cries of the fishermen can be
heard through the windows.

"What a pity Victor Hugo is dead! I would have enjoyed telling
him about this evening, and above all sending him your poems."

"That would be lovely, a little volume of poems printed here. Just
think, Monsieur de Mayrena: if Alfred de Musset had had his first
poems printed in Venice."

"Pretty, but little read, madame. And your poems are better than
that flowery tomb."

"Ah! we've lost the habit of gallantry here. You knew Victor Hugo?
How lucky you are! Tell me, was he anything like people say?"

"People say many things, madame. Like my grandfather, whom he
resembled, he was a man of another age: refined and courteous, very
formal at his grand dinners, and very simple in private. The last
memory I have of him is an amusing one, and may perhaps disillusion
you."

"Oh no, do tell me!"

"It was, as it happens, at the end of one of those grand dinners.
The master was always the last to leave the great dining room in the
Avenue d'Eylau. We had just moved into the drawing room when I

found that I had dropped my handkerchief. I was very attached to it:
it was a . . . souvenir. So I come back with my eyes on the ground.
I find it, pick it up, and when I raise my eyes I see the master, standing
up in his seat, with his back to me since he was facing away from the
door. (He was very greedy.) So, from the back, I had the impression
that he was looking at all those empty seats, a little in disorder, as if
it were a supper of ghosts. He leaves his place, still without noticing
me, takes a few paces and sadly picks up a bowl of cakes, like Hamlet's
cup; then puts it down again and says aloud, in his fine, deep, slightly
cracked voice: 'The swine! They've eaten all the cakes . . .' Those
were the last words I heard him speak."

"And Madame Drouet? Tell me, tell me."

"A little white-haired old lady, sitting impassively by the fire; she
was dying of cancer. We all looked on her with reverence. For each of
us, madame, she represented fifty years of love! And the ghost of her
beauty was still such that she represented those years worthily."

> Répondez, vallon pur, répondez, solitude,
> O nature abritée en ce désert si beau
> Lorsque nous dormirons tous deux dans l'attitude
> Que donne aux morts pensifs la forme du tombeau;
> Est-ce que vous serez à ce point insensible,
> De nous savoir couchés, morts avec nos amours,
> Et de continuer votre fête paisible,
> Et de toujours sourire et de chanter toujours?

While he recites, images of France covered in roses, the tall carts
groaning under the sheaves of corn in the setting sun. Big horses, the
cool of the evening, stone villages.

Between the sea and the Annamite Chain, the solemn chorus of
frogs in the warm night.

Thalie, in medium close-up, motionless and deeply melancholy. She
still looks like the Madwoman of Chaillot, but dead. She replies:

> Je ne veux rien savoir, ni si les champs fleurissent,
> Ni ce qu'il adviendra du simulacre humain,
> Ni si ces vastes cieux éclaireront demain
>   ce qu'ils ensevelissent . . .

"One day, when I was rereading *Souvenir*—one gets so bored here!—I realized that Alfred de Musset wasn't addressing Dante at all, as he claims, but *Olympio*."

"Splendid idea! And no one has noticed! Why don't you write an article about it?"

She makes a vague gesture of discouragement, then gets up: "Will you excuse me? I must give a few orders."

The two men go outside to smoke the traditional cigar. Tall fronds, lianas, frogs, cicadas, surf.

CHAMINADE: In the army of the Loire I met a woman who . . . Do you know, it was the only time I've been happy. It would certainly have been the love of my life . . . It's nearly twenty years ago now . . . Only I was married.

A lizard screeches. The Resident lowers his voice still further: "It was too late . . . At our age, we have so many dreams behind us. Still, you have one in front of you . . . You're lucky."

"But you run this region! When I ran my newspaper campaign, I was thinking of gold. But since then, and, just imagine, after my interview with your bishop, I've been saying to myself that to get rid of slavery from a territory as big as half of France is something rather more worthy of me than the destiny I have been pursuing for ten years on a razor's edge! And we're doing it together!"

The nearest frogs fall silent: Mayrena has begun to raise his voice in the darkness. His exaltation dies away with their regular croaking.

CHAMINADE: Sometimes I tell myself that. Yes, I run this region as well as I can. But the sad truth, as you well know, is that I'm a kind of police superintendent. One thing used to interest me very much at the beginning—exploration. Now it depends on Hué, even Hanoi. I was informed of your arrival the day before yesterday; yet given time, I could have helped you. And we're so exhausted by the climate, my wife and I. You must watch out for dysentery, you know.

Silence. Cicadas.

CHAMINADE: So settle in here. It will be a pleasure for us. We'll organize the work together: we shall have a lot to do in common when you're up there. I shall have many things to ask you, partly for my collection, but mainly for the '89 Exhibition, if it takes place.

They are at the end of the garden. A voice behind them calls: "Monsieur de Mayrena! Did you know Alfred de Musset?"

Thalie comes out of the Residence, silhouetted against the lights of the verandah, then disappears into the darkness. The sound of her heels comes toward them. She joins them, dreamy but out of breath.

"Ah, Musset! He's the one I should really have liked to know."

"How I would like to be a poet, madame, so that women like you would dream of my damned soul at the farthest ends of the earth! No, I know nothing of him. But how he would have loved your poems! 'Frenzied hearts.' "

"Do you know Charpentier?"

"The publisher?"

"Yes, his publisher."

"A little. I could easily scribble a note to him, if you like."

"Oh, that would be so kind of you!"

"Your French perfume is competing with the perfume of the trees."

Chaminade takes Thalie's arm. They go in.

Chaminade's study. Mayrena has taken a sheet of the Resident's letterhead paper, and reads aloud as he writes:

Dear Sir, I am, as you see, a long way from our last conversation. But only in space; for it is still French literature, that France which is everywhere present, that I have heard discussed this evening among the statues of a vanished people, by the finest French poetess, I swear, in this part of the world: Mme. Thalie de Sombreuse. I am sending you her poems, which she aspires to the honor of reading under your imprint. She unites with a sure sense of form the Indochinese inspiration which our poetry still lacks. But I will say no more: this letter has no other purpose than to beg you on no account to leave the reading . . .

"Excuse me," he asks the Resident, "what is the name of Mme. de Sombreuse's collection?"

"*Enchanted Lotuses.* I preferred *French Lotuses;* we hesitated between the two . . ."

. . . on no account to leave the reading of Enchanted Lotuses in inferior hands.

Read, judge, and thank me.

Marie-David de Mayrena.

"We're very grateful to you," says the Resident.

"Not at all. The least I could do."

"Listen," says the Resident, "there is one thing that you might perhaps do. One of the principal chiefs of the lower region, called Phim, is in process of organizing a federation of chiefs. He is devoted to me: the Residence has done him various favors.

"Phim cannot read, but he can recognize seals, and knows mine.

See him (and I beg you to mention in high places the fact that I helped you), get his federation finally under way: everything is ready. That will be a first success, and a worthwhile base. There is a tip of Jarai territory lying between Phim's Moïs and those of the missions."

Mayrena looks at the map of the province on the wall.

"That's devilish interesting."

"We must look into all that more closely, as well as the arrangements for your expedition. I believe . . ."

Thalie comes in. She sees the finished letter on the desk, and seizes Mayrena's hands: "Come, come now, he's right! Do you know what you should do, Monsieur de Mayrena? Move in here. You would be better off here than staying with the shipping agent, an excellent man, but still . . . It will be more appropriate to the dignity of your mission. We shall talk of poetry. Come, do come!"

Clappique places his hands on his manuscript. In the warm night, a dozen guests on their way back from a reception or from the cinema return to the hotel without distracting the ephemerids flitting round the lamps.

"Here," he says, "the second part begins. I won't go on reading, because we would never get to the end."

"I'm in no hurry."

"And because some scenes are only sketched in. I'll give you a summary, with excerpts. The atmosphere must change entirely. Up to now, it was the old colony, tropical boredom, the Cochin-China of the whites at the end of the nineteenth century. Now, everything is timeless.

"God knows I've seen some forests in the cinema! The camera always seems to be taking a stroll there. One must convey impression of penetration. It's nothing but endless leaves among endless treetrunks, but the shots must be closer and closer together, because after three days you get the feeling that the forest is closing in. An occasional clearing: mountains and the sparkle of valleys. Three thousand feet below, Annam. One goes back into the forest as if one were going underground. Always tracks, never footpaths. Inside there, everything pullulates. There'll be the usual methods of showing that the days are passing; but right from the beginning there must be insects. The thatched villages look like wood lice. The camera must zoom down on leeches and flabby, almost transparent frogs. As the caravan advances, the spectator must stifle. A tiger will carry off a child brought with the guides. But the coolies will know of the tiger's presence beforehand, because they will have found the skeleton of a buffalo, picked quite clean. The white chest cage, the big black crescent of the horns on the skull swarming with insects. The tiger is the Lord of the insects. And the convoy must plunge into the Moï world at the same time as it plunges into the forest.

"I call it the Moï world, because it isn't only savagery, you'll see."

Mayrena is at the head of the convoy. Next to him, M. Minh, the Annamite interpreter, a big forty-year-old baby with tortoise-shell spectacles, and the Bahnar guide. Evening is about to fall. From time to time, an almost naked savage leaning on his spear and a red outcrop of rock. Above the convoy, huge bamboos. Above them, the transparent needles of the leaves, and farther up, the gnarled branches. Higher still, like crystallizations in the ocean deeps, the pentagonal spiders' webs two stories high; on the highest threads, from which the webs hang down like canopies, the fugitive red glow of evening. With tiny sounds of branches tapping against each other, the treetrunks are beginning their evening assembly. Everything comes from the forest, and everything goes back to its undersea vegetation out of which there loom at intervals treetrunks dead of old age.

Here, absurd or no, magic is a living thing. Sometimes a wild peacock goes shrieking by. "We are afraid," the guide says; for the peacock is the tiger's companion. Mayrena, behind this savage who smells like a wet dog, is finally discovering his youth. How many years has he been waiting for it? This time it is here, in spite of all those absurd years that must be obliterated.

The forest ceases and the fields begin, little fields cleared with spear blades. They are crisscrossed with cracks caused by the drought. The guide points them out with his spear.

"He says, M. de Mayrena, that there must be many spiders. He says this because of the drought."

"They nest there?"

The Bahnar makes a fairly lengthy reply.

"No: he says that the cracks are the drought. Drought near a village means there are many adulterers. Adultery is when a spider has dropped on to the bed."

"His Grace told me there was no adultery among the Moïs."

"In some tribes."

"Does the guide really believe what he says, or is it a bit of folklore?"

"He says: In your country are there different spirits?"

"It isn't spirits. It's that the clouds have stayed away too long."

"He says: Of course. But why are there no clouds?"

"Because there's not enough evaporation."

Explanation (?) in Bahnar of evaporation.

"He says he understands very well. But he says: Why is there not enough evaporation?"

"I'll explain it to him when I can speak his language."

"He says thank you. He says that where you come from it must be as you say. But that here, adultery is spiders."

The Annamite abandons his interpreter's voice.

"He isn't a wise man, M. de Mayrena. He's very animal. Perhaps they're superstitious prejudices; but perhaps not . . ."

"Do you also think that drought is caused by adultery, M. Minh?" Mayrena asks, flashing his teeth in a smile.

The trees have reappeared: the fields are no longer visible. The Annamite makes a vague gesture and seems vexed.

"The savages believe in many fables, M. de Mayrena. But they also have many just beliefs about their country. They know the animals better than we do, and even in Saigon, the pearl of the Far East, the French also believe in fables."

"Are you referring to our holy religion?"

All-in shot from the front: Don Quixote and Sancho Panza.

"But I am baptized, M. de Mayrena!"

"Well, then? Do Frenchmen believe absurd things when it's a question of ascertainable facts?"

"You agree, M. de Mayrena, that nearly all Europeans smoke opium after being in the colony for a while?"

"Well, many."

"All the Europeans, they say that opium gives great visions. Opium never gives great visions, and yet many smoke, and all say this."

Mayrena reflects. M. Minh goes on: "He says: Drought is not always spiders. Sometimes it is scorpions. After all, the frogs . . . what do you call them? Tree frogs, yes . . . certainly climb their ladder when it is going to rain?"

Mayrena, Mercurol, the guide, M. Minh, round a campfire. The dogs, hair standing on end, tails between their legs, bark softly.

MERCUROL: The tiger certainly got that kid all right, just now.

The guide says a few words. M. Minh translates.

"He is prowling round us. He is watching."

He raises his voice, which is drowned by the crackling of the fire.

"The child was doomed. Death at the hands of the Master is hereditary."

Mayrena shrugs his shoulders. M. Minh continues: "I read in the library at Saigon, in a respected French book, that suicide is hereditary. Why not death at the hands of the Master as well, M. de Mayrena? All the Moïs say so. They are very animal, but among us Annamites in the plantations, people say it too."

The muffled barking rises and falls, then stops.

"It is not wise to believe that it is just another animal, M. de Mayrena. Since we do not know where dead men go, why shouldn't the ones that He has killed go into him?"

The dogs' confabulation grows fainter and fainter, slower and slower; one senses that it will go on all night. They talk at the fire, heads cocked sideways, while their ears are on the alert for something or other.

"Do you know why the Moïs all say that the Master is not an animal? And we Annamites too, a little? Because He can make man traps."

The hammocks are slung, the militiamen mount guard by the fires.

When they wake up, forty-three coolies and one militiaman have fled.

Morning. The convoy (not so long) in the forest. More animal skeletons. "The Master's tongue is a rasp," says M. Minh. Insects. Man trap: an uprooted tree, hairpin track round it, tiger's lair at the apex of the hairpin.

Shouts, confusion, halt. Coolies and militiamen pick themselves up, one militiaman remains prostrate. Killed: an arrow in his eye. Hurriedly, they make a hurdle and carry the dead man away. One arm is already twisted like a root.

"Jarai arrows are always poisoned," says M. Minh.

The arrow has not been pulled out. The convoy moves off again. Rapid shots of the journey. Halt. In the forest, the yelling of an entire tribe. Militiamen taking aim. Messengers. It is not the Jarais, but chief Phim's Bahnars. Long spears, round shields, yataghans slanting across their waists, short red loincloths, tightly wound double turbans. No crossbows.

Arrival at the village. Straw huts on piles, beautiful breasts of the women. Except for the weapons, a gentle peasantry. The guesthouse overlooks the village. Mayrena, Mercurol, and Minh on the balcony.

Mayrena disappears, comes back dressed in a pale blue military tunic covered with gold braid, and white trousers with a gold stripe. They sit down on wooden cubes, facing a vacant cube. Around them, the population of the village. The crowd makes way respectfully for a stiff-jointed old man, dressed like the other warriors. He sits down on the vacant cube. It is Phim.

Salaams. Chaminade's note. Translation.

MAYRENA: Foreigners have allied themselves with the Siamese. They are preparing to cross the Mekong and will try to seize the villages of the Bahnars. In the name of the French governor who is the great chief of the Resident of Binh-Dinh, I propose to protect them. We will lend them a rifle to learn with. Later we will teach them the European way of making war, and we will arm them.

Translation.

The old man, squatting down, wraps himself in a blanket with geometrical designs from which only his amiable monkey's head and the knee on which he is supporting it now emerge.

"I, Chief Phim, have no chief. I am willing to treat with the French chief at Binh-Dinh, or the chief here present. But only with them, not with the other French chiefs whom I do not know."

That need be no obstacle.

"Are we in agreement with the Fathers?"

Of course, of course! Minh explains that he is a Christian, and so is Mayrena. How long has Chief Phim been a convert? But that's just it, he isn't! The missionaries refused.

"The chief, he says, M. de Mayrena, that he believes in God and Our Lord Jesus Christ his only begotten son. But the Fathers want him to throw away his fetishes. So he says he wants to believe in Our Lord, but he does not want to throw away his fetishes. Which is pagan. So the Fathers, they do not want to baptize him, and he says that they are not wise men, but they will understand in the end."

A pause. Then a speech from the old man, which boils down to: "Will the French chief demand forced labor?"

"No."

"Will he demand tribute?"

"Four elephant tusks a year. But Chief Mayrena will at once give a necklace per head; and a kilo of quinine for the village, yes, a kilo. And Chief Phim will also be able to get quinine from the hospital at Binh-Dinh when he needs it. But he will not have the right to trade in it."

"Do we also have cures for rheumatism at Binh-Dinh?"

"Yes."

The tribute is laughable, but the Bahnars have never paid tribute to Siam.

On the word quinine, pan round the circle of heads listening below: one face in two has a feverish look.

"We will not make the Bahnars hunt elephants for us?"

"No."

"Nor hand over young girls?"

"No."

"We will swear by the oath of the rice alcohol?"

"Yes."

"Will we be able to set the village free from the slave trade, if it accepts the alliance?"

The Jarais periodically carry off Bahnar slaves and sell them in Laos.

"Either we will come to an agreement with the Jarais and they will stop attacking the Bahnars, or else we will make war on them: the slave trade is forbidden among the allies of France."

The old man, puzzled, gazes at the fat white clouds above the dead trees of the forest.

"For the military training, we will send Frenchmen, not Annamites?"

"Yes."

Mayrena is thinking of the Algerian riflemen.

"We will lend them rifles with bullets?"

They must have swiped some rifles and been unable to use them for lack of ammunition.

"Yes."

"You will also swear not to make us treat the fetishes with dishonor, or throw the spirits in the river?"

"Yes."

"No interference with customs (that still means the fetishes, perhaps) even if the Fathers request it?"

"The Fathers will not request it."

"M. de Mayrena, the chief says that he would like to talk to the Elders. And to those of the neighboring villages. And to the great dead chiefs."

"If the dead are favorable, Phim will receive a revolver for them, when the arms arrive; I shall hand the arms over to him, as well as the quinine."

("Here," says Clappique, "we must be careful to see that the scenes of magic are shot in a perfectly casual way. He is off to have a few words with the dead in the same way we go to a funeral.")

* * * *

Twelve more coolies gone. Mercurol makes the militiamen hand over their papers.

Phim's return is announced.

Mayrena writes to Father Maranges, Superior of the mission, to ask for some Christians and a few elephants.

Return of Phim, toes in the air and heels in the dust, on a little Bahnar horse. He brings back the sheet of Residence notepaper, the text of which Minh had translated.

They have signed Phim with a lozenge, the other big chief with a square. Other small signs. Fourteen villages, approximately four thousand souls. Mayrena examines the signatures by the dim glow of a resin torch.

MAYRENA (to Mercurol): We must drop a line to Chaminade to get an Algerian military post set up here as soon as possible. And to send a doctor too.

On screen, the text rises and there remain only the shapes of the signatures.

Fade to the page of Bonaparte's notebook at Brienne: "St. Helena, little island."

Some hours later. Nocturnal hubbub. It is not the Superior, it is Father Georges.

"Thank you for coming, Father. His Grace asked me to deliver the mail for the mission."

"You did not have the misfortune to lose your baggage, I hope? Your message worried us deeply; we all prayed for you."

"I've lost more than half my bearers," says Mayrena, "but I've restored the situation. Our fine friend Chaminade was incapable of giving me reliable men!"

"My dear sir, no caravan has ever been known to arrive here intact."

Rapid diction, in spite of the unctuous vocabulary.

"First of all, Father: has the Siamese mission left Siamese territory?"

"Oh, assuredly."

"In what strength?"

"According to our information, sixteen elephants, two hundred soldiers, and the usual mob of bearers. Two or three European ethnologists."

"They are not European ethnologists, they are German officers."

"Even here! I was a soldier at fourteen before entering the seminary, and I am from Metz."

The reddish flames of torches flicker inside invisible straw huts, under the swollen white stars.

"Missionaries everywhere have the right to the motto, 'God and country.'"

"The motto of the Mayrenas is, 'Never give in, always give help.' The two are complementary, Father! And it will be the very devil, and no mistake, if we do not bar the way to those damned Prussians with our united mottoes.

"This magnificent country is very unhealthy. All the Fathers who came here before us died of jungle fever, with the sole exception of Father Maranges. With or without Prussians, I don't think a column of that size could get as far as here. And the good Lord is helping us, since here you are. Perhaps it is none too early."

They arrive at the guesthouse, where the resin torch makes it possible to distinguish their faces: the priest's is large, with light-gray eyes and a thin blond beard. He is as tall as Mayrena, and his Clemenceau-like eyebrows are bushy, as the bishop said.

"I am going to ask you to examine at once the mail which is addressed to you personally, Father: you may find there some information in addition to mine, and which we will need if we are to act together."

Father Georges holds out a small parcel: "It is an exchange! You have brought my colleagues and me a sad piece of news, but also some very precious news; for the latter, the good Lord presents you with some sausages! He forgives a little sin of greed to the Fathers of the savages from time to time! Our flock rear pigs."

Dinner. Mayrena apprises the Father of what he has obtained from Phim.

"Félix Faure told me, at a time when all this was not yet on the cards, 'My dear young fellow, we must act in Asia, but we must do so with extreme caution.' Come, Father, let us act for France, cautiously but without flinching, like true cavaliers! By the way, you will have to legalize the chiefs' signatures for me. How much are Phim's promises worth?"

"He claims," says Mercurol, "that you haven't been able to hit it off religion-wise."

"Only God gives faith. Not that Phim is in the least antagonistic to the word of God; but, like many others, he wants to be Christian and pagan at the same time, and not give up his fetishes. Pshaw! We've seen countless others further away than he. In the day-to-day workings of his Providence," the Father adds, smiling, "God leaves it to the zeal and perseverance of all his apostles to use the means they consider most suitable to further the workings of grace."

Under the bamboo floor of the communal house, a black pig wakes up, disturbs the poultry, and goes back to sleep amid a flapping of hens' wings.

Very tall trees. A bare, primitive night, like the night over high seas or plowed fields.

"Beneath the same sky," says the missionary, "along a Latin road, the Apostle Peter arrived in Rome, barefoot. Consider, there is not a single word here that signifies 'God.' When the savages understood the meaning of the word 'Almighty,' we were a little less advanced than before: for the God of the Christians was all-powerful, but everyone saw that the converts were poor and unfortunate like everyone else. But the savages love their children, especially when they are small. If you tell them: Jesus loves men as you love your little boy, they understand. And through that doorway you can get a lot of grain into the barn. But the poor savages are terrorized by their jinns. If there are good ones, they say, why bother with them, since they will do no harm. It is the others that have to be exorcised. There is one thing that they all understood at once: hell. Wherever the devil is master, he brings fear with him. There is nothing to be done with your convoy. We shall leave tomorrow, we shall stop at Kong-Jeri—our place, if I may venture the expression—and we shall organize a convoy of Christian Bahnars. Then you will be able to get down to work. You will keep only your soldiers. The mission has a small store of trade goods with which we will pay your new porters."

"So have we."

"I'm afraid I won't get my new chapel next year. Ah, well! It's for France. Do you know what the mission's budget is? Six hundred and forty piastres! For everything. But agriculture helps us, and everything is making progress, thanks be to God."

"And how much will the building of your chapel cost, Father?" Mayrena asks.

"Oh, a great deal. I would like a chapel that is more than a straw hut, you see. I'm sorry to say that the savages will understand God better if they see him well housed. Three hundred piastres, at least."

"Thirty louis? As you say, it is God who has sent me: allow me to present him with his chapel."

Mayrena takes a small wad of notes from his pocket and hands it to the missionary.

Father Georges thanks him and stands up, accompanied by Mayrena. Mercurol holds his friend back while the Father climbs down the ladder of the guesthouse.

"How much did we have left?"

"Four hundred."

"And you give him three hundred piastres, as if he couldn't go on using the chapel he's got!"

"God and luck are on our side, and as for you, shut your trap!"

"Do I go round building chapels?"

The Father and Mayrena are walking in the open space around which the huts are laid out.

"No European has ever crossed the high Moï plateaus from Siam to the sea. You can penetrate the Moï country provided you don't frighten the natives; in other words with a small escort, not a column. All the Moïs will desert their villages in the path of the Siamese. Moï guides only escort you from one village to the next. Therefore, as soon as the mission leaves the area traversed by Siamese hunters, it will have no more guides, and one does not make very fast progress with a compass in a forest of thorny rattans. On top of that, the arrows of the invisible Jarais. On top of that, and above all, jungle fever."

Shots of the dead coolie, the others in flight, the wall of the forest.

"And do not forget, my dear sir, that you only encroached on Jarai territory by accident, whereas the path of the Siamese crosses it from end to end. The Siamese mission has been planned in total ignorance, since it is venturing first among the most dangerous and most powerful tribes."

"According to the last letter from Faure, I mean the President, Germany is not thought to be contemplating any direct colonial action."

"However the Prussians have arranged their cards, we must nonetheless aim at creating a buffer with the Sedangs."

Mayrena has at his disposal fifteen Annamite soldiers, whom he cannot use against the Siamese without being immediately disowned: he has no orders to make war on Siam.

"In short, Father, I have soldiers but am forbidden to use them. To what extent could we rely on the Bahnars to mobilize the Sedang tribes?"

"Unfortunately, my dear sir, tribes do not exist. Especially among the Sedangs. Here there are dialects, races perhaps, but not tribes. No real chiefs, except for Phim and the Sadets. And these poor savages forget what they have signed, or rather lose interest in it, unless the agreed course of action is immediate. Everything must be done village by village, and even then the chapel must be built and the deacon left there, otherwise . . ."

"Could we not instruct and arm the Christians, first to get rid of slavery, and then to make them instructors?"

"We have no other choice. But the obstacles will come thick and fast, once they are armed. However, God will provide. But you will see what a slow business it is!"

"With an Algerian regiment or a battalion of legionnaires, it wouldn't take long."

"Since you know some members of the government I cannot urge you too strongly to draw their attention to the difficulties which any attempt at a military occupation of these regions will run up against. Annam, at the height of its power, tried to conquer them. Siam as well. In vain. The occupation itself will be a comparatively simple matter, for the bravest clans will abandon their villages. But guerrilla warfare will begin at once, and in that guerrilla warfare, only Moïs will be capable of fighting other Moïs. If the soldiers of the invading country cannot leave their encampments, what use will they be? And if they do leave them, the little crossbow arrows will soon begin to fly. Organize a modern gold-mining development? Perhaps. The construction of the road will cost many a life. Undertake the development of agriculture, using methods less primitive than theirs? There is no shortage of land either in Annam or Laos, in peaceful regions. As long as it is recognized that if we are attacked, we will take our breviaries in one hand and our rifles in the other, well and good. Beyond that—caution."

The orange flame of the torch, still burning at the guesthouse, reveals the dim outline of its massive bulk, like a great tomb. From one end of the mountains to the other all is wrapped in sleep.

"In these sequences," says Clappique, "I'm chiefly concerned with conveying the atmosphere and the difficulties. It is 1888, four years after the defeat of Langson. The first priority is to federate the Bahnars, Christians and non-Christians."

The former are willing. The latter, more than anxious to have done with the Jarai raids. The slowness of the action is due to the palavers— but the palavers have an objective. And adherents are coming in thick and fast, partly because Mercurol, in a British officer's red uniform which he picked up God knows where before his departure, is beginning to train the Christians, but mainly because the news of the approach of the Siamese expedition has reached the region. It is more or less lost in the Jarai country, where the natives have abandoned their villages. It will not be long before it is hit by jungle fever, Father Georges says. Mayrena buys a little Sedang slave girl, in order to try to give her back to her parents. He devises a Bahnar flag, while waiting for the others. He reaches Kontum, the mission headquarters, and makes contact with Father Maranges, a very old man. The latter had always dreamed of creating a Christian country, and is ready to help Mayrena. His Christians work the land with plows, he has founded village after village, but emphasizes the difficulties Mayrena will meet in getting the Moïs to work. They are peasants, who owe obedience only to the dictates of the land. Even the artisans (the blacksmiths are Sedangs) only work when they deem it absolutely necessary. The taboos against work are legion, and even the Christians are only half-Christians. Mayrena's tour is a long one, and the film must convey, with a small number of intercut shots, the sensation of the boring slowness of the endless repetition of ceremonies in the forest. In the "frontier villages," Mayrena sees the first Sedangs, who are bigger than the other Moïs, and who carry shields shaped like escutcheons. They await the coming of a Messiah, who will make them rulers of all the Moïs. Mayrena thinks modestly of the prophecy which heralded Cortez.

The ceremony of the Rolang, the ritual killing of a buffalo. It is a cruel ceremony, and in some villages the victim is still a slave. Clappique is not too sure if he wants to shoot this scene, which has the advantage of revealing the ferocious side of the Sedangs. "What bothers me is that at that rate you could get the most ridiculous ideas about the Spaniards by showing bullfights. However, we shall have to see."

A great reunion of the principal chiefs, or those who are alleged to be so, is to take place at the end of the month in Kong-Gung. Mayrena and Father Georges make their way toward this village.

They cross the Dak-Henui, a *gold-bearing* stream. They are now in Sedang country. In every village, the mothers of children carried off by the Jarais come to see the little girl. The child, sitting motionless on the blanket which the bearers lay down at each resting place, her legs crossed like a tiny Buddha, says nothing.

Some of the Sedangs wear gold nuggets on their tiger's-teeth necklaces. They attach no greater importance to them than to the teeth. The little convoy approaches Kong-Gung. A hut piled full of bones, very white, those of sacrificed animals. The augur birds are flying in the right direction. Nevertheless, no guide, and the track is beginning to bristle with caltrops. The Father's men slowly push before them a sort of rake.

A wall of enormous treetrunks, joined together by rattans, and disappearing into the forest on either side. Behind the wall, the shouts of children, the grunting of black pigs, and a regular clanging of hammers on anvils: the blacksmiths. The sky is overcast. There is no gate, but a triangular hole through which can be seen a second wall, this time of bamboo. On a platform to the right of the hole, like sentries at the postern gate of a rampart, dark against the gray sky, two characters with huge spears are yelling that the village is djeng.*

The Father gets the Sedang guide from Kong-Jeri to talk. "He's saying that our birds were very favorable, that he saw it himself." The spear men yell again. "Listen to that!" says the Father. "The birds, favorable? they keep saying. How extraordinary! But the fact is that we are djeng, and very much djeng: not only can you not come in, but we cannot even give you rice. And furthermore, we cannot give you a guide. And furthermore, we're djeng for another two days."

It only remains to leave. But the Father has taken up the dialogue of yells again. Yes, they are expecting an assembly of all the Sedang chiefs of the region, as soon as the djeng is lifted. A great chief of the Keniong tribe ("there, they have real chiefs," says the Father) whom the Laotians appointed to rule long years ago is also expected.

The guide knows the route to a neighboring village, Kong-Ye.

Twenty minutes after the arrival of the convoy, the inhabitants know that the little girl is with them. She is waiting for her rice, her legs crossed on the blanket.

As usual, the women whose children have been kidnaped by the Jarais come one after the other to look at her; some of them hang around, talking and pawing her. Shouts of jubilation from the porters: here is the mother at last!

The father was killed by the Jarais and the child carried off two years ago. At first the mother had not recognized her; it is the strange bow made of colored threads that the little girl wears through her ear that did the trick (my-mother's-crucifix!). The porters calm down. The mother obdurately turns her back on Mayrena. But she holds the child in her arms, and does not let go of her.

At last she makes up her mind to turn round. She is a plump-cheeked, flat-nosed peasant with wiry hair, big for a savage. She is crying. How alike tears are everywhere!

* Forbidden.

"When are you leaving?" the Father translates.

"She could at least thank me!" says Mayrena.

"You have paid for the child: she thinks you're going to take her away with you. Perhaps, too, some of the porters told her that the girl was to go to our orphanage."

She can keep the child. Stupefaction, and exclamations of gratitude. The entire little village rushes off (the child still in her mother's arms), then comes back, and there is much bowing and scraping.

The first women to come and greet Mayrena are the four women with their heads shaved in mourning for their lost children who had been the first to come and look at the girl. The convoy has seen this procession of unhappy women in several villages; Mayrena, who has always assumed that they came to seek their child, now knows that they only came to see her passing by . . .

On their return to Kong-Gung, the interdict on the village has been raised. Two warriors come to pilot the convoy through the caltrops.

The chiefs will be here tomorrow. And the Laotian governor.

Nearly all the Sedang villages we have seen since the River Pekau (and the others, it is said) are built on hilltops. This one is a peninsula in the clouds, and overlooks all the foothills of the Chain in the direction of the Pacific.

Like so many mountain huts, the guesthouse is built on the edge of the cliff. It is open onto the void. The ceiling and the three walls—the fourth being replaced by this huge gap opening onto infinity—are "decorated" with the skulls of animals. The village appears to be somehow sacred. Is it because of this atmosphere as of a holy place that the Sedangs have decided to hold the council of the entire region here?

The chief welcomes Mayrena. About thirty-five years old, very tough, his body covered with white spots like burns: traces of an old skin disease.

The Sedangs who have abandoned their villages in the path of the Siamese are squatting on vacant land. They are not authorized to receive gifts. The chiefs who have already arrived with their escorts are also camping out there. Mayrena gets Mercurol to distribute some junk. Only the women come. In the thick of the henhouse squawking and fluttering, Mercurol, overwhelmed, slips off his jacket, then slides his thumbs under his suspenders and pulls on the elastic to let in some air. Great gusts of laughter, which start up again frenetically as soon as Mercurol, seeing what it's all about, pulls at them again.

When he opens a bottle of Pernod, the corkscrew is a great hit. Then there is a relapse into torpor. A hammer strikes an anvil. Soon others reply, like cock-crows.

Opening a new crate, Mayrena finds some Japanese paper parasols, bought on the advice of Chaminade. Minh offers one to the spotted chief, and this leopard-man accepts it with obvious pleasure.

Vultures hover. Opposite the guesthouse is a platform which is loaded with meat for them after the sacrifices.

The men have decided to wake up. They are tougher than the Bahnars. And darker (their color is that of the Cambodians and the Malays, not of the Annamites). Once again, peasants, in spite of their weapons. But murderous peasants, dedicated to sorcery.

Distribution of quinine to the sick. Most of them have never taken it, but know of its existence. The ones who have received it disappear.

A group of old men arrives, with a few young ones. One of the young men speaks for them all. They have come to ask for their parents to be rejuvenated. "But look at those very old men," says Minh, "look at them: they are really too old, I assure you!" Eventually they go away, convinced that their guests have refused. But apparently they think it is their right to do so.

A woman asks questions about the disease that makes holes (small-pox). It is the great scourge here; it carries off a third of the villages. Vaccination is needed. Impossible: the Sedangs, like the rest of the Moïs, regard vaccination scars as a sign of slavery.

Courtyard of Miracles: the limbless, the one-eyed, the blind, in groups. They ask for arms, legs, eyes. Then three lepers. Frightful, like all lepers. The Father gives them some of the melissa cordial of the Carmelites.

For all the diseases of which he knows nothing, the Father distributes what he calls water of hope.

Behind the lepers, as if they were an integral part of them, stands a group of women. They wait. Finally, one of them makes up her mind, comes up to Mayrena, and silently shows him her unornamented ears, with broken lobes.*

Why not stitch them up? The Father agrees.

There are a good dozen of these women.

All of them have earlobes hanging down on their shoulders, or tied together like two pieces of string.

* To beautify themselves, the young Moïs introduce bigger and bigger ornaments into their pierced ears, and gradually distend the lobes. If they break, the woman is blemished and condemned to spinsterhood.

In ten minutes, it will be dark. The Father starts organizing the transfer of their belongings to the hut assigned to them. The spotted chief comes up. The guests cannot go into this hut; there is no hut for them, and so on. Why? Because they have cured half the village? Really! The Father, indignant, flourishes the big flask of paregoric elixir and one of the bottles of absinthe. "If you do not keep your promises," Minh translates, "I will break these two healing flask spirits, and those who are cured will become ill again, and the earlobes will split of their own accord, and the Bearded Ones will no longer be able to make cures!" And crash! this discobolus of the Lord. . .

("There! I'm writing the way Mayrena speaks," says Clappique. "I'm not surprised!")

. . . dispatches the Pernod over the roof of the house into the chasm . . .

The chief leads the travelers to their hut, and leaves them.

In the distance, toward the open country, glow the little fires of fleeing Sedangs. A whinnying of horses rises up from the valley: one very far away, then a dozen, nearer and nearer; no doubt they are answering the first, muffled by the mist like the calls of the men. A long convoy is approaching.

At the far end of the village, banks of low clouds drift by, glowing a dull red from the refugee fires; against them are silhouetted a few roofs, tall trees draped with lianas, and palm trees, in the nocturnal mist of the high mountains.

Shadows, bent under the weight of overloaded baskets, are climbing toward the encampments where the chiefs wait. This antlike exodus before the Siamese advance does not resemble a flight; it is a movement as silent as the growth of trees. A call goes up, the modulated call of the hillmen, and the infinitesimal, distant sound of shields struck by spears reaches Mayrena's ears.

A very wideawake-looking youth, arms and torso swathed in wrappings, climbs the little ladder.

"He is a witch doctor who has just been officiating at a ritual," M. Minh says.

The Moï points at something in the distance, with the gesture of a Red Indian chief.

The bonfires made by the peasants for clearing the land a little farther to the left continue to advance toward the east, behind the ridge of the mountains, like a flame licking at the edge of a sheet of paper. The lights to which the witch doctor is pointing are numerous and still.

"The encampment of one of the chiefs summoned to the meeting, or of the escaping Sedangs?" asks Mayrena.

Sedang chiefs do not have big enough escorts for twenty fires, and the fires of the refugees are scattered.

"The witch doctor, he says: A big camp."

"Whoever they are, those people coming that way will have a devil of a road to get through!"

Minh waits a moment for the reply.

"He says: "Yes. But they will do it in three days.""

"The Siamese? Or this Keniong chief they're waiting for. . .""

The witch doctor's answer is a long one. He talks with his thumbs stuck into the wrappings round his armpits, like Mercurol with his braces.

"He says: He does not know what it is. But it is very significant. Every lifetime (he means every fifty years, perhaps), a great red light appears in the east. And it is not very long since the light came."

Mayrena asks to have this repeated.

"But he also says: The Siamese have never taken the land of the Sedangs or the Jarais. They will never take them. If they come, they will die. That is all."

"Just ask him this: Does he believe that a man will come to make the Sedangs masters of the other Moïs?"

"He says: Of course!"

To the left, very far off, two more horses whinny: another chief is arriving.

"How does one become a witch doctor?" Mayrena asks.

"He says that his father was a *bojaou*. But also, if you are one, it is easy to see."

The Sedang adds a speech.

"He says that he cannot see your red and white face, but that he knows you are smiling. But that as for him, it makes him laugh to think that the jinns will allow power to be brought to the Sedangs by a man with a red and white face." (Laughter.)

Without giving Mayrena time to answer, the witch doctor turns his back on them and mingles with the shadowy figures of fugitives.

"What do you think of those fires?" Mayrena asks the Father. "The Siamese?"

"We are in God's keeping."

"Are the witch doctors violently hostile to us?"

"Only a few will come tomorrow, but the others will have talked. They are the guardians of what is most ancient here. What have we come for, if not to destroy what they wish to preserve?"

"Yes, yes. But what can they do against us?"

"Oh, their power is far from being limitless: once a village believes that the spirit has left its witch doctor, you'll see them drive him out with the most intense hatred, you'll see them throw into the river the pebbles which they used to pray to as jinns. The Château de Mayrena is in Franche-Comté, didn't you say? You must surely have come across village witches thereabouts? I sometimes used to spend my holidays with some kind relations in the Pyrenees; I went back to stay with them before I was sent to work in the Lord's Vineyard; well, I don't think the witches here are so very different."

Trumpetings rise from the depths beyond the guesthouse. The hut overhangs the chasm. The fugitive Sedangs have no elephants. How many chiefs have arrived?

"Here, I have heard dead men speak," the Father says at last.

"And what the devil did you do?"

"What? I said my Rosary, of course, and put my trust in God's will. You look astonished. After all, what a lot of fuss about a laggard soul! The supernatural? But good Lord, good Lord, my dear sir, do you find the world natural? And what does it matter? When you are up to your neck in the supernatural and you have to act, believe me—take care not to harm anybody, but, that said, take no notice of the supernatural, and carry on as if it did not exist."

Elephants arrive: chiefs from a big village, no doubt. The shouts of elephant drivers and the little grunts of the animals can be heard: massive dark shadows pass by against the moon.

"When I say a laggard soul, don't misunderstand me: I certainly do not believe that it's the wretched dead who speak: it is clearly a trick of the devil: to our knowledge, the greatest number of strange happenings occur around the deaths of converts. I am convinced that the Evil One sometimes plagues these poor savages.

"But one must be sensible. You realize, of course, that we have no desire to lend credence to old wives' tales. In creating this mission from nothing, with God's help, Father Maranges has shown that he knew about the ways of the world. But in this country the rationalist approach is a pretty pitiful one! Think of the lives of us missionaries. Phim was the principal enemy of the Christians, and he mirac . . . inexplicably made friends with us from our first meeting, as if Providence had not wished to leave to human calculations the glory of founding the mission to the Savages.

"And after all, what does it matter if the Evil One decides one day to push his power to the point of speaking with the voice of the dead? I have heard the Lord's voice. I was at Kong-Trang. I had not seen

my colleagues for over a month. I had left before daybreak. I lost my
way, and I had nothing left to eat. After four hours I found the way
again. Two hours later I lost it once more. I tried to cut across the
forest. Still lost, this time among some wild boar traps. I put myself
under the protection of the Blessed Virgin, and I extricated myself, I
found the path again. It was four o'clock in the afternoon, and I had
had nothing to drink for twenty hours. At last I reached a village where
I asked for water: it was refused me. I lost my way yet again, and got
bogged down to the waist! I wanted to climb a tree to get my bearings:
I was too weak. Night was approaching. I was lost, drenched with sweat
and mud, alone with the turtledoves cooing their evening prayer in the
silence of the forest. I tried to light a fire: I managed to ignite the
tinder I had with me, but it went out before it had set fire to the leaves
I had collected. Nothing to eat, not even a wild pumpkin gnawed by a
monkey; nothing to drink. And you know the terrible weakness the
mountain cold induces in one. I was so poor, so lonely, so like the first
men on earth. 'O my God,' I said, 'in this utter destitution of mine,
do you at least acknowledge me a little as your missionary?' And suddenly I was overwhelmed by a supernatural happiness. I could not contain my joy. I had collapsed on to an overturned treetrunk. I stood
up to sing the canticle, 'Let us forever bless the Lord in his goodness!'

"I must have been in the middle of a mountain crater overgrown
with forest. Scarcely had I summoned up the strength to sing 'Let us
forever bless' at the top of my voice and get my breath back—for my
newfound strength was leaving me once more—when from all sides an
immense echo gave voice to every created thing; a voice which was no
longer my own but that of the rocks and trees answered me: 'forever.'

"I had closed my eyes to listen; when I opened them again, my son,
I could see luminous pinpricks in the shadows: the eyes of animals
which had not run away, and were perhaps listening too."

As if they could hear him, the elephants start trumpeting again, very
close now. Shadows, indistinct among the shreds of mist, run to and
fro, with a clinking of bracelets, and the invisible long-houses creak on
their piles.

Mayrena jumps to his feet. From somewhere close by, doubtless from
the guesthouse, a sound like that of some enormous gong fades into the
echoless mist. Then two more strokes, softer and close together, then
once more the booming sound whose depth and volume are intensified
by the two little preceding strokes.

"The war drum," says the Father. "Perhaps it is to guide the chiefs
on their way through the mountains. And yet I doubt it . . . If it's a
fire, the omen is terrible, and we can leave."

Shadows run through the darkness toward the guesthouse, the naked feet striking the ground noiselessly.

"They have no weapons," he says.

How many are they? More than the village seemed to hold. Below the hut, the shadowy multitude is now stamping and jostling like a crowd on a staircase. Under the floor, the black pigs, awakened once more, have started grunting, and it seems as if they too are answering the drum. When the guesthouse toward which these shadows are thronging was built, the first pile was thrust into the body of a living slave. And if Mayrena and the Father are attacked at night, their escort will be useless.

"What is happening?" shouts the Father in Sedang.

"*Khang*," reply four or five shadows as they run past.

"Come on," says the missionary hurriedly. "The recited fragments are never chosen haphazardly."

"What fragments?"

"It's their epic poems, you might say. They are rarely recited, and tonight it's certainly not without a purpose. It's the strangers, the new arrivals, who have organized it. We must find out what they want."

It is not the African tomtom, the hollow treetrunk, but a great Tibetan booming, carrying endlessly in the mist. Mayrena and the Father go down the ladder and circle the hut. Shadows are still running, but fewer now. Between the strokes of the war drum, a voice can already be heard reciting.

"You must not expect anything direct," the Father says. "The chant itself is clear enough, but what it alludes to will no doubt be obscure."

They pass the corner of the hut. By the reddish gleam of the torches, a few figures are moving about on the invisible verandah of the guesthouse, itself lost in the darkness, suspended over the void. Mayrena, as he draws nearer, sees the head and shoulders of a man emerge from the darkness, leaning against one of the main beams wrapped in a blanket and stretching out an arm covered with bracelets. This apparition, the only shape outside the darkness, is intoning—three high syllables and three low—taking a breath at the end of each verse with the hoarse wheeze of a consumptive, without stirring. Suddenly he stretches out his arm in a Roman salute, and stops speaking. A silent crowd advances toward him in the darkness. Mayrena, who has approached with some difficulty, can make him out dimly: old, muffled up in his blanket with the geometric designs, his arm outstretched, he resembles Phim. Although it is impossible to see his eyes, Mayrena is certain that he is blind.

"A great dead chief is about to speak through his voice," the Father whispers.

The war drum has stopped. Women, foreign chiefs, elephant drivers, all the Moïs are there. The blind man begins his invocation, letting each syllable of this language with its gong-like sonority die slowly away into the mist.

Verse by verse, the Father translates in a low voice.

" 'O youths, go and unearth the balm of invincibility from the foot of the lilac tree!

" 'Go and unearth the balm of invulnerability from the foot of the banana trees! Strike the gong-spirit with the iron cymbals, bind him with his cord, hang him up—so that the terror-stricken Bahnars may hear it and bring buffaloes!—that the terror-stricken Laotians may hear it and bring elephants!—that the poor may hear it and bring us pigs and jars of rice wine.' "

He stops, then resumes in a higher voice:

" 'He brandishes his shield—and the brass plates make the sound of seeds [I don't know the French word] in their dry husks. The hair on his calves is so thick that it seems to have been curled.'

"There are some passages in an ancient language which I cannot quite grasp," the Father says. "It seems that the hero has just arrived at the village of the abductor who comes out on to the verandah of his hut, I think:

" 'O friend, O friend, come down to earth and I will decapitate thee cleanly . . .'

" 'O friend, I cannot come down—my hands are straying between thy wife's breasts.' "

The Father goes on translating, in an expressionless voice, engrossed in the effort of understanding.

"Now the hero has run the other one, who had called himself his ally, through the thigh. He's being ironical, you understand:

" 'Why then is thy thigh pierced, O my ally? What is this blood, O my ally?'

" 'This red is the fringe of the blanket of our woman in my house.' "

The old man alters his voice for each role.

"The abductor has just fallen," the father continues, "and the other has placed his foot on his body. The abductor begs for mercy.

" 'Why should I leave thee when thou art wounded already—when thy thigh is broken—when thy blood is inundating the village!—I shall throw thy head into the straw hut—I shall leave thy jaw-bone outside where the ants will assail it—thou the great fierce chief who took my heart and bore it away beyond the great mountain—thou who hast stolen my wife from me—torn out my thigh—torn my heart from my belly. Nowhere—up among the Jarais or down among the Bahnars—is there anyone like thee.—O children, children—place his head above the door and leave his jaw-bone outside—so that the ants large and small may swarm over every one of them and devour them—O birds in your thousands, dappled turtledoves, O you his servants, every one of you, come with me!'"

The blind man has lowered his voice for the servants' reply, and as the Father translates, he too lowers his voice:

" 'How can we not follow him?—Our Lord is already putrefying . . .'"

The Moïs round the Father and Mayrena are standing stockstill, but in the shadow others are arriving, and the inhuman stillness of the reciter glued to his beam seems as though linked with the trees and the mountains, above the stealthy listeners.

"In short," says Mayrena, "they seem to be counseling submission to the conqueror? And no quarter! But on whose behalf?"

"Very hard to say," and the Father quickly resumes his listening. "Wait, wait! We'll try to interpret later."

He does not translate for a long while. The tone has become narrative again. Caught by a gust of wind, the vertical plumes of smoke from the torches droop like whips' tails.

" 'Let those who make the burial stakes go and prepare them . . .'" the Father resumes. "This is what it's all about, I think. The hero is dead. He wanted to take to wife the daughter of the Sun. She refused, and commanded him to escape before daybreak. For only the night allows the hero to return to earth, and if the light appears, the hero's life will depart with the night.

"He has remained. Now a woman, his sister or his sister-in-law, I think, is weeping:

" 'I had thought that thou wouldst die with funeral sculptures—and a fine coffin prepared during a year's moons—and now thou art dead in the road of black wax, thou, beloved of the spirits on the mountain!'

"The road of black wax is the night," the Father adds.

" 'I had thought that thou wouldst die fighting thine enemies—I had thought that thou wouldst perish while invading the territories of the great chiefs. Come back to eat the heart of one of our oxen on a tray—come back to eat the heart of one of our buffaloes in a cup! come back to drink rice wine in a jar.

" 'I shall not see thy face again, I shall meet thee no more—for thou art dead, little brother . . .'"

The voice has grown louder and louder, with the slow, intense, restrained deliberation of an orator adjuring a crowd—the deliberation which makes a voice carry a long way. The narrator's voice now carries as far as the forest where the monkeys are asleep in the mist. "Now it's the hero's wife—the real one—who is weeping," the Father says. Still glued to his beam, his mouth wide open, the blind man looks like a prophet.

" 'Thy mother gave thee advice and thou didst not listen—thy father commanded and thou didst not obey—thou didst play the wild flute until thy body's death. The water of my nose would fill a flower vase— the water of my face would fill a decorated bowl—I weep all the tears of my eyes—all the tears of my body.—Thou wilt not eat rice again— thou wilt not drink water again—thou wilt not pick the flowering liana again!—The flesh of oxen and of buffaloes will never again appease the hunger of thy belly.—And now my cooked rice grows dry in the plate—the roast chicken remains in the dish, dried up like the male vulture.—I had thought that thou wouldst die fighting thine enemies— invading the Jarai lands—and thou didst die, thou didst die bemired —in the road of black wax.' " The bard stretches out both arms in an imploring gesture:

" 'Call the Mnong chiefs who wear necklaces of serpents' teeth— summon them from east and west—and you, multitudinous birds, turtledoves with speckled wings, my servants—come and see, we are about to fight!' "

The blind man falls silent, as motionless in his silence as in his incantation, and the war drum begins to boom again through the mist.

"It's over, I think," says the Father.

The Moïs begin to chatter.

"Moral: We must fight?" suggests Mayrena.

"Yes."

"Against the Siamese or against us?"

"Not us: they would have driven us away."

A quick rat-a-tat on the drum, drowned by a full-blooded boom.

"Let us pray for the travelers," says the Father.

A metal gong echoes in the distance outside the wall. The booming recommences, and the metal gong answers again, then the war drum once more, until approaching tribesmen answer from three remote but separate points.

"Are they still on the way?"

The Father replies in an abstracted voice, probably continuing his prayer:

"They will march all night."

Now there is a rapid tattoo on the war drum, as if the drummer is bouncing his stick on the stretched hide. Then a single mighty blow, at the limit of the gong's resonance, obliterates this thrumming. The man lets a silence follow this blow, as if waiting for the last vibration to fade into the night; then he strikes again, and the longhouse trembles. Gong-beats answer him from the forest, muffled and near at hand; others from the bottom of the chasm, clear as distant cymbals, together or separately, sometimes almost silvery. When the war drum starts up again, and the approaching tribesmen wait for it to fade before replying, horses whinny in the depths of the night. The entire Sedang country is on the march.

Through a gap in the mist the line of the Siamese campfires can be seen glimmering.

"Everything works out satisfactorily: the enemies of the Moïs are indeed the Siamese, and the Confederation will be established the following day. To this day, we do not know to what Mayrena owed this sudden success. His promises? Phim's trust? The legend of the Sedang Messiah? The appeal of an alliance with the whites, distant and powerful, against the Siamese, nearby and well known? All these factors together? The text of the charter has been published several times. It is extremely generous. Mayrena reserves for himself only the exploitation of the gold-bearing lands."

Clappique closes his portfolio in which there are chapters which he has not read.

"But this is where you see me hang my head. We have reached the hole in my magnificent chasuble. Nothing is down on paper: these pages here are about Mayrena's return to Paris. Now, the reign begins. Down, Pen-Wiper!"

He then proceeds to outline the following, with no clowning.

People believed in Mayrena's kingship because it corresponded to an established romantic image. *Nobody*, with the exception of the Fathers, knew anything about the Sedangs. The hotheads who had tried to cross their land had been killed, as was, later on, the administrator Odend'hal, notwithstanding his escort. The kingship, which lasted six months, starts with the first "signatures," the first acts of vassalage. When Mayrena narrates the legend, Clappique would film it, but by way of counterpoint, he must also film the truth.

"What's that, Pen-Wiper? Enough of these abstractions? An example! Quite right, old chap. So, an example: the little Cham mistress died up there in childbirth and Mayrena really took it into his head to have her buried beneath the royal towers of My-Son. He set off with a large escort of warriors. But after a week they absentmindedly abandoned him; and he found himself in the depths of the forest with a dozen men. He decided to bury her there, and to go back. When he tells this story, I should like to have shots of the royal funeral as he imagines it, and at the same time of him and his remaining chaps with their spades, the immensity of the forest, and a cross made of two branches tied together with string."

It is difficult to film the reign, because there is none. It will exist only in Mayrena's imagination and his listeners' dreams. Clappique therefore has to film what took place during these six months in a rapid rhythm. And create an antiromantic exoticism. In short, an outlandish documentary. That is why he has written almost nothing. He is counting on what no logic can foresee, on the sort of unexpected things that will attract the camera. He will certainly have to show three palavers, to suggest the long tour through the villages. Palavers still happen; he will have to take contrasting ones—for instance, the funereal mass of the guesthouses among the Bahnars make a strong contrast with the longhouses of the Sedangs. He is counting on animals, plants, some native customs perhaps. "But not a buffalo sacrifice; a documentary, not an ethnographic lecture! We'll have more than enough with what is strictly necessary." The dripping forest, the insects, the giant spiders' webs, the green night: the camera must render all this, by smothered images intercut with shots of the mountains in the distance with clearings in the forest. The higher one goes the cooler it becomes, and the more the forest takes on a familiar French look. But it is very different. And it should be possible to make something out of a near-normal vegetation juxtaposed with naked bodies, huge animals, native huts, and above all the villages of the dead. "You know them: high palisades of treetrunks, surmounted by fetish weepers and huge masks. I should like to convey the atmosphere through very boring scenery, Picardy style, null in every way, from which there would emerge some nightmare thing that becomes as natural as Père-Lachaise, and by way of contrast, a dotard more or less in the buff, with his hands folded on his grubbing-spear like one of our rustics leaning on the handle of his spade."

There must be plenty of mist (mist on the plateaus, like heat on the coast), little clouds wandering around like idiotic cattle. Above all, it must be well understood that these characters are peasants. They invent their dreamworlds, they have fetishes, their wives are delivered of children by witches, motionless witch doctors recite their *Chanson de Roland* by night, but their life is the village, the fields, the animals.

At the same time, these primitives must not be simpletons. Their sagas must suggest the depth of their tradition—an aura which should accompany Mayrena's whole adventure. "In short, I have to depict an absurd epic—not a word!—but an epic all the same. So, no romanticism, but a good dollop of the supernatural. I don't remember those villages too well. I shall have to go back there. With what the imagination cannot imagine, but which reality provides us with galore, one can always capture the unusual. When I went there, the thing that gave me the most powerful impression of plunging into time, into the unknown, was the cleanliness of the huts."

He is all the more obliged to search for the supernatural, he says, because the scenes he cannot dispense with do not express it in the least—in fact he must carefully exclude it from them. He cannot avoid either the duel with the Sadet of Fire or the elephant hunt in which Mayrena has a brush with death.

The duel seems clear enough. Mayrena's idea of conquest was romantic and military. The idea of tackling the great witch doctor in single combat must have attracted him. The Sadet of Fire—for other reasons—must have thought that the fight was a matter of course. The Jarais had never seen any whites other than the missionaries. It is they who bother Clappique in this story. Could they not have prevented the fight? They were far from having converted the majority of the Moïs, the Sadet probably detested them—competition!—and Mayrena was perfectly capable of disregarding them, confident in his skill and in the length of his cavalry sergeant's sword. And then again: "killed in single combat by the Sadet of Fire, whose enslaved people he came to set free"—that wouldn't have been bad either.

The fight must have resembled a *corrida*, like all vaguely ritual combats. It can easily be filmed: saber fencing is still practiced among the Moïs. It is a solemn sort of fencing, like that of the Chinese theater. As background, the enclosure of the dead with its horned fetishes, or one of the tiny straw huts where the spirits shelter. Preferably the dead. Against this background, the almost naked Sadet beginning his barbaric dance, and silhouetted against the mist, Mayrena, as rigid and upright as the long blade which covers him. There must be a close-up of the hand and arm—naked—which hold the Moï saber. Mayrena is well aware that he must not kill his adversary. "I studied saber fencing a bit for the film." Mayrena must finish a feint with a hit. The Sadet's swordsmanship will be clear because at this point the camera will be looking through Mayrena's eyes. Slow-motion shots, a maximum of a minute in all, will make the whole thing comprehensible. Mayrena must be hit twice, once across the tunic, ripping two buttons off and drawing blood. But the Sadet only uses his saber to slash, and now Mayrena protects himself, his arm almost straight. He feints in his turn, changes his guard, the point of his saber slides down the entire length of the Sadet's forearm and he drops his weapon. The wound is deep, the blood flows copiously. Mayrena's little troop shower the Sadet with tokens of respect, and one of the Fathers dresses his wound. In the crowd, neither enthusiasm nor hostility; a taboo has been lifted, that is all.

Clappique does not know what to do with the war between the tribes. In his opinion it never took place, either because the Fathers did not want to make converts through war, or because Mayrena left the Moï country too soon. He certainly made preparations for it: what fitted in best with his visionary idea of kingship was the role of the warrior chief. But what interest can there be in filming the victory of men armed with rifles over spearmen?

On the other hand, there is much to be got out of the elephant hunt, conducted at a terrific pace. Mayrena is a very good shot, his Colt is excellent, and the ejected cartridges will make remarkable ornaments for pipe stems. This time he has decided that he too will hunt with the spear. There, Clappique envisages three shots: the elephant charging, trunk in the air, taken from ground level—the Sedang who throws himself on top of Mayrena's fallen body, buttressed by his lance—and the close-up of the elephant's rutted foot as seen by Mayrena, a yard above him. The charging mass of the beast suddenly stopped by the lance, its swaying (but above all, the sudden halt), can provide riveting images. Mayrena, while the elephant is expiring on the lance of the Sedang who is risking his life, has rolled clear, and finding the Moï who is carrying his rifle, fires. The beast, which up to this point has been tottering, sinks on its side. Finally, there would have to be a scene, like something out of the *Ring*, presented without any suggestion of irony, showing five or six near-naked warriors against the background of the Annamite Chain, and Mayrena hooking a medal representing the elephant's foot on to the loincloth of the man who saved his life: "In the name of the Ancestors and of the warriors of the future, I name you Knight of Sedang Valor." This would doubtless be the last image of the Moï country.

Clappique would like to fade straight into a scene which is written, and which takes place in the Chaminades' house.

Thalie is in the middle of concocting a ravishing imaginary outfit for a ball which takes place in Paris, when the Resident calls to her

from his study—something he never does. He hands her a piece of
paper:

NO OFFICIAL SANCTION MAYRENA MISSION STOP DISOWN HIS ACTIONS
AND TAKE DISCIPLINARY MEASURES.

He gets up and paces around the room.

"What the devil does that mean! I ask you, what does it mean!
Disown what? You miserable cretins, what do I know about his actions?
You made me organize his convoy, I sent him off into uncharted terri-
tory on your orders, and now that he's in the middle of nowhere . . .
Disown a needle in a haystack, take stern disciplinary measures against
a drought, idiots! Iddiots!"

"If we lose the sea, Henri," she murmurs, "we'll have fever and
dysentery again inside six months."

"And it's a telegram!" he shouts, waving the blue paper. "A telegram! To get here faster!"

"But if I lose the sea, I shall be an old woman when I go back to
France! An old woman! And what have we done to deserve this!
What . . ."

Something strikes her, and she suddenly regains her normal voice:
"Perhaps he's dead," she whispers.

"It's a little bit healthier now, up there: the previous missionaries
nearly all died of fever, but these are surviving."

The causes of the break between Mayrena and the Governor General
have been exhaustively investigated. Clappique's hypothesis is perhaps
the most convincing. Faced with the evacuation of the Sedang villages,
disease, and perhaps the news that some of the Moïs now possessed
rifles, the Siamese expedition, with or without Germans, had returned
to Bangkok. At the same time, Constans had ceased to be Governor
General of Indochina. The Moï hinterland having lost its pressing
interest, Constans's successor, an anticlerical to boot, had abandoned
Mayrena as cheerfully as his predecessor had sent him. The break may
have had nothing to do with Mayrena's action, whatever judgment may
have been passed on them. But solely with the fact that at a time when
relations with Germany were bad, the new Governor General was more
timorous than Constans had been. And more hostile toward rough-
necks. Constans had been Minister of the Interior.

"Mayrena," Clappique adds, "could not part company with the Fathers, because he was ignorant of the dialects, and because the soldiers he had trained were Christians. The Fathers would follow the orders of the hierarchy, which was not very interested in a struggle with the French government for the Sedang kingdom. They were opposed to a real war of the tribes, that is to say the military conquest of the Jarai country, which would have lasted a long time. The Confederation once created, at least in appearance, what was to be done? Mayrena was no administrator. He would never put an end to slavery if he was precluded from making war. He no longer wanted to become a gold prospector, and could never succeed in making his subjects work. 'Offer vast concessions, and import manpower!' The missionaries would never agree."

The big concessionary companies in colonial territories had their headquarters in Paris. The colonization charter had no value except to the Minister for Colonial Affairs; perhaps, in a pinch, to the big foreign companies. And the seat of Mayrena's kingdom was no longer the duchy of Kontum, but the Place de l'Opéra. So he went back to France.

No tragedy for Thalie. When he passed through Qui Nhon again, the Resident had been posted to Hanoi.

He was thwarted from the start. The Minister for Colonial Affairs regarded him as a tool of the priests. The Moï country might perhaps be of interest to Germany or England; not through Mayrena. Siam was far away. But the newspapers glorified, as against the stick-in-the-mud spirit and bureaucratic passivity, the splendid adventurer who wanted to give France a new Indochina. The Revolt of the Literati was barely over. The more Mayrena found himself doomed to obscurity, the more the legend grew. He became very Parisian.

Clappique wants to construct this sequence out of a series of shots of the Paris of 1890: cafés, carriages, men in tophats in the restaurants and the theater foyers, women with long gloves: the sequence ending with a frantic cancan in the Moulin-Rouge, which stops when Mayrena enters amid loud applause, the dancers rushing up to him with flowers.

The turning point comes in the Chamber of Deputies. According to the legend, Mayrena, dressed as a tropical general, is sitting in the diplomatic gallery. (It would be worth looking up this session of March 18, which must have been spectacular since he had chosen it.) While Clemenceau is demolishing Ferry, or the other way round, an usher comes up, followed by two police inspectors, and mutters, "Monsieur, the President requests you to leave this gallery for the public one." Mayrena smiles contemptuously, and leaves the Chamber.

"There could be similar scenes in the Tabarin or the Moulin-Rouge; I should like lots of paper streamers, and especially paper moons. There's one scene, whose real hero is Lautrec, that I'd love to have. Somewhere near the Rat mort, the Moulin-Rouge, or some other night spot, a bedraggled flower seller holds out a bunch of flowers. He takes it, pays her, and says: 'Thank you, madame.' 'Madame? You must be a prince or an artist.' 'I am a king.' By the way, do you know who was the director of the Tabarin, before the war? Dubout, yes, the caricaturist of the fat ladies and little ferrety men, who used to spend his afternoons eyeing the beauties. Actually that's untrue: it was another man with the same name. But it's more amusing that way. Not a word! So, paper moons. (That would all be cut very fast, like the signature scenes in the Moï country.) Up to the main scene, the one in the Rat mort."

The Place Blanche: terraces, night walkers, flower sellers. The Moulin-Rouge is already in existence, and its sails are turning. The sign of the Rat mort. The bottom of an evening gown and tails, going up the dark red velvet staircase. The sound of tsigane music drawing nearer. The first floor room. Dancing. Around Mayrena—in evening dress, wearing the ribbon of the Royal Order of Valor—only men, some elegant, others phantasmal. Champagne. At the other tables, women with violet eyelids.

"Out there, at this very moment," Mayrena is saying, "Colonel Mercurol, Duke of Kontum, dressed in a khaki bush-jacket, and M. Minh, the simple-minded interpreter, their cigars glowing in the mist, are strolling around Kong-Gerang, as inconspicuous as a pair of elephants strolling round the Place Blanche. Colonel Mercurol, then a captain, has captured the most ferocious figure in the war, the De-Tham. Those chair-borne puppets who consider me an interloper in the diplomatic gallery were incapable of giving him anything more than a decoration!"

"Here," says Clappique, "I'll have to have a good look at what the editor can do intercutting the shots of the Rat mort (no problem), shots of what's happening outside (tiny problem), what Mayrena is describing, and what really happened.

"It's obvious that right through the film, Mayrena tells lies. But not all the time, or at least not always undiluted lies. I'm afraid I'll only be able to suggest this by a bit of exaggeration on the actor's part. For example (to gratify you, Pen-Wiper!), he knows Félix Faure about as well as I know General de Gaulle: he has heard him talking to journalists. He knews the publisher Charpentier even less. His information about the departure of the German-Siamese mission was a shot in the dark, and he realized that the Governor thought that he was as well 'informed' as himself. But he doesn't do much bragging over what he really has accomplished. He never speaks about his generosity. He really did fight the Sadet, he really did stand up to hellish conditions, and diseases which he never mentions."

Clappique puts on his monocle.

"I wonder whether some beady-eyed little doctor mightn't see the development of a sort of paranoia in many of the things that intrigue me. Then there are the techniques he used. Thin as our documentary evidence may be, there's obviously some pretty extravagant eccentricity there—Mercurol's dummies, the illusionistic methods that you used in your *Voie royale*, the buffalo skull that bleeds when a bullet hits it."

"I found them in the *Memoirs* of Robert Houdin, who was instructed to use them against the marabouts during the conquest of Algeria."

"They used to teach the missionaries little conjuring tricks to combat the witch doctors. And there's another world I should like to bring out, after Mayrena's return to Paris: the world of the magnificently eccentric Bohemians, dear to my heart, those of Nina de Villars's salon, Baudelaire's excessive heirs. Mayrena probably knew this milieu, which was enchanted by Aurelius I, king of Araucania, an ex-notary. The Sedang anthem was composed, to words by MacNab (absolutely!), by Charles de Sivry, Verlaine's brother-in-law. That should make you sit up!

"Among other jobs, I am the correspondent here of the Agence Française de Presse. One of the characters I had in tow used to tell me that Forain had told him the following: 'One snowy day he goes to visit Nina de Villars, Manet's *Femme aux éventails* . . .'"

"The one whose carpet was full of holes because her kangaroo had eaten the green bits of it during the siege."

"You really know your authorities—splendid! Standing in front of Forain, without overcoats, hands in pockets, worn tophats, turned-up collars (you see the type: Daumier's gentlemen tramps under gaslamps), two indignant characters:

'The ladders had ninety rungs, monsieur!'

'Eighty-four, monsieur!'

'My ancestor was there, monsieur!'

'At the storming of Byzantium by the Crusaders? Oh, oh! Well, mine too, monsieur!'

'Who are you?'

'Auguste de Châtillon. And you?'

'Villiers de l'Isle-Adam.'

"And they embrace each other in the snow, and go off to Nina's together. I shall not introduce these historic figures into my film, for I despise Hollywood's well-tried methods. Frightful. But I like Villiers. And for a descendant of Renaud de Châtillon, that colossal pimp, to write *La Levrette en Pal'tot!* But I should like something of that atmosphere round the Parisian Mayrena, perhaps through a series of brief flashes, perhaps through the scenes themselves.

"But to return to the plot of the film, and to Mercurol. He really did capture the Dé-Tham. But he wasn't a colonel: he was a sergeant, acting head of his outpost. What I'd like best would be, once Mayrena and the atmosphere are established, to have the gypsy music continuing, muffled and languorous—I repeat: languorous! Not a word!—and Mayrena's voice, and on the screen the truth: the Mercurol who was known as the Frightened One, and not the captain. All the more so because the person whom Mayrena quotes and describes *is* the Frightened One, and not his imaginary captain or colonel.

"I must also have the metaphors in direct images. (What, Pen-Wiper, you still want examples! When I write 'the hour when the monkeys sleep,' we must see on the screen monkeys sleeping on misty branches. Got it? Right: stop meowing!) I'll have to find out more about the Dé-Tham: he must have been extraordinary. So Mayrena is in the middle of his tale.

"The Dé-Tham was the piratical chief who held Upper Tonkin against the French ten years before. His marauding was made the easier by the fact that he could slip into China after each raid. But the viceroy of Yunnan, appointed to another post, was replaced by an enemy of the Dé-Tham, who fortified the Chinese frontier against him. So the rebel chief found himself shut up in Tonkin with its little Annamite dragon pagodas, knowing that he couldn't hold out there. Naturally the French were unaware of this.

"One day the native mistress of Captain Mercurol, a descendant of the imperial family of Annam—like all native mistresses, of course!—informs him that provided he was sure of being amnestied, the Dé-Tham would surrender. (Mercurol had a well-established reputation among the Annamites as an honest soldier, not too bright and a bit crazy.) He wires Hanoi. He is ordered to guarantee the amnesty: someone will be sent to negotiate the surrender. The following day he learns that the Dé-Tham, apprehensive, is about to skip. So off he goes to the mess to receive an unmerciful ragging.

"The only way to prevent the rebel leader from running away, according to the counterespionage service, would be to send a Frenchman to his camp. But the Dé-Tham has had many relatives killed by the whites; the envoy would be a tempting hostage, especially if the information was false; and lastly, the Dé-Tham has a habit of crucifying his more distinguished prisoners on rafts and launching them down the Red River. So Mercurol's suggestion, put forward at the Pernod hour, that someone should go, is received with great slappings of the thigh and references to a 'touch of the sun.'

" 'Bet you a round of drinks that I'll go,' he says on his second Pernod. 'A round of drinks you won't.' 'A round of drinks I will.' That same night, he sends a message to the Dé-Tham, and the following day he leaves with one of the Dé-Tham's envoys.

"Having sobered up, he has second thoughts. Dying of heat under his fantasy uniform, as colorful as a stage musketeer, caressing his red mustache and whiskers meditatively ('for the Duke of Kontum, gentlemen, not only resembles d'Artagnan but has the soul of a d'Artagnan—the d'Artagnan of *Twenty Years After*'), greeted from time to time by a severed head hanging from a bough, he devotes the best part of his energy to not thinking about what is going to happen. It was he who telegraphed Hanoi: he's not going to let some headquarters lounger think he's a chump, and he has committed himself vis-à-vis his colleagues.

"A twisted body succeeds the severed heads. He must be getting close. Not so much courageous as obstinate—the obstinacy of a donkey.

"The Dé-Tham is waiting for him in a large hut made of branches, open at either end. Behind him, outside the hut, a dead white man hangs crucified in the sun on an enormous treetrunk. The Dé-Tham, a cultivated chief, points out the body with the gesture of someone waving a fan; to which Mercurol answers in Annamese something signifying roughly: 'So what?' Torture fills him with horror and contempt. 'Since this legendary man is responsible for this crucifixion, all the feelings Mercurol had about him, even fear, are crushed beneath a single irremediable absolute, gentlemen—disgust.' "

In the silence which follows the end of the dance, only Mayrena's voice is heard. Couples have come and occupied the neighboring tables, and the diners have drawn closer.

For Mercurol, confronted with this crucified body, with the two white slits of the eyes between the lids, the great Dé-Tham is lower than the lowest of native servants. And for the first time his stumbling Annamese really sounds like something; and he has over the rebel chief what he has never had except over his riflemen: authority. He confirms the amnesty (but all the same, if someone put a dozen bullets in your hide, it would serve you damn well right), confirms to the Dé-Tham that he will be sent to another colony, a free man. The chief makes a long speech about nothing, followed by a silence filled with the buzzing of flies. The tropical sun lights up the crucified body. Then the Dé-Tham says, "Will I be in a prison or a cage?" "I told you, a free man," Mercurol replies, motionless as a judge. Ten minutes later another long palaver, "Will I be bound with ropes or chains?" "I told you, free." Surrounded by rebel chiefs who are wondering whether his enormous stripes are not those of a general, drunk with disgust, Mercurol scratches his chin through his red beard, and waits for the illustrious chief of the northern insurrection to finish havering.

The palaver lasts three hours. The Dé-Tham agrees to send a representative to Mercurol's camp, as soon as the envoy from Hanoi arrives, to negotiate his surrender.

The Governor General was anxious to give Mercurol his due for the surrender. Summoned to Hanoi and congratulated, he gets his reward. For a long time ("Got to try everything once") he has dreamed of taking hashish, which is expensive. This time, no sooner said than done!

"An hour later, he is bouncing about on the switchback railway of hemp. This is followed by an erotic frenzy. The effect of hashish, as you know, gentlemen, is cyclical, made up of great whirls of intoxication separated by lucid intervals. Coming out of the first cycle, he makes a dash for the nearest straw hut brothel."

Three hours later he returns, having performed doughty deeds, slept badly, and eaten one on top of the other two meals which have not appeased the hunger pangs of hashish. Stretched out on his bed, he is wolfing down, one after another, a bunch of pink bananas, when an orderly brings him an urgent summons to the general's house.

He, like everybody else, questions the hero of Cao-Bang on his exploit; the hero, his mustaches symmetrical and his beard dead straight, standing stiffly to attention in spite of the general's invitation to sit down, scarcely makes a reply. Very intimidated. He would be quite capable of bawling out a cantankerous Governor General, "but the benevolence of the great disarms him—as it disarms us all, gentlemen!" For some minutes, he has been staring at the general's chest. All at once he said,

"Your buttons don't look right, sir."

The general, taken aback, fingers them. Mercurol, somewhat stiff and awkward up to this point, smiles like a cherub.

"Funny thing, buttons. One, two, three, four."

And he bursts out laughing, splitting his sides.

"What's the matter? Have you got a touch of fever?"

It looks not unlike it. But this is only a beginning. The laugh disappears as if by magic. Mercurol goes on, sentimentally:

"Ah, that little fourth one, gen'ral, you can't imagine how much I like it. Oh yes, I do love the little fourth one. Just like a little sun."

In spite of being protected by his desk, the general backs away. But Mercurol, who had been leaning toward him, snaps back to attention, while at the same time his grimacing face takes on a dreamy calm, very slightly tensed by an effort of memory.

"Thank you," he says, recollecting the moment at which the general had invited him to sit down. He sits down. Then the general's question filters into his awareness.

"So, what was it that most impressed me, general? Well, sir. When it's got to be done, you do it. My way—I sneaked in."

But the hashish cycle, starting up again, though gently as yet, begins to restore his confidence.

"There was one thing, though—the time they all left. 'Cause he was suspicious, see, the Dé-Tham, suspicious as anything, all the time. So he wanted me to stay in his camp the last night. It was in a clearing, not very big, the camp, very badly kept, piles of empty cans, 'cause they'd robbed a . . ." (he cannot think of the word, makes a sweeping gesture: the return of the hashish is ridding him of his stammer and his shyness) "Well then, as he was suspicious, see, all his chiefs were in the wood. There was only him in the clearing, and of course me as well, with a can sticking into my rear end, only I couldn't budge, see, because . . . well, anyway. So I look at him, well, sort of, I couldn't really see him, not his face at any rate, only his big shadow—he's tall for an Annamite. And he was yelling at them that they'd fought together, they'd all defended Annam together against the French, and it was a good thing, and that he might be going to die, perhaps, perhaps not, and that . . . Right! Then he yelled out that he didn't think he'd be tortured, because they'd promised. But perhaps they'd torture him just the same, to find out where his chiefs were. So the only sure way for him not to tell (because he was still suspicious) was not to know. So he said: 'Now go away forever and leave me.' Five minutes later, he shouts, 'Who's left?' A good fifty voices came from the woods, hardly any of them had gone. So he yelled at them again, then waited, then asked again. From the voices, less than half had gone. Then he called again. This time it took longer."

The return of the hashish gives the narration, along with a precision of which Mercurol would ordinarily be incapable, the disturbing intensity of madmen's tales.

"But there was still a lot of them left. Maybe ten. So he shouted again. After that, only about three voices left. That took even longer; that lot certainly didn't want to go. One time, nobody answered; then he shouted again, to make sure. What a silence there was. Then he tapped me on the shoulder. There was only us two left, in the middle of all those empty cans. I took him off with me."

His musketeer mustaches twitch nervously, as if his lips were hesitating between laughter and sobs; his gaze has once more alighted on the gilt buttons, and a tear trickles down toward his trembling beard.

"My little sun, my poor little sun!"

"Are you, by any chance, just plain drunk?"

One of Mayrena's more seedy looking guests—Daumier's tail-coated tramps, like the heroes of the story about the ramparts of Byzantium—has gone downstairs and returned with seven Bohemians who stand there listening.

"By the way," says Mayrena in a different tone of voice, "champagne please, waiter! Take a seat, gentlemen, and let's get back to the captain."

"Now he is actually shedding warm tears!

"'That's a pointless question, gen'ral, a very pointless question. It'll never be settled! Never, the poor question! But the fourth little button, why are you so hard on it, button-button, why aren't you nicer to it, putting it in a box, leaving it without a drink for a week.'

"And sobbing with compassion, he stretches out his two hands over the desk toward the general's chest. The latter backs away and rings for an orderly.

"'Oh, I do love it so, gen'ral, that little button, because I had one like it when I was eight, just like it, on my little trousers.'

"The orderlies arrive in time to stop him licking the general's tunic, but his advancement has become doubtful.

"The general, gentlemen, has no experience of hashish. But we are not unaware how much fantasy owes to God, and that is why we regard the Duke of Kontum as one of us!

"This desperado, a condottiere in spite of his slightly moth-eaten look, used to give me food for reflection by the way he used to update Perrault's fairy tales for his brat of a son in Toulouse. This was how he went on with *Little Red Riding Hood*, just after the little girl has been eaten. Then your dad passed by on his way home from the colonies. In the cavalry, they'll tell you that a squadron commander is higher than a major, but don't you believe it! Then he saw there was a light in the grandmother's house, so he crept in, and of course he caught on at once. The wolf said to him: "So you're the sergeant, I mean the captain, who arrested the Dé-Tham?" The Dé-Tham is a big wolf even wickeder than all the others. So your dad answered him modestly: "Yes, it was me." So then the wolf curled up and howled, and your dad turned him over on his back and cut open his belly with his big saber that he'd brought back from Tonkin and pulled out the grandmother and Little Red Riding Hood. And he said to them, "You must be mad!" and took them to the Place du Capitole, to buy sugar violets for the little girl and roast chestnuts for the grandmother, because she said, "I was cold in the wolf's belly." ' "

While Mayrena is speaking, the Bohemians go downstairs to fetch more of their friends. Everytime a new guest arrives, Mayrena tells him to take a seat and goes on. Two couples are still dancing, and the orchestra is still playing softly in the background. All the waiters, their shirt fronts more and more crumpled, have come up to the table.

"The Revolt of the Literati has only just been crushed, the bush is the bush, and the last Resident's wife, Mme. de Sombreuse (we must do something about her poems, incidentally), is reciting sublime verses with the face of a lingerie saleslady and the voice of Sarah Bernhardt. Immediately afterward, leaves everywhere, a horse sinking into the undergrowth, skeletons of animals covered with insects, rasped by the tiger's tongue. And the man traps, and the shrill cries. One doesn't see any of this. And nor does one see the sharp teeth of the thorny brambles, which slit your throat. One sees only the huge patches of blood on the ground, where the tiger and the elephant met. And the spiderwebs two stories high! And the porous treetrunks. And the marshy smell of tracks cut with a machete. And then a bearer is killed and he is taken to the next village to be buried, a crossbow arrow in his eye. Ten bearers running away, charges on the spongy track, and in the night the Fathers' elephant caravan, arriving in a hubbub like that of a village wedding.

"For there are the elephants. When they are tamed, you can do anything with them except lead them along beside telegraph wires; they tear the poles up! Wild elephants are hunted with the lance, and with a huge bow worked by two men. But I'll talk about that hunt some other time. Let's just say that it was to reward the hunters that I instituted the Order of Sedang, which represents the imprint of an elephant's foot, such as any defeated hunter has seen a few moments before dying! And there's not a single warrior who wears it who hasn't had a brush with death, there's not a single Order, since Napoleon, which has so exclusively honored valor!"

He takes a medal out of his waistcoat pocket and throws it on to the table. The medal is passed round from hand to hand.

"I've had enough champagne. Hallo there, somebody! Get them to bring me an absinthe!"

"Kingship, what about kingship? It's everyday life, once the negotiations are over. The men, fighters or not, bewildered athletes who expect magic seed from their king. And the animals. Tame blackbirds on the loincloth driers. Whirlwinds of gnats over animals wallowing in mud. To steal rice is sacrilegious, but the rice crops have to be protected against the peacocks, the shoals of parrots as thick as shoals of fish, and the monkeys. The monkeys hold their revels with the dogs, and the ones in the forest take refuge in the villages when they are harassed by leopards. And there are cats—funny black ones who don't play either with the monkeys or with the dogs, but who aren't wild. And the most extraordinary thing is finding those amiable tomcats out there where the dead are no longer the dead, in the depths of the Annamite Chain.

"I conquered the Sedang country, where one often has to crawl on one's belly because of the bamboos and the rattans. One gets up covered with blood: there are leeches everywhere. Lashed by the rains as if by a cat-o'-nine-tails, I did it behind the flag bearing my own coat of arms, since I was forbidden to unfurl the Tricolor of France. I saw gold-bearing streams, tigers hunted with lances, fireflies rising toward the stars. I saw blind bards wrapped in their blankets, arms outstretched to call the dead. I heard the tintinnabulation of the little war-gong, which they call the cry of the water frog. I heard the hallucinating

borborygms of fettered elephants. I lived in the midst of the supernatural: the proximity of the tiger, the bloody sacrifices after which
the Moïs resume their peaceful peasant expressions once again, the
torches of the houses of the Dead. The work of the first missionaries
was held up for a year because some rascal claimed that bearded men
brought bad luck: and later because another one said that the Christian Moïs couldn't marry, because the Mother of God was a virgin!
The Father Superior told me that when the faithful reaped three times
more rice than the others, thanks to their plows, the Fathers were
accused of selling the souls of the Moïs to their God: this God gave
rice to eat souls.

"I saw the houses of the Dead. Next to a chick in a cage, a corpse
stretched out, knees and toes bound with cotton, over copper bracelets
and necklaces. The shades bury this barbaric king when the chief takes
up his torch again, and says, 'You are too close, beware of the spirits
of the dead.' The chick is the soul.

"I met the witches swathed in mummy cloths, with their cheerful
peasant mugs and their madhouse shrieks; and all those dullards of
village headmen! I heard speeches being addressed to the trees, the
tigers, the dead. And I heard the Moïs who had taken part in the
sacrifice of buffaloes or slaves recite their *Chanson de Roland*: 'Go
and unearth at the foot of the lilac the balm of invincibility.' Why
do they have to help Brazza and not me? He brings in four or five
hundred thousand men, I bring in more. The warriors of Makoko are
nothing! I have ten thousand warriors as brave as Sikhs, and I shall
have a hundred thousand in five years if they wish. Is there less need
to truckle to all that Germanry along the Congo than along the
Mekong? Savorgnan obtained acts of submission or alliance, as I did.
I followed the banner of the Mayrenas and not the Tricolor because I
had been enjoined to do so. And I had to fight the Sadet of Fire, with
my own hands I had to stop the Jarais, the most dangerous fighting
men in the Indochinese peninsula; I was on the way to suppressing
slavery! Instead of handing over all our money to the Russians, or building that ridiculous Eiffel Tower, could we not keep back a few louis
for the Empire—that Empire which may well weigh more heavily in the
balance than General Boulanger, on the day of vengeance. It is the
centenary of the Revolution. Yesterday I watched Liberty, that great
whore, on her way to America, looming out of Javel's sheds, and I said
to her: 'Raise your torch over the New World, but look at what they're
doing to you.'"

He waves for another absinthe. He is not in the least drunk, and has hardly raised his voice.

"I am neither that poor Raousset-Boulbon who they so kindly allowed to be shot, nor Aurelius I, king of Araucania on holiday, who is worth more than they are, by God! I can launch an expedition, an army, from Siam to Annam: Who else could? I was ordered to pin down or drive off a Siamese expedition (let's call it Siamese) with the most paltry resources. Did I do it? So they want to treat me as a crackpot? Did they give me an escort or not? Did I come to Qui Nhon with Governor General Constans? Did I arrive among the missionaries with instructions from the bishop? When it was necessary to fight, did we do honor to that flag which I did not even have the right to unfurl? And yet, all in all, did I not achieve a peaceful infiltration? Always the same thing: Dupleix died, deserted, the pillow on which his head rested stuffed with the shares of the East India Company, and with the state bringing a case against him! Think of Balboa, discovering the Pacific: 'Long live the king of Castile, sovereign of this sea and of all the continents it bathes!' In face of Stanley, they will abandon Brazza as they abandoned me! I bring rubber, coffee; my trees range from palm to pine. All that colonial produce can be had for the asking. Gold! What do they think I had the medals of my orders struck in? They found ten times less gold in the Transvaal when the gold rush started five years ago than was found in the Sedang country! And that insolent president of their Chamber has the nerve to say I have no right to be in the diplomatic gallery! I was in the diplomatic gallery at the exhibition! Those ghastly looking puppets failed me and I'm burning to give them a lesson they'll remember! What were those apes doing when the war drum was rumbling in the mist on the mountain peaks?"

The Bohemians have come closer, still standing. The last dancers and the new arrivals have also come up, and all of them are conglomerated round his table, except for the musicians, who have not dared to leave the orchestra, but who are listening. He speaks without histrionic gestures, surrounded by a captive audience.

"Was there a queen?" asks a Bohemian, innocently.

"Yes, my lad, there was a queen! And wipe that leer off your face, for everything I have done I did to give people like you something to dream about, and you might get a good thrashing! They're prepared to hand over the Sedang kingdom to anyone at all, even to the Germans, as long as it isn't me. But who will drive me from men's dreams? The bourgeois can laugh when Villiers de l'Isle-Adam asserts his rights to the throne of Greece, but we will not!

"So, then, there was a queen. Maddeningly beautiful with her coral diadem, she was the last descendant of the Cham kings, and the Sedangs were vassals of the Chams. She came with me, and was never afraid. And some days were really very hard. She died in childbirth: she insisted on being looked after by the witches—and no doubt we would not have been able to look after her. I shall spare you the witches. I assembled the warriors, and we crossed the mountains with the elephants, to the great ruins. Flocks of white butterflies settled on us like mayflowers and when they had gone, my companions were pierrots and our elephants white elephants! The queen was buried beneath the ruins of the palaces and temples of her race. A priestess sang the obsequies; all the warriors, their lances at rest, held torches which they extinguished at the last spadeful of earth. It was five hundred years since a Cham princess had been buried beneath the towers of My-Son. That is all."

While he speaks, the last shot of the solitary burial, with the cross made of branches. Return to the table. Rapid pan over the empty champagne bottles and the saucers of absinthe glasses. The bill is brought. It is more than he has left. He smiles bitterly, tears off the golden plaque of valor which hangs at the end of its great ribbon. He looks at the imprint of the elephant's foot—a flashback to the raised foot, and the tableau of the warriors he had decorated in the mountain mist. He lays the plaque on the bill, tells the waiter, "Change it by weight!" and stands up. The Bohemians scatter, his guests go to get their overcoats. Mayrena's change arrives. He gives a tip to the red-capped pageboy, who says, shyly,

"You wouldn't happen to have another medal, a smaller one?"

"There are still some out there. Gold too."

"There are? I'd like to go back there with you."

The Malay coast. Mr. William Moran, assistant administrator of the Straits Settlement, is walking down a street lined with huts and banana trees (in the distance, the China Sea), a copy of a telegram in his hand: "WILLIAM, EMPEROR, BERLIN STOP LAST WISHES STOP BEQUEATH YOU PROTECTORATE SEDANG KINGDOM STOP YOUR COUSIN STOP MARIE." Mr. Moran looks like a white-haired Shelley.

He arrives at Mayrena's hut, which gives on to the sea. Mayrena watches him approach.

"They told you about my telegram, and you've come to see if I'm mad?"

"The telegram only concerns Germany, and perhaps France. But I feel that if you were ill we should have to help you, and you're a long way from everything. Are there many birds of paradise at the moment?"

"See for yourself."

There are numerous paradise feathers on the partitions of the straw hut, and on the table, an entire bird wrapped in a newspaper. Mayrena pushes it aside, takes a bottle of whisky and two glasses from a chest, and puts them down in its place. On the main partition, a framed photograph of Marie I in military uniform. Some large feathers stick out behind it.

"Do you like birds?" Mayrena asks.

"When I was stationed in San Salvador, I used to love to see the quetzal hunters. You know that it's the bird of freedom, which dies when caged. I saw a very fine one sticking out from behind a photograph like your bird of paradise: it was a photograph of the dictator. The hunters are smugglers, because the export of quetzals is banned."

"The bad part was 'delivering' the feathers to Singapore. I'm beginning to detest towns."

"Have you any news from . . . over there?"

"It's lost. And yet, some day, there will be a Moï confederation. I came too soon. My compatriots haven't the colonial bent. Alsace is an excuse."

"Then why?"

"I'm a patriot, but I want the Sedang kingdom to exist, I want them to know that I wasn't a crackpot. Had I been English, I would have got help. You didn't disown Brooke, far from it. Germany, you, Russia, Siam, perhaps even France. By God, the door I opened will never close again!

"Do you sometimes have the feeling that you can see life behind you, like something over and done with?"

"One drinks a lot in these tropical countries."

"The fire of Prometheus is accommodating, even if one can't get hold of Pernod, only vile whisky, in your Malaya! Have you ever taken hashish?"

"You're sure you don't need anything? We have the best English preserves."

"Nothing: I shall be dead in an hour. I've been bitten by a tedong-hiar snake, so . . . You know as well as I do that there's no cure. And I no longer want a cure."

"May I suggest that the telegram seems to me unwise?"

"It doesn't matter. You know that death from the bite of the tedong-hiar resembles the effects of certain vegetable poisons well known among the natives. And the death pangs do not differ greatly from hashish bouts. That is why I asked whether you had tried it."

"No."

Mayrena stares at him: he has the complexion of an opium addict.

"Opium and hashish don't exactly go together."

"Opium is peace."

"I'm not addicted to hashish, that infernal companion, as the Arabs call it. I became very interested in it in Indochina, in the lands of obligatory ecclesiastical service, where the bonzes use it to bring picked subjects toward ecstasy. It is an insolent multiplier of what it encounters —music if you make musicians play, a god if you think strongly about him, and eroticism if you have nothing better, since it is an aphrodisiac. I talked about it with the pope of the bonzes, in Cambodia. I told him that I liked religion, not drugs. He answered, 'If you give it to a stupid young bonze, he will not become less stupid. Hashish does not carry illumination within itself. But we are separated from it by a shell, and it destroys the shell.' I know nothing about music, and even less about Asian music; yet I have heard songs of Paradise.

"My enemies take me for an impostor. You too, probably. A duel with a witch doctor is not something to make a fuss about. All right. I fought in the war. And I have fought several duels, like all journalists of my age. But I would have you realize that with the Sadet the risk was not of being wounded or killed—mere bagatelles!—but of being wounded enough to fall into the hands of the Sedangs. Torture still exists in those regions, and the Christians could have done nothing for me, for my defeat would have forced them to take flight, and fast! I hardly thought about it. But I felt Father Georges's fear, and the confidence, as palpable as joy or sorrow, manifested by the Sedangs who surrounded the Sadet; and the forest, which was his and not mine. Time and again I have lived in the supernatural. If I were a great poet, I might be able to express it. By God, my master and friend Victor Hugo would have done so! I cannot express it, but *I know it*. It is for that whiff of the supernatural that I have lived, like an addict for his drug. If I had to do it again, I would act more cleverly, learn Sedang, get away from the Fathers gradually, obtain arms at the start, and so on. To what end? In flashes I have known what I wanted to know.

That is my truth, in the sense in which love is one. They can call it absurd and extravagant—why should I care? You can see that I'm perfectly lucid. I can think hard about what has been my own world, and I have only to think of it to possess it. The poison is beginning to take effect. I am about to grasp my whole life. Not in its individual moments, but in what it will be later, for a destiny like mine creates of necessity its own legend. Every past is absurd, isn't it?"

"Like everything else."

"Bravo! But I, bird hunter, wreck, I die a king. I still have three-quarters of an hour left. You're wondering whether I'm not dreaming once again. Do you not feel that I pity you? I want to give you presents."

"No one knows how he is to die, and I have sometimes regretted not having any morphine. What is that poison called?"

Once again, Mayrena stares straight at his visitor. He takes a metal box from a chest and opens it. It holds a small bottle and a syringe. Mayrena holds out the bottle to Moran.

"It is of crystal, and the stopper is pure gold. It was my last souvenir of the Château de Mayrena. The poison is the same as that of the Sedang witch doctors: the exact equivalent of snake venom. Fifty drops, two hours.

"You didn't bring a dog with you? I should like to stroke a gentle animal. I am going to give you something else, since you have taken the trouble to come and see me. One day it will be rare. And a kind of testimony. This sheet, in the box, is a sheet of the stamps I issued during my kingship. I hope you're a stamp collector. Thank you again. Goodbye."

He goes out. The metal box remains open on the table. Moran gazes dreamily at the syringe; there is still a little liquid left in it.

"After that," Clappique goes on, "I should like to be able to shoot the rest myself, because the scenario can only give general indications.

"Mayrena arrives at a pleasant cove; the sea is beating against the rocks, covered with vegetation that seems to reach right down to the water. He falls onto the soft ground, panting a little. The camera sees through his eyes: mosses at eye level, tiny plants, seaweed, shrubs, giant trees hung with lianas. A few insects. After the noise of his fall, silence, then the thud of the sea breaking against the rock.

"The song of a distant bird, on three notes. They are repeated, pure, then mixed, then sung: 'Your king-dom . . .'

"The camera shows the mosses, which begin to whisper: 'Your kingdom . . .' Montage of all the plants, in time with the music, each plant repeating these words in a voice suited to its image. When an insect passes, the sound is cut off.

"For the mosses, little girls' voices, then, accompanying the succeeding images, little boys' voices, choirs of children, women, men which fade as the plant recedes from the camera: close-up whispering for the mosses.

"The thick vegetation murmurs: 'When the war drum growled in the mist . . .'

"Then 'Your king-dom' is taken up by a solemn chorus streaked with the few sharp voices of the trees overgrown with lianas.

"A palm tree with its slender trunks says: 'I'd like to go out there with you.'

"Finally the immense trees repeat: 'Your king-dom!' leaving only the empty sky on the screen, with the superb cumulus clouds of the equator.

"Distant chorus of women: 'Go and unearth at the foot of the lilac —the balm of invincibility.'

"Mayrena has raised himself on to his elbows. He watches the waves surging in to break against the rocks roaring: 'Your king-dom!'

"The waves flow back.

" 'I should like to stroke a gentle animal.'

"The Sadet. The elephant, trunk uplifted; the elephant's foot; the warriors being decorated in the mist.

"A buffalo skull, swarming with insects.

"The semicircle of the Chamber, a speaker on the rostrum.

"The burial of the queen: the elephants turned white, and the cross of branches.

"Mayrena's listeners at the Rat mort.

"The waves surge back, break with a roar, ebb.

"A motionless monkey in a tree.

"The camera zooms. Close-up of Mayrena. When the entire face fills the screen, the wave striking the rock cries 'Your king-dom!' and the chorus follows its ebb while the face is magnified on the screen until only the eyes remain, closing on the fading cry. The waves also recede, and only the ebbing sound remains as the camera, following the movement of the eyelids, rises (the human eye closes upward) toward the sky and its cumulus clouds.

"End of *The Devil's Kingdom*."

"What do you think of it?" asks Clappique.

*   *   *   *

At last, the plane takes off for Hong Kong. The Pacific. Islands. Over there, there is an island called Balé-Kambang, which Eddy du Perron gave me when I dedicated *La Condition humaine* to him. He died when the Germans entered Holland. He thought all politics meaningless, and history too, I believe. He was my best friend. I am told that the Dutch now recognize him as one of their great writers. What has become of his family's plantations? And his *Letter to the Liberator Shariar?* He did not believe in politics, but he believed in justice. What has become of my island? Will I visit it before I die, with Sukarno's blessing? The coconut palms grow thickly there, it seems.

Eddy du Perron used to tell me that *La Voie royale* was worthless, and could only be justified if it became the fantastic prologue to subsequent volumes. (These became *La Condition humaine.*) In the airplane, I reread the main scenes of my novel. Clappique is right in thinking that in many respects my character Perken was based on Mayrena. More exactly, on what Mayrena has in common with a vanished breed of adventurers. In 1929 his crazy side was unknown. He was identified with a white adventurer in Sumatra, and some of those men who dared, like Mercurol, to venture unarmed among unsubdued or insurgent peoples.

The book and the character arose from a speculation on what man can do against death. Whence this prototype of the hero without a cause, ready to risk torture simply for the sake of his own conception of himself, and perhaps for a kind of blinding perception of his destiny —because the risk of torture alone seems to him to triumph over death. "If I kill myself, I become a tsar," said Kirilov. The man who kills himself does not become a tsar at all, he "becomes free." But the man who accepts the risk of torture—even if *only* for his own arbitrary conception of himself and, more deeply, for a cause which is not the defense of his own kin but the human condition—does not commit himself alone, like Kirilov, or his near ones, like the traditional hero, but the human condition, like Prometheus—or the supreme illusion.

Since then, torture has become terrifyingly commonplace, and we have no time for heroes without a cause. But in 1965, over the Pacific, I think of the young man of 1928 on his way to Batum, pacing the deck of a cargo boat in the Straits of Messina, one of the most beautiful landscapes in the world, thinking up this character, or rather this holocaust in a radiant Italian morning. I look for the passage where Claude watches the unarmed Perken walk toward the armed Moïs to try to rescue their companion Grabot.

I am flying over the land of the Möis, the forest still as tangled as it

was in the last century, in spite of Ban-Me-Thuot and a few other bases.
The administrator who had devoted himself to the Moïs was removed
by the French, and no Vietnamese has replaced him. We are crossing
the Annamite Chain. Here is Qui Nhon, and the shadow of Thalie.

And a little farther on, here is Danang, which was once Tourane;
around the port, the American battle fleet lies motionless.

La Condition humaine

1

Hong Kong. I am alone in the drawing room of the consulate general. The entire gulf is framed in the windows. A warm haze bathes the aggressive skyscrapers which crush the imperial waterfront of the days of *Les Conquérants* and outflank and beleaguer the peak; the mist transforms the ships and junks into gray silhouettes under a ruffled sky. I passed through Hong Kong in 1958 on my way from Nehru's India to Japan. The thick-leaved plants on the fretted balconies of the Chinese hotels in Queen's Road tumbled as of old over the thousands of little porcelains in front of the antique shops. I remember a day in 1925 or 1926. The sun was shining over the gulf; the blue air quivered. The colonial administration had succeeded in preventing every printer in Saigon from printing the newspaper of the Young Annam movement, *L'Indochine*, at the time of the Bac Lieu spoliations. The militants had reassembled some old presses, and I had come to buy type from the only type founder from Ceylon to Shanghai: the Hong Kong mission. I returned to Saigon with some English type, without accents. Impossible to print the paper. One day, an Annamese worker came in, pulled out of his pocket a handkerchief knotted into a bundle, the corners standing up like rabbits' ears. "They're all e's," he said. "Grave and acute accents, and circumflexes too. The diaereses will be more difficult. Perhaps you can do without them. Tomorrow some press workers will bring all the accents they can." He emptied the characters, jumbled up like jackstraws, on to a press stone, aligned them with the tips of his expert fingers, and left. His comrades followed him. They all knew that if they were caught they would be sentenced, not as revolutionaries but as thieves.

Forty years ago. Below me now I can see the roofs of the mission. Still farther below, down as far as the sea front, the gigantic bamboo scaffoldings are being hastily dismantled, for typhoons blow them down, and a typhoon is hovering round the island at the moment. I have seen again the Chinese women with their embroidered sheath dresses reminiscent of the days of Nanking, and the old tradeswomen with their stumps of feet. The adventurers who are no longer to be found in Singapore are here in plenty—they are all Chinese. And I have just been listening to stories like those I used to hear in Shanghai before 1930: the shipload of blind people arriving at the nuns' hospice after escaping from Canton, where the police no doubt organized the escape to get rid of them; the young Chinese from Borneo who came to participate in the building of the new China and, loathing it, have escaped penniless and taken refuge with the missionaries, who got them jobs in firework factories where they steal the crackers to gamble; and the junks loaded with clandestine passengers which the captain scuttles (the bottom of the junk opens) if he is stopped by the people's police or the British police.

In front of me, across the bay, the "New Territories" stretch to the black bar which closes the horizon: Communist China. It is present even in the city, through its discreet control of all the unions, and through the spectacular store it has just opened. Imagine, in the middle of an opulent Monte Carlo, the *Samaritaine** of a communist Europe. Red China sells what it makes. It is not very much, but every little things represents another battle won. In the background, the atom bomb; in the foreground, the Spartan smiles of the shop assistants. Even the toys are austere, and the trappings of the perfect communist housewife seem like an offering before the portraits of Mao and the images of the Long March.

Above this accumulation of fiber suitcases and Thermos bottles, all the emporium goods of which the people's democracies are always so proud, these mythological images hold sway. The suitcases and furniture of the capitalists may be less crude than these, but then who was it who crossed the rivers, who was it who trudged through the Tibetan snows? After a quarter of an hour, what is sold here pales before what is dreamed about. All the better for the fact that, though the brave militiaman and the heroic militiawoman of the posters are socialist-realist, nearly all the images of the Long March are in traditional Chinese style. For the millions conglomerated on the rock of Hong Kong, the vastness that stretches behind the black bar of the horizon is not the land of the people's communes, the individual blast furnaces and the giant factories, nor even of the atom bomb, it is the land of the Long March and of its leader; just as Russia, beyond the triumphal arch of Niegoreloïe, was not the land of the kolkhozes but of Lenin and the October Revolution.

There are now no more than twenty thousand survivors of the Long March—and eight hundred "responsibles," it is said. On the other side of the bay, it pervades the popular imagination as the *Ramayana* still pervades the imagination of India, as Olympus once pervaded the imagination of Greece.

Everything had begun with victories.

In the autumn of 1928 the Sixth Congress in Moscow finally recognizes the importance of peasant action in the revolutionary struggle.

* A big department store in Paris. (Tr.)

It is the end of the first schism. Red armies spring up: mutiny after mutiny breaks out in the armies of the Kuomintang, and the mutineers join Mao in the Chingkang Mountains. But his supplies will not feed an army.

In January 1929 Mao's principal general, Chu Teh, breaks through the blockade and joins up with other Red troops. In December, the whole of southern Kiangsi is conquered, and the first provincial soviet government proclaimed.

The Kuomintang, now the Nanking government, opens the first "Encirclement and Annihilation Campaign" with one hundred thousand men against Mao's forty thousand. By a war of maneuver, in which the bulk of the Red forces is always brought to bear on isolated columns which Mao has lured deep into his territory, and thanks to the support of the local population, the army of Nanking is scattered in two months.

Four months later, the Second Campaign commits two hundred thousand men in seven separate columns. Same tactic, same results.

A month later Chiang Kai-shek takes personal command of three hundred thousand men. Mao's forces attack five columns in five days, capture a considerable amount of war material, and in October Chiang withdraws the forces of the Third Campaign of Annihilation.

The Chinese Soviet Republic is proclaimed under the chairmanship of Mao.

In December 1931 two hundred thousand men come over to him from Nanking. The Red Army starts offensive operations of its own. In 1933 Nanking opens the Fourth Campaign of Annihilation, loses thirteen thousand men in a single battle, and sees its best division destroyed.

But Chiang Kai-shek's advisers (among them Von Falkenhausen and Von Seekt, former chief of general staff of the German army) have taken part in the campaign and learned its lessons. For the Fifth Campaign of Annihilation, Nanking assembles nearly a million men, with tanks and four hundred airplanes. Mao has at his disposal one hundred eighty thousand soldiers, about two hundred thousand militiamen—armed with pikes!—and four aircraft captured from Nanking. No fuel, no bombs, no artillery, little ammunition. Chiang Kai-shek no longer advances into communist territory: he surrounds it with a ring of blockhouses, a new Wall of China hemming it in. The Red Army realizes that it is trapped.

Was it then that Mao thought of Yenan? Japan had declared war on China, and Mao wanted to become the symbol of the Chinese people's resistance to aggression, for Nanking was doing far less fighting against the Japanese than against the communists. In that case it was essential to get to the north, the real battlefield; yet at first for thousands of miles, the Red Army thrust westward toward Tibet. In spite of all the obstacles, in spite of the opposition of various tribal chiefs, Mao remained confident that the whole of peasant China was on his side, provided the message got through to the people. Somewhere or other a region favorable to the establishment of a communist government would be found, as in Kiangsi. There was in the Long March an indubitable element of romantic adventure, reminiscent of Alexander's expedition, which is by no means foreign to Mao's character.

But first of all, *they must get out.* The Red Army, under constant bombardment, had already lost sixty thousand men in this vast siege.

Ninety thousand men, women, and children would attempt to break through the blockade, as Chu Teh had done in the Chingkang Mountains. Little by little, the front line army was replaced by partisans. On October 16, 1934, concentrated in southern Kiangsi, it took the enemy fortifications by storm, and veered westward. The Long March had begun.

Mules were loaded with machine guns and sewing machines. Thousands of civilians accompanied the army. How many would remain in the villages—or in the cemeteries? How many of the dismantled machines carried on muleback would be found again one day, buried along the seven-thousand-mile route? The partisans with their red-tasseled pikes and their hats topped by leaves which shook like feathers would hold out for a long time yet—some of them for three years. The Nanking forces killed them, but Mao's army marched on.

In one month, harassed from the air, it fought nine battles, broke through four lines of blockhouses and a hundred and ten regiments. It lost a third of its men, decided to keep only its military equipment and a few field printing presses, stopped advancing toward the northwest (which baffled the enemy but slowed its march considerably). Chiang Kai-shek had gathered his forces behind the Yangtze and destroyed the bridges. But a hundred thousand men and their artillery were awaiting Mao before the Kweichow River. The Reds wiped out five divisions, held a meeting of their Central Committee in the governor's palace, enrolled fifteen thousand deserters, and organized youth cadres. But the "golden sands river" of the poems had yet to be crossed. Mao turned southward, and in four days was fifteen miles from Yunnanfu, where Chiang Kai-shek had established himself. It was a diversion, for the main body of the Red Army was marching northward to cross the river there.

It was the Tatu River, no less difficult to cross than the Yangtze, and where the last army of the Taipings had been wiped out by the imperial forces. Moreover it could only be reached through the vast forest of the Lolos, where no Chinese army had ever penetrated. But a few Red officers who had served in Szechwan had once set free some Lolo chiefs, and Mao negotiated with these unsubdued tribes as he had done with all the villages his soldiers had passed through. "The government army is the common enemy." To which the tribes responded by asking for arms, which Mao and Chu Teh ventured to give them. The Lolos then guided the Reds through their forests where the Nanking air force lost all trace of them—to the Tatu ferry, which together they captured in a surprise attack.

It would have taken weeks for the army to cross the river by means of this ferry. Chiang Kai-shek's airmen, reconnoitering the river, had found the columns again. His armies had bypassed the forest and would soon be ready to give battle once more. This was the time when Nanking spoke of the funeral march of the Red Army.

There was only one bridge, much farther up the river, between steep cliffs across a rushing torrent. The army, exposed to continuous bombardment, advanced by forced marches through a storm along a narrow trail above the river, which by night reflected the thousands of torches tied to the soldiers' backs. When the advance guard reached the bridge, it found that half the wooden flooring had been burnt out.

Facing them, on the opposite bank, the enemy machine guns.

All China knows the fabulous gorges of its great rivers, the fury of the waters pent up by sheer peaks which pierce the heavy, low clouds under the echoing cries of the birds of prey. It has never ceased to picture this army of torches in the night, the flames of the dead sacrificed to the gods of the river; and the colossal chains stretching across the void, like those of the gates of Hell. For the bridge of Luting now consisted of the nine chains which supported its plank floor and two chains on either side which served as handrails. With the wooden roadway burnt, there remained these thirteen nightmare chains, no longer a bridge but its skeleton, thrusting over the savage roar of the waters. Binoculars revealed the intact section of the roadway and a voluted pavilion from behind which came the crackle of machine gun fire.

The Red machine guns opened up. Under the whistling hail of bullets, volunteers dangling from the freezing chains began to advance, link after enormous link—white caps and white cross belts standing out in the mist—swinging their bodies to heave themselves forward. One after another they dropped into the raging waters, but the lines of dangling men, swaying from their own efforts and from the force of the wind whistling through the gorges, advanced inexorably toward the opposite bank. The machine guns easily picked off those who were clinging to the four supporting chains, but the curve of the other nine chains protected the men advancing below them, grenades at their belts. The most dangerous moment would come when they reached the fragment of roadway still in place and hoisted themselves onto it—which would only be possible, at best, for nine men at a time. The prisoners were later to declare that the defense was paralyzed by the sight of armed men suddenly springing up from the chains over the middle of the river; perhaps most of Chiang's mercenaries, accustomed to fighting Tibetan "brigands" armed with flintlocks, had no stomach for hand-to-hand combat with soldiers who had carried out such a legendary exploit before their very eyes. The first volunteers to hoist themselves onto the bridge had time to fling their grenades at the enemy machine gun nests, which were firing blind. The enemy officers ordered barrels of paraffin to be tipped over the remaining planks of the roadway, and set fire to them. Too late: the assailants dashed through the curtain of flames. The machine guns fell silent on both sides of the river, and the enemy retreated into the forest. The army crossed the bridge beneath the ineffectual bombing of the air force.

It is the most famous legend of Red China. In the communist store in Hong Kong I had seen, first of all, the exodus, strung out for mile upon mile; the peasant army preceding the civilians bent double under their burdens like rows of men hauling barges; a multitude as bowed as that which accompanied the Partition of India, but resolutely prepared for battles unknown. Three thousand miles they traveled, liberating village after village on the way, for a few days or a few years; and here were those stooping bodies which seemed to have risen from the tomb of China, and beyond the gorges, those chains stretching across history. Everywhere, chains belong to the darker side of man's imagination. They used to be part of the equipment of dungeons—and still were, in China, not so long ago—and their outline seems the very ideogram of slavery. Those hapless men with one arm hanging limp under the bullets are still watched by the wretched masses of China as the other hand opens above the roar of an ageless gulf. Other men followed them, whose hands did not open. In the memory of every Chinese, that string of dangling men swaying toward freedom seem to be brandishing aloft the chains to which they cling.

Nevertheless, this famous episode cost the Red Army fewer men than those which followed. It reached a region where the blockhouses of Nanking were still few, and regained the military initiative. But it still had to cross the high snow-covered passes of the Chiachin Mountains. It had been warm in June in the Chinese lowlands, but it was cold at fifteen thousand feet, and the cotton-clad men of the south began to die. There were no paths; the army had to build its own track. One army corps lost two-thirds of its animals. Mountain upon mountain, soon corpse upon corpse: one can follow the Long March by the skeletons fallen under their empty sacks; and those who fell forever before the peak of the Feather of Dreams, and those who skirted the Great Drum (for the Chinese, the drum is the bronze drum) with its vertical faces in the endless jagged immensity of the mountains. The murderous clouds hid the gods of the Tibetan snows. At last the army with the mustaches of hoarfrost reached the fields of Maokung. Down below, it was still summer.

There were forty-five thousand men left.

The Fourth Army and the vague soviet authorities of Sungpan awaited Mao there. The Red forces now mustered a hundred thousand soldiers; but after a disagreement which allowed Nanking a successful offensive, Mao set off again toward the Great Grasslands with thirty thousand men. Chu Teh stayed behind in Szechwan.

The Great Grasslands also meant dense forest, the sources of ten great rivers, and above all the Great Swamplands, occupied by autonomous tribes. The queen of the Mant-ze tribe gave orders that anyone who made contact with the Chinese, Red or otherwise, was to be boiled alive. For once, Mao failed in his efforts to negotiate. Empty dwellings, vanished cattle, narrow defiles in which the tribesmen rolled boulders down on them. "A sheep costs a man's life." There remained fields of green corn, and giant turnips each of which, Mao said, could feed fifteen men. And the Great Swamplands.

The army advanced, guided by native prisoners. Anyone who left the trail vanished. Endless rain in the immensity of the sodden grasslands and stagnant waters, under the white mists or the livid sky. No firewood, no trees—and the army had no tents. As protection against the rain, the white caps had been replaced with big sun hats. The clouds drifted low over the marshes, and the horses stumbled in the bottomless mud. At night the soldiers slept on their feet, tied together like bundles of fire-wood. After ten days, they reached Kansu. The Nanking forces had abandoned the pursuit, or were buried in the marshes. Mao now com-manded no more than twenty-five thousand men. The field theater started up again, in front of soldiers dressed in animal hides turned inside out. And the ragged lines advanced at last among stones, their flags threadbare like those of our maquis.

New forces were mustered by Nanking, supported by the Chinese Muslim cavalry who were to "finish the Reds off once and for all." But in spite of their exhaustion, no mercenary force could have beaten these volunteers who were only a battle away from the Red bases in Shensi. The horses captured from the Tartars of the Chinese steppes were later to form the cavalry of Yenan. On October 20, 1935, at the foot of the Great Wall, Mao's horsemen, wearing hats of leaves and mounted on little shaggy ponies like those of the prehistoric cave paintings, joined up with the three communist armies of Shensi, of which Mao took command. He had twenty thousand men left, of whom seven thousand had been with him all the way from the south. They had covered six and a half thousand miles. Almost all the women had died, and the children had been left along the way.

The Long March was at an end.

When you go into the communist store, when you look at the moun-tains beyond the New Territories, People's China is the March. And Mao would be inconceivable without it. Nothing remained of the na-tion except shame, nothing remained of the land except famine. But while tens of thousands of dead men or deserters had been replaced, tens of thousands of absent comrades were neither dead nor deserters. They had stayed behind because they belonged to the third order of peasant emancipation. In many regions, the guerrilla warfare stirred up by the Long March was to last for two years, holding down whole enemy divisions, sometimes whole armies. The repression in Kiangsi—a million victims—had left the peasantry of that province without a voice, but not without hate. The Long March had brought hope to two hundred million Chinese, and this hope had not disappeared with the last com-batant. This tattered phalanx followed by its last stragglers had played the role of the horsemen of Allah; on its arrival at the Great Wall, it declared war against Japan. The military retreat had ended in political victory. Wherever it had passed, for the Chinese peasants the Red Army had become the army that defended the peasants, and China.

At eleven o'clock at night, as I travel across the harbor in a sampan as at the time of the first strike, the electricity is switched off in the skyscrapers. There remain the "flower boats," outlined against the bay by their lightbulbs, with a few glimmers in the Chinese back streets and the dotted line of the lamps along the road to the peak. On the water, the city of the junks continues its life in death. It seems to be unaware of the land, and many a traveler has written of its hubbub of former days. This evening, only a few shadows glide from junk to junk. The carved bows succeed one another, separated by the alleys of sampans. A few dim lights appear, then fade. Merchants glide past in rowing boats, carrying lanterns like the merchants on the lakes of the emperors long ago. And the tall decorated prows which will never take to sea again seem to muffle their almost secret calls beneath the last dragon's-wing sails whose tatters are hidden by the darkness, and which once were the sails of the most numerous fleet in the world. At dawn, as mammoth China slowly awakens yonder, the skyscrapers will set off again with a bang on their assault against the peak, and the antique dealers will hang above their devalued treasures the photograph of Chiang Kai-shek which carries a picture of Mao on the back and which they will turn over whenever necessary. Around me there remains nothing but the trembling dotted line of the lamps on the road, fading away in the distance until it merges with the stars—and the faint call of a tradesman through the night and the silence.

Canton

"*General strike declared in Canton.*"
1925. It was the first general strike, and the first sentence of my first novel.

Not a sign is left of the Chinese of the East India Company, of the moneychangers' quarter whose tintinnabulation could be heard along the riverside as they hammered on the coins with their little hammers— or of the amorphous bazaar which still filled the center of the town on the eve of the revolution. Not much sign of the revolution either—except its museums. The Cadet School has been demolished, I am told, and Borodin's house, and . . . Asphalt streets with low, uniform houses, immense parks "of culture." In spite of the banana trees, in spite of the heat, there is a sense of vastness reminiscent of Russia. A hotel with endless staircases, endless corridors; Russian in its size, in its purple carpet, in a dreamlike emptiness unlike that of the West, but which I have not seen in Russia. Shameen, the former island of the consulates, is intact—like the body of a murdered man. Its houses, which no longer resemble those of the town, are peeling above the little square with its serried rows of flowers; engineless junks, their sails a patchwork of Bengal pink and smoke-gray, are rounding the point of the island, chimeras in Harlequin costume; in the gathering dusk, Marco Polo's fleet is setting sail on the Pearl River, past the old docks and the new shipyards, across the Siberian wilderness. Here is the bridge on which Colonel Chiang Kai-shek's machine guns opened fire.

The Museum of the Revolution is laid out in the circular hall of the monument to Sun Yat-sen. Close by is the mausoleum of the political martyrs, reminiscent of the mausoleums of the emperors of ancient China (the whole park seems to be its sacred wood), before which the communist pioneers come to be sworn in.

In the museum there are photographs of the leaders of the 1925 strike, the first strike against Hong Kong; all of them are dead. Beneath a strip bearing the date May 4, 1919, there is the prison gate, like a network of black crosses against a blur of faces; on the ground, the medieval irons which the prisoners wore at the time of the repression of the Canton commune. Everything is outside time: a village of partisans which resisted the Kuomintang forces for ten months, the women's units in which termagants mingled with typists; the executions in Shanghai during the repression narrated in La Condition humaine, the condemned men on their knees, blindfolded with black cloths which hang like cowls back to front; a model of the capture of Hainan by an army of junks (what were the Kuomintang warships doing at the time?); and all the photographs of the peasant movement—of which no one spoke in 1925. Here are the pikes with the short red tassels, for the long ones are those of Yenan; and the "Tonkinese" hats. (One of my grandfathers had brought one back which was called the Black Flag hat.)

As in the Soviet Union, these photographs and these objects are mixed up with a whole folklore of the revolution. This people which had no minister of justice, but a minister of punishments, assembles the same photographs as Moscow and, even more obscurely, as the denizens of our cathedrals. They are supposed to teach revolution, and they teach martyrdom. The Taipings ruled for ten years, and were wiped out beside that same river which Mao crossed. Obviously it is his political genius which distinguishes him from them; but what this museum shows is almost exclusively what links him to them.

As in Moscow, the pictures are intended not so much to make the course of the revolution intelligible as to create a past amenable to the victors. How much more effective than this propaganda would be a museum which clearly explained Mao's complex achievement to these young people around me who can only guess at it all and accept it with vague reverence.

I only see the people who are hidden. Lenin is never accompanied by anyone except Stalin: there never was a Trotsky. Or a Borodin, for that matter. Or a Chiang Kai-shek. The photographs of the Cadet School show only Chou En-lai, as a political commissar. In a photograph of fifty officers I recognize Galen, the future Marshal Blücher, and point him out to the French ambassador who is with me. Up comes the interpreter, who had seemed no longer interested in us, as if on roller skates. "Which one is he?" he asks, wide-eyed. Galen does not reappear in any other photographs. There were no Russians in Canton in 1925.

Next Day

Yesterday evening, in the Sun Yat-sen mausoleum, a hall seating five thousand people, the theater was playing *The East Is Red*. It started three quarters of an hour late because it was raining—during the rainy season. Like Russia, China unaccountably combines a nonexistent sense of time (theaters, airplanes) with the strictest punctuality (railways, army). While we waited, the three hundred singers of the chorus were in their places on either side of the stage—blue trousers, white shirts— and as they were ranged in tiers one could only make out an immense white cloth dotted with heads.

At last, the announcer began. He was wearing the high-necked jacket of the cadres, but pearl-gray and nipped at the waist. The entire chorus accompanied him, and the first sentence of the play came out with the full-throated roar of a crowd:

"*In the time of Mao Tse-tung . . .*"

One tableau followed another, very effective as long as they were only proffered as tableaux. The subject was the legend of the liberation, treated both as ballet and as Peking opera. The slogans corresponded to the subtitles of silent films. Words have no place in this imperious stylization except as song. The port of Shanghai was the stem of a liner, the *President Wilson*, moored to a pier by colossal and vaguely live chains like the chains over the Tatu River. On the pier, a Westerner in a pale blue costume and soft boots, a Russian of the time of Peter the Great or a colonial Englishman of 1820, represented imperialism. He ran off before a group of Chinese soldiers who wore garlands of camouflage leaves on their helmets, and resembled the crowned jester whom Lorca calls Pampre.

"What army do these soldiers symbolize?"

"The university," my interpreter replied.

When the stage is filled with actors, the stylization at once begins to work. This revolutionary imagery, intended to symbolize the creation of the Chinese Communist party, shows none of the obstacles it had to overcome. All the ballets are naïve; and last night this naïveté was at the service of traditional China, which emerged in the fan scenes where the throng of actors would be shot through with a unanimous tremor, or the dances in which the performers' sleeves were elongated by undulating fabrics like those of the Tang funerary dancers, or in which the convulsions of a crowd would be halted by a sudden petrification. All this sustained by a music unfamiliar to me, which mingles the Western scale with the meowings and shouts of the old Chinese opera. But these choruses, these admirable voices, are to Chinese music what jazz is to African music. Of the revolution, there remains nothing but museums—and operas.

In an hour the plane leaves for Peking.

From my window I look out over the factories and buildings of a tropical Siberia, stretching to a horizon of chimneys still dominated by the pagoda of old. The banana trees are rustling, though it is not yet raining. In front of me are the woodlouse roofs, their vermilion faded by the sun and verdigrised by the rain, traversed by a muddy alleyway in which half-naked children are playing: the last enclave of the Canton of yesterday, when fragments of the ramparts still jutted out from the weeds? The baking wind makes the struts of a long scroll depicting a military scene bang against my wall, and gives the pink bathrobe on a hanger the undulating movements of the Chinese theater. So much death, so much hope and blood, all that I have known and dreamed about Canton ends in my absurdly pink phantom flapping at the window in the livid haze of the storm.

Peking

The city was once orientated by the crossing of two roads without pavements, Tartar dust in which the ramparts of the citadel and the voluted bastions of the gates appeared as if through rain. The haughty camels from the Gobi Desert loped past one after another, and their attendants accompanied them slowly. The dust, the caravans, and one wall of the ramparts have gone. Here are the gates, in the pale blue morning. Around the city, endless avenues bordered by squat buildings remind me, like the main streets of Canton, of the Siberian immensity —but the baking heat has gone. The car passes enormous bamboo scaffoldings above tiny willows, then pink acacias which are not acacias, and everywhere the scythelike swooping of the martlets. When the engine stops, a great chorus of cicadas fills the silence.

The corridors of the palace of foreign affairs have the same desolate vastness as those of the hotel in Canton. After innumerable seemingly empty rooms, the office of the minister, Marshal Chen-yi; wicker armchairs, wash drawings, under-secretaries, interpreters. The Marshal is jovial and smooth faced (the Chinese often age within a few months), with a big piercing laugh. He wears the almost Stalinian costume of the cadres and seems, like the Soviet generals of yore, to have retained nothing of his origins (he is the son of a magistrate); indeed, to have no origin. He began his career as assistant to a Szechwan warlord. He went through the military college, joined Chu Teh in the darkest days of the struggle, then commanded the rear guard of the Long March under continual attack. Victorious over the Japanese, commander of the Fourth Army, then of the People's Liberation Army of West China, it was he who took Nanking and Shanghai in 1949.

"How is General de Gaulle?"

"Quite recovered, thank you. And Chairman Mao?"

"Very well."

The preliminary exchange of courtesies over, I realize I have forgotten the health of the President of the Republic, Liu Shao-ch'i. This does not appear to disturb the Marshal, who proceeds to expound the basic principles of Chinese policy. His interpreter, occasionally assisted by ours, translates:

"On the home front, the People's Government is anxious to get rid of poverty and ignorance, to see to it that everyone is assured of the necessities of life and that there is a general blossoming of progress on the basis of the socialist system. Capitalism presents some interesting aspects, notably in the technical sphere, but it must be rejected as a system, because the director of an industrial concern ought not to be solely responsible for the fate of a million men. M. Malraux, who has studied Marxism as thoroughly as anyone, will understand that even though capitalism might have been able to obtain a few incidental results here, only communism could insure the progress and development of the country as a whole."

Quite so. As for Marxism, while we were indulging in our preliminary salutations, we had exchanged compliments on our respective works. Like Mao, the Marshal is a poet—and the husband of a well-known actress, who is at the moment working (as a propagandist?) in a people's commune.

"In short," he stresses, "the Chinese government is determined to build up China through its own efforts in a few decades."

To anyone who knew the China of old the phrase, however jovially pronounced, takes on a historic grandeur.

"Externally, the Chinese government is pursuing a policy of peace. It wants a peaceful world in which the peoples choose their own political systems. China, which has borne its share of colonialist and imperialist exploitation, has the duty of supporting liberation movements everywhere. From 1840 to 1911, it suffered the ravages of British imperialism, then of Japanese imperialism, and now of American imperialism. Sato is a satellite of the United States; he cannot make a move independently of Washington. France withdrew from China after the Second World War; she has adopted a realistic policy. On the European front, as on others, she is pursuing a policy of self-defense with regard to the United States."

"Of independence, Marshal."

He was a member, together with Chou En-lai, of the "student-workers" group at Billancourt who had formed one of the first sections of the Chinese Communist party. He was deported in 1921. Forty years later, as a minister, he represented China in Geneva. Did he see Paris again?

No doubt he has talked like this to a hundred left-wing journalists, and to all the ambassadors he has received. I have had enough experience of the Soviet Union not to be surprised by these phonograph records; but when the Marshal opens his mouth I still half expect that he himself will speak. I felt closer to him when we were exchanging compliments on our writings. His genuine warmth enlivens what he says, but still . . .

Suddenly he becomes more animated:

"The reports on Vietnam are contradictory," he says. "Mr. Harriman really did go to Moscow to talk about Vietnam! The American papers ought to get their facts straight."

"Don't you think there's far more to it than a disagreement between newspapers? People in France also talk of American policy as if there were only one; but the forces at work in the United States with respect to the Vietnam war are probably fairly divergent."

He spreads a small fan, fans himself smilingly, looks at me as if to say, "It's possible," and inquires, with rugged affability:

"Are you in favor of the neutralization of the country?"

"To begin with."

"Our Vietnamese friends are afraid that it would mean permanent partition. Ever since the Americans intervened directly, neutralization has become a hollow word. There is only one solution: the withdrawal of the American forces. Conditions are more and more favorable. This war is developing. The more it escalates, the more the obstacles multiply; the determination of the Vietnamese people is growing stronger, and will end by forcing the Americans to quit the country."

"Do you think it impossible for a great power to maintain one hundred and fifty thousand men in a theater of operations for ten years?"

"Ah! So there are one hundred and fifty thousand now!"

He knows this as well as I do. Probably better.

"Soon there will be more," I say.

"The Americans have imposed war on the Vietnamese people. We are taking its side. If they leave, they will still be a world power. If they don't withdraw their forces, they will lose still more face. For the Vietnamese nation, it isn't a question of face, but of life or death. The Americans are bombing where they please."

"In their view, the whole of their policy in Asia is at stake."

"The loss of one mah-jongg domino doesn't finish off the game for the man who loses it. And the United States will not be able to keep troops stationed abroad indefinitely; sooner or later they will have to evacuate Taiwan and Berlin."

"Would their withdrawal from Formosa involve a Russian withdrawal from Siberia, in your view? There are more open spaces in the North than in Southeast Asia."

The Marshal laughs, his mouth opening from ear to ear.

"All the same," he answers, "Taiwan is not part of the United States; Siberia is part of the Soviet Union, and has never been Chinese."

Let us suppose . . . On the subject of Bandoeng, I use the expression "China's global policy."

"In every sphere, China has considerable leeway to make up," he goes on, "and it will still require a big effort before she is capable of conducting a global policy. Meanwhile, we know who we are with and who we are not. What I told your ambassador on July 14 is still true. The Vietnamese have no other choice but to continue the fight. If the United States are sincere in their desire to negotiate, why do they talk about sending two hundred thousand men, a million men, to Vietnam? They have got into the habit of making threats. Ho Chi Minh and Pham Van Dong said in May and June that in 1960 they were not certain of the outcome of the war, but they are now. Our experience gives us the same certainty.

"The American forces are scattered all over the world. Look at a map: they are in Formosa, where they are propping up the dictator Chiang Kai-shek, in Vietnam with the dictator Ky after the dictator Diem, in Korea with the dictator Rhee and others, in Pakistan with the dictator Ayub Khan, in Laos with Phoumi, in Thailand with the king. Are we in Hawaii or Mexico or Canada?

"Our experience with Chiang Kai-shek taught us that one must alternate periods of fighting with periods of negotiation. In Korea, fighting and negotiations took place simultaneously, to the point where the sound of the voices sometimes drowned that of the guns. The Vietnamese are wise and farseeing, they were Marxists before we were, we have every confidence in them. On the twentieth, President Ho Chi Minh proclaimed his determination to carry on the struggle for five, ten, twenty years until the last American leaves Vietnam and reunification is achieved."

For the rulers of China, escalation is the Long March of Vietnam.

"It's always the same thing," the Marshal continues. "Look at the Korean War, the intervention of the Seventh Fleet in the Taiwan Straits, the occupation of Taiwan—and then the U.N. rushing to the assistance of the capitalist aggression in the Congo! The aim of the American attack on North Korea was to threaten our security; we were forced to intervene to defend ourselves. Afterward, we set American prisoners free. Without reciprocation. After the Korean War, the Americans stepped up their meddling in Vietnam, where the situation is not dissimilar."

"But better for you."

"If the United States does not extend its aggression, it will not be necessary for China to take a hand in the operations; but if it does, she will."

"On Chinese territory?"

"And perhaps on Vietnamese territory also."

A pause.

I doubt this. Mao has always followed Lenin's maxim about the *defensive* tactics of revolutionary armies against the foreigner and has always stressed that Stalin only fought to defend Russian territory. Lenin said, "People who believe that the revolution can be launched to order in a foreign country are either fools or provocateurs." But in Vietnam it is no longer a matter of launching the revolution: the Marshal speaks as if he held himself responsible for the Vietnam war. Such a responsibility would redound to his credit. But what are the facts? The French attributed Dienbienphu to Chinese artillery, which was not there at all. Are the Vietcong guerrillas armed by China? Partly, no doubt. But they have also been armed to a considerable extent by the Soviet Union and by arms captured from the French and the Americans, as the Chinese communists were by arms captured from Chiang Kai-shek. Their ideology, their tactics, their confidence come from Mao; as do a certain number of their organizers and liaison officers. But no one here has asked me, "Do you believe that the guerrillas of the South are trained, or at any rate directed, by the Northern troops, who are satellites of the Chinese forces?" The Marshal would not be averse to giving me that impression. And yet? Vietnam seems incapable of producing a national government; the Americans are forced to intervene directly in the war; the prisoners are not Chinese. "It is a Western obsession," Nehru had said to me, "to believe that wars of liberation are conducted from abroad." I know from experience the limits of the help that guerrillas can receive, the "advice" they can accept. So I do not believe that escalation, even as far as Peking (nuclear war aside), can save a Saigon government which resembles that of Chiang Kai-shek, only worse.

"The Americans," the Marshal continues, "never cease to violate our air space. Do Chinese spy planes fly over the United States? They have declared that there can be no 'sanctuary' as there was at the time of the Korean War: very well. Under the pretext of supporting South Vietnam, they bomb the North. Who is to say that tomorrow they will not take the pretext of China's support for North Vietnam to bomb us?

They think they can do whatever they like. We must weigh the consequences of future incidents. And in the end we shall win, as we did against the Japanese, and against Chiang Kai-shek.

"Look at their intrigues in the Dominican Republic, in the Congo: they stir up trouble everywhere, unlike Great Britain and France. They must be resisted. As soon as European colonialism leaves Asia, American imperialism takes its place. The Vietnamese are fighting not only for themselves but for China and for the whole world, and they deserve all our admiration and respect."

When I met Gide for the first time, it was the author of *Les Nourritures terrestres* I saw, not the man waiting for me outside the Vieux Colombier munching a brioche; when I met Einstein, it was the mathematician, not the amiable, shaggy violinist who greeted me at Princeton. I am well aware that the Marshal is not Mao. But he is the foreign minister of People's China—one of the figures around whom history prowls; he commanded the rear guard of the Long March, under continual harassment. The writer quickly came to the surface in Gide, and the scientist in Einstein. In Chen-yi, where was the conqueror of Shanghai? China is conditioned to the phonograph record as she is conditioned to ceremonial; and in spite of a certain unbuttoned quality, the Marshal is obviously on the job. Valéry used to say of General de Gaulle, "One would like to know what it is in him that springs from the man, the politician or the soldier." In the Marshal, everything springs from convention—and this is accentuated by translation. There is no real dialogue. Obviously I cannot say to him, "Marshal, the United States only dominates the Vietnam game through their air power, and it is not the Chinese who are fighting that air power, but the Russians." I retain only his mixture of firmness, caution, and half-hinted pledges; the limits he sets, openly or tacitly, to the conflict between China and the United States. I only heard his real voice when he said, "And on Vietnamese territory too." Is his type, so different from the one I used to know, that of the new Chinese authorities? The Chinese ambassador in Paris, who was also one of the generals of the Long March—and who produced a book of almost humorous drawings about it—displays this same invulnerable and slightly sham joviality. I am familiar with the foreign-affairs social circuit; he does not belong to it, because he has substituted a military heartiness for reserve.

"General de Gaulle is right to resist the United States in Europe. They are not omnipotent, but they have profited from two wars: in the First World War, they lost a hundred thousand men, in the Second, four hundred thousand. In Korea they lost three hundred thousand fairly profitlessly, so they made a miscalculation. Now they are going to do their arithmetic in Vietnam."

"Nehru felt that colonialism dies when the victory of a Western expedition over an Asian army ceases to be a foregone conclusion. I think so too."

But why does the Marshal seem not to envisage the use of atomic bombs by the Americans, if they came into conflict with China?

"We hope France will use her influence to get the United States to withdraw. We must face up to the Americans to bring them to leave the country. The American people are good; they have produced remarkable achievements in two centuries, but the policy of their recent leaders have gone against their deepest aspirations. China does not seek a large-scale war, she wants a coalition of peaceful forces to compel the United States to abandon its policy of aggression. This could only benefit the world, and the United States itself."

The United States would find his solicitude touching. Our ambassador watches for my reaction. None of this is new to me. The Manichean monologue, which always seems to be addressed to the "masses," still goes on. This intelligent man, a chess champion, at the peak of his dazzling career, is not talking to convince me. He is performing a ritual.

I tell him that the United States, as I said to Nehru, seems to me to be the only nation ever to have become the most powerful in the world without seeking to; whereas the power of Alexander, Caesar, Napoleon, the great Chinese emperors, was the consequence of deliberate military conquest. And that at present I cannot discern any American global policy comparable to that of imperial Britain, or the Marshall Plan, or what President Kennedy was after. That the United States seems to me, for the moment, to be repeating the mistakes which are all too familiar to us, for our Fourth Republic committed them before they did. I add:

"As for the influence we may be able to bring to bear on the United States, I believe that it is of the same order as that which you can bring to bear on the Soviet Union."

"China adapts her feelings to the facts. After the October Revolution, under Lenin and under Stalin, the U.S.S.R. was sympathetic to the Chinese people, and we were to them. After the defeat of Japan, we became accustomed to the idea that the U.S.S.R., exhausted by the war, had no desire to intervene in Far Eastern affairs, and we did not pin any hopes on help from her. The socialist construction of China cannot be based on the assistance of the U.S.S.R., under whatever form.

One must rely on oneself above all. The Russians got things under way, but we can carry on without them. And by 1964 we had paid all our debts. When Khrushchev tried to smother us. . . ."

He stops, then resumes: "Since Khrushchev, the Soviet leaders have wanted the world to be dominated by two great powers, which is unthinkable, for every country, big or small, is equally a part of the world."

I am surprised, not by these asseverations, but by the level of the conversation. As I used to be in the Soviet Union when I heard Marxists, intellectually rigorous or subtle in private, sink in public to the level of *L'Humanité*. Does the Marshal believe in the Manicheism he professes? After all, Manicheism works better in action than in speech. And for him the United States is not the nation that twice saved the freedom of Europe, but the nation that supported Chiang Kai-shek.

"General de Gaulle has never been in favor of a dual hegemony."

He laughs: "But neither do we support a fivefold hegemony"—no doubt he means the United States, Soviet Union, Britain, France, China —"with India scratching at the door!"

"Two's company, three's a crowd."

"However, there will never be too many allies on behalf of peace."

"If we were to combine our efforts to bring about peace, would you envisage negotiations after a pledge to withdraw or following an actual withdrawal of the American forces?"

The Marshal reflects. "The question must be studied; perhaps I shall be in a position to give you a reply in a few days. The decision is one for Ho Chi Minh and Pham Van Dong. As far as I know, they still insist on withdrawal as a prerequisite. Have you brought any proposals with you, Minister?"

"None, Marshal."

He was expecting one—in order to reject it? But no doubt he was also anxious to discover the nature of the discussions I am to have with Chou En-lai, with the President of the Republic, and possibly, with Mao; and to give himself time to prepare for them.

The door through which the ambassador and I leave opens on to the old Forbidden City. The palaces reminiscent of the Siberian wastes (the Palace of the People, the Museum of the Revolution) are behind us, and I rediscover the imperial city of old. It ruled over a proliferation of low houses with voluted roofs, since no unauthorized gaze was allowed to plunge into its courtyards. The recumbent skyscraper from which I have just emerged now overlooks it. Inside, the splendid courtyards are empty: it is noon. Weeds are growing in front of the sacred bronze jars. In the rooms there is a jumbled museum with a few unique pieces; in the background, the apartment of the last Empress. Snug little rooms—one would like to see them when the snow is falling —with their flea-market lanterns and the vulgarity which the Victorian and Second Empire styles spread all over Asia. I am reminded of the Chinese Museum of the Empress Eugénie at Fontainebleau, of the chinoiseries brought back from the sacking of the Summer Palace and the conquest of Cambodia, where only the king possessed a few silver ingots. Who still knows the Chinese Museum at Fontainebleau? But the Forbidden City has not been abandoned. It was in its great hall that Loti found the remains of the banquet of the departed spirits, eaten by the European soldiers on the first day of their conquest; and the musical instruments which the Empress had set out there for the shades. At the time of her flight, she had placed a bouquet in front of her favorite Kwan-yin, and hung one of her pearl necklaces around its neck. The Kwan-yin is there. Statues of gods were piled up in the courtyards, so that the soldiers could sleep on the altars; in the temple of Confucius, there was a scroll which read, "The literature of the future will be the literature of compassion." It was in the days when the insurgent barbarians were beginning to call themselves foreign powers, but when it was still believed that the Christians killed and ate children for their bloody sacrifice, which was called the Mass.

Long ago I saw the old China come to an end, and the shadows of foxes flitting across the violet asters of the ramparts, above a procession of Gobi camels covered in hoarfrost. I remember the pigs' bladders lit by candles, and decorated with Chinese characters that identified the hotels on the platforms of Kalgan station kept by Russian hoteliers whose beards alone, lit up from below, were visible in the darkness— and those Hieronymus Bosch lanterns seemed to be keeping a solitary vigil, in the snow and the gloom, over the death throes of White Russia, outside the little restaurants with a single table where phonographs with trumpet-shaped horns would play *Under the Ramparts of Manchuria*. I remember the wooden enclosures of Mongol villages opening like the gates of a corral, and the Genghis Khan horsemen charging out on their little shaggy ponies with foreheads shaved from ear to ear and their gray locks, as long as a woman's, streaming out horizontally in the wind of the steppes under the livid sky. I remember the old princesses of the snows, like queens of the Casamance already marked down by the horsemen of death. Mongolia, Tibetan marches, Visigoth headdresses—and above the putrescent villages, the monasteries smelling of wax, with the parquet reflecting the yellow lamas and the blue of the Himalayas. And the great mausoleum of Sun Yat-sen, and the soldiers of the warlords with their umbrellas. Finally I witnessed the resurrection of the Chinese army. There, in the flooded river, where the red-clad executioner's boat passed by me through the drifting corpses, his short saber gaily reflecting the rain-washed sky, I landed beside the blast furnaces of Hanyang.

When we turn round and look back after leaving the majestic court-yards, the orange roofs gently curving over the ox-blood walls give an impression of such architectural power that the giant characters ex-tolling the People's Republic seem to have been fixed there from time immemorial, and the terrace seems to have been specially built for Mao's speeches.

While waiting for Chou En-lai's return to Peking, we are invited to visit Lungmen; it will allow us to go through Loyang and Sian, which are usually forbidden to foreigners.

Loyang was the city of purple-tiled palaces which housed the most exquisite art in the world, during our Carolingian era. It was renowned as far as Byzantium. And it was renowned all over China, for this was a city of poetry, the Chinese Isfahan. Here were found the skeletons of the Empress's favorites pinned to the wall by arrows weighted with foxes' tails. There remains only a sleeping countryside through the round gates.

A people's commune clean as a new pin, where famine is unknown. They want me to admire their tractor, and do not realize that it is they themselves whom I admire.

This is the departure point for the Buddhist caves of Lungmen. They are now protected by glass, and the statues are on show there as in a shop window. Above other statues which have lost their heads ("It was the Americans," the guide says), in the unprotected amphitheater, the crowd huddles below the Great Buddha, astonishingly Indo-Hellenistic by comparison with the sculptures of the Wei caves. On the sides are the tutelary giants who symbolize the cardinal points: one of them is crushing a poor tearful dwarf beneath its medieval boot. Some visitor has left one of his shoes nearby, so that the stone dwarf seems to have lost one of his. As in India, the cave has been carved out of the very mountain, but never have I felt so strongly the extent to which divine figures lose their souls above an indifferent crowd. The colossal Buddha was sculpted on the orders of the Empress whose lovers were nailed up with arrows. The squawks of hens contend with the creak of cicadas and the radio of an inn weaves and unweaves the airs of Peking around the sacred rock.

We leave for Sian.

The museum, which gives on to an ancient square the color of clay, is at once genuine and fake, a wonderful ensemble of classical pavilions with burnt orange and turquoise tiles, round gateways opening on to the countryside or on to unfinished gardens heavy with hibiscus, gladioli, and enormous odorless lilacs. On the way, the interpreter had said, pointing out half-wild parks, "Here stood a summerhouse of the Emperor T'ai Tsung." The first pavilion of the museum houses a forest of steles, and suddenly I realize the identity of this city of a million inhabitants with its administrative skyscraper, its clocktower and its museum even more unreal than the Summer Palace: Sian is Singanfu, which was eleven times the capital of China.

Here are the stone animals which led to the tomb of T'ai Tsung, the Charlemagne of China. Here is the rhinoceros, on whose back children are perched while the parents stroke its horn and a friend photographs the family. In the main gallery are the four bas-reliefs from the emperor's tomb, said to depict his four favorite horses. The tomb was neglected for several centuries. Two of the bas-reliefs, now in the United States, have been replaced here by life-size photographs below the caption, "Stolen by the Americans."

The anti-American propaganda is meticulous and all-pervasive. The imagery which covers the walls of towns is determined by it, even when the brave militiaman and the heroic militiawoman, who are products of the American films even more than of socialist realism, are portrayed without enemies. In the smallest people's communes—low houses, chickens running about in well-swept yards, reapers in the fields in the distance—one sees, drawn in colored chalks on a large slate for the use of the illiterate, the intrepid little pioneer driving his spear through the big paper tiger.

Tomorrow, Chou En-lai will be back in Peking.

Peking

The same endless corridors as those I went through to reach the Marshal (it is the same building, the same succession of empty rooms and, in the Prime Minister's office, the same cane armchairs with the same covers, the same wash drawings, and the same photographers when we shake hands). The interpreter—this time a woman—speaks French without an accent (she is probably Tonkin Chinese) and the political vocabulary is familiar to her; the attitude of the Prime Minister is amicably distant; hers, almost hostile.

Chou En-lai has changed little, for he has aged naturally: the hollows in his face have deepened. He is dressed like the Marshal, but he is thin. It is difficult to guess the origins of most of the Chinese leaders, but he is obviously an intellectual. The grandson of a mandarin. He was the political commissar in the Canton Cadet School when Chiang Kai-shek commanded it. Among his successive functions—including the premiership—he preferred that of foreign minister. I am reminded of a diplomat who welcomed me to Moscow around 1929: he was wearing a monocle, in a town where Lenin's wife wore a cap. I have known for a long time that diplomats are a race apart—a race to which Marshal Chen-yi does not belong but to which Chou En-lai, Mao's right-hand man on the Long March, does.

Neither truculent nor jovial: faultlessly urbane.

And as reticent as a cat.

"I was very struck by General de Gaulle's criticisms, in his last press conference, of the Russian and American plans for world hegemony. And also by the phrase: the Pacific, where the fate of the world will be played out."

A pause. I answer: "Lenin once said that joint action was perfectly conceivable provided the slogans and the flags are kept separate."

Chou, absently: "We haven't forgotten that you are familiar with Marxism, and with China. Nor have we forgotten that you were on the run at the same time as Nguyen-Ai-Qoc.* You wanted dominion status for Indochina: the French would have been well advised to endorse you."

"I am grateful to you for remembering. The more so because the other founder of the Young Annam movement, Paul Monin, died in Canton."

"Did you see Chiang Kai-shek again?"

"Never. It's a pity."

"Oh!"

An evasive gesture. I should have liked to ask him, "And you?" For nobody knows what happened at the "Sian incident." And that is not the least of the reasons for the complex feelings my interlocutor inspires in me.

*   *   *   *

* Ho Chi Minh.

In December 1936 Chiang Kai-shek, while on an inspection tour of the anticommunist forces in the north, was arrested by the leader of the Manchurian forces, the "Young Marshal" Chiang Hsüeh-liang. It was generally assumed that he would be executed; but an envoy (from the Russians?) intervened, and the Generalissimo was released against his promise that at last he would fight the Japanese and not Mao's forces. On his return to Nanking he kept his promise, which flabbergasted everybody—not least the Americans. What pledge could possibly have bound him to this extent?

That envoy was Chou En-lai.

On my visit to Sian I saw the Baths of the Favorite, where Chiang Kai-shek was living at the time of his arrest. He escaped into the wood which overlooks the pavilions and the marble junk, and was captured there.

"I was here at the time," the curator told me. "This is his bed." (It was a European campbed.) "When we came in, with the captain and the soldiers, there was nobody here, but he had left his false teeth on the bathroom shelf.

"And I was on the big bridge over the river when the female student threw herself in front of Chiang Hsüeh-liang's car and shouted, 'Don't let the Japanese crush China again! Blood will be shed here! Let our blood flow to stop our humiliation!' She was crying and everyone who heard her was crying, and the Young Marshal started to cry as well."

This palace, a copy of the palace of a great emperor's favorite, resembles, like everything which was copied in the nineteenth century (especially the Summer Palace) a chinoiserie stage set. But on the little terraces, above the weeping willows, the pink summer mimosa bushes looked like those of the eighth century. There was a pagoda where a stage general had become an irrigation god. And in the distance, the burial mound of the founding emperor.

The captive Generalissimo had begun by snapping at Chiang Hsüeh-liang, who addressed him as "General": "If I'm your general, you can start by obeying my orders!" Then Chou En-lai had arrived.

"One of President Mao's expressions," I said, "has caught on in France, though the French are a little puzzled by it: that the United States is a paper tiger."

"The United States is a real tiger, and has shown its teeth. But if that tiger comes here, it will change into a paper one. Because the most powerful army in the world can do nothing against universal guerrilla action. Our rifles, our tanks, our aircraft are nearly all American. We took them from Chiang Kai-shek. The more the Americans gave him, the more we captured. Not all Chiang's soldiers were that bad, you know! The Americans are better? No matter. Every Chinese knows that the People's Army is the sole guarantee of the distribution of lands. And the war will take place here."

That war will be a continuation of the wars against Japan, Chiang Kai-shek, and the Americans in Korea, in Taiwan, in Vietnam. Although the minister thinks that negotiations on Vietnam are not even imaginable, he makes it clear that Ho Chi Minh could not be the sole representative of the anti-Saigon forces. "There must be negotiations with those who are fighting, in other words, the National Liberation Front and Hanoi, but the Front first."

It is a tactic similar to the one I saw the French Communist party attempt in 1944: overall control of the guerrillas being out of the question, delegate guerrilla leaders of Chinese persuasion, who will keep a check on Ho Chi Minh.

He also talks about the United Nations, which he thinks China should not join before Formosa leaves, and he seems to be torn between an Afro-Asian organization more or less controlled by China, and the transfer of the U.N. from New York to Geneva.

I ask him, "Do you think the present policy of Japan can survive your possession of the bomb?"

He looks at me sharply: "I don't think so."

He knows as well as I do that in the United States he is thought to be the original of one of the characters in La Condition humaine. I am reminded of the photograph in the Canton Museum in which he alone remains visible among the Cadets, surrounded by blurred figures like the shades of Hades—who were Borodin, Galen, and Chiang Kai-shek.

"General de Gaulle," I tell him, "is of the opinion that the contacts established through our ambassadors are at a standstill."

His thick eyebrows, pointed toward the temples like those of the characters in the Chinese theater, underline his air of a studious cat. He muses, with a bizarre attentiveness, without any object.

"We are in agreement," he says, "on the terms which define our peaceful coexistence. We want independence, and we do not want the dual hegemony. You asked the foreign minister if we would agree to negotiations on Vietnam prior to the withdrawal of the American troops. We will not negotiate, either about Vietnam or anything else, until the Americans go home. That means not only quitting Saigon, but dismantling the bases in Santo Domingo, Cuba, the Congo, Laos, Thailand, and the rocket-launching sites in Pakistan and elsewhere. The world could live in peace; if it doesn't, it is because of the misdeeds of the Americans, who are everywhere, and create conflicts everywhere. In Thailand, in Korea, in Taiwan, in Vietnam, in Pakistan—to name but a few—they are subsidizing or arming against us 1,700,000 men. They are becoming the policemen of the world. What for? Let them go home, and the world will have peace again. And for a start, let them observe the Geneva agreements."

He throws up his hands, the image of the innocent man who calls on the whole world to witness his good faith.

"How can one negotiate with people who do not respect agreements?"

Grieved by so much perfidy, he is the perfect embodiment of the Confucian sage faced with the regrettable barbarism of those who do not observe the rites. An unexpected mask, on that samurai face. As with Nehru some years ago, I notice that when a shamelessly realistic politician appeals to virtue, he goes to fetch the mask of his ancestors: Soviet communists disguise themselves as priests of Holy Russia, Frenchmen as revolutionary democrats, Anglo-Saxons as ironclad Puritans.

He suggests that France should advise her ally Great Britain, as China might her ally the U.S.S.R., to take up a common attitude against the aggressive policy of the United States and the presence of American military bases on foreign soil.

And yet he is one of the premier diplomats of our age. As when I listened to the Marshal, I wonder what he is leading up to. Neither Great Britain nor the United States solicit our advice, and France's position is generally known. He makes much of Chinese aid to the underdeveloped countries, and I point out to him that the percentage of our own aid to Africa is the highest in the world. But only Chinese aid is disinterested. In what sense, I ask him, is our aid to Algeria interested?

"Oil," he answers.

There is a strange remoteness in what he says, quite different from the impression of distance which General de Gaulle conveys. I am reminded of the withdrawnness of a man struck down by misfortune. His wife, one of the party's foremost orators, is gravely ill. When he says something conventional, he seems to be "putting a record on" so as not to have to think—in spite of his extreme courtesy. This discussion seems to tire him, but also to rivet him, as if he were afraid of finding himself alone again.

"You were foreign minister for a long time," I say to him, "and you know better than I do that some positions are taken up as a basis for discussion, and others simply as a matter of principle. I don't believe that the United States has any intention of disputing yours."

He makes a dismissive gesture, and replies: "Do you believe in the atomic menace? The autonomy of the people's communes is assured. China would survive the death of a hundred million people. And sooner or later the Americans are bound to have to reembark. China will never accept the return of Chiang Kai-shek. She has found freedom. It isn't America's freedom, that's all."

I think of Sun Yat-sen's lecture a year before he died: "If we spoke of freedom to the man in the street . . . he would certainly not understand us. The reason why the Chinese do not in fact attach the slightest importance to freedom is that the very word which designates it was only recently imported into China." The revolution freed the wife from her husband, the son from his father, the farmer from his overlord. But for the benefit of a collectivity. The individualism of the West has no roots among the Chinese masses. The hope of transformation, on the other hand, is a very powerful sentiment. A husband must stop beating his wife in order to become a different man, who will be a member of the party, or simply of his people's commune, or of those which the army will set free: "Gods are all right for the rich, the poor have the Eighth Route Army."

Chou En-lai has resumed: "One of your generals in the 1914 war said, 'It is wrong to forget that gunfire kills.' Chairman Mao has not forgotten. But that sort of fire cannot kill what it does not see. We will only commit our armies against the invading army at the right time and in the right place."

"Like Kutuzov."

"In the first place we will not forget that any invading army becomes less strong than the people invaded, if that people is resolved to fight. The Europeans have ceased to rule in Asia, and the Americans will follow them."

Does he believe there will be a war, or not? What puzzles me is that, like the Marshal, he does not seem even to consider the possibility of a war in which the United States—even without atom bombs—would be content with destroying the ten principal Chinese industrial centers, thus delaying the building of a new China by fifty years, and then go home without imposing a Chiang Kai-shek.

His thinking is based on a theory of Mao's which I am surprised not yet to have heard aired. Imperialism numbers six hundred million men;

the underdeveloped countries, socialist and communist, two billion. Victory for the latter is inevitable. They surround the last imperialism, that of the United States, as the proletariat surrounds capitalism, as China surrounded the armies of Chiang Kai-shek. "It is always men," says Mao, "who win in the end."

Yenan

The arrival of the Burmese military leaders, and of a Somali president, seemed to have driven the foreign affairs staff to distraction. Nobody knows whether Chairman Mao, having recovered, will proceed to Peking, or whether the audience will take place at his villa in Hangchow. When? Soon. How soon? Three days, four, maybe less. I had expressed a wish to visit Yenan, and an airplane is put at my disposal.

Here, then, is Sparta. The truth, the legend, and the obscure force which prolongs past battles into an epic—it all comes together in these jagged mountains. At their foot is the Museum of the Revolution.

Almost everything it portrays or evokes happened here, thirty years ago. It is already a vanished era. Here are the black cavalry riding through the gorges, the soldiers racing along the Great Wall, the field-guns made of treetrunks bound with barbed wire, the hats camouflaged with leaves like primitive helmets, mixed up with the medieval pikes of the partisans with their red tassels much bigger than those of the militiamen of the south, and the wooden rifles for drill; here are the home-made grenades. Here are the pieces of birch bark which served as paper, and the wheels on which each man spun his own uniform. But it is a far cry from Gandhi. Here is the machine for printing bank-notes—modest little notes, and a modest little machine sent in separate pieces by the workers of the provinces occupied by the enemy. Before Mao, all this was the age-old equipment of the defeated. I had come across souvenirs of this primitive guerrilla warfare in Siberia, but the Siberian partisans were not fighting against odds of a hundred to one, and did not suggest what everything here proclaims: the Jacquerie transformed into the revolution. Chinese museums display the iron crowns worn by the Taiping chiefs before their defeat: they are the same barbaric crowns which the chiefs of the Jacques also wore, and which the kings' troops replaced, when they captured them, with crowns of red-hot iron. The timeless Chinese peasantry, the peasantry of every nation in its peasant era, is pinned down here at the moment when it is about to rise and conquer China, below the mountain cave of the only man who was capable of leading it to victory: after the pikes, in these glass cases, come the rifles and machine guns captured from the Japanese and from Chiang Kai-shek's soldiers. The female guide, a mouse with the two traditional little pigtails and a rasping voice, narrates this epic—up to the last room, which displays the stuffed figure of the brave horse which carried Mao during the Long March.

It is the Napoleonic epic as narrated by a veteran of the Old Guard to the illiterate peasants which Balzac borrowed from Henri Monnier in *Le Médecin de Campagne*: it is *Orlando Furioso* as presented by the Sicilian puppeteers. But beyond the pedantic fetishism illustrated by Mao's horse and Mao's inkwell arises the real emotion inspired by the liberation itself. These wooden rifles, these pikes, are not the same kind of testimony as the muskets and halberds of our museums: they are the actual weapons of the revolution, as the cave is Mao's cave. Would we regard bayonets from Fleurus or Austerlitz as "models of weapons"? In the Museum of the Resistance in Paris, the bullet-riddled execution post speaks to us in the same way as the great totem poles with their tops hidden by the low clouds spoke to the redskins. This China, so unreligious but so strongly bound to its earth, its rivers, its mountains, and its dead, is linked to its resurrection by another form of ancestor worship, in which the history of the liberation is the gospel and Mao the son, in the sense in which the Emperor was the Son of Heaven. Here, as in every Chinese city, one sees the poster on which a brave youth with flashing teeth joyously flourishes a rifle, while his left arm encircles the waist of a militiagirl with a submachine gun. They do not look at each other; they are looking at the future, of course. And this socialist-realist idealization symbolizes the dream of millions of Chinese. Are we so distant from Mars and Venus? It is a far cry from the yapping phonograph record of the girl with the little pigtails: this couple are a god and a goddess of antiquity.

Nowhere does the mythological power of Chinese communism come through so strongly. Yenan is a small town, and its factories, its bridge, its electric light do not obliterate those gaps in the mountain where the destiny of China was forged (Mao was ruling a hundred million people by the time he left), that pagoda which those who rallied to Yenan greeted with a shout as our pilgrims greeted the walls of Jerusalem. The yellow earth is everywhere, the dust of the steppes advancing on the tilled land clinging to the riverbanks, and the old headquarters are of beaten earth, as clean as stone—schoolyards or prisonyards. They are now deserted: "The masses come at other times of the year." Here, bombed but rebuilt, are the hall in which Mao made his speech on literature, the Red Army staff room with its benches and its ceiling of treetrunks, the offices of the leaders in the caves sheltered from winter by partitions of wood or glass, like immaculate street stalls. The word caves is inadequate to suggest these troglodytes' dwellings dug out of the rock like those of the wine growers of the Loire. If Mao's shelter, near the museum, seems like an Egyptian burial chamber, most of the others are workplaces whose austerity alone is surprising. When it settled in here, the army had just covered six thousand miles. Mao lost Yenan, and retook it. And the whole place betokens the dialogue between army and party, the military character of this political conquest, the legacy of the conquerors of the steppes—only without the carpets and the furs. Here, on a shabby red felt tablecloth, sputtered the candles of the Central Committee. The army was passing through: here, it stopped a little longer. Until Peking was taken, the supreme head of the peasant army was a nomad chieftain.

I am shown a few old newsreels. Yenan empty as Chiang Kai-shek's army approaches, and the exodus, doubtless toward other nearby caves, for the peasants are transporting tables on the backs of their donkeys. Then the return of the army of liberation and its entry into all the cities of China, from the Shanghai waterfront to the ramshackle wooden porticoes of Yunnanfu, and eventually to the Tibetan ribbon dance danced in front of the Dalai Lama's palace in Lhasa by girls with the gestures of Tang statuettes, overshadowed by the Red soldiers marching past with fixed bayonets.

One of my companions, a vague party official, tells me he saw the survivors of the Long March entering Yenan.

"When did you first see Mao?"

"When he called on us all to fight the Japanese. I was surprised, because he seemed so simple. He was dressed in blue, like ourselves, but he had brown socks. I had placed myself at the back: I had been among the first to arrive, but I was only seventeen. He spoke well: we were convinced at once that he was right."

The mountain looms over us, receding in fold after endless fold. I am reminded of Lungmen.

"There was no electricity at the time. The town was no longer lived in, because it was being bombed all the time. At night, lights glowed on in all the caves."

Peking

Return. Yesterday evening I received a telephone call requesting me not to leave the embassy. At one o'clock this afternoon, another telephone call: they are expecting me at three. In theory, it is for the audience with the President of the Republic, Liu Shao-ch'i; but the "they" leads our ambassador to suppose that Mao will be present.

Three o'clock. The pediment of the Palace of the People rests on massive Egyptian pillars, with lotus-capitals painted red. A corridor over a hundred yards long. At the end, against the sunlight (but in a room, I suppose), about twenty people. Two symmetrical groups. No, there is only one group, which seems to be split into two because the people facing me are standing some way behind the central personage, probably Mao Tse-tung. As I enter the room I can distinguish the faces. I walk toward Liu Shao-ch'i, since my letter is addressed to the President of the Republic. No one moves.

"Mr. President, I have the honor of delivering to you this letter from the President of the French Republic, in which General de Gaulle empowers me to act as his spokesman with Chairman Mao Tse-tung and yourself."

When I reach the phrase which concerns Mao, I address it to him, and find myself in front of him, after handing over the letter, at the moment when the translation is completed. His welcome is both cordial and curiously familiar, as if he were about to say: "To hell with politics!"

But he says, "You have just come back from Yenan, have you not? What is your impression?"

"A very powerful one. It is a museum of the invisible . . ."

The interpreter—the one Chou En-lai used—translates without faltering, but is obviously expecting an explanation.

"In the Yenan Museum, one expects photographs of the Long March, Lolo tribesmen, mountains, swamps. But the expedition itself is relegated to the background. In the foreground are the pikes, the fieldguns made of treetrunks and telegraph wire—a gallery of revolutionary penury.

When one leaves it for the caves where you lived with your colleagues,
one has the same impression, especially when one remembers the luxury
of your opponents. I was reminded of Robespierre's room in the house
of the cabinetmaker Duplay. But a mountain is more impressive than
a workshop, and your shelter, above the present-day museum, is reminiscent of the tombs of Egypt."

"But not the party assembly rooms."

"No. First of all, they are protected by panes of glass. But they give
an impression of a deliberate, a monastic bareness. It is the bareness,
reminiscent of our great monasteries, which suggests an invisible power."

We are all seated in wicker chairs with little white cloths on the
arms. A waiting room in a tropical railway station. Outside, through the
blinds, the immense August sun. Now I can make out Mao against the
light. The same type of face, round, smooth and young-looking, as the
Marshal's. The famous wart on the chin, like a Buddhist sign. A serenity
that is all the more unexpected because he is reputed to be violent.
Beside him, the equine face of the President of the Republic. Behind
them, a white-clad nurse.

"When the poor are determined to fight," he says, "they are always
victorious over the rich: look at your own revolution."

The stock phrase of all our staff colleges rings in my ears: irregulars
will never defeat a regular army in the long run. And how many Jac-
queries for one revolution! But perhaps he means that in a country like
China, where the armies resembled our great medieval companies, what
was strong enough to raise volunteer forces was also strong enough to
insure victory: one fights better to survive than to conserve.

After the crushing of the communists by Chiang Kai-shek in Shanghai and Hankow in 1927, Mao organized peasant militias. Now all the
Russians, basing themselves on Marxism-Leninism, and all the Chinese
who were directly dependent on them, Trotskyists and Stalinists alike,
laid it down as a basic principle that the peasantry can never win on
its own. Mao's certainty that a seizure of power by the peasants was
possible changed everything. How did it arise? When did he oppose
the peasant multitudes armed with spears to all Marxists of Russian,
hence Comintern, persuasion?

"My conviction did not take shape: I always felt it."

I remember General de Gaulle's answer to the question, "When did
you think that you would return to power?": "Always."

"But there is a rational answer all the same. After Chiang Kai-shek's
coup in Shanghai, we scattered. As you know, I decided to go back to
my village. Long ago I had experienced the great famine in Changsha,

when the severed heads of rebels were stuck on poles, but I had forgotten it. Two miles outside my village there were trees stripped of their bark up to a height of twelve feet: starving people had eaten it. We could make better fighters out of men who were forced to eat bark than out of the stokers of Shanghai, or even the coolies. But Borodin understood nothing about peasants."

"Gorki said to me one day, in Stalin's presence: peasants are the same everywhere."

"Neither Gorki, a great vagabond poet, nor Stalin . . . knew anything at all about peasants. There is no sense in confusing your kulaks with the poverty stricken people of the underdeveloped countries. And there is no such thing as abstract Marxism, but only concrete Marxism, adapted to the concrete realities of China, to the trees as naked as the people because the people are busy eating them."

After "Stalin" he hesitated. What was he about to say? A seminarist? What can he think of him today? Right up to the communist entry into Peking, Stalin believed in Chiang Kai-shek, who would crush this ephemeral, not even Stalinist party, as he had crushed it in 1927. At the secret session of the Twentieth Party Congress in 1956, Khrushchev asserted that Stalin had been ready to break with the Chinese communists. In North Korea, he had left the factories intact; in the regions which Mao was to occupy, he had destroyed them. He had sent Mao a work on partisan warfare, and Mao had given it to Liu Shao-ch'i: "Read this, if you want to know what we ought to have done—in order to end up dead." If he had to trust a Chinese communist, Stalin preferred Li Li-san, who was Moscow-trained. Mao had probably been indifferent to the purges—more so than to the rejection of criticism, and to the contempt for the peasant masses. And no doubt he appreciates the immense services rendered to communism by the campaign against the kulaks, the struggle against encirclement, and the conduct of the war. Above me, as in all official rooms, hang four portraits: Marx, Engels, Lenin—and Stalin.

Although Mao belonged to the group of young Chinese who were to go to France one after the other, after picking up a few words of French, to get their revolutionary training in French factories (Chou En-lai founded the Chinese Communist party at Billancourt), he never left China, and never abandoned his mistrust of most of the revolutionaries who came back from abroad, nor of the envoys from the Comintern.

"Around 1919, I was in charge of the students of Hunan. Before anything else we wanted autonomy for the province. We fought alongside the warlord Chao Heng-ti. The following year, he turned against us. He crushed us. I realized that only the masses could overthrow the warlords. At that time I was reading the *Communist Manifesto*, and took a hand in the organizing of the workers. But I knew the army; I had been a soldier for a few months in 1911. I knew the workers would not be enough."

"With us, the soldiers of the revolution, many of whom were the sons of peasants, became the soldiers of Napoleon. We know roughly how. But how was the People's Army formed—and reformed, since only seven thousand of the twenty thousand fighting men who arrived in Yenan came from the south. People talk of propaganda, but propaganda produces supporters, not soldiers."

"First there were the party cells. There were more workers than they say in the revolutionary army. We had a lot of people in Kiangsi: we chose the best. And for the Long March, they chose themselves. Those who stayed behind made a mistake: Chiang Kai-shek wiped out more than a million of them.

"Our people hated, despised and feared soldiers. They soon realized that the Red Army was their own. Almost everywhere it had a friendly reception. It helped the peasants, especially at harvest time. They saw that there was no privileged class among us. They saw that we all ate the same food and wore the same clothes. The soldiers were free to meet and free to talk. They could inspect the accounts of their company. Above all, the officers did not have the right to strike the men or to insult them.

"We studied the relations between classes. When the army was present, it wasn't difficult to show what we were defending: peasants have eyes. The enemy forces were much more numerous than ours, and helped by the Americans; yet we were often victorious, and the peasants knew that we were victorious on their behalf. One must learn to wage war, but war is simpler than politics: it is a question of having more men or more courage in the place where you give battle. An occasional defeat is inevitable; you simply need to have more victories than defeats."

"You turned your defeats to great advantage."

"More so than we had foreseen. In some respects the Long March was a retreat. Yet its results were those of a victory, because wherever we went . . ." ("six thousand miles," the interpreter interjected) "the peasants understood that we were with them, and if ever they doubted it, the behavior of the Kuomintang soldiers soon persuaded them. Not to mention the repression."

Chiang Kai-shek's. But he might also mention the efficacy of his own: not only did the liberation army confiscate the big estates, it also exterminated the big landowners and canceled debts. Mao's war maxims became a popular song: "The enemy advances, we retreat. The enemy camps, we harass. The enemy tires, we attack. The enemy retreats, we pursue." I know that his "we" includes not only the army and the party, but the workers of today and those of eternal China. Death has no place there. The civilization of China had made every Chinese a naturally disciplined individual. And for any peasant, life in the People's Army, where you were taught to read, where there was great comradeship, was more honorable and less harsh than village life. The progress of the Red Army across China was more powerful as propaganda than anything conceived of by the party; along the whole length of this trail of corpses, the entire peasantry rose when the time came.

"What was the pivot of your propaganda?"

"Just visualize the life of the peasants. It had always been unpleasant, especially when armies were living off the land. It had never been worse than during the last days of Kuomintang power. Suspects buried alive, peasant women who longed to be reborn as dogs so as to be less miserable, witches who invoked their gods by singing like a funeral dirge: 'Chiang Kai-shek is coming.' The peasants knew little of capitalism: they found themselves faced with a feudal state reinforced by the machine guns of the Kuomintang.

"The first part of our struggle was a peasant revolt. The aim was to free the farmer from his overlord; to win not freedom of speech, voting or assembly, but the freedom to survive. Fraternity rather than liberty! The peasants had tackled it without us, or were on the point of tackling it. But often in a state of despair. We brought hope. In the liberated areas, life was less terrible. Chiang Kai-shek's troops were so well aware of this that they put it about that the prisoners and peasants who came over to us were buried alive. That is why we had to organize a war of slogans, having the truth propagated by people who were known to those who listened to them. And only by those who had left no relatives on the other side. It was in order to sustain hope that we developed guerrilla warfare as much as we could. Much more than for punitive expeditions. *Everything arose out of a specific situation: we organized peasant revolt, we did not instigate it.* Revolution is a drama of passion; we did not win the people over by appealing to reason, but by developing hope, trust, and fraternity. In the face of famine, the will to equality takes on a religious force. Then, in the struggle for rice, land, and the rights brought by agrarian reform, the peasants had the conviction that they were fighting for their lives and those of their children.

"For a tree to grow, there must be seed, there must also be soil: if you sow in the desert, the tree will not sprout. The seed, in many places, was the memory of the liberation army; in many others, our prisoners. But everywhere the soil was the specific situation, the intolerable life of the villagers under the last Kuomintang regime.

"During the Long March, we took more than a hundred and fifty thousand prisoners, a few at a time; and many more during the march on Peking. They stayed with us for four or five days. They could see the difference between themselves and our soldiers. Even if they had almost nothing to eat—like us—they felt liberated. A few days after their capture, we would assemble those who wanted to leave. They would go off, after a farewell ceremony, as if they were our own men. After the ceremony, many of them gave up the idea of leaving. And with us, they became brave. Because they knew what they were fighting for."

"And because you distributed them among experienced units?"

"Of course. The soldier's relationship to his company is as important as the army's relationship to the population. That is what I called the fish in water. An army of liberation is a soup into which prisoners dissolve. Likewise, new recruits must only be committed to battles they can win. Later on, it's different. But we always looked after the enemy wounded. We couldn't have dragged all those prisoners along with us; no matter. When we marched on Peking, the defeated soldiers knew that they ran no risk by surrendering, and they surrendered in droves. The generals too, in fact."

To give an army the feeling that it is inevitably destined for victory is certainly no mean feat. I remember Napoleon, during the retreat from Russia: "Sire, our men are being massacred by two Russian batteries." "Order a squadron to capture them!"

I tell this to Mao, who laughs, and adds: "You must realize that before us, among the masses, no one had addressed themselves to women or to the young. Nor, of course, to the peasants. For the first time in their lives, every one of them felt involved.

"When Westerners talk about revolutionary sentiments, they nearly always attribute to us a propaganda akin to Russian propaganda. Well, if there is propaganda, it's more like that of your revolution, because, like you, we were fighting for a peasantry. If propaganda means training militiamen and guerrillas, we did a lot of propaganda. But if it means preaching. . . You know I've proclaimed for a long time: we must teach the masses clearly what we have received from them confusedly. What was it that won over most villages to us? The expositions of bitterness."

The exposition of bitterness is a public confession in which the speaker confesses not his sins but his sufferings in front of the whole village. Most of the listeners realize that they have undergone the same sufferings and recount them in their turn. There is a familiar poignancy in many of these confessions, the immemorial lament of immemorial misery. Some of them are appalling. (I was told of the one by a peasant woman who goes to ask the warlord what has happened to her imprisoned husband: "He is in the garden." She finds the body there, decapitated, with the head lying on the stomach. She takes the head, which the soldiers try to snatch from her, cradles it, and defends it so fiercely that the soldiers recoil as if the woman was the object of a supernatural possession. This story is very well known, because the woman repeated this exposition of bitterness many times—and because when the warlord was brought to public trial, she tore out his eyes.)

"We organized these expositions in every village," Mao says, "but we didn't invent them."

"What discipline did you have to impose in the early days?"

"We did not impose much discipline over the settling of that kind of score. As for the army, its three principles were: no individual requisitioning; all goods confiscated from landlords to be handed over to the political commissariat; immediate obedience to orders. We never took anything from the poor peasants. Everything depends on the cadres: a soldier attached to a disciplined unit is disciplined. But all militants are disciplined, and ours was an army of militants. It was the famous 'brain-washing' that brought most of our prisoners over to us. But what did it consist of? Saying to them, 'Why are you fighting us?' and telling the peasants, 'Communism is first of all an insurance against fascism.'"

I think of the men eating the bark of trees, and of what Nehru said to me about famine. But I know that brain-washing was not limited to these manifestations. The sessions of self-criticism were often sessions of accusation, followed by expulsions, arrests, and executions. "Turn resolutely against the enemy lurking inside your skull!" In 1942, at Yenan, Mao ordered the militants to become like the workers and the peasants. (I was shown the field he himself used to cultivate in the valley.) Later he was to order the "reconditioning" of all the Chinese. When he enjoined them to "surrender their hearts" there began the ritual oaths of the crowds "whose hearts beat only for the party," and the ecstasies of big Red hearts, some of which became kites.

"We lost the south," Mao continues, "and we even abandoned Yenan. But we recaptured Yenan, and we recaptured the south. In the north, we had the possibility of direct contact with Russia, and the certainty of not being encircled; Chiang Kai-shek still had several million men. We were able to establish solid bases, develop the party, organize the masses. As far as Tsinan, as far as Peking."

"In the Soviet Union, it was the party which made the Red Army; here, it seems as if often it was the liberation army which developed the party."

"We will never allow the gun to rule the party. But it's true that the Eighth Route Army built up a powerful party organization in northern China—cadres, schools, mass movements. Yenan was built by the gun. Everything can grow in the barrel of a gun.

"But in Yenan we came across a class we had hardly ever come across in the south, and not at all during the Long March: the bourgeois-nationalists, the intellectuals,* all those who had sincerely accepted the united front in the struggle against Japan. In Yenan we were confronted with the problems of government. What I'm going to tell you will surprise you: if we hadn't been forced to it by the enemy offensive, we would never have attacked."

"Did they think they could wipe you out?"

"Yes. Chiang Kai-shek's generals lied to him a great deal, and he lied a great deal to the Americans. He thought we were going to give battle in the traditional manner. But Chu Teh and Chen-yi refused to take up the challenge except when our forces became superior to his. He immobilized a lot of men for the defense of cities, but we never attacked cities."

"Which was why the Russians . . . neglected you for such a long time."

"If revolution can only be brought about by the workers, obviously we couldn't bring about revolution. The Russians' friendly feelings were for Chiang Kai-shek. When he escaped from China, the Soviet ambassador was the last person to wish him goodbye. The cities fell like ripe fruit."

"Russia was mistaken, but we too would have been mistaken. Nineteenth-century Asia seems to have been stricken with a decay which colonialism doesn't sufficiently explain. Japan was the first to Westernize herself, and it was prophesied that she would very quickly become

* By this, Mao means, apart from the liberal professions, students and teachers, technicians and engineers: the mass of those who are neither workers, peasants, nor former compradores or capitalists.

Americanized. The truth is that, in spite of appearances, she has remained profoundly Japanese. You are in the process of restoring Greater China, Mr. Chairman; that is evident in all the propaganda pictures and posters, in your own poems, in China herself, with the military adjuncts of which tourists are so critical."

Here the ministers, sitting in a circle, prick up their ears.

"Yes," he replies calmly.

"You are hoping that your ancient agriculture, in which manual labor is still so widespread, will catch up with mechanization?"

"It will take time. Perhaps decades. We shall also need friends. First of all there must be contacts. There are various kinds of friends. France is one kind. Indonesia is another. Aidit* is here. I haven't seen him yet. There are still some points in common between him and us, and others between you and us. You said very . . ."—the interpreter is trying to think of the French—"pertinently to the foreign minister, that you did not want a world subjected to a dual hegemony of the United States and the Soviet Union, who will end up, in fact, by establishing what I called two years ago their Holy Alliance. You have shown your independence with regard to the Americans."

"We are independent, but we are also their allies."

Since the beginning of the interview, he has made no other gesture than to raise his cigarette to his lips and put it down on the ashtray again. In the general stillness, he does not seem a sick man, but a bronze emperor. Now, suddenly, he raises both arms in the air and lets them drop.

"Our allies! Yours and ours!"

As much as to say, a fine lot they are!

"The United States simply means American imperialism, and Great Britain is playing a double game."

For the first time, the Marshal takes the floor: "Britain supports the American imperialists."

Almost in the same breath as I reply, "Don't forget Malaysia . . ." Mao says, "Returning the compliment." But he lowers his voice as though talking to himself as he goes on. "We have done what had to be done, but who knows what will happen in a few decades?"

I am thinking not of what will happen tomorrow but of what happened yesterday, when the Russians, at the same time as they were constructing giant steel plants, were moving the frontier posts on the Turkestan steppes while all the Chinese guards were dead-drunk, in

---

* Leader of the Indonesian Communist party.

order to lay hands on the uranium mines—the frontier posts returning to their original positions a little later on as a result of a comradely tit for tat which had put the Russian guards to sleep.

"Is the opposition still powerful?" I ask.

"There are still the bourgeois-nationalists, the intellectuals, and so on. They are beginning to have children."

"Why the intellectuals?"

"Their thinking is anti-Marxist. At the time of the liberation, we welcomed them even when they had been involved with the Kuomintang, because we had too few Marxist intellectuals. Their influence is far from disappearing. Especially among the young."

I suddenly notice that the paintings on the wall are traditional scrolls in the Manchu style—as in the Marshal's office and Chou En-lai's. There are none of the socialist-realist pictures which cover the walls of the town.

"The young I have come across in the course of my travels," says our ambassador, "are nevertheless deeply devoted to you, Mr. Chairman."

Mao knows that Lucien Paye was minister of education and rector of Dakar University. He also knows that he takes every opportunity to make contact with teachers and students. The ambassador speaks a little Mandarin, which several of the members of our embassy, Chinese-born, speak fluently.

"One can see things in that way also."

It is not a polite phrase meant to ward off discussion. Mao attaches the same importance to youth as General de Gaulle or Nehru. He seems to think that there can be several opinions on the youth of China, and to wish that some other view than his own were tenable. He knows that our ambassador has studied the new Chinese educational method: the "half work, half study" system, and the system whereby students are allowed to bring their textbooks with them for examinations. He questions the ambassador closely: "How long have you been in Peking?"

"Fourteen months. But I have been to Canton by train; I have visited the central south, which enabled me, Mr. Chairman, and not without emotion, to see the house where you were born, in Hunan; I have seen Szechwan and the northeast. And we saw Loyang and Sian on our way to Yenan. Everywhere, I have been in contact with the people. A superficial contact; but the contact I established with teachers and students was a real one—and in Peking, fairly durable. The students are oriented toward the future which you envisage for them, Mr. Chairman."

"You have seen one aspect. Another could have escaped you. And yet it has been seen and confirmed. A society is a complex organism. Do you know what the chrysanthemums were called, at the last Hang-chow show? The drunken dancer, the old temple in the setting sun, the lover powdering his fair one. It is possible that the two tendencies coexist, but there are many conflicts in store."

In this country where people talk of nothing else but fraternity and the future, how lonely his voice sounds when confronting the future! I think of a childish picture from my first history book: Charlemagne watching the first Normans in the distance sailing up the Rhine.

"Neither the agricultural nor the industrial problem is solved. Still less the youth problem. Revolution and children have to be trained if they are to be properly brought up."

His children, entrusted to peasants during the Long March, were never found again. Somewhere, perhaps, in a people's commune, there are two young men of thirty, left behind years ago with so many others, alive and dead, and who are the nameless sons of Mao Tse-tung.

"Youth must be put to the test."

A sudden change in the atmosphere seems to intensify the stillness of our audience. Something very different from the uneasy curiosity which set in when they were waiting to hear what he would say about the resurrection of China. It is as if we were talking about secret preparations for an atomic explosion. "Put to the test." There are twenty-five million young communists, of whom nearly four million are intellectuals; what Mao has just said suggests, and surely heralds, a new revolutionary development comparable to that which instigated the "Hundred Flowers" campaign and its subsequent suppression.

"Let a hundred flowers bloom, let a hundred schools contend!" Mao launched this slogan, which seemed to be a proclamation of liberalism, at a time when he believed China to have been "remodeled." The kind of criticism he was inviting was the "constructive" criticism so dear to communist parties: his intention was to use it as a basis for necessary reforms. He found himself faced with a mass of negative criticisms, which even went so far as to attack the party itself. The return to Sparta was not long delayed; the intellectuals were sent to remodel themselves in people's communes. Critics of the regime have seen in the "Hundred Flowers" campaign a bait intended to lure opponents out into the open. But Mao had been sincerely anxious to relax the party line, just as he decided sincerely, and firmly, to reestablish it as soon as he realized that the criticism he had aroused was not "self-criticism." In many respects the situation would be the same today if the slogan were "Let youth blossom." Does he consider communist youth capable of carrying the young along with it in a campaign comparable to the "Great Leap Forward"? Moreover, the party doubtless needs to be put to the test again. The repression which followed the "Hundred Flowers" eliminated not only the protesting young but also the party members who had allowed them to protest: two birds with one stone. The whole of Chinese youth must be worked upon, in order to put the party to the test. The beleaguerment of the West by the underdeveloped nations to which Chou En-lai alluded—"hence," says Mao, "the fate of the world"—is inseparable from the youth of China. Does he really believe in the liberation of the world under the leadership of China? Revolution brought about by the evangelists of a great revolutionary nation certainly seems a more grandiose and thrilling policy than that of the United States, which can be defined simply as the prevention of such an expansion. Borodin, the Soviet envoy to Sun Yat-sen, answered the *Hong Kong Times* interviewer: "You understand the behavior of the Protestant missionaries, don't you? Well then, you understand mine!" But that was in 1925. Two thousand dancers and three hundred thousand spectators are mobilized for the President of Somalia—and then what? Stalin believed in the Red Army, not the Comintern, and perhaps Mao believes in the seizure of world power by the underdeveloped countries only in the same way that Stalin believed in the seizure of power by the international proletariat. The revolution will conquer: but in the meantime Somali presidents, Vietnam war, war propaganda down to village level, these are the justification for Sparta. Mao blesses Hanoi, Somalia, Santo Domingo, and "liquidates" his Tibetan adversaries. The defense of Vietnam and the communization of Tibet are connected, at a far deeper level than the symbolic aid to the Somalis or the Congolese, like twins at the breast of the Old Empire. Every Vietnamese guerrilla fallen in the bush around Danang vindicates the toil of the Chinese peasants. China will go to the aid (up to what point?) of all the oppressed peoples struggling for freedom, but the struggle of these peoples is the cement that keeps her together. "Strategically," says Mao, "imperialism is doomed—and no doubt capitalism with it; tactically, it must be fought as the troops of the liberation army fought those of Chiang Kai-shek." And tactically, the decisive battles will take place in China, because Mao will not commit himself decisively outside. But already the Long March has taken on the aura of a legend, and the survivors of the end of the war against Chiang Kai-shek are called the Veterans.

Mao said that the industrial problem was not yet solved, but I do not believe he is worried about it: in his mind, China's conversion is already a fact. He said that the agricultural problem was not yet solved; yet there are those—he himself first and foremost—who maintain that nearly all the arable land in China is under cultivation, and that its yield can only be increased to a limited extent; while others proclaim the imminent development of the steppes, and a doubling of the yield. The atom bomb and the hand cart will not always coexist. But Mao envisages the modernization of agriculture, and industrialization, only in terms of the powerful Chinese structures in which the party expresses, guides, and directs the masses as the Emperor directed the forces of the earth. Agriculture and industry are linked, and must remain so; politics comes before technology. Perhaps the Soviet state is strong enough for Russian youth to become to some extent indifferent to a policy which nevertheless fills them with pride; but the Chinese state is still no more than the daily victory won by China in the glorious struggle. Like the Soviet state before the war, the Chinese state needs enemies. Was the austerity which brought with it the daily bowl of rice really austerity, compared to the poverty which brought hunger? But poverty is receding, the landowners of the days of the Empire and of the Kuomintang are dead, the Japanese and Chiang Kai-shek have gone. What is there in common between the illiterates of Kiangsi who still resemble the Taiping revolutionaries, the Tibetan serfs freed by the liberation army and trained by the School of National Minorities, and the students interrogated by Lucien Paye? The menace of revisionism of which Mao speaks surely lies there, far more than in nostalgia for a past of which only the worst aspects are now known. More than two hundred and eighty million Chinese under seventeen years of age have not a single memory prior to the capture of Peking.

Since the interpreter's last sentence, no one has spoken. The reaction which Mao inspires in his companions intrigues me. There is first of all a kind of friendly deference: the Central Committee around Lenin, not Stalin. But what he has been saying to me sometimes appears to be also addressed to an imaginary contradictor, to whom he is replying through them. He has a slight air of saying: this is how it will be, whether you like it or not. As for them, their attentive silence gives them, fleetingly, the aspect of a tribunal.

"By the way," says Mao suddenly, "a few months ago I received a parliamentary delegation from your country. Do your socialist and communist parties really mean what they say?"

"It depends what they say. The Socialist party is primarily a party of white-collar workers, whose influence is exerted through the unions of the Force Ouvrière, which have a considerable membership in the administration. It is a liberal party with a Marxist vocabulary. In the south, there are quite a few vineyard owners who vote socialist."

My interlocutors seem thunderstruck by these elementary truths.

"As for the Communist party, it still has a quarter or a fifth of the vote. Brave and devoted militants, under the apparatus which you know as well as I do. Too revolutionary a party for another militant party to develop, too weak to bring about Revolution."

"The revisionism of the Soviet Union may not make it lose votes, but it will make it lose teeth. As a party, it is against us. Like all the others, apart from Albania. They have become social-democratic parties of a new type."

"It was the last great Stalinist party. Individually most of the communists would like to have you kiss them on one cheek and the Russians on the other."

He is not quite sure he has understood. The interpreter enlarges. He turns toward the Marshal, the President, and the other ministers. Mao's laugh is said to be infectious. It is true: they all roar with laughter. Serious again, he says, "What does General de Gaulle think of it?"

"He does not attach any great importance to it. It is nothing more than an electoral factor. At present, the destiny of France is being worked out between the French people and him."

Mao reflects. "Plekhanov and the Mensheviks were Marxists, even Leninists. They cut themselves off from the masses and ended up by taking up arms against the Bolsheviks—or rather they mainly ended up exiled or shot.

"There are now two paths for every communist: that of socialist construction, and that of revisionism. We are beyond the bark-eating stage, but we have only got as far as a bowl of rice a day. To accept revisionism is to snatch away the bowl of rice. As I told you, we made the Revolution with peasant rebels; then we led them against the cities ruled by the Kuomintang. But the successor of the Kuomintang was not the Chinese Communist party, however important that may be: it was the New Democracy. The history of the Revolution, like the weakness of the proletariat of the big cities, forced the communists into collaboration with the petty bourgeoisie. For that reason, too, our revolution, in the last analysis, will no more resemble the Russian Revolution than the Russian Revolution resembled yours. Even today, broad layers of our society are conditioned in such a way that their activity is necessarily orientated toward revisionism. They can only obtain what they want by taking it from the masses."

(I think of Stalin: "We did not bring about the October Revolution in order to give power to the kulaks!")

"Corruption, law-breaking, the arrogance of intellectuals, the wish to do honor to one's family by becoming a white-collar worker and not dirtying one's hands anymore, all these stupidities are only symptoms. Inside the party and out. The cause of them is the historical conditions themselves. But also the political conditions."

I know his theory: you begin by no longer tolerating criticism, then you abandon self-criticism, then you cut yourself off from the masses, and, since the party can draw its revolutionary strength only from them, you tolerate the formation of a new class; finally like Khrushchev, you proclaim peaceful coexistence on a durable basis with the United States —and the Americans arrive in Vietnam. I have not forgotten his old saying: "Here seventy per cent of the people are poor peasants, and their sense of the Revolution has never been at fault." He has just explained how he interprets it: one must learn from the masses in order to be able to teach them.

"That is why," he says, "Soviet revisionism is an . . . apostasy." (The interpreter hit on the word "apostasy" almost at once. Brought up by the nuns?) "It is moving toward the restoration of capitalism, and one wonders why Europe isn't satisfied with it."

"I don't believe they are contemplating a return to private ownership of the means of production."

"Are you so sure? Look at Yugoslavia!"

I have no desire to talk about Yugoslavia, but it crosses my mind that the two major rebels, Mao and Tito, are both strangers to the cadres of the Gray House in Moscow—both guerrilla leaders.

"I believe that Russia wants to extricate itself from Stalinism without returning to straight capitalism. Hence a certain liberalism. But this entails a metamorphosis of power; there is no such thing as liberal Stalinism. If what we call Russian communism means Stalinism, we're facing a change of régime. The end of encirclement and of the primacy of heavy industry, the abolition of the political police as a fourth power, the victory of 1945, have brought about a metamorphosis in the Soviet Union at least as radical as the transition from Lenin to Stalin. Brezhnev is the successor of Khrushchev and so will all the Brezhnevs be. I remember a time when one didn't talk politics even with one's wife; when I heard that people were daring to make fun of the government in the underground, I realized that there hadn't simply been a 'softening' of what I had known, but a radical transformation."

"In other words, you think they are not revisionists, because they are

no longer even communists. Perhaps you're right, if one thinks of"—
the interpreter cannot think of the word; "hurly-burly," our interpreter
suggests—"if one thinks of the hurly-burly which reigns over there, and
which has no other aim than to deceive the whole world! Yet the ruling
clique allows the formation of strata of the population which are not yet
classes, but which influence communist policy."

Rome betrays as soon as it eliminates Sparta. For a Chinese Sparta
cannot comfortably be maintained beside a Rome which in any case it
identifies with Capua. I know the exasperated answer of the Russians:
"Mao is a dogmatist and a visionary. How can revolutionary fervor be
maintained fifty years after the revolution! There are no tsarist defeats
or capitalists or landowners to revive the feeling of October 1917. China
is going through the trials we went through thirty years ago. She has
nothing, whereas we have something, and we cannot return to nothing.
A new factor outweighs all ideologies: nuclear war will annihilate every
nation involved in it. Khrushchev put an end to the terror and the
concentration camps, and believed in the possibility of disarmament
agreements. He governed injudiciously, but we too, like him, want to
establish communism in the world while avoiding war." I also know
Mao's answer. He will quote Lenin on his deathbed: "In the last analysis, the success of our struggle will be determined by the fact that
Russia, China, and India constitute the overwhelming majority of the
population of the globe." He will recall that the Chinese party has ac-
cumulated more experience than all the others. He will think of the
saying of the man beside him, Liu Shao-ch'i: "Mao's stroke of genius
was to transpose the European character of Marxism-Leninism into its
Asian form." He will repeat that Khrushchev's abandonment of China
over the affair of the offshore islands of Quemoy and Matsu was a be-
trayal, and that Soviet support for the United Nations action in the
Congo was another. That the conditions of the recall of the Russian
experts were calculated to force the relinquishment of all the public
works that had been begun. That every intervention of the United
States makes them an object of hatred for the poor and revolutionary
majority, and that the disintegration of the colonial world now demands
rapid action. That Khrushchev was a non-Leninist petty bourgeois, who
graduated from fear of nuclear war to fear of revolution—and that the
Soviet government is henceforth incapable of appealing to the masses
because it is afraid of them.

The sending of city dwellers, of engineers and factory managers into
the people's communes here is as banally rigid as was compulsory military service in Europe. The party's slogans are never questioned; not even

the absurdities which accompany an epic, such as the campaign "against bourgeois sentiments such as love between parents and children, or between people of opposite sexes when they are carried to extremes of emotional feeling." But slogans are only followed if the masses remain mobilized. Mao can only build China with volunteers. He is more anxious to make China than to make war, and he is positive that the United States will not use nuclear weapons in Vietnam any more than in Korea. He still believes in the permanent revolution—and what most separates him from it is Russia.

For the third time, a secretary has come to speak to Liu Shao-ch'i, and for the third time the President has come to hold a low-voiced conversation with Mao. The latter makes a tired gesture, and levers himself up with his hands on the arms of his chair. He is the most upright of us all: monolithic. He is still holding a cigarette. I go to take leave of him, and he holds out an almost feminine hand, with palms as pink as if they had been boiled. To my surprise, he accompanies me out. The interpreter is between us, a little to the rear; the nurse, behind him. Our companions precede him, the French ambassador with the President of the Republic, who has not said a word. Some distance behind us is a younger group—high officials, I presume.

He walks one step at a time, as stiff as if he were not bending his legs, more than ever the bronze emperor in his dark uniform surrounded by light-colored or white ones. I think of Churchill at the time he received the Cross of the Liberation. He was to review the guard which had just presented arms to him. He too could only shuffle forward step by step, and he stopped in front of each soldier to examine his decorations before going on to the next man. He seemed, then, to be at death's door. The soldiers watched the stricken old lion pass slowly by in front of them. Mao is not stricken: he has the uncertain equilibrium of the statue of the Commendatore, and walks like a legendary figure risen from some imperial grave. I quote to him Chou En-lai's remark a few years back: "We began a new Long March in 1949, and we are still only on the first lap."

"Lenin wrote: 'The dictatorship of the proletariat is an unrelenting struggle against all the forces and traditions of the old society.' Unrelenting. If Khrushchev really believed that all the contradictions had disappeared in Russia, it was perhaps because he thought he was ruling a revived Russia."

"Which Russia is that?"

"The Russia of victories. That can suffice. Victory is the mother of many illusions. When he came here for the last time, on his return from Camp David, he believed in compromise with American imperialism. He imagined that the Soviet government was that of all Russia. He imagined that the contradictions had almost disappeared there. The truth is that if the contradictions due to victory are less painful than the old ones, luckily they are almost as deep. Humanity left to its own devices does not necessarily reestablish capitalism (which is why you are perhaps right in saying they will not revert to private ownership of the means of production), but it does reestablish inequality. The forces tending toward the creation of new classes are powerful. We have just suppressed military titles and badges of rank; every "cadre" becomes a worker again at least one day a week; whole trainloads of city dwellers go off to work in the people's communes. Khrushchev seemed to think that a revolution is done when a communist party has seized power— as if it were merely a question of national liberation."

He does not raise his voice, but his hostility when he refers to the Russian Communist party is as obvious as Chou En-lai's hatred when he refers to the United States. And yet, in Loyang or in the back streets of Peking, the children, who took us for Russians (they have not seen any other whites), smiled at us.

"Lenin was well aware that at this juncture the revolution is only just beginning. The forces and traditions he was referring to are not only the legacy of the bourgeoisie. They are also our fate. Li Tsung-jen, who was vice-president of the Kuomintang, has just come back home from Taiwan. Another one! I told him: 'We still need another twenty or thirty years of effort to make China a powerful country.' But is that merely in order that this China should become like Taiwan? The revisionists mix up cause and effect. Equality is not important in itself; it is important because it is natural to those who have not lost contact with the masses. The only way of knowing whether a young cadre is really revolutionary is to see whether he really makes friends with the workers and peasants. The young are not Red by birth; they have not known Revolution. You remember Kosygin at the Twenty-third Congress: 'Communism means the raising of living standards.' Of course! And swimming is a way of putting on a pair of trunks! Stalin had destroyed the kulaks. It isn't simply a question of replacing the Tsar with Khrushchev, one bourgeoisie with another, even if it's called communist. It's the same as with women. Of course it was necessary to give them legal equality to begin with! But from there on, everything still remains to be done. The thought, culture, and customs which brought

China to where we found her must disappear, and the thought, customs, and culture of proletarian China, which does not yet exist, must appear. The Chinese woman doesn't yet exist either, among the masses; but she is beginning to want to exist. And then, to liberate women is not to manufacture washing machines—and to liberate their husbands is not to manufacture bicycles but to build the Moscow subway."

I think of his own wives, or rather what one hears about them. The first had been chosen by his parents. It was under the Empire—Mao could have seen the last Empress. He draws aside her veil, finds her ugly, and has not stopped running since. The second was the daughter of his master. He loved her, and refers to her in a famous poem as "my proud poplar" (a play on her name). She was taken as a hostage by the Kuomintang, and beheaded. I remember the photograph in which he is seen raising his glass face to face with Chiang Kai-shek at Chungking: much icier than Stalin face to face with Ribbentrop. The third was the heroine of the Long March: wounded fourteen times. He divorced her (divorce is rare in the Chinese party); today she is governor of a province. Finally he married Chiang Ching, a Shanghai film star who found her way to Yenan through the lines to serve the party. She directed the army theater. Since the capture of Peking she has lived only for Mao, and has never again appeared in public.*

"Proletarian China," Mao goes on, "is no more a coolie than it is a mandarin; the People's Army is no more a partisan band than a Chiang Kai-shek army. Thought, culture, customs must be born of struggle, and the struggle must continue for as long as there is still a danger of a return to the past. Fifty years is not a long time; barely a lifetime—our customs must become as different from the traditional customs as yours are from feudal customs. The basis on which we have constructed everything is the real toil of the masses, the real struggle of the soldiers. Anyone who does not understand that puts himself outside the Revolution. It isn't a victory, it is a mixing of the masses and the cadres over several generations."

Thus, doubtless, did he speak of China in the cave at Yenan. I think of the poem in which, after evoking the heroes of Chinese history and Genghis Khan, he adds, "Look rather in the present."

"And yet," I remark, "it will be the China of the great empires."

"I don't know; but I do know that if our methods are the right ones—if we tolerate no deviation—China will be restored to greatness."

* She has since played an important role in the Great Proletarian Cultural Revolution.

Once more I am about to take my leave of him: the cars are at the bottom of the steps.

"But in this battle," he adds, "we are alone."

"Not for the first time."

"I am alone with the masses. Waiting."

The tone is a surprising one, in which there is bitterness, perhaps irony, and above all pride. One might think he had spoken these last words for the benefit of the others, but he has only spoken with passion since they moved out of earshot. He is walking more slowly than his illness compels him to.

"What is expressed in that commonplace term 'revisionism' is the death of the revolution. What we have just done in the army must be done everywhere. I have told you that the revolution is also a feeling. If we decide to make of it what the Russians are now doing—a feeling of the past—everything will fall apart. Our revolution cannot be simply the stabilization of a victory."

"Doesn't the Great Leap Forward seem much more than a stabilization?"

Its edifices surround us as far as the eye can see.

"Yes. But since then . . . There is what one sees, and what one doesn't see. Men do not like to bear the burden of the Revolution throughout their lives. When I said, 'Chinese Marxism is the religion of the people,' I meant—but do you know how many communists there are in the countryside? One per cent!—I meant that the communists express the Chinese people in a real way if they remain faithful to the work upon which the whole of China has embarked as if on another Long March. When we say, 'We are the Sons of the People,' China understands it as she understood the phrase 'Son of Heaven.' The People has taken the place of the ancestors. The People, not the victorious Communist party."

"Marshals have always liked stabilizations; but you have just eliminated ranks."

"Not only marshals! Besides, the survivors of the old guard have been molded by action, like our state. Many of them are empirical, resolute, prudent revolutionaries. On the other hand, there is a whole generation of dogmatic youth, and dogma is less useful than cow dung. One can make whatever one likes out of it, even revisionism! Whatever your ambassador may think, this youth is showing dangerous tendencies. It is time to show that there are others."

He seems to be struggling simultaneously against the United States, against Russia—and against China: "If we tolerate no deviation . . ."

Little by little we approach the front steps. I look at him (he is looking straight ahead). What an extraordinary power of allusion! I know that he is about to intervene anew. Through the young? Through the army? No man will have shaken history so powerfully since Lenin. The Long March portrays him better than any personal trait, and his decision will be brutal and ruthless. He is still hesitating, and there is something epic in this hesitation whose object I do not know. He wanted to re-create China, and he has re-created it; but he also wants the "uninterrupted revolution" with the same determination, and it is essential to him that youth should want it too. I think of Trotsky, but the "permanent revolution" related to a different context, and I only knew Trotsky after his defeat (that first evening, at Royan, the shock of white hair, the smile, and the little wide-apart teeth in the glare of the car headlights). The man walking slowly by my side is haunted by something more than the uninterrupted revolution; by a gigantic conception of which neither of us has spoken: the underdeveloped countries are far more numerous than the countries of the West, and the struggle began as soon as the colonies became nations. He knows that he will not see the global revolution. The underdeveloped nations are at the same stage as the proletariat in 1848. But there will be a Marx (he himself first and foremost) and a Lenin. A great deal can be done in a century! It is not a question of the alliance of such and such an external proletariat with an internal proletariat, the alliance of India with the British Labour movement, of Algeria with the French communists; it is a question of the vast tracts of misery against the little European headland, against hateful America. Proletariat will unite with capitalism, as in Russia, as in the United States. But there is one country dedicated to vengeance and justice, one country that will never lay down its arms, will never lay down its spirit, before the global confrontation. Three hundred years of European energy are now on the wane; the Chinese era is dawning. He reminded me of the emperors, and he now reminds me, standing there, of the rust-covered shields of the army chiefs which belonged to the funerary avenues of the emperors, and are to be found abandoned in the sorghum fields. Behind our entire conversation the hope of a twilight world stood watch. In the vast corridor, the dignitaries have stopped, without daring to turn round.

"I am alone," he repeats. And suddenly he laughs: "Well, with a few distant friends: please give General de Gaulle my greetings. As for them" (he means the Russians), "the revolution doesn't really interest them, you know."

The car drives off. I draw back the little curtains on the rear window.

As when I arrived, but this time in broad daylight, he is alone in his dark costume at the center of a slightly withdrawn circle of light-colored suits. Silky tufts of mimosa drift past on the wind like snowflakes, like the tufts of kapok above the queen of the Casamance. Overhead, an airplane flashes past. With his hand to his forehead in the age-old gesture, the Old Man of the Mountain watches it recede, shading his eyes from the sun.

For a few hours, our interpreter will be transcribing his shorthand notes. I suggest to the ambassador that we should go and visit the tombs of the Ming emperors. I have not seen them for over twenty years. How will they have changed? I remember my dialogue with India after leaving Nehru. *He* saw himself as the heir of Ellora, and Mao sees himself as the heir of the Great Founders. But the Ming tombs are mausoleums reminiscent of Versailles, unlike that of Tai Tsung abandoned amid the close-cropped flowers of the steppes under its guard of sculpted horses.

We come first to the Great Wall. The tangled dragon stretches out across the hills as it did of old. Here are the same hollyhocks, the same willow paths: but the stone roadway built for the war chariots is today as clean as a Dutch dresser. Are these wastepaper bins set out like mileposts to be found along the entire length of the Great Wall? Here, as before, are the herds of little Manchu ponies, the dragon-flies, the russet-colored Mongolian birds of prey, and the large butterflies of a warm brown similar to the one I saw alight on the rope of the bell tower at Vézelay on the day war was declared in 1939.

The tombs are still approached by way of the funerary walkway, which begins after the marble portico and the rostral columns. Along its entire length are the famous statues: chargers, camels, dignitaries. These statues have neither the grace of the figurines of the classical periods nor the taut majesty of the chimeras abandoned in the millet fields of Sian. They are eternity's playthings, a Père-Lachaise presided over by the postman Cheval.* We stop the car in front of a tortoise of longevity straddled by children, and walk through former outbuildings delivered over to the cicadas, the swifts and the sparrows. But just inside the great entrance there appears the meticulously kept garden which I knew in its wild state: red and orange flowerbeds, cannas and gladioli, make the glazed tiles of a paler orange, and the walls of dark purple, seem almost

* Monsieur Cheval, a postman who lived at Hautes-Rives (Drôme), spent thirty-three years (1879–1912) building in his garden one of the great follies of the world—a palace constructed of local stones and cement. (Tr.)

matt. Raised on its high marble base—the plinth of Angkor and of Borobodur—the tomb seems to entrap the mountainous countryside which surrounds its solitude. In front of it, the dark green of the pine trees and the bright green of the oaks twisted like decorative rocks; behind, the somber mass of the sacred wood. It is not a temple, it is a gateway of death; a tomb like the pyramids—but which draws its eternity from living forms. Two tiny girls are clambering over it like blue cats, followed by a mother with twin pigtails. Behind the archway, the immemorial fields, the immemorial peasants with their immemorial hats, the reapers who survive empires and revolutions. (And yet, at the foot of the hills, already there looms the great dam.)

The sun is sinking lower in the sky. Let us go and see some other tombs. Here is the one whose barbaric trapezoid base reminds one of the gates of Peking. The red gladioli are infiltrating among the thujas of its sacred wood. The burial chambers have been cleared, and we can enter upright, whereas one almost has to crawl to enter the Han tombs at Loyang, as one has to stoop in the corridors of the pyramids. But there remain only stone slabs; in the wood, a little edifice houses the Empress's tiara of kingfishers' feathers.

The roofs have only the slightest of curves, but it is enough to free them from the earth. Here is one of the deepest expressions of the soul of China. It is no longer the Erebus of the founders with their war chariots, their steles, and their bronze boar spears. On the painted beams, the white-bordered bestiary still proliferates. But these tombs, like the Temple of Heaven, proclaim the supreme harmony. All earth is the earth of the dead, all harmony unites the dead with the living. Each tomb reveals the accord of heaven and earth. The harmony is the presence of eternity, to which the Emperor's body is visibly returned—as all other bodies are returned to it invisibly.

A little farther on lies a ruined tomb. Chinese ruins belong to death, because once the roof has collapsed, the building, deprived of its volutes, is nothing but bare walls. The sacred wood hems in the tomb, but without invading it as the jungle invades the temples of India. Above the stone base and the high, crimson walls, the fading daylight lingers on a pink faience surface.

Let us go back. The paths leading off the main road are forbidden to foreigners. Dahlias in profusion, blooming like those of June 1940. I thought the dahlia had come to Europe from Mexico. In the evening light, a long string of horses preceded by two sad-looking donkeys slowly wends its way back to Peking, passed by vanloads of soldiers who have finished their day's work in the nearby people's communes.

We pass the first temples of the city. I have visited nearly all of them again, as intrigued as ever by their folding-screen decor. With the exception of the Temple of Heaven and the Forbidden City, geomancers' edifices, traps for the cosmos in spite of their rooftop menageries, the pagodas of the last dynasty preserve (badly) a mid-Lent pantheon to which are added the Tibetan monsters and the gigantic black statue of the temple of the lamas, which are no longer addressed to anyone. It is easier, for a Frenchman, to make the transition from the crusades of religion to those of the revolution than from the art of Louis IX to the rococo of Louis XV; now that China has become China again, all its bric-à-brac of porcelains, of agricultural gods and of little potbellied Buddhas forms a weird interlude, from the first Manchu Emperor to the Empress Tzu Hsi, between the great faceless emperors and Mao. The interval seems to end not with the bloody tumult of 1900, but with the storming of the Summer Palace. I must somewhere have told the story of the night during which the English soldiers searched for the pearls of the concubines of old, while the zouaves threw into the woods the mechanical figures collected by the emperors over the centuries. Amid the shouts of the soldiers, a toy rabbit ran about on the lawn, striking its little golden bells which reflected the light of the conflagration.

Above the Forbidden City, I have seen the tree loaded with chains on which the last Ming emperor hanged himself on the entry of the Manchus. But I have also found (was it in the Museum of the Revolution?) the photograph of the two sisters who led the Boxer Rebellion with the courage of prophetesses, and fell into the hands of the Europeans. Loti saw them at Tientsin, huddled in the corner of a room as Joan of Arc must have been in the corner of her last dungeon. Those women foreshadowed Mao. Although he is better suited to the tomb of Tai Tsung in the wilds of the steppes than to those of the Mings, no doubt a prodigious tomb will be erected for him. He is unsuited to harmony, to the libations poured out by the emperors to unite men with the earth; still less to the China of puppets or of overrefinement. And many of his adherents would like to destroy the whole of the past, as is the way of nascent revolutions. What he himself wishes to destroy and to preserve sometimes seems to be determined by the opposition of yin and yang, the two fundamental movements of the earth's pulsation. "If we do what we should do, China will become China again."

As the car passes through the great Square of Celestial Peace again, night has fallen. A last glimmer outlines the Forbidden City, opposite the Palace of the People whose shapeless mass is lost in shadow. I think of the Old Man of the Mountain, of his two black-clad arms ponderously raised above all the motionless shoulders in white linen: "Our allies!"

"Our allies . . ."

I think, too, of the Glières chaplain—his arms raised toward the stars of Dieulefit: "There are no grown-ups . . ."

2

I return to France "over the Pole."

White expanses. Anchorage. When I first went through here, I expected a fishing port and a few Eskimo. I found a military base and innumerable avenues, dead straight and empty. Festoons of electric lightbulbs, a few red-light bars (it was three in the morning) and, in the middle of the snow-covered main square, tall totem poles whose redskin animal figures watched over a St. Joseph and a kneeling Virgin. They belonged to the mock isba which serves as the tourist information bureau. They had put up a crèche, taken it down again, and left the statues behind in the lonely square at the foot of the magic animals. There was one solitary car on the avenue. It was December 26.

This time we do not change planes. We take off again over the white immensity. When I arrive in Europe tomorrow, I shall be a day younger. Before the ice shelf, there are still large tracts of ocean. I have no desire to take my notes out of the little traveling case. I think of the Glières chaplain and of the German one who felt it was such a sad thing for my family; of the Guatemala Indians, the queen of the Casamance, the wall against which I was to be shot, the bathroom at Toulouse, Elephanta and the tanks of 1940, Mao's trees whose bark had been eaten by the peasants, the American fleet off Danang. Just as Asia rediscovered after thirty years communed with the Asia of yesterday, all my surviving memories commune with one another—but perhaps all that I retain of my life are its dialogues. But in this polar night, above the last primordial waters similar to those of India, on which an infant god as yet invisible lies cradled, the dialogue which seems to me the most agonizing of all is one I know only through having heard it. It is not directly linked with my life—although . . . If it comes back to me now as the secret arbiter of so much remembrance in this long night, it is surely because the dialogue of the human animal with torture is more profound than that of man with death.

A December night in Paris, frozen stars above a fretwork of Daumier chimneys. At the tip of the île, in the place where the morgue once was, the Crypt of the Deportees, with its portcullis of black blades, its two hundred thousand symbols representing the two hundred thousand missing, its earth from the camps and ashes from the crematoria, and its unknown corpse. In the little garden over which the shadowy bulk of Notre Dame towers in vain (tonight, death is below ground), the delegations of survivors surround the tank which is about to bear the ashes of Jean Moulin* to the Panthéon. The electric light will only be switched on again when the tank has left, escorted by five thousand young torch bearers sent by Resistance organizations. The eye grows accustomed to the lunar haze: old comrades recognize one another. The ashes are brought in a child's coffin. The tank's engine starts up, and the delegations fall in behind it. The torches are lit. The flames of torches manufactured today have the bluish quivering dazzle of acetylene lamps; feet still drag along in darkness, below heads which are brightly illuminated. Those who have just recognized one another, so like what they remembered in the moonlight (the torch bearers are their sons), discover that they nearly all have white hair.

Mounted guards precede the tank, which rumbles off at a dead slow pace. Many of the men following it cannot walk any faster. All lights are extinguished as it goes by. The torches, which now light up only the young faces, frame the blurred, silent mass of marchers. I think of Michelet's account of the duel between Jarnac and La Châtaigneraie— Henri II discovering the survivors of Pavia and Agnadello with their Louis XII clothes and white beards on horses that have been lame since Italy. The torches are reflected in the Baudelairean Seine, and between the cafés of the Boulevard St. Michel, whose lights go out one by one, the tank draws along behind it its train of shadows.

I make my way to the Panthéon, to see that the alterations have been completed. From the bottom of the Rue Soufflot comes a sound I remember from my childhood: the trampling of horses, which the mounted guards are keeping at walking pace. Only the streaks of moonlight on the upright sabers can be seen, then the flames of the torches which at this distance no longer illuminate the bearers' faces.

The noise of the tank, which has just left the boulevard, drowns the clatter of the horses' hooves.

The little coffin is carried on to the catafalque. General Koenig takes the first watch. People disperse; in a corner of the emptying square, a pyre of torches which have now served their purpose will soon be consumed.

The following morning, as I pronounce the funeral oration, the icy wind blows my notes against the microphone with a sound as of breaking surf.

* Most famous of all French Resistance leaders, parachuted into France in 1942 to coordinate the underground movements under Gaullist leadership. Betrayed, arrested, and tortured in June 1943, he died on the train in which he was being transferred to Germany. (Tr.)

To right and left, but in the background, are the flag bearers and the Companions of the Liberation; in front, at the foot of the two palaces, the representatives of the state. General de Gaulle, in the long great-coat which I have only seen him wearing in photographs of the landing, has remained on his feet, and no one is seated. In the Rue Soufflot, the crowd. Gossec's *Marche lugubre* comes echoing down from the dome with the solemn throb of its war drums. The wind whistles in the microphone, and raises little whirlwinds of frozen dust on the pavement stones. There is something dreamlike about this solemn, windswept square, with that music from beyond the grave, the emptiness, the uniforms in the distance; behind me, the massive pillars of the Panthéon, and everywhere an attentiveness as urgent and alive as a presence in the night. For most of the men listening in the invisible Rue Soufflot, I am speaking of their own dead. And of mine:

"*It was the time when, in the depths of the countryside, we strained our ears at the barking of a dog in the night; the time when the multi-colored parachutes laden with arms and cigarettes dropped from the sky in the glow of the signal flares in the glades and on the heaths; the time when the cellars resounded with the despairing screams which tortured men utter with the voices of children . . .*

"*The great battle of the darkness had begun.*

"*And then that day at Fort Montluc in Lyons, when the Gestapo interrogator, after having had him tortured, handed him something to write with because he could no longer speak, and Jean Moulin drew a caricature of his torturer. For the terrible sequel, we need only listen to the words of his sister, so poignantly simple: 'His mission is over, his calvary begins. Jeered at, savagely beaten, his head covered with blood, his organs shattered, he reaches the limits of human suffering without ever betraying a single secret, he who knew them all.'*

"*But behold now the victory of that silence which was so terribly rewarded: the scales of destiny swing over. Resistance leader tortured in foul cellars, look with your vanished eyes on all these black-clad women who watch over our companions: they are in mourning for France, and for you! See the men of the maquis steal through the scrub oak of Quercy with a flag of knotted muslin, invulnerable to the Gestapo who believe only in tall trees!*

"*See the prisoner entering a luxury villa and wondering why he is given a bathroom—he has not yet heard tell of the bath torture.*"

Despite the loudspeakers, the remoteness of the crowd forces me into a vociferous chant.

"*Poor tortured king of the shades, see your shadowy people rising in the June night spangled with tortures. Listen to the roar of the German*

tanks moving up toward Normandy amid the long drawn-out complaints of the awakened cattle: thanks to you, those tanks will not arrive in time. And when the Allied breakthrough begins, look, Prefect,
as the commissaries of the Republic spring up in every town in France
—unless they have been killed! You envied, as we did, the epic rabble
of Leclerc: look, fighter, at your own rabble crawling out of their oak
maquis and with their peasant hands trained in the use of bazookas
hold up one of the foremost armored divisions of the Hitlerian empire,
the Das Reich division!

"As Leclerc entered the Invalides with his retinue of glory glittering
from the sun of Africa and the Battles of Alsace, enter here, Jean
Moulin, with your fearful retinue. With those, like you, who died in
the cellars without having talked; and even, what is perhaps more
agonizing still, with those who died after having talked; with all those
in prison stripes and shaved heads from the extermination camps, with
the last stumbling body of the dreadful files of Nacht und Nebel who
fell at last under the rifle butts; with the eight thousand Frenchwomen
who did not come back from the labor camps, with the last woman
who died in Ravensbrück for having sheltered one of our men! Enter
with the race that was born in shadow and disappeared with the
shadow—our brothers in the Order of the Night."

The band strikes up the Song of the Partisans. How many times have
I heard it hummed softly on nights of parachute drops as cold as today;
and one day aloud, in the mist of the Alsace woods where it mingled
with the faint bleating of the sheep of the Moroccan cavalry.

"It is the funeral march of the ashes which you see before you. By
the side of those of Carnot with the soldiers of the Year II, those of
Victor Hugo with the Misérables, those of Jaurès watched over by the
spirit of Justice, may they lie here at rest with their long retinue of
disfigured shades."

The soldiers prepare to march past. Everything seems suspended;
there is no applause after a funeral oration. The Song of the Partisans
rises in plaintive waves, a lullaby for all the war dead. The body is
borne into the nave, where General de Gaulle goes to greet Jean
Moulin's family. Behind a theater curtain, the band of the guard is
still playing. There is no amplifying system inside the Panthéon, and
this real music sounds like the fragile and meditative echo of the vast
lament which fills the frozen streets through the loudspeakers. (I had
come here in 1933; in the middle of the Roman nave, a solitary little
girl was playing with a red balloon.) The body is taken down into the
crypt. I go up again with Laure Moulin. The musicians have departed;

from the monumental doorway open to the square comes the tramp of the last troops marching off. I say to Mlle. Moulin, "The General told me, 'For the record, you should see his sister: she resembles him.'" She understands what he means, for their features are not alike. She answers, "When he died, he was forty-five years old; and I'm seventy-two." (She hardly looks sixty.) The square is not yet open to the public: the diplomatic corps leaves; there remain the men with the old flags, the men of the liberation, of the maquis, the survivors of the camps—here in the icy daylight, those who recognized each other in the darkness.

This daylight is death. Not the death of torture or war: the death that has need of nothing. Ten million Frenchmen have followed the ceremony on television. But the television did not show that all these flag bearers are old men; that there is not a young man left in the square. In order that they may recognize one another, the daylight must fade.

I said in the course of my funeral oration:

"With Jean Moulin, the prehistory of the Resistance had come to an end."

At the beginning of 1944, after the Germans had laid hands on one of our parachute drops, I had inspected the hiding places of all our maquis for the first time. Some of them contained the arms which were intended for the volunteers who would join us when the landing was announced. There are numerous caves in Périgord, and we climbed the iron ladders placed there for prewar tourists to locate our hidden weapons in a honeycomb of cavities like the boxes of a Magdalenian theater. But the biggest cave, at Montignac, was underground, and the cache a long way from the entrance. We carried powerful flashlights, for night had fallen, and anyone who got lost there was a dead man. The passage became so narrow that soon we could only advance sideways. There was a right-angled turn, and on the rock which seemed to bar our way a vast drawing appeared. I took it for a guide mark made by one of our guides, and shone my torch on it. It was a frieze of superimposed bison.

At Font-de-Gaume, the prehistoric paintings were blurred. These bison, on the contrary, were stamped in the rock like seals, their sharpness all the more remarkable for the fact that the walls were great smooth stones, now rounded, now hollowed out, not like rocks but like physiologic organs. These petrified entrails through which one had to worm one's way, for the rock fault did not form chambers, seemed like the bowels of the earth. The bison, if not now a guide mark, had perhaps been one some twenty thousand years earlier. All subterranean caverns arouse disquiet, since a sudden cave-in could bury one alive there. Not death, but entombment; and the bison gave this tomb a mysterious soul, as if they had risen up from the ageless earth to guide us. Over our heads, perhaps, German patrols were prowling; we were advancing toward our weapons; and the bison had been prancing on the stone for two hundred centuries. The crevice widened out and ramified. Our flashlights did not illuminate these chasms: their beams guided us through them as a blind man is guided by his stick. We could no longer distinguish the rock except by the gleaming fragments of the walls which surrounded us. In each cleft, one's light would pick out another cleft—reaching down into the heart of the earth. This darkness had nothing to do with the night; it belonged to chasms as enclosed as the sky is open, succeeding one another endlessly, and ever more disquietingly because they appeared to have been consciously fashioned. My companions had ceased to talk except in whispers. Then a passage so narrow as to be encompassed by the halves of our lights, and in which we had to stoop, led to a crevasse about a hundred feet long and thirty feet wide. The guides stopped, and all the beams converged. On red and blue parachutes spread out on the ground lay container after container. Suggestive of two animals of some future era, a pair of machine guns on their tripods, like Egyptian cats on their forepaws, kept watch over them. On the roof, clearly visible this time, immense horned animals.

This place had undoubtedly been sacred, and still was, not only because of the spirit of the caverns but also because an inexplicable bond united these bison, these bulls, these horses (others receded beyond the circle of light) and these containers which seemed to have come here of their own accord, and which were guarded by these machine guns pointing at us. On the vaults, covered in a kind of saltpeter, ran somber and magnificent beasts, carried along by the movement of our beams of light like a flight of heraldic emblems. The man next to me lifted the lid of a container full of ammunition, and the light which he put down cast an enormous shadow on the roof. Doubtless the shadows of the bison hunters cast by the flame of their resin torches had been the shadows of giants long ago.

We went down by a knotted rope into a fairly shallow pit, on the wall of which was an elementary human form with a bird's head. A pile of bazookas fell over with a weird clang which faded into the shadows, and the silence returned more desolate and more menacing than before.

As we went back, the rock here and there suggested limbless animals, as old walls suggest human figures. And we emerged to find the little trees on the hillside white with frost, the River Vézère, the wartime darkness over the dim hump of Montignac, the stars, the transparency of the terrestrial darkness.

"Are you interested in the paintings?" asked the guide. "Some kids found them when they went in there to rescue a puppy in September 1940. It's very very old. Some scientists came, but then, in 1940, you can imagine!"

It was Lascaux.

Troops, officials, police have all gone.

I remember that electric light glowing in the center of the earth, that primordial flight above the two machine guns like dogs at point, and a real dog howling on the banks of the Vézère. Was it on emerging from such a place as that, beneath a similar sky, that a kind of gorilla who hunted like a wild beast and painted like a man understood for the first time that he would have to die?

In the Place du Panthéon life has resumed its ambling course, free of battles and of funerals. "Jeered at, savagely beaten, his organs shattered . . ." During this funeral ceremony which would undoubtedly not have been the same if Jean Moulin had died, not a martyr, but a minister or a marshal, the shadow that looms over the shadow of death passed slowly over the Panthéon—eternal Evil, which all the religions have confronted in their turn, and which this child's coffin confronted with its invisible guard of ghosts who had fallen in the Baltic night, with these survivors who had only recognized each other before they saw each other clearly, and who would perhaps never see each other again.

Passing the church of Saint Séverin, I remember Bernanos and those heavy eyelids of his, the day I said to him, "With the camps, Satan visibly reappeared on earth."

I have not been back to Saint Séverin since his funeral. The church was full, but there were no writers there, I believe. It was a day in March, with the lowering, tattered clouds that are a feature of the finest scenes of his novels, and sudden bursts of sunshine. Some days earlier, at the American Hospital, he had said to me, "Now it's for Him to decide what He wants me to do." He was referring to a Life of Christ which he thought he would have to write if he survived; his recovery would be the sign. The Abbé Pezeril had reached the point in his funeral oration where he recalled that, when he was administering the last sacraments, Bernanos had said to him gently, referring without any doubt to God, "And now it's between us two."

At that moment the sun had come out, and a ray as straight as an arrow had alighted on the coffin.

I am on my way to join the committee formed to erect a monument to Jean Moulin. It is made up of delegates from the Resistance organizations, the deportees, and the survivors of the extermination camps.

For twenty years I have been thinking about the camps. Horror and torture filtered into nearly all my books, at a time when as yet only penal settlements were known. My experience is almost valueless, although I have not forgotten the curly haired little Gestapo man, or the torture victims glimpsed through the open doors in Toulouse, or the woman with the spoonful of tea. And in any case it is not a question of experience, but of the sole dialogue that is more profound than that of man with death.

Like all the writers of my generation, I had been struck by the passage in The Brothers Karamazov where Ivan says, "If the divine will implies the torture of an innocent child by a brute, I'm handing back my ticket." I had lent Karamazov to the chaplain of Glières, and he had written to me on returning the book, "It's first rate, but it's the eternal problem of evil; and for me evil is not a problem, it's a mystery."

Dostoevsky, Cervantes, Defoe, Villon—the men of the penal settlements, the pillory, or the jail. As I descend from the Panthéon toward the Seine—for the committee is meeting in the Crypt of the Deportees —I think of the garden in the Crimea where Gorki told me, "I asked a komsomol member, in about 1925, what he thought of Crime and Punishment, and he answered, 'What a lot of fuss about one old woman!' "

Did that komsomol die in a Russian labor camp, in a German concentration camp? Has he, at least, learned something since then? There was an invincible hope in Dostoevsky which emerges only in fits and starts in his books. Meyerhold once showed me, after the old quarter of Crime and Punishment in St. Petersburg (endless iron staircases losing themselves among the haunted shadows of the canals), the writer's adolescent home in Moscow, where his father was a doctor at the military college. On the wall of the study, in a plush frame, there was an enormous enlargement of a discolored photograph. I knew those shoulders bowed by every form of misery, that death's head trimmed with a straggly beard, but they haunted the desolate half-light as if the discoloration of the bromide paper had re-created the past in a more convincing manner than any costume. It was in truth the image stolen from the living which was once such a source of terror to the Asians, stuck on the wall of the room with its sorrowful gaze and gray complexion. But it was also a resurrection, this life-size image, all the more striking in that it manifestly belonged to death, in that it embodied that Lazarus whose mantle Dostoevsky had long ago assumed, not in order to console the murderers and the prostitutes but to shake the pillars which uphold the riddle of the world: beyond even the adjurations of love, the shadows of the irremediable and of human suffering, the supreme riddle of "What am I doing on this earth where sorrow reigns?" The most profoundly urgent questioning since Shakespeare's gasped out its tragic message in this concierge's lodge. The caretaker took a book from the desk and handed it to us: "It is the Bible he brought back from prison," she said. It was covered with annotations: the word *Niet* again and again. To foretell the future, the Russians used to open the Bible when they woke up: the first paragraph on the left-hand page foretold what was to happen. And so, always in the same handwriting, opposite some such passage as "*Mary Magdalene saw that the stone had been taken away from the sepulcher*," after weeks or days the prisoner had sadly written "No."

As I leave Rue St. Jacques, I remember that portrait between the windows framing the barrackyard with its bleak paving-stones, the somnolent sweeper in the fog, that communist lady with the black shawl of old Russia over her white hair, waiting for Meyerhold to give her back the book. I think of you now, Dostoevsky, with your buffoons drunk with alcohol and brotherhood in the St. Petersburg evening, your saints and your madmen, your tedious political theories and your prophetic soul. I think of you now, freed from your translations of Balzac and your Dickensian novels by the revelation of the gallows. I do not yet know that in ten years' time I shall find myself facing a mock execution, and that perhaps one no more believes in fictitious gallows than in rifles aimed at one. I think of you, now, Orthodox and Tsarist, with all that makes your characters fling themselves with arms outstretched into the mud of public confessions—but also with the terrible silence of your discolored face on which night is falling, your lips which need not speak for us to hear those words that have haunted our century; the only reply, since the Sermon on the Mount, to the holy barbarism of the Book of Job: "If the order of the universe must be paid for with the torture of one innocent child . . ."

You did not invent the mystery of evil, although you gave it its most poignant expression. It is not your anguish, prophet, which fills this shabby room, even if it is the anguish of our time: for all life becomes mystery when it is questioned by pain. It is the voice of Lazarus, against whom neither misery nor death prevails; the indomitable reply of Antigone or Joan of Arc before the tribunals of the earth: "I was not born to partake of hatred, but to partake of love"; it is the eternity which the psalmist sang, and which Shakespeare rediscovers two thousand years later beneath the enchanted stars of Venice: "In such a night . . ."—the lovers who sense the resurrection of vanished lovers in the perfumed night, and the cries rising from the prison camps as they did toward the Assyrian constellations. I think of the German rifles pointing toward me. It was on such a day as this, Dostoevsky, that you stepped on to that gallows which resembled a goalpost, of which I was once shown a clumsy drawing.

That gibbet reminds me of the one at Nuremberg. The rope was put round the prisoners' necks as they stood on tiptoe, so that exhaustion would force them to kill themselves. I saw that framework of tubing, without ropes and without corpses, in the deserted camp; it was like one of those metal scaffoldings which firemen use in their exercises.

I have read everything there is to be read about the deportation, in particular the accounts written by survivors of the camps where my brothers died. I have questioned all my friends who were saved. Oral accounts are more sketchy than written ones, but they have that density of truth which our interminable chronicle of the inhuman does not always have. What are the memories which blend in my mind? First of all, the *Song of the Partisans*:

> Ami, entends-tu
> Le vol noir—des corbeaux—sur nos plaines . . .
> Ami, entends-tu
> Les cris sourds—du pays—qu'on enchaine . . .*

* Friend, do you hear/The black flight—of the crows—on our plains . . ./Friend, do you hear/The faint cries—of the country—in chains . . .

perhaps because I have just been listening to the music; and the *Song of the Marshes*, bequeathed to us by the communists arrested in 1933:

> *Loin vers l'infini s'étendent*
> *Les grands prés marécageux*
> *Pas un seul oiseau ne chante*
> *Sur les arbres verts et vieux*
> *O terre de détresse*
> *Où nous devons sans cesse*
> *Pi-o-cher . . . ***

Sores, snow, hunger, lice, thirst; then thirst, hunger, lice, snow, sicknesses, and sores. And corpses: "You can choose between grave-digging fatigue or ash disposal at the crematorium." The hallucinations which caused the murderous truncheons of the kapos to be taken for bars of chocolate; the perpetual sucking on a little piece of wood; the sensation that one's body was nothing but an aching lump of hunger; the thirst which after four days and nights in the death trains drove the unfortunates to the latrine buckets; and above all, the organized degradation. Hunger was the deportees' daily companion right up to the verge of death, with obsessive competitions for imaginary feasts which made the competitors laugh with a tightening of the heart-strings ("Anyway I don't care, there's nothing better than a good glass of *rouge* with steak and chips") and ended in altercations and blows. Edmond Michelet told me of the ravings of a dying priest in the Dachau famine: "Give my sugared almonds and caramels to so-and-so, my condensed milk to . . ." He had never had any sugared almonds, or caramels, or condensed milk, and Michelet did not know any of the intended recipients. The priest, who did not die, said later, "They were the names of my old classmates . . ." Sexual imaginings and desire had long disappeared, to leave room exclusively for the two most common-place furies.

There was the destruction of time, which gives slow-motion torture the semblance of the human condition itself; the body becoming the most insidious enemy, the terrible awakening which brought back all the novelty of misery day after day, the suppression of any sign of

---

* Far into the distant stretch/The great swampy meadows/Not a single bird sings/On the green old trees/O land of distress/Where we unceasingly/Must dig . . .

individuality, the transformation of men into derelicts and the incessant blows in a world where death was the only consolation. And an occasional memory of a world in which woman had been desirable and man had had a heart, in which hatred had had the hope of one day being appeased—for the man deprived of all hope is beyond hatred.

The setting for hell, in the accounts I remember, is not the mine, the quarry, the camp: it is insanity. The main street was called Liberty Street, which was also the name given to the path of the clippers across the skull from the forehead to the nape of the neck. The houses of the Germans were surrounded by "trim little gardens," as the survivors put it, and one saw kittens playing in them amidst the screams of prisoners being beaten to death—just as one might see convent flowers in the middle of dormitories whose bunks swarmed with lice. There was the wildness of the blows dealt by the half-crazy German *political* detainees. It was a world in which the impossible was always possible, a nightmare in the strict sense of the word: a delirium in which the dreamer was imprisoned, an *organized* chaos in a world where "organizing" was the euphemism for filching from the enemy: the lumps of sugar stolen to give to the dying were "organized." There was the recovery of gold teeth and of shaved hair; there were the arbitrary departures (but the SS knew that separation weakened the prisoners); among the women, there was the German thief with the black triangle who washed the floor with the left-over coffee so as not to give it to her French fellow prisoners; the call for volunteers for Bordeaux, which the SS confused with *bordel*; the question "Can you play the piano?" put to the women prisoners sent to the earthworks; the walking skeletons, seven or eight at a time, pulling their ground roller, like something out of a Mesopotamian bas-relief. In the women's section and the men's, there were the loudspeakers which broadcast *Schön ist das Leben*; the stealers of spectacles—destined for whom?—and the curiously phosphorescent slices of sausage. There were the prisoners who tied their boots round their necks by the laces when they were going to sleep, and who were nearly strangled by the thieves. There were the medical certificates of fitness to be beaten. There were the women who told fortunes in exchange for bread, and those who did not weep under the most agonizing beatings, but wept when they lost at a clandestine card game. There were the bullies who, during air raids, asked those they had beaten to say a prayer for them too. There was the *Schwester* whom the women in labor were threatened with to make them keep quiet. There was that marvel of black humor—punishment for "laughing in the ranks"—and the enthusiasm, shared by the jovial warders, for boxing matches between prisoners still bloodstained from the beatings of the SS. There were the theatrical performances (*Romeo and Juliet* at Treblinka!) and the orchestras in prison stripes who played while the excavators tore bunches of half-dead prisoners out of the ditches and threw them on the pyre, which roared like a giant blowtorch.

There were the scenes which I noted down after listening to the accounts of the survivors. I notice that three of them were scenes involving oral discourse.

First of all, the quarantine compound.

The prisoners who are still idle watch the files of unfortunates in prison stripes, heads shaven, hobbling along on crutches; or the troops of skeletal convicts on their way back from the labor kommandos. Each of them tells his stories (not personal ones), which finally run out. There are picturesque professions: an animal tamer has a great success as he explains that small animals can only be tamed if you pretend to be afraid of them. People play at training a rabbit, while the SS on the other side of the barbed wire, to encourage them, bludgeon a prisoner with a spade. After ten days, silence sets in. Three of those whom the others affectionately call the Raving Intellectuals are lying on their crepuscular straw mattresses. One of them, beaten almost to the point of death during an interrogation in the Avenue Foch, is about to die, and his death-rattle blends with the Germanic yells from outside. Further on, those who know songs begin singing them. They are songs about home, or about sleep. Sung in chorus and in slow motion, *Le P'tit Quinquin* becomes an endless lullaby. Someone tells the story of *Macbeth*. Those who know poetry recite it. The Raving Intellectuals know a great deal. One of them, unseen, recites fragments of Péguy.

The thick smoke from the crematorium merges with the low clouds drifting across from the forest of Bavaria and the mountains of Bohemia. The French prisoners listen, astounded. The others sense the groundswell, and fall silent. A second Raving Intellectual takes up the Péguy ballad, declaiming passionately. This one can be seen: standing on something, in his underpants, tufts of hair over his ears, the figure of a terrifying mad clown:

> *Vous nous voyez marcher, nous sommes la piétaille.*
> *Nous n'avançons jamais que d'un pas à la fois.*
> *Mais vingt siècles de peuple et vingt siècles de rois,*
> *Et toute leur séquelle et toute leur volaille*

Et leurs chapeaux à plume avec leur valetaille
Ont appris ce que c'est que d'être familiers,
Et comme on peut marcher, les pieds dans les souliers,
Vers un dernier carré le soir d'une bataille . . .*

Outside, the shouting of orders has stopped, and the crowing of a cock is heard. A prisoner produces a piece of mirror, and they all want to look at themselves in it. What they call boredom is not so much enforced idleness as a continual foreboding: and now, what is going to become of us? Rumors—sprung up from whence?—run through the crowd from time to time like little animals.

Christmas Day, 1944. In the men's hospital, there is a sermon by a Resistance priest. Dysentery, typhus, tuberculosis, sores, limbs broken while working or beneath the blows of the kapos. A single thermometer, no more medicaments. Skeletons with shriveled skin showing through striped rags. An almost silent hell. Only the bizarre cries of hunger, or, when black-clad peasants pass by on the road outside the barbed wire, a man with a broken leg screaming: "You're free! FREE!" The lavatory pails are the lids of containers from captured parachute drops. This morning, the German doctor asked my neighbor, who was spitting blood as the result of beatings, "Are there any bad consumptives in your family?"

"It doesn't matter," says the priest, whose clothes are falling to pieces because they gave him rags instead of the striped prisoner's uniform. "It doesn't matter. Tonight, in France, families are reunited around their tables. Our empty places are there. And on earth there is an immense family, the family of the camps: those who have died, those who are going to die, those who will see the liberation."

He recites the Gospel of the Nativity, adding the shepherds of Luke to the magi of Matthew, and the donkey and the ox to the sacred text: the gospel of the childhood of the men listening . . .

"And thus He came into this world, to be condemned to death so that we should not die alone.

* You see us march, we are the footsloggers./We never take more than one step at a time./But twenty centuries of the people and twenty centuries of kings,/And all their hangers-on and all their hens
And feathered hats and flunkeys/Have taught us what it is to be too familiar,/And how a man can march, his feet in his boots,/Towards a last billet, the night before a battle . . .

"They made him carry the cross. Somewhere, believe me, he is making a great cross out of what we are bearing.

"He fell for the first time, as you know.

"A man named Simon helped him carry his cross; we have all met Simons. A pious woman wiped his face. They are not exactly legion, but when we were leaving the Gare de l'Est at the beginning of May, the women selling lilies of the valley brought us some, and people immediately bought the rest . . .

"He fell for the second time, as we know. He consoled the women of Jerusalem who were following him; at Fresnes, and here, many have taken great risks to comfort new arrivals through the walls. May God grant each one of us grace to comfort his fellow.

"He fell for the third time. He was stripped of his clothing. They nailed him to the Cross and he died there.

"He was taken down and laid in his mother's arms; it is a great mercy that our mothers have nothing to do with this place."

Not always: in some camps, there are often both mothers and daughters, when they have been arrested together.

"They laid him in the sepulcher."

Opposite, a second crematorium is being built.

"A bicycle! If I only had a bicycle!" screams the man whose leg has been cut off.

A skeletal patient gets up screaming: his bed fellow has just died, and the lice are emigrating onto him.

"It is the Stations of the Cross. When we left, the German chaplain at Fresnes (he was a good man) said to me, 'The important thing is never to despair, and never to doubt God . . . And over there it will be difficult, perhaps . . .'

"Yes, it's difficult. But later, we will understand. That is why we must accept death as if we understood. Make it welcome.

"When I was a boy, we used to sing a carol which . . . It is God who sings."

His voice, which had become lower, rises again to sing, to a tune reminiscent of *There Was a Little Ship*:

I have a little journey to make

The little journey is the Incarnation, it seems.

There are those who feel that no one has made all that much fuss about them. And those who remain silent.

"For Christmas, the crematorium really ought to take a day off," a voice says.

Ravensbrück. The women prisoners have been assembled in front of the commandant, a white-haired figure who is like an actor playing the part of an SS officer. There is a microphone plugged into the loudspeaker. The prisoners translate:

"In letting you live, the Great Reich has shown unprecedented restraint. You antisocials are a leprosy on the body of Germany. You politicals have been responsible for the cowardly murder of German soldiers. You have been allowed to live. It is a pity. But I submit to it. You must do the same. Those who try to resist the discipline of this camp will come to me on their knees, I tell you, to ask for it to be enforced on them. SS discipline is a steamroller, and nothing grows again where it has been. Dismissed!"

The women immediately christen him Attilaminoir.*

Next, for the Frenchwomen only—this second puppet show is probably addressed to each category of prisoners separately—an SS man without stripes. He is not wearing the death's-head cap, but is bareheaded: the shaved skull, thick neck and watchful Great Dane's face of Eric von Stroheim. He stands with his legs wide apart, swaying backward and forward. The translator is an Alsatian girl who cannot weigh more than ninety pounds.

"Bunch of whores! You were dolled up and painted, you wanted to be taken for women! You talked against Germany. As the commandant said, you treacherously tried to murder us. What are you? Look at yourselves—just shit. The pretending is over. The only way you leave here will be up the chimney. Get ready for a shock! Jew-riddled, all of you! Up the chimney!"

He is swaying more and more. Will he fall? He is at an extreme stage of drunkenness, which is intensified by his harangue:

"Over with the pretenses! Up the chimney! First of all, you're too fat! Your bones should hurt when they touch the bed! Eat clover, it's good for the health!"

The Alsatian translates; her expressionless voice is addressed to no one:

"He says that we are dirt and we will only leave here when we are dead."

* Compound of Attila, the Hun, and laminoir, roller. (Tr.)

Legs still wide apart, but not looking as if he will fall, he goes up to the first row of prisoners. The others can no longer see him. But they can hear him.

"Ach! my pretty French cows, I'll teach you to be beautiful!"

Translation. He walks away, framed between two SS women. From behind, his drunkenness is more obvious. It is not the drunkenness of the music hall but the slow and menacing Nordic drunkenness. Not a tippler, a maniac. He steadies himself with his hands on a shoulder of each of the SS women, wheels them round and turns to face the prisoners:

"The first woman who moves goes straight into the madwomen's cell."

A pause.

"Into the dirt and up the chimney! I'll teach you to be beautiful!"

No translation. He walks off, now slightly atilt, but nevertheless as stiff as if he were wearing a corset, leaning on the two shoulders, like an ignoble King Lear supported by his two hateful daughters. The parade ground is of an exemplary cleanliness. One of the prisoners is seized with a fit of the giggles; the others, exasperated but loyal, close up around her. He does not turn round again and walks heavily away under the smoke of the crematorium.

The female camp commandant rides her bicycle alongside a column of prisoners on their way to work. She gets off, walks up to a prisoner and slaps her face, perhaps for being out of line. The latter, leader of a Resistance network and aware of the consequences of what she is about to do, slaps the SS woman back with all her strength. The whole column gasps. SS men and women lash out wildly with their whips. They set the dogs on the prisoner, but her blood is trickling over her feet, and instead of biting her the dogs lick it up, as in the Christian legends. The SS, not so sentimental, drive the dogs away and beat her to death. The tears flow silently down the cheeks of the prisoners standing there at attention.

When I wrote all that down some years ago, I also made notes about the women prisoners sitting on the dead bodies of their companions in the snow; the women for whom the old life stopped at ten thirty by the clock at Fresnes; the wordless sound ("talking verboten") of kisses that filled the main hall on the occasion of a mass departure; the obsession with dancing; the nocturnal arrival in the darkness pierced

with the luminous pinpricks of the torches of the SS; the walls vibrating
with the throes of fever. And I thought of Pasternak at the time when
he came to recite his poems in Russian before the subdued students in
the Salle de la Mutualité, of the singers in our barrack-rooms and in the
prisoner-of-war camp in 1940, of the frescoes of the Guiana convicts
and the man "who was such a good announcer" at the prefect's reception; of Thalie, inspired, answering Mayrena beneath the friendly lizards
on the ceiling: "I want to know nothing, neither if the fields are in
bloom—nor what will become of the human spectacle . . ."; of Ehren-
burg, superintendent of circus animals under the supreme direction of
Meyerhold, and quite crushed because the spectators were filching his
rabbits' slices of carrot; of my Spanish republican priest: "And when
the last column of the poor began to march—an unknown star rose
above their heads . . ." But torture has existed for centuries—and even
people who have sung in chains. What had not existed before was this
organized brutalization.

Hell is not horror; hell is being degraded to the point of death,
whether death comes or passes by: the appalling abjection of the victim,
the mysterious abjection of the executioner. Satan is the Degrader. The
degradation of the camps lay above all in the combination of madness
and mockery: the recaptured prisoners to whom labels were attached
reading "Here I am again," the bread thieves who also wore labels, and
whom each convict had to slap after spitting in their faces (then a
kapo would beat them senseless). Even worse than the meeting of the
torture victims with Gestapo guards playing leapfrog: the mockery of
Christ. Conversions were rare, but nearly all the atheist prisoners took
part in the semisecret religious ceremonies, for as soon as the priest
spoke of the Passion he was speaking to them about themselves. The
perfection of the concentration camp system was no doubt reached at
Dachau, when the SS ordered the imprisoned German priests to expel
from the chapel all the foreign laymen who came to pray there. (In
front of this corrugated-iron chapel was the notice in Gothic lettering:
"Here, God is Adolf Hitler.")

Those who refused were shot, but there were always prisoners on
their knees around the chapel. The system whereby the political prisoners were subordinated to the common-law prisoners—thieves and
murderers, and among the women, prostitutes—has been carefully
studied. But the effects of the admixture, which changed considerably
during the course of the war, have not been so closely analyzed.
Triangles of material sewn on to the clothing designated the origins of
the prisoners: the Resistance worker had to have it brought home to

him that he was subject to an assassin or a pimp, and every German, whether guard or prisoner, had to be able to recognize the "terrorists." But many of those who wore the red triangle of the political prisoners were not Resistance fighters but peasants who had refused to inform, or young people who had scrawled the Cross of Lorraine on walls, or schoolteachers who had organized the singing of the *Marseillaise*, or hostages, or even, among the Poles and Russians, entire villages. Those who wore the black triangle of the "antisocials" were sometimes semi-lunatics, but often simply gypsies. And nothing could prevail against the astonishment all these men felt at the discovery that they were at once irreducibly different and irreducibly alike in the same shared homeland of misfortune. And then, heroes are not always heroes, and whores not always whores: there were some who became resisters. Killing all these unfortunates in the long run could have been achieved by other means; there was a more obscure purpose, which humanity had not previously thought of, for the aim of torture in the old days had been to extract confessions or to punish a religious or political heresy. The supreme objective was that the prisoners, in their own eyes, should lose their identity as human beings. Hence the spilling of the soup onto the ground so that some of the hungrier prisoners should come and lap it up; hence the cigarette butts thrown into the dogs' vomit, the shutting of prisoners in with madmen, and more insidiously atrocious, the "experiments" and sterilizations. (With an excruciating pity, the other prisoners called the girls destined for the experiments "the little rabbits.") The ideal was to bring the resisters to hang themselves or throw themselves on to the electrified barbed wire. But then the SS felt cheated.

The demoniacal efficiency of it all was blunted by the fact that the worst tortures or the most abject degradation were not reserved for Resistance prisoners but for those who retaliated against the blows of the guards, who were often Polish peasants, men or women, deported when half their village had taken to the maquis. For years, a dour struggle went on, in which the first victim was death. Death reigned physically and constantly through the clinging smoke of the crematoria; yet the furious determination to survive which animated most of the resisters was not primarily concentrated against it. They had grasped that in every man there is something more profound. "The ability to accept it," the priest who preached at Christmas would have said; this was only true for those who welcomed it as God's will. The battle was not being fought on that ground. It consisted, for the prisoners, of putting up with what was imposed on them as they would have put up with cancer, but never participating in it. "I don't care," in the sense of "it does not concern me, it did not happen," was probably the prisoners' most constant thought. "The slap in the face takes the form of the man who receives it, not the one who gives it," Alain used to say, thinking of Christ. One had to survive at all costs. Live for the moment. Never give anything away in face of torments, in face of horror, in face of a kapo's treacherous smile. Sabotage them. Don't lap up spilt soup. Death was one element among others. Those who were liberated say that the will to survive is perhaps man's most powerful passion, but the only ones who did survive were "those who refused to let themselves go." In this world which was crazed both because of what it owed to deliberate organization and because of what it owed to chance, an absurdity as intense as that of the camp itself *protected* the victims: the absurdity of their persecutors. Each hideous day legitimized the Resistance. The priest had joined a network when he had heard of the existence of camps where the SS only allowed the prisoners to go around on all fours.

Probably the most profound conflict was played out between two forms of sacrilege. Between the corpses and the refuse, there was little room for the spirit. Hitler had organized his barbarity as all states have organized their penal settlements, but no state would have promulgated the slogan on which the camps were based: "Treat men like dirt, and they will really become dirt." This was the treatment that was to be meted out to the men who by their behavior or their mere existence denied the Nazi idol. And the SS guards, like the German thieves or murderers, unremittingly avenged the idol, with a sacrilege which nothing could expiate.

Yet even among the dying there remained enough humanity to divine that the will to live was not animal, but obscurely sacred. The mystery of the human condition manifested itself there, far more than in the cosmic groundswell which sooner or later would sweep tortured and torturers alike to their deaths; the abjection of the prisoners who informed on their fellows was of a piece with that of the SS flogger who had been told by a prisoner that the translation of *Schnell* (quick) was "take it easy," and who bludgeoned the prisoners mercilessly while yelling at them to go slowly. The wretched ghosts who called themselves "walking trunks," because they kept their heads drawn in between their shoulders against the perpetual blows, had not lost their contempt —in other words the profound but vague idea of man for which they had fought, and which now became clear: man was what "they" were trying to take from them.

The human condition is the condition of creaturehood, which dictates man's destiny as mortal illness dictates the destiny of the individual. To destroy this condition is to destroy life—to kill. But the extermination camps, in endeavoring to turn man into a beast, intimated that it is not life alone which makes him man.

When I arrive at the meeting of the committee, after passing through the walls of the Crypt of the Deportees, then the grilled doorway reminiscent of barbed wire and butcher's hooks, it is almost over. Leaders of Resistance or deportees' associations, Edmond Michelet, a few women and a few soldiers, a Dominican. They summarize for me what I already know and what I do not yet know:

A monument is to be erected to the memory of Jean Moulin, near the spot where he was parachuted. At the expense of three ministries, the Bouches-du-Rhône and the local municipality: a lot of people, a lot of antagonisms. A captain who was arrested by the Gestapo as a member of the Resistance and who concealed his rank in order to stay with his comrades is carrying on a bitter argument with the Dominican, who is the priest who preached the Christmas sermon at Dachau. The word emaciated would be sufficient to describe him, were it not that it is usually applied to long faces, whereas his round face with its dark eyes looks like a death's head on which there flickers a smile of spirituality. The others are trying to calm them. I think, alas! of the dinner table of the *Prix des Vikings* at which Fernand Fleuret prophetically told two members of the jury who were getting to grips with one another during the hors d'oeuvres: "Have a little patience! Why yell at each other when you know very well that when you're even drunker you'll be falling on each other's necks." Here it is not a question of drunkenness. The Father has suggested that we should decide to erect the more or less abstract monument favored by Mlle. Moulin; the captain is demanding a competition. He does not know that the official jury will choose according to their friends, since great artists do not waste their time on competitions. But the Father, who at first had been thinking only of Jean Moulin's memory, is beginning to get angry. He knows all about competitions. A specialist in Romanesque art, he also knows the profound incompatibility between the portrait and modern art, especially when it comes to a "heroic" monument. He does not want a tin soldier. The other members of the committee simply want a monument. The two adversaries hurl government pledges and garbled texts at one another.

I think of the captain in prison stripes. At Stuttgart, the day when General de Lattre invited Rommel's son to dine with us—the Field-marshal had committed suicide—a French general in civilian clothes whom we had liberated said to me superciliously: "Of course they didn't put us in with the people in stripes." Slaps soon fade, and one man can only shrug two shoulders.

I think, too, of the Father in prison stripes: "I have a little journey to make." He is wearing the white robe of the Dominicans, on which the rosary has taken the place of the sword for so many years, and is smoking a short pipe. He would like to see the monument entrusted to Alberto Giacometti. I have met him on similar committees, and remember hearing him say, "If Christians put into their lives the virtues that Cézanne and others put into their art, God would be well content." I think especially of Jean Moulin as he crossed out the "s" of MOULINS on the document which one of his torturers handed him. I find it difficult to imagine a monument to the deportation, because I remember all too well the execution post exhibited at the Invalides: a plain stump squared off at the base, which the bullets of the firing squad had transformed into a shapeless sculpture up to the height of the victims' stomachs.

The discussion continues. Dachau, Ravensbrück, Auschwitz. I get up to take a pill: the mineral water is on another table. It is always odd to watch a gathering which one formed part of a few minutes earlier. I feel it every week at Cabinet meetings. Sitting down, I see all my companions around the table at my own height; standing, and removed from them, I see a group carrying on its discussions as if it existed autonomously and will never come to an end. "A competition is fair; a commission is arbitrary!" No doubt I should have made the ceiling of the Opéra the subject of a competition, instead of entrusting it to Chagall. "Rise, Lazarus!" In place of the great sinister mockery which death brings in its train comes the everyday mockery of life. Neither the voice which silenced the hell of Dachau nor that which volunteered to accompany comrades into hell can silence touchiness. "My dear chap," says the captain, "you would have done better to stay in your monastery." The Father replies sadly, "In spite of everything we went through, I thank God for having made us lay aside our uniforms for a time, you and I."

We sign the minutes. The captain has put on record "the wish of all the friends of Jean Moulin to rediscover his likeness" in the monument erected to his memory. Will he get his tin soldier? Why am I struck by this unexpected absurdity? Because a puerile bone of contention sets men against each other who should be joined in fraternity? They have never claimed to be heroes or saints. What distresses me is to see Lazarus risen from the dead to argue angrily about the design of tombs.

Did I ever believe that the most terrible ordeal guaranteed the most solemn wisdom? In 1936, in the company of Marcel Arland, I met Arthur Koestler, freed from the Francoist prison cell where he had spent months under sentence of death. "It's always the same," Arland said to me after we left him. "One imagines they must be the bearers of a sort of revelation, and then they talk as if nothing had happened to them." I remember, too, a wartime companion of my father who came to visit him in 1920. He was accompanied by his wife, and tea time was the occasion for a continuous smoldering domestic wrangle. "And yet," my father told me after he had seen him off, "he is a fine man and a brave one—one of the bravest officers I have known." And courage was not rare in the tanks in 1918. I remember seeing one of my uncles, an NCO in the flame throwers who on returning home had married a woman who had been waiting for him for twenty years, deeply happy, every week, sipping his Sunday aperitif. Heroic fighters stripped of what they had once been at the same time as of their uniforms, commando leaders transformed into grocers or publicans, were common in the aftermath of the First World War. Because courage had, as it were, been grafted on to them? Courage is worth no more and no less than the man—provided one does not forget what it brings to him; sacrifice is never contemptible. All those men had been stripped not only of the experience which death had brought them, but of that which life had brought them too.

The comedy of the monument draws a net from the depths of my consciousness of whose contents I am only faintly aware. It is not the memory of misfortune or bravery which haunts me, it is the insidious power of life, capable of obliterating anything—except, perhaps, in the case of the deportees for whom the memory of the camp actualizes the Passion—when the body is no longer simply a vehicle for suffering. For these bourgeois ex-heroes, peace had made physical bravery superfluous, and brought about a dispersal of friendships, a return to wives and children, a substitution of social life for the irresponsibility of the soldier. Life had enveloped these survivors as the earth had enveloped the dead. Eighty per cent of the political deportees, male and female, died in the camps; almost all the others sooner or later gave evidence of an exemplary courage, if only a passive one. But it is not in terms of war that all this obsesses me. For several years, the shadow of Satan stretched literally, visibly, over the world, and even those upon whom it fell seem to have forgotten it. Is it that they can only live again to the extent that they forget? I had believed the experience of the extermination camps to be a deeper one than that of the threat of death. But extreme misfortune leaves a less visible scar than the most commonplace wound.

We are left on our own—Brigitte, who has been representing her camp and a Ravensbrück group (it was she who had had that fit of giggles after the drunken SS man's address); Edmond Michelet and a Spanish republican representing Dachau; the Dominican Father and myself.

How did they get back to life again? What did they bring back from the inferno? Many deportees, from all over Europe, have written about their experiences; their return to humanity is hardly ever mentioned. It is not easy for a diver to bring back from the deeps what he finds there without recognizing it.

And they say even less about it than they have written.

"For me," Brigitte says, "it was rotten, because I came back in May. I was the only deportee on my train. The others were STO's* and I don't know what else. The fellow at the Lutetia† started off by not believing a word I told him. And after that, when I went to draw my military pay as a deportee, the clerk told me I only had a right to the basic rate, 'since I had been lodged, fed, and clothed by the Germans.' I was a bit angry. Then, another cretin: I'm queuing up at the Crédit Lyonnais in the Place Victor Hugo, to change the first thousand franc notes. I suddenly feel faint. A charitable lady comes to my aid. I explain to her that it's nothing, that I'm just back from deportation. The lady insists that I should go first, and calls the assistant. They take me up to the front. An elegant person of about fifty protests. What right have I to go before him? They explain. 'She should have stayed in her camp.'

"I was freed more quickly from memories than from dreams. At night I would find myself back in the camp, and in the evening, under the

---

* French workers conscripted for forced labor in Germany under the *Service de Travail Obligatoire*. (Tr.)

† One of the officers to whom the deportees reported at the Hotel Lutetia.

chestnut trees on the Avenue Henri Martin, I was certain that I was going to wake up in Ravensbrück. I used to cry in my dreams, whereas I never did in the camp. And then, you know Nelly Sachs's poem:

> Leave us quietly to learn to live again . . .
> Do not yet show us a dog that bites . . .

"But all that was Paris. At the frontier, I was just horribly afraid."

"Of what?"

"Of what I was going to find, of what I had become. I don't know."

"When the first group was repatriated," Edmond Michelet says, "De Gaulle was waiting for the deportees on the station platform."

"He should have stayed there, as my idiot said."

"For us, people had made flags, and we passed under a hedge of whatever those things are."

"Because you came back much earlier than I did. In Ravensbrück, on July 14, 1944, we made costumes out of bits of paper, and managed to dress ourselves, one in blue, one in white, one in red. All the women hummed the *Marseillaise*. It was rather risky, and it seems odd to me today: it isn't like the camp."

"What *is* like the camp?" asks the Father.

"I can imagine much worse prisons than the one I had," I observe. "And as for torture, I never underwent it, but I witnessed it. But there was something more—the attempt to force human beings to despise themselves. That is what I call hell. We all know what existed elsewhere. I heard the famous international experts at Nuremberg and at the Masuy trial: 'Against timebombs left in cafés and what is commonly called terrorism, equally effective measures have been taken by every counterespionage service.' These high-flown terms obviously stand for torture. But you underwent something which never existed in Russia or Algeria or Italy, something which seems to me to have to do with the very nature of Nazism. It was aimed at making you lose your soul, in the sense in which one talks about 'losing one's reason.' (What does 'soul' mean?) It might be said that you came back to earth, as I did after they had pretended to execute me, or when I escaped from a tank trap. But what you are all suggesting without managing to express it fully—can it be expressed?—is something different. At Bône, when I came back from the other side (when my plane got caught in a cyclone), I was amazed to see women ironing clothes, and small animals trotting around, and most of all the huge red sign of a glovemaker. The earth was strange. In your case, it wasn't the earth that was strange, it

was men, the human feelings from which you had been cut off as completely as I was when my plane was spinning like a top in the cyclone.
I quite see how you found the earth again: the same way as I did, after
all, though more painfully. But I can't quite grasp how you rediscovered life."

"In the first place, my dear man," Edmond Michelet says, "don't
forget that everything was mixed up. Are we the pensioners of hell?
I'll never forget the German priests who were given the job of throwing
us out of church! But when we came back, what we felt to begin with
was that life was a bonus. First of all, we should have been dead; after
that, everything else was a jumble.

"Another thing. For me, who always plows into things like a clumsy
lout, the infernal, or metaphysical, absurdity—call it what you will—
was always mixed with a common-or-garden idiocy which diluted it,
surprising though it may seem: the idiocy of stupidly wiping out one's
labor force! We felt it every day, and everything else went with it."

For me, too, the patient tide of life had blurred everything, in the
same way as the Red Sea had washed away the plan of the city of
Sheba on the sands of the beach. What is left to me today of the land
of death? A jaded sense of surprise, which would not even stop me
from getting worked up in my turn over the monument. I have studied
the vanished civilizations, observed foreign civilizations, and even my
own, like the shades silently descending the staircase of the Cairo
Museum. Thus did the intellectuals of Altenburg study historical
barbarisms as particular civilizations. But the true barbarism is Dachau;
the true civilization is first of all the element in man which the camps
sought to destroy. The Christian can offer up his suffering, the ascetic
can deny it—on condition that he dies fairly quickly. Civilizations flutter like huge moths around this conflagration. In the cold, transparent
light behind the spiked bars of the windows, what counterbalances the
atrocious images of Dachau is a scene described to me by Czapski,
General Anders's aide-de-camp and one of the few survivors of the
Katyn massacre. In the Russian concentration camps of 1941, in the
depths of the forests, the Polish officers were allowed occasional visits
by their wives, and were left alone with them. Hunger destroys sensu-
ality. The women smeared their bodies with a thick belt of flour, which
the prisoners scraped off and which prevented them from starving to
death. The men, being taller, knelt down, and I have retained in my
mind's eye a picture of these motionless Valkyries in the shadow of the
cells that is as clearcut as the image of the black-clad women in the

cemetery in Corrèze. Had they been denounced, they would have been shot or beaten to death. For me, they blend with the striped populace of the snow and darkness into one and the same mystery; for if it is true that for a religious spirit the camps, like the torture of an innocent child by a brute, pose the supreme riddle, it is also true that for an agnostic spirit the same riddle springs up with the first act of compassion, heroism or love.

"For me," says Brigitte, "it's very jumbled too. First of all—I suppose it was the same for you, Michelet?—we didn't expect to survive. At the Lutetia the good doctor who X-rayed me told me, 'In any case, you'll all be done for inside ten years.' You couldn't accuse him of fobbing off his patients with evasions. We were in that period of extra time you were talking about just now, even in the most elementary sense. And then, I didn't feel so completely back home as all that, since every time I smelled the chestnut trees and the wet pavements of the Avenue Henri Martin I thought I was going to wake up in the camp, and pinched myself to make sure I wasn't dreaming. The passersby used to look quite sorry for me. What you are talking about took a bizarre form: I found people childish. Not the officials I came across when I got back: I simply thought *they* were a bunch of idiots. When I went home, everyone thought I was dead, because of the delay. My father had been silent for two months. All the same, I felt that my parents had turned into kids. Out of delicacy, they didn't talk to me about the camp; my father said little, in the early days, but his silence also seemed childish to me. Where was the reality? Before the war? In the camp? Now? It didn't last. One clear memory, I'm not sure why, was my rediscovery of men's cuff-links. Out there we had the feeling that if we had been men, we would at least have had the hope of rebelling."

"Not much question of that when you weigh under a hundred pounds," said Michelet.

"Were there any successful uprisings other than that of the Jews of Treblinka?" I ask.

None of us know.

"And there were also the tarts who didn't come home," Brigitte says. "Really, I don't know when I became reconciled with the human race."

The deportees never seem to know that. Can the conscience bear this end-of-term examination? I think of Möllberg: "If civilizations survive only through metamorphosis, then the world is made of oblivion." What if our friends *cannot* remember their return among men?

"In the great Buddhist parable," I say, "those who have embarked in the ship of deliverance can only make out the opposite bank of the river when the land is out of sight."

"A Warsaw Jew," the Father says, "told me that after his arrest he had crossed the empty ghetto, with its doors open and meals on the tables, as if it hadn't been abandoned, as if life was simply suspended. And that when he was liberated by the Americans he had felt something similar, a sort of dissociation from life."

During my escape in 1940 I went into the first cinema I came across to take my shoes off, because they were too small for me and agonizingly painful. It was showing a German film of the bombing of Warsaw. The view was taken from an airplane: black plumes of petrol, and an Apocalyptic pall of smoke over the line of burning houses. The aircraft crossed the screen; and higher up, this murderous Golgotha sky became an immaculate sea of cloud.

"And in Spain?" asked Michelet.

"I didn't come across any prisoners."

"Usually the fascists executed them," the Spaniard said.

"There were ours. But we aviators had no occasion to take any."

It is not hell which Spain brings back to me. I have never forgotten the immense procession of the peasants behind the biers of the airmen, at Teruel. Nor have I forgotten a very different picture. It was dawn— the hour when we usually arrived over the enemy lines. I had come from the castle of white stone and black ironwork in which the pilots slept, and walked along the edge of the vast orchard where I had often come in the morning to eat the tangerines sprinkled with hoarfrost. On my right, tall sycamores concealed a fighter aircraft whose aluminum fuselage glittered in the rising sun. It was covered with dew which was colorless near the tail and pink, then red, as I approached the cockpit. It was the aircraft of a comrade killed the day before, whose blood had gushed over the fuselage. The night had washed it clean, and the blood of the battle had mingled with the dew which gathered over the fields of Spain as far as the Pyrenees.

"It was a mixture of the profound and the ludicrous," Brigitte says. "In the camp, we lived in a state of indignation. A steady, constant indignation. It was peculiarly scandalous that human beings should be treated like that. And we found ourselves back here with our indignation undirected. As if we had brought our shovels with us. We never really had much faith in the trials of the war criminals. And then, at a certain level, the desire for vengeance wears off too. Killing the torturers doesn't negate the torture.

"One talks mainly about the dramatic side of it all, because it's easier to get across. There are things you only become aware of afterward, which haven't even a name. For instance, not knowing our fate, or the fate of our friends, or of our families left behind in France, or the course of the war. It was a permanent anguish, and yet we were in the highest degree irresponsible. Coming back to life meant a bed, a bath, a tablecloth—what everybody imagines. And silence. Silence! They used to scream and shout at us the whole time. All this was complicated. Hell ends up by seeming simple. Over there, on some days, I used to look at the trees as if to embrace them—it was a way of escaping; it took me at least a week before I was able to look simply at a free tree."

I think of Nehru's trees and little animals.

"It seems to me," says the Father, "that the worst of it all arose from the fact that life was not, for us, the memory of the time when we were alive. It was the memory of that time seen from the camp. Seen from the camp, which creates more unreality than prison. Real life could not coincide."

"As regards physical life," Brigitte said. "But in the camp I never imagined the moral life of people outside."

"When a person has narrowly escaped death," I remark, "he lives in a state of continual surprise in face of the obviousness of life. But not in the moral sphere, if we can so designate people's feelings, their relationship with life. The length of time spent in the vicinity of death must play a part."

"Don't forget that we had no ideas," Brigitte replies. "It was an experiment, you see: a very long experiment. Fourteen months of concubinage with death, and for some, much more. Death was present within us because we were always threatened, and in front of us because we never stopped seeing it. We touched the heart of the matter. We were perfectly aware of our struggle. But we were struggling with some kind of support—faith, patriotism, solidarity, call it what you will, friendship often, responsibility."

"That's true," Michelet says. "I often used to wonder how so many people with responsibility had survived, since they enjoyed no special privileges. Our responsibility kept us going."

"And humiliation does not destroy pride," says the Father.

"But pride which survives destroys humiliation," says the Spaniard. "I'm not speaking for myself. I was a turner and I got through all right by making toys for the kapos' kids. What I say is true all the same."

"When we came back from the moon," Brigitte goes on, "there was no longer any camp—long live sheets and Eau de Cologne! But the self-defense which had been protecting us had become purposeless. We came back expecting a world dominated by it. It wasn't quite like that! We had climbed the Stations of the Cross, we had been crucified, and it all ended up in Mary Magdalene's bed."

I glance at the Father. No sign of annoyance, whereas ten minutes ago he was acutely exasperated over the monument. His sad smile seems to say: my poor little girl!

"It certainly wasn't the Resurrection. And all this came about, make no mistake, with a huge measure of acquiescence. That was the worst thing. Everything which should have preserved us, feelings and memories, was no longer any use. There was no longer a hell, and there was no longer anything to counteract hell. We had reached the nadir, and we found ourselves back in a world for which it did not exist. People beguiled themselves with trifles, but why? In order not to have to face up to a reality which for us was a great deal more than skin deep. It was like Dante's return among the indifferent. And there was one weird thing. We all came back looking like corpses. After quite a short time, mostly spent in the relative solitude of bed, we seemed . . . recovered. And our families thought that we had become morally like them again, too. But we were like our fellow deportees, and no one else. The family was like the bed—warm and extraneous."

"Do you agree?" I ask.

Even the Father nods sadly.

"How we came back was something I thought a lot about beforehand," she continues, "and I had no need to think about it afterward. Just as there had been the sheets and the forks, there was the crazy restlessness we all suffered from, the mirthless fun and the nightclubs. All that did not last long, because it isn't terribly amusing, and because the fleshpots attracted us but also disgusted us. But you know, we all caught on pretty quickly. What did living involve? Being blind. So we became blind again. Sooner or later."

"Not altogether," says the Father.

"No, but quite enough. For you it's different, because faith is your very life, in the camp or elsewhere."

"Anguish always finds its form. I have frequently come across the fear of losing one's faith. To me, it's incomprehensible. We shall probably never again encounter evil in such a diabolical form; but evil is impotent against faith. The Bible has given its answer in advance in the Book of Job."

I think of the chaplain of Glières saying that for him evil was not a problem but a mystery.

"How did our people die?"

"My dear man," Michelet says to me, "the Reverend Father hardly ever attended anyone but believers. So of course *they* repented. When he said to them: 'Will you forgive all your enemies'—a tall order, God knows!—they answered before God."

"Did you see a single man die in hatred?" the Father asks him.

Michelet reflects, then turns to me: "The Father is right, old man, he's right. As the man responsible for the French inmates of Dachau, I probably saw more people die than he did. Naturally not in the same way—naturally! It wasn't my job to confess them, or to forgive them. Nevertheless you'd have thought they might have had a thing or two to say about the Fritzes. Never! They were beyond all that. Their last words were always for their families: 'When you get home, go and tell my wife to dig under the third pear tree from the left,' or, 'Tell the kids I did what I could.'"

"Does death forgive—or despise?"

"Forgives," the Father says. "At least for those who were vaguely Christian. I was in the presence of grace."

"There wasn't room for many sins."

"Just theft and murder!" Brigitte says.

"And the others?"

"It must have been the same," says the Father, "only they didn't know it."

"I was on deathbed duty too," says the Spaniard. "There isn't a great deal to say to a dying man. You have your words, Padre, but my people would no longer have wanted to hear them."

"If death is not . . . an outlet toward God, perhaps there's nothing to be said. But I believe there's always a place for Charity. Being an atheist is not that simple!"

"With us," says Brigitte, "in spite of the communal life, death was personal. As in ordinary life."

"In ordinary life," says the Father gently, "it isn't particularly personal . . . I have seldom seen hatred hold out against the approach of death. In the camp, death wore itself out. Here, no; and the approach of death is like nothing else. But out there, Satan held horror in one hand and forgiveness in the other."

I think once more of Spain. President Azaña, as he lay dying, in Andorra I think, said, "What is the name of that country . . . you know, that country where I was President of the Republic?"

Behind the bars, the crowds file past as if on a pilgrimage. Those who have come to salute the ashes of Jean Moulin in memory of their own dead pass slowly against the sky of death—as in the cities of Egypt and

Mesopotamia in the year 1965 before Christ. There is no coming back from hell any more than there is from death.

I went back to Lascaux. Since people had been allowed to enter freely, tiny fungi had begun to proliferate in the cave, flaking the Magdalenian bison and horses. Twenty thousand years of survival without men, fifteen years of survival with men, and destruction. (It cost a hundred and fifty million old francs to arrest it.) Lascaux is saved, on condition that people stop going there as they please. The sight is almost as surprising—in a different way—as it was in wartime. The crevices in the strangely smooth rock have lost their mystery, because their limits can be dimly discerned, thanks to the invisible reflectors which illuminate the paintings as nightlights illuminate icons. One goes down the shaft by a metal ladder. The figure with the bird mask no longer stands guard over weapons. Four-bladed ventilators, connected to generators, revolve slowly, and seem to bring their incongruous protection to the bison as did our machine guns standing like watch dogs. I ask the friendly and intelligent guide, "What became of the kids who were trying to rescue their little dog?"

"It was me."

He is about forty.

"You know, they always blame it on the pup. What my pals and I were looking for was adventure."

"And what about them?"

"One died in the Resistance, the other's a contractor."

We go outside. The little trees on the hillside are no longer so small, Montignac has spread, and the road comes as far as the cave.

"When the accident happened . . ."

(The accident is the spread of the fungi.)

". . . on some Sundays, as many as fifteen hundred people used to come . . ."

Two long corrugated iron huts have been erected near the entrance.

"Huts for the specialists?"

"No, they only come from time to time. They're for the conscientious objectors. The conservation work has been entrusted to them."

Index